Tennessee's Forgotten Warriors

Tennessee's Forgotten Warriors

Frank Cheatham and
His Confederate Division

Christopher Losson

The University of Tennessee Press
KNOXVILLE

Copyright © 1989 by the University of Tennessee Press / Knoxville.
All Rights Reserved. Manufactured in the United States of America.
First Edition.

Frontispiece: Major-General Benjamin Franklin Cheatham.
              (Virginia Cheatham Van Ness)

The paper in this book meets the minimum requirements of the
American National Standard for Permanence of Paper for Printed
Library Materials. ∞ The binding materials have been chosen
for strength and durability.

Library of Congress Cataloging in Publication Data

Losson, Christopher, 1954–
   Tennessee's forgotten warriors : Frank Cheatham and his
Confederate division / Christopher Losson.—1st ed.
      p. cm.
   Bibliography: p.
   Includes index.
   ISBN 0-87049-615-8 (cloth: alk. paper)
      1. Cheatham, Benjamin Franklin, 1820–1886. 2. Generals—United
States—Biography. 3. Generals—Southern States—Biography.
4. Confederate States of America. Army of Tennessee—Biography.
5. Tennessee—History—Civil War, 1861–1865—Campaigns. 6. United
States—History—Civil War, 1861–1865—Campaigns. I. Title.
E467.1.C516L67 1989
973.7'68-dc20   89-33944 CIP

In memory of my grandparents:
Mary C. and Thomas D. Hagan and
Catherine M. and John C. Losson

Contents

Acknowledgments   xi

Introduction   xiii

1   From Nashville to Mexico City   1

2   "One of the Wickedest Men I Ever Heard Speak":
The 1850s and the Onset of the Civil War   20

3   "Old Frank Is One of the Boys":
Shiloh and Its Aftermath   40

4   "The Most Exciting Few Moments of My Life":
The Kentucky Campaign   60

5   Controversy at Murfreesboro   77

6   "Give Them Hell, Boys!":
The Battles for Chattanooga   98

7   "This Is Old Joe":
From Dalton to Kennesaw Mountain   132

8   The Fight for Atlanta   166

9   "I Don't Like the Looks of This Fight":
Spring Hill and Franklin   195

10   Disaster at Nashville   232

11   The Postwar Years   253

Epilogue   280

Notes   289

Bibliography   333

Index   343

Illustrations

PLATES

Benjamin Franklin Cheatham   ii
Westover   6
Cheatham in the Mexican War   13
Highway Marker for Camp Cheatham   29
Alfred Tyler Fielder   34
B. F. Cheatham   42
General Braxton Bragg   54
Battle Flag of First Tennessee Regiment   72
Sketch of Officer on Horseback   103
General Preston Smith   108
General Leonidas Polk   114
General Joseph E. Johnston   134
W. H. T. Walker   138
Sketch of Attack on Kennesaw Mountain   158
Cheatham in Uniform   164
General Alfred J. Vaughan   167
General Alexander P. Stewart   185
General George E. Maney   191
John C. Brown   211
General John Bell Hood   214
Map of the Battle of Franklin   220
General Patrick Cleburne   222
Reverend Doctor Charles Todd Quintard   229
Map of the Battle of Nashville   235
Anna Bell Robertson Cheatham   255
James D. Porter   263

Railroad Pass   270
Ribbon from the 1883 Reunion   271
Children of B. F. and Anna Bell Cheatham   282
Tombstone of B. F. Cheatham   285
Confederate Monument in Nashville   286

MAPS

1. Cheatham's Division at Perryville, October 8, 1862   68
2. Confederate Attack at Stones River,
   December 31, 1862   86
3. Cheatham's Division at Chickamauga,
   September 19, 1863   105
4. Cheatham Hill, June 27, 1864   156
5. Spring Hill, November 29, 1864   206

Acknowledgments

Any author who takes as long as I have to write a book acquires an immense debt to dozens of individuals and institutions. Though I can never adequately repay that debt, I wish to extend my appreciation to those who helped me along the way.

Two of General Cheatham's granddaughters — Alice Parker of Charleston, S.C., and Virginia C. Van Ness of Seattle — were kind enough to provide family data and other information. Mrs. Van Ness also made available photographs of General Cheatham and his wife, Anna Bell.

I was the beneficiary of assistance from librarians and archivists throughout the country. Each of the repositories listed in the Bibliography or in the photo credits aided me in my endeavors. I am particularly indebted to the Tennessee State Library and Archives. The staff there was invariably cordial and helpful and responded to numerous requests for information. I am especially grateful for the aid rendered by Senior Archivist Marylin Bell Hughes. Another Tennessean who provided valuable assistance was Anne Armour, archivist at the University of the South at Sewanee.

The Southern Historical Collection at the University of North Carolina at Chapel Hill provided me with much useful information. Mr. Richard Shrader kindly arranged a loan of the Cheatham papers which are on microfilm at Chapel Hill.

National Park Service employees aided me during my visits to Civil War battlefields. I would like to acknowledge in particular the assistance of Dan Brown at Stones River National Military Park, Robert Housch and Ed Tinney at Chickamauga-Chattanooga National Military Park, and Dennis Kelly at Kennesaw Mountain National Battlefield Park. Messrs. Tinney and Kelly went above and beyond the call of duty by escorting me on the battleground at their respective parks.

A number of persons read various drafts of this manuscript. Dr. Harry P. Owens of the University of Mississippi and Timothy D. Johnson of Montgomery, Alabama, read an early draft of this work and made many valuable suggestions. The latter was also gracious enough to share the results of his research into General Cheatham's early career. Dr. James Lee McDonough, formerly of David Lipscomb College and Pepperdine University and now with Auburn University, read two versions of the manuscript. Dr. Richard McMurry of North Carolina State University and Joseph Johnson of the University of Tennessee at Knoxville also read the manuscript, and their suggestions, like Dr. McDonough's, greatly strengthened it.

In addition to the institutions cited in the Bibliography, I am also indebted to the staffs at the Coffee County (Tenn.) Public Library, the Maury County (Tenn.) Public Library, the Public Library of Nashville and Davidson County, and the John D. Williams Library at the University of Mississippi. A number of persons and institutions also assisted me in St. Joseph, Missouri. Dr. Warren Chelline of the English department at Missouri Western State College read a draft of the manuscript. Both the St. Joseph Public Library and the Missouri Western State College Library staffs rendered valuable assistance. Missouri Western's enlightened policy of allowing volumes of *The Official Records of the War of the Rebellion* to circulate proved a godsend during the research phase of this project. Bray Photography Studio and Prompt Printing Company provided advice and assistance relative to photographs and maps, respectively. Despite their Yankee antecedents, my colleagues at Bishop Le-Blond High School were good enough to refrain from physical violence when I took to extolling the virtues of the South in general and Frank Cheatham in particular.

Working with the staff at the University of Tennessee Press has been a pleasure. I am especially indebted to Cynthia Maude-Gembler, Carolyn Moser, and Lee Campbell Sioles.

Though they are listed last in this compilation, my foremost debt of gratitude belongs to my family, who have steadfastly encouraged me in my pursuit of General Cheatham. My sister, Anne Minsterketter, generously provided food, lodging, and other support during research forays to Nashville. My wife, Deanna, may have had an inkling of what the future held in store during our honeymoon ten years ago. Our romantic excursion was interrupted by visits to three Civil War battlefields, the Confederate Cemetery at Franklin, and a search for General Cheatham's grave at Mount Olivet Cemetery in Nashville. She has long since become resigned to summer vacations given over to Civil War research and travel; my children likewise think journeys to battlefields and libraries constitute a normal part of summertime routine. Needless to say, I could not have completed this biography without Deanna's patience, tolerance, and encouragement.

The people closest to me did all they could to make this a good book; if it is not, the fault is strictly my own.

Introduction

Mourners who accompanied Benjamin Franklin Cheatham's remains as they were borne to Nashville's Mount Olivet Cemetery on September 6, 1886, had reason to expect that Cheatham's name and reputation would be long remembered. The funeral itself was evidence that Cheatham had been an extraordinary man. Behind Cheatham's casket sprawled a funeral procession which extended more than a mile. Onlookers jammed the city to catch a glimpse of the cortege as it passed. Newspaper correspondents estimated that as many as 30,000 people were either funeral participants or spectators. The size of the crowd was attributable in large measure to the affection which many Tennesseans felt for Cheatham, but this alone does not account for the vast interest in his funeral proceedings. Such attention was generated by the presence of several hundred men who marched two abreast during the initial stage of the funeral procession, as Cheatham's body was conveyed from the Senate chamber of the State Capitol to a local church. These men were dressed in civilian clothes, but a ribbon pinned to each of their jackets identified the military connection which had united them over twenty years earlier: Cheatham's division. They were former Confederate soldiers, and they represented the thousands of men who had served under Cheatham in the Army of Tennessee.

Therein lies the key to understanding Frank Cheatham's prominence. Cheatham's elaborate funeral display is inconceivable without the backdrop provided by the Civil War. He first won renown in the Mexican War, but it was his Confederate service which propelled him into the limelight, as he commanded successively a brigade, a division, and a corps in the Army of Tennessee. He was a major-general in charge of a division from the spring of 1862 through mid-summer 1864 and led his men through some of the war's most bitter fighting. Cheatham and his men left their mark at Shiloh, Perryville, Stones River, Chickamauga, and in the Georgia campaign. As a corps commander, he was a major figure in the final year of the war, as the army fought its last major engagements at Franklin and Nashville. Cheatham's surviving veterans were convinced that his exploits had secured him (and by extension themselves) a permanent place in Tennessee history. Cheatham's wartime aide James D. Porter neatly summarized this view: "When the part taken by Tennessee in the war is written, he will be named as her representative soldier, and none can dispute his title."

Today Porter's words sound flat and hollow. The title predicted for Cheatham as Tennessee's representative Confederate military hero has long since been bestowed on the cavalryman Nathan Bedford Forrest. Despite the expectations of his contemporaries, Cheatham lies buried today beneath a simple rectangular headstone, forgotten by all by a handful of state residents. Even Civil War historians tend to reduce him to a caricature, focusing less on his military talents than on his reputation as a profane, hard-drinking officer. Such a stereotype has obscured the real Frank Cheatham, who was a man of more substance and complexity than most scholars have assumed. Historians may have based their conclusions, in part at least, on Cheatham's self-assessment that he was a simple man, a characterization echoed by many of those who gathered at his funeral. Yet contradictory impulses abounded in Cheatham, although he and his friends never fully comprehended the dual nature of his personality. One example might illustrate the point. Porter related a story about an elderly Georgia couple who met with Cheatham, probably in 1864, to complain that their sheep had been stolen the night before. The entire army had encamped near their farm, and it was impossible to locate the soldiers who had carted off the animals. Moved by the couple's plight, Cheatham quietly pulled out his pocketbook and paid for the missing sheep from his own funds. Yet the same man who could be swayed by such an appeal calmly plotted the destruction of hundreds of Yankees when they assaulted his position at Kennesaw Mountain a few weeks later. He accomplished his task so thoroughly that the bluecoats were unable to recover the bodies of their fallen comrades until a formal cease-fire went into effect two days later. Compassion and fury. Both emotions coexisted within Cheatham, and he could swing from one to the other in a matter of minutes.

That Cheatham's historical light has dimmed is by no means unprecedented; one generation's hero is likely to become another's trivia question, and vice versa. Several factors contributed to Cheatham's slide. One was the postwar preoccupation with Robert E. Lee's Army of Northern Virginia, a phenomenon which overshadowed their less successful counterparts in the Army of Tennessee. Not until this century, and particularly until works by Stanley F. Horn and Thomas L. Connelly appeared, was the imbalance in coverage addressed. Even so, the renewed interest in the Army of Tennessee did not fully restore Cheatham to prominence. A lack of postwar political success did not enhance Cheatham's prestige, as the offices he held after the conflict were relatively minor compared to those claimed by many former generals. In addition, Cheatham apparently accepted the end of the war with remarkable equanimity. Such an attitude endeared him to former Federals, whom Cheatham warmly greeted whenever they met, but it paled in comparison to the rancor felt by many of his army colleagues during Reconstruction. In short, his postwar years were not as lively or colorful as those experienced by many of his military associates.

That Cheatham survived the war may have made him somewhat less attractive to potential biographers. As morbid as it sounds, there is a certain gory fascination attached to men who die in battle. Often a mystique surrounds high-ranking officers who died during the Civil War, as is the case with Cheatham's close friend Patrick Cleburne. For some generals, dying in battle provoked arguments later about their relative military talents. This is especially true of those who died early in the conflict, with Albert Sidney Johnston the prime example, but it applies also to a man like Leonidas Polk, who was killed in 1864. Literary remembrances often followed those generals killed in battle. Cleburne, Johnston, and Polk all were subjects of sympathetic biographies written in the postwar period. Cheatham exposed himself to fully as much danger as the aforementioned trio, and his singular good fortune in escaping battlefield hazards was simply a case of beating the odds. This nonetheless did deny writers a bloody climax with which to stir their readers.

Not all of Cheatham's fellow generals had to die to merit attention from postwar scribes. Army commanders were particularly well-regarded subjects, and two of them, John Bell Hood and Joseph E. Johnston, understood the interest in their careers well enough that they penned their own autobiographies. Others, such as Braxton Bragg, provided documents and other assistance to would-be biographers. Porter came closest to serving as Cheatham's literary booster when he contributed a volume on Tennessee's role in the war to the "Confederate Military History" series published in 1899. Cheatham was given favorable coverage in the volume, but since it covers so many other personalities and events, it does not have the full range of anecdotes and insights that a book strictly devoted to Cheatham would possess. Porter never chronicled the life of his wartime chief in a separate work, although it is impossible to say if this was due to Cheatham's modesty or Porter's time constraints.

As the decades passed, a paucity of readily available sources may have daunted some who hoped to learn more about Cheatham. The family retained possession of his memorabilia well into this century, and there are tales that fire consumed many of General Cheatham's wartime papers. The Cheatham Papers now on deposit in the Tennessee State Library and Archives contain much valuable information, but only the existence of isolated documents and the assistance of librarians and archivists throughout the country has allowed a portrait of Cheatham to emerge. Even so, the portrait is incomplete. As with any biography dealing with a subject who has been dead for over a century, there are frustrations. There is no way to conjure up the nuances which comprised Frank Cheatham; we cannot know what his voice sounded like, the way he looked on horseback, his gait, or many of the other individual mannerisms which help define a person. What is left is the broad outline of Cheatham's life—and my firm belief that within this framework Cheatham deserves more attention than he has received. Certainly the Army of Tennessee was affected by his presence.

As the allusion to the army suggests, this is more than the story of one individual. In the course of resuscitating Frank Cheatham, I found myself reviving thousands of other men along the way—those who served under his command. They appear in this book as well, particularly his beloved Tennesseans, through the words they jotted down in diaries, letters, memoirs, and articles. Their perceptions help breathe life back into Cheatham and, in turn, into themselves. Frank Cheatham would approve of their inclusion, since he always understood that whatever fame he won in the war was due to the sacrifices and devotion of his men. He would be glad that their story, like his, was finally being told.

Chapter 1

From Nashville
to Mexico City

The Civil War had been over for two and a half years when Confederate chieftain Joseph E. Johnston, one of several men who commanded the Army of Tennessee, penned a letter to a former associate. Johnston remarked, "That Army of Tennessee never received justice," and added that the troops who fought for the Confederacy in the western theater "were not inferior to those that fought under General Lee." Convinced that the Richmond government slighted his command during the war, Johnston became an enemy of President Jefferson Davis long before the conflict ended. After the war Johnston found other targets of disdain, notably John Bell Hood, who replaced him as army commander in July 1864. Seeking allies in his bitter postwar feuds with Davis and Hood, Johnston urged his correspondent to set a few hours aside to record wartime recollections. The Virginia-born Johnston was especially interested in events tied to the 1864 campaign from Dalton, Georgia, to Atlanta, when he first directed the main Rebel host in the west. Johnston sought to cajole the letter's recipient by noting that "the noble Tennesseans you commanded" would prize such a work by their battlefield leader and that the exercise would highlight the contributions of westerners who served in the Army of Tennessee.[1]

Unfortunately for both Johnston and historians, his entreaties failed to elicit the desired manuscript. Major-General Benjamin Franklin Cheatham, Johnston's correspondent, apparently never felt inclined or could not find the time to attempt such a literary endeavor. In the end Johnston was not deterred by Cheatham's failure to forward his reminiscences. The Virginian later wrote a book which savagely assailed Davis and Hood, and thus added to his wartime prominence. The same cannot be said of the letter's recipient. As the years progressed and old Confederates passed away, Cheatham's considerable lifetime famed waned. This was especially true for the years after Cheatham's death. Eventually much of his life was an enigma, including some aspects of his service in the Army of Tennessee.

Benjamin Franklin Cheatham was born October 20, 1820, near Nashville, the son of Elizabeth and Leonard Pope Cheatham. He was one of eleven children and the first of three sons. Only a sister, Medora Charlotte, preceded him in birth. "Frank" and his siblings represented the eighth generation of Cheathams born in this country, as the Cheathams moved from the British Isles in the 1600s. His first American ancestor of record was a Thomas Cheatham born in Henrico County, Virginia, in 1645. For several generations, the Cheathams lived in Virginia, where some members of the family acquired land along the Appomattox River. Like other Americans who moved westward across the mountains, the Cheathams emigrated to Tennessee around 1793, when Archer Cheatham and several of his sons arrived in Robertson County. Successive generations established themselves in Middle Tennessee, where they became involved in local society as agrarians, merchants, and lawyers.[2]

As an adult, Frank Cheatham dabbled in local and state politics. This is not surprising given the political background on his paternal side. Frank's grandfather Anderson Cheatham served in the Tennessee General Assembly off and on from 1801 to 1825, a practice which was emulated by various uncles and cousins of the Confederate general. The Cheathams generally represented Robertson County, and several were influential in Tennessee political life. Frank's great-uncle, Richard Cheatham, served five terms in the state legislature and was a member of the state Constitutional Convention in 1834. Elected to the U.S. House of Representatives in 1837 as a Whig, he was a political opponent of James K. Polk. Edward Saunders Cheatham, a first cousin to Frank, was a state legislator in the 1850s and 1860s, affiliated at various times with the Whigs and the Know-Nothings. Yet another cousin, Richard B. Cheatham, was a Nashville alderman in the 1850s and was mayor when the city surrendered to the Union army in early 1862.[3]

Leonard Pope Cheatham, Frank's father, embodied many of the characteristics found in other members of the Cheatham clan. Born in 1792 to Anderson and Sarah Pope Cheatham, Leonard was shaped by a diverse array of interests and pursuits. Although he is typically referred to as a lawyer, Leonard's activities were by no means confined to legal affairs. He was, at one time or another, a merchant, a financier, a military veteran, a politician, a slaveowner, a horse breeder, and a respected member of Middle Tennessee's plantation aristocracy. Leonard served with Andrew Jackson at the Battle of New Orleans, and it may be that this proximity to the future president led Cheatham into later political ventures. While he shared the family passion for politics, Leonard broke from relatives such as Richard Cheatham by allying himself with the Democratic party, where he became a firm supporter of James K. Polk.

Leonard's personal triumphs in the political arena were modest. He served as Davidson County court clerk in 1834 and made a run at the state legislature the next year. Leonard lost the election, despite the approval of one Nashville newspaper editor, who wrote Polk that Cheatham was "the truest man in the field." After the defeat, Leonard turned to behind-the-scenes work. He served as presiding officer of the Tennessee Democratic convention in 1843 and labored for Polk's nomination as vice-president on an 1844 ticket with Martin Van Buren. Leonard was probably surprised, if heartened, when Polk secured the presidential nomination instead. His interest in politics remained even after Polk's term in the White House ended. Leonard was a delegate to both sessions of the 1850 Nashville Convention, where he typified the majority of those in attendance by his allegiance to the Democratic party, his ownership of slaves, and his prominence in local affairs. The Nashville Convention was dominated by moderate Tennesseans, who during the two sessions advocated the extension of slavery below the Missouri Compromise line of 36°30′ all the way to the Pacific Ocean, "denounced the recently enacted Compromise of 1850," and "affirmed the right of secession." Given Leonard's enthusiasm for politics, it is not surprising that his eldest son, Frank, later continued his father's association with the Democratic party and made his own forays into political campaigns.[4]

Politics was one of several areas where Leonard's activities influenced Frank. A second was military service, a role shared by relatives on both sides of Frank's family tree. Leonard never devoted himself to army life in the same manner his son would, and his societal prestige did not stem from a strong military connection. Still, indications from the Mexican War era that Frank corresponded with his father about strategy and other military affairs imply a respect for Leonard's acumen in regard to army matters. It would be interesting to know if the elder Cheatham ever discussed the possibility of a West Point education with his son, but for whatever reason Frank did not enter that institution.

Besides the military, agriculture and horses were two cornerstones of Frank Cheatham's life that must have been influenced by his father. A large plantation which the Cheathams maintained in Frank's youth provided an opportunity to learn about crops, livestock, and the operation of a sizeable estate. Family wealth also afforded both Leonard and Frank the chance to purchase, train, and breed thoroughbred horses. Although Frank's financial status as an adult did not keep pace with the wealth Leonard enjoyed, farming and an eye for good horseflesh were two of the most important legacies bequeathed by Leonard to his eldest son.[5] While it is impossible to assess exactly the extent to which Leonard influenced his son, there is little doubt that he played a significant role in shaping the type of person Frank ultimately became, and that Frank lionized his father.

If the Cheathams were somewhat prominent, the lineage on Frank's maternal side was even more impressive. His mother, Elizabeth, was the granddaughter of General James Robertson, one of the most imposing figures in early Tennessee history. A contemporary of Daniel Boone, Robertson played a pioneer role in Tennessee akin to the one held by Boone in Kentucky. The diverse Robertson was an Indian fighter; was one of five judges of the Watauga Association, which organized an independent government in what is now northeastern Tennessee; and led a party which settled present-day Nashville in 1779–80. He eventually served in the North Carolina legislature from 1784 to 1789, was a member of the 1796 Constitutional Convention at Knoxville, and was a U.S. agent to the Chickasaws. Frank had a military role model in Robertson as well, since his great-grandfather served at Kings Mountain, was an officer in the militia, and was elevated to the rank of brigadier-general. A description of Robertson by Elizabeth Cheatham depicted him as being "five feet nine . . . heavy build, but not too fat," with a "very fair [complexion] that was darkened and reddened by exposure." The description is startlingly similar to Frank Cheatham's own adult physique. The distinguished ancestor was a source of family pride, and the nickname "Father of Middle Tennessee" is an index of the leading role Robertson played in the development of the state.[6]

General Robertson sired a family as well as a state; he and his wife Charlotte had eleven children. The eldest son, Jonathan Friar, was the father of Elizabeth Cheatham. Jonathan Robertson was also responsible for the development of a plantation, Westover, where Frank Cheatham and his siblings were born and reared. Westover originated in a 3,000-acre land grant first provided to General Robertson in 1784 by the state of North Carolina. The land was situated in a horseshoe bend of the Cumberland River near Richland Creek, known for years afterward as "Robertson's Bend." Biographical sketches of Frank Cheatham habitually refer to his boyhood home as a family farm, which is a gross understatement. Jonathan Robertson controlled 2,400 acres of the original tract in 1801, when he erected a huge two-story mansion in the center of the property. Westover was a plantation, not a mere farm, and both the Robertsons and the Cheathams employed slaves to assist with the operation of the house and grounds.[7]

Westover was bequeathed to Elizabeth Robertson in 1814, when both her grandfather and father died. General Robertson died on September 1, 1814, while serving as agent to the Chickasaw Indians. Jonathan Friar Robertson survived his father by not quite a month and a half, dying at Westover on October 14, 1814. The dual tragedy left teenaged Elizabeth the heiress to Westover. When she married Leonard Pope Cheatham on September 11, 1817, she provided her husband not only with a mate but with an estate as well. The marriage was between two of Nashville's most prestigious families, but was particularly advantageous to Leonard, who instantly became proprietor of a handsome plantation.[8]

Within two years of the marriage, Elizabeth and Leonard began raising a family. Medora Charlotte was born in January of 1819, and Frank made his appearance the following October. Over the twenty years following the birth of their first daughter, the Cheathams had eleven children. The youngest child, Samuella, was born in 1839, and like the rest of her siblings, she survived infancy and childhood. Westover was a busy spot during the early years of Frank's life. An extended family was present under the roof of the mansion because Jonathan Robertson's widow, Ciddy, lived at Westover with the Cheathams. Several of her younger children also stayed at the plantation, with the result that the place was filled with the sounds of youthful merriment. Visitors who paid their respects to Ciddy at Westover contributed to the social atmosphere of the plantation. Young Frank and his brothers and sisters undoubtedly heard tales of General Robertson and pioneer days in Tennessee from grandmother Ciddy, and gleaned other family information as they grew older.[9]

The few sources on Frank's boyhood reveal that it was a happy one. His early years at Westover were probably spent in pursuits such as farm chores, learning to ride, and assisting in small ways with the rearing of the younger children. At some point Leonard hired an accomplished Englishman to tutor Frank at home, another indication that the family was prosperous. In addition to farm work and lessons, Frank took advantage of the opportunities the region afforded for fishing, boating, and swimming. All of these delighted the boy. One of the swimming expeditions almost ended in disaster when a slave companion who had "gone beyond his depth" faltered, and called on his master Frank to save him. Frank unhesitatingly plunged into the water and rescued the black youth. The incident was recounted to the tutor, who was justly proud of his young charge's "heroic conduct."[10]

While Frank and the other Cheatham progeny grew up in the hospitable climate at Westover, Leonard Cheatham sought other avenues for his energy. Records reveal that Leonard purchased several pieces of Nashville real estate from 1818 to 1835. The slave population at Westover increased from a dozen in 1829 to seventeen by 1840. Leonard contracted with the U.S. government in 1832 to supply steamboat transportation for the removal of Cherokee Indians from Alabama to Oklahoma. The arrangement was utilized in 1832 and 1834, but eventually the government

An imposing mansion house dominated Westover, the plantation on the Cumberland River where Cheatham spent his childhood. (Tennessee State Library and Archives)

opted for other means of transportation. Aggrieved by the loss of the profitable contract, Leonard "filed a petition arguing breach of contract." The government heard the claim, but denied Leonard compensation despite his contention that he lost $35,000 to $40,000 in estimated profits when the Cherokees were shipped westward by other means.[11]

Among the personal issues Leonard grappled with in these years was the education of his children. He no doubt sought to provide adequate training for the children that would allow them to maintain a certain social status. For Frank, the eldest son, a proper education was especially vital. It would allow him to help in every aspect of Westover's operation and prepare him to assist Leonard in managing the family's other real estate holdings. It is also reasonable to assume that Leonard and Elizabeth placed greater expectations on Frank's shoulders than may have been the case with the younger children. In the mid-1830s, Leonard attempted to broaden Frank's academic skills by enrolling him in a school for boys in Nashville. The school was run by Nathaniel Cross, a New Jersey native and Princeton graduate who had arrived in Nashville in 1824. Cross opened his academy in 1832 on Vine Street, "between Church and Broad Streets," though later he moved it to his residence. How long Frank remained under Professor Cross's tutelage is unknown, but a receipt from Cross to the elder Cheatham indicates that Frank attended school there for at least part of 1834. At age seventeen, Frank was sent away to school in Kentucky to complete his education. The school he attended is unknown, but it may well have been St. Mary's College in Lebanon, for his brother Felix later attended that institution.[12]

The Kentucky interlude ended in two years, when Frank was called home. Leonard Cheatham suffered some unspecified adversity while his eldest son was in Kentucky, possibly related to his speculation in real estate, and financial reverses spurred him to summon Frank back to Nashville. The implication is that the young man's education costs could no longer be borne comfortably. An indication of the family's weakened financial state was readily apparent when Frank went to Philadelphia to work in a wholesale dry goods store, a position almost assuredly garnered for Frank by a brother-in-law, Samuel Riggs, a wholesale merchant in Philadelphia, who married Medora in 1835. The Philadelphia hiatus was a relatively short one, lasting not more than two years. There are indications that Frank felt the job was unsatisfactory and not in keeping with his previous expectations. When the proprietor of the firm sent Frank home to Nashville, a note to Leonard concluded that Frank was "a fine fellow" but considered himself destined for a higher position than that of a dry goods clerk. It is not hard to imagine that Frank, raised in a mansion at Westover and used to a plantation society, found work in the store relatively menial and degrading. Leonard may have acquiesced in Frank's homecoming because his own financial circumstances improved, albeit temporarily; he was granted sizeable acreage in three counties in south-central Tennessee in the 1840s and 1850s.[13]

Upon his return to Nashville, Frank received an opportunity to join a military company for the first time. The Nashville Blues was a group of young men from the area who formed an independent volunteer company. In essence a militia group, the Blues drilled, elected officers, and participated in various social events. Cheatham attached himself to the Blues in the early 1840s as a private. After two years he was elevated to the post of second lieutenant, and was subsequently promoted to first lieutenant. He remained with the Blues for five years before resigning his commission. Sources give no reason for the resignation, but it coincided with his father's appointment as postmaster of Nashville by President Polk, who thus rewarded Leonard for political efforts on his behalf. Between duties at Westover and assisting his father at the post office, Frank was unable to devote as much time to the Blues as he had before.[14]

Up to this time Frank Cheatham's life had been one of relative contentment, if lacking in excitement. He apparently resented the Philadelphia job somewhat, but otherwise he was regarded as a popular young man and a hard worker. Nonetheless, he had not yet been able to distinguish himself in any military or mercantile pursuits. It may well have galled Frank to realize that he was not living up to the record of achievement carved out by a number of his ancestors and living relatives. Frank was rescued from an otherwise obscure career by developments in foreign policy. James K. Polk heeded the sentiments of the expansionists who had helped him win the White House and stirred up war talk in the wake of border disputes between the United States and Mexico. When war was declared in May of 1846, Frank was in Mississippi, but the prospects for military service compelled him to hurry home to Nashville. When he arrived, he discovered that the Nashville Blues had reorganized and named him captain of the unit, which numbered around a hundred men. For Frank and the rest of the Blues, the Mexican conflict represented an opportunity for combat, recognition, and an exciting break from the seemingly dull routines of Nashville life.[15]

Cheatham was not alone in responding to the call to arms. Congress asked for 50,000 men and allotted quotas to various states. On May 21, 1846, Tennessee governor Aaron Brown formally requested enough troops for three regiments, two of infantry and one of cavalry. Filling the units required 2,800 men, with volunteers enlisted for twelve months. Tennesseans earned their "Volunteer State" moniker during this era, as nearly 30,000 men expressed a willingness to join the service. Because of the overabundance of volunteers Brown divided the state into four recruiting areas and resorted to ballots to fill the ranks. One observer noted that those not selected often expressed "chagrin and disappointment" at the unfavorable results.[16] For Cheatham and the other members of the Nashville Blues, the selection process was easily expedited. The Blues, composed of ninety-one officers and men, was one of two companies drawn from Davidson County. The Blues and the Harrison Guards under Captain Robert C. Foster were accepted "on account of their previous organization and excellence in drill." Other units rendezvoused near Nashville by June 1, and elections were held for officers. William B. Campbell of Smith County was chosen colonel of the newly formed First Tennessee Regiment.[17]

Events moved forward with amazing rapidity. In a week and a half the regiment was gathered, organized, supplied, and prepared to leave Nashville. On the evening of June 3, the 1,040 soldiers marched to the Nashville Female Academy, where several speakers addressed the regiment and a large group of citizens. The highlight of the ceremony was the presentation to the regiment of the "Eagle Blue Banner," a flag depicting an eagle on an azure background with the motto "Weeping in solitude for the fallen brave is better than the presence of men too timid to fight for their country." The troops embarked for New Orleans in the next two days, "a vast throng" witnessing their departure.[18]

Cheatham and his compatriots no doubt felt exhilarated by the swift transformation from civilian to military life, and their enthusiasm did not wane in the Crescent City, where they arrived June 11, 12, and 13. The Tennesseans were all in "fine spirits and health" as they stepped off the transports, and after they were taken to a large warehouse two miles below the city, many of the men, in violation of orders, slipped away to sample New Orleans's amenities, such as juleps.[19] Not until they set out in three ships for Mexico on June 17 did they get an inkling that war's adventures were not all pleasant.

Over five hundred men, including Cheatham, were crammed into one of the vessels, the *Charlotte*, and seasickness broke out shortly after the voyage commenced. The crowded conditions were especially troublesome at night, when men lay "in every position imaginable" within the ship and on the wet deck. The doctor on board was inattentive and stayed in his berth, avoiding the hundreds of wretched soldiers. The seasick Tennesseans were enraged with him and with the quartermaster at New Orleans, who was responsible for the transportation arrangements. The water turned bad after being stored in "improper casks," and only an unspecified suggestion by Cheatham, which provided the men with ice, alleviated the sufferings. The miserable voyage lasted a week, and even then the ordeal was not over. A violent three-day storm and rolling seas prevented the regiment from landing, and not until June 30 did the last soldiers get ashore. Their landing site was Brazos Saint Iago, a small, sandy island south of an estuary at Port Isabel.[20]

Not long after their debarkation, the unit shifted to Lomita, thirty miles north of Port Isabel. An ominous series of developments ensued, as warm weather, the rainy season, and the first outbreak of measles all coincided. In August, Zachary Taylor summoned the regiment to Camargo, 125 miles up the Rio Grande, where he was assembling a force for a campaign against Monterrey. Camargo was a drab city located on the San Juan River near the confluence of that stream and the Rio Grande. Recently receded floodwaters had damaged a large portion of the city, and the waves of mud quickly dried into a fine dust as the thermometer soared as high as 112 degrees. The Tennesseans sweltered in the blistering heat, and disease spread swiftly through the ranks. Ignorant of sanitation procedures and lacking in camp discipline, the Tennesseans were ravaged by measles and diarrhea, "the most dangerous disease that a man can have in this country," Frank recounted in a letter.[21]

Frank was among the hundreds stricken. "I have just had a high rub [fever] for four days as ever a man had in the world," Cheatham related to his brother Felix. Despite his bout with this fever, which recurred weekly throughout his first months in Mexico, Frank knew he was fortunate. The regiment lost four or five men to disease each day during their weeks at Camargo. An inspection revealed that "out of one thousand men we could muster but scarce five hundred fit for duty," Cheatham lamented. Taylor decided to discharge the men who were too ill to take up the march for Monterrey. Before ever reaching the enemy, the regiment's numbers were scythed in half. Cheatham wrote discharges for twenty-one of his men on September 5, and they joined the nearly three hundred who were sent home. Others were too dangerously ill to move and languished in hospitals, while one hundred luckless Tennesseans were already dead.[22]

Taylor moved to Monterrey with just over six thousand men, almost equally split between Regulars and volunteers. The Regulars comprised two divisions, the volunteers a third, Texas cavalrymen a fourth. The First Tennessee and Colonel Jefferson Davis's Mississippi Rifles joined to form a brigade under Major-General John A. Quitman. The target of the campaign, Monterrey, was the leading city of northeastern Mexico, and contained about ten thousand inhabitants. It was an attractive city, arranged around a central plaza and several smaller ones to form a crude rectangle stretching a mile in length. There were roughly seven thousand defenders in Monterrey, well supported by artillery. Major-General Pedro de Ampudia led the Mexican forces, and his men worked hard to fortify the city.[23]

General Taylor made a number of miscalculations and errors during the campaign. He maintained that the Mexicans would not defend Monterrey, and one Tennessean noted that only when a cannonball landed near Taylor during a reconnaissance mission did he realize that Ampudia would resist the American advance. He failed to bring siege guns and heavy artillery, an omission which Cheatham savagely assailed in a letter home. "I consider, that old Taylor committed one of the greatest blunders that ever a General was guilty of, in coming here to attack one of the strongest fortified towns in Mexico, with nothing . . . but small artillery."[24]

Cheatham's criticism was not without merit. Monterrey's defenses were indeed formidable. A thousand yards north of the city stood an imposing citadel built around the ruins of an unfinished cathedral. Dubbed the "Black Fort" by Americans because of the citadel's dusky walls and pillars, the structure covered roads to the north and east by its position on a slight elevation. Elsewhere, a chain of fortifications featuring infantry and artillery commanded other approaches into Monterrey. One of these forts, called La Teneria after a nearby tannery, guarded the northeastern part of town.[25]

Taylor divided his army and sent one half under Brigadier-General William J. Worth to attack from the west. The other half he directed to mount a demonstration against the city's eastern approaches. The battle opened in earnest September 21. Worth's western attack inched forward against strong Mexican opposition. Fearing that Ampudia would withdraw men from other sectors of the city to reinforce his threatened line, Taylor changed his tactics and converted the demonstration from the east into a full-fledged assault. Cheatham and his fellow Tennesseans were a portion of his group, and they waited nervously as other units advanced. Not yet under direct Mexican fire, the regiment suffered its first casualty when an errant cannonball sheared off a man's leg. The delay in attacking unnerved some of the men, who grew increasingly apprehensive as noise from the battle escalated. Lieutenant S. M. Putnam of the Blues was so convinced that he would die in the battle that he wrote some friends regarding the disposition of his personal effects.[26]

Around noon, General Quitman at last received orders directing his brigade to move forward. The unit marched over a mile across a plain as Mexican artillery fire opened upon them. Their route was slightly different from previous unsuccessful assaults, and shielded them to some extent from the citadel's destructive fire. Eventually their line of march brought them to Monterrey's outskirts, where they rushed towards the La Teneria redoubt in the northeastern angle of the city. Here the attack sputtered. Caught in a murderous crossfire from several Mexican positions, the Tennesseans and Mississippians suffered heavy casualties. The losses mounted as the column halted and fired several ineffectual volleys against the fort. To remain stationary was suicidal, and Colonel Campbell and several of the other officers urged the men on. The din was too overwhelming for the commands to be heard until a slight lull allowed Campbell's order to register, and the regiment surged forward.[27]

Cheatham was in the forefront of the attack, springing ahead and crying, "Come on, men! Follow me!" His impetuosity was not without its risks. Three men were shot from Cheatham's side in the assault, and Frank himself narrowly escaped death as he raced towards the fort. A cannonball landed about twenty paces in front of him, and he dropped instantly to his knees to let it bound over him. He "scarcely touched the ground" when a musketball grazed across his back. The shot felt "as if a coal of fire had been dropped upon my back" where it broke the skin. Frank later marvelled, "If I had been standing I would have been shot through." He regained his footing and leaped across two deep ditches as he and other members of the brigade finally reached the enemy stronghold. Assisted by the fire of isolated Regulars who worked their way into the city, Quitman's force at last drove the Mexican defenders from La Teneria. The Tennesseans promptly hoisted the "Eagle Blue Banner" above its walls and exchanged fire with Mexicans entrenched in another nearby fort.[28]

The conquest of La Teneria, encouraging as it was, did not end the battle. Quitman's men could make no further advance and were relieved at nightfall by a Kentucky regiment and some Regulars. Though he must have been tired by his exertions, Cheatham volunteered to remain with a detail caring for the dead and wounded. This dangerous duty was complicated further by a heavy, chilling rainstorm, but Cheatham and the others groped their way around the dark battlefield. They were guided in their ministrations by the moans of the wounded. When daybreak arrived, he returned to La Teneria, which was again occupied by Quitman's brigade.

On September 23, the third day of the battle, Americans occupied several works near La Teneria which the Mexicans had abandoned during the night. On September 24, Ampudia opened negotiations for the city's surrender. Taylor agreed to an armistice of eight weeks' duration and allowed the Mexicans to take their arms, accouterments, and one 6-gun battery. Satisfied with these generous terms, Ampudia and his men vacated the city on September 25.[29]

Despite the victory, Cheatham questioned the manner in which Taylor and other superior officers had handled the battle. Frank contended that his division was "badly managed . . . we were rushed headlong into the fight, even our Generals did not know where we were going," or what

Cheatham entered the Mexican War as a captain and emerged as a colonel of the Third Tennessee Regiment. (Tennessee State Library and Archives)

situation they would meet. The failure to reconnoiter properly and the lack of artillery combined to boost American casualties. The loss was heaviest in Quitman's brigade, and the Tennesseans were particularly hard hit. Of 340 men in the regiment, 104 were casualties, nearly a third of the force. In an era where smoothbore weapons were often inaccurate, the high casualty rate was "a thing almost unheard of," as Cheatham mourned to one of his sisters. Frank's Nashville Blues suffered relatively light casualties, with 3 men slain. Among the trio was Lieutenant Putnam, whose eerie premonition of death was realized when a musketball pierced his heart. Morale was somewhat shaken after the battle; Cheatham related that there was a wave of "homesickness in camp since the battle," although he did not share this anxiety to any great extent. Instead, he was weakened by a ten-day bout with cold and fever brought on by "exposure, fatigue, and excitement."[30]

The triumph was also marred by a violent controversy between the Tennesseans and Jefferson Davis's Mississippians, who were not content merely to fight the Mexicans but also squabbled over which regiment was the first to enter La Teneria. Each claimed the honor, but Cheatham was contemptuous of the rival boast. He scathingly characterized the Mississippi claim as the "most rascally, ungentlemanly and unsoldierlike piece of conduct that was ever heard of." Any honor and glory had been won at the expense of "many of Tennessee's noble sons." Other members of the regiment shared Cheatham's indignation. One wrote later that General Quitman, himself a Mississippian, congratulated Cheatham and several other officers for being the first regiment to enter the fort. The unseemly row was never really settled, as both regiments advanced arguments in their behalf for years after the war.[31]

Certainly, all was not bleak in the battle's wake. The Tennesseans took justifiable pride in their achievement, though they were sobered by the high cost. The regiment's veterans dubbed themselves "The Bloody First" after the action, an apt nickname in light of the severe losses. Cheatham wrote that the Mexicans were astounded by the courage of the Tennesseans. Having witnessed the impetuous Americans "run up into the cannon's mouth," the Mexicans "wanted to know where we came from and what kind of people we were." Another U.S. officer labelled the Tennesseans the "d[amn]dest men that he ever saw," and that once "told to charge, h[el]l [itself] couldn't stop them." For Frank there was personal glory as well. "I was the first Captain in the fort," he proudly wrote Medora, and indeed he proved courageous in his initial military action.[32] Cheatham's postbattle tending of the wounded also reflected favorably with his compatriots.

Still, the war continued. Indeed, Monterrey's conquest accomplished little save to boost Zachary Taylor's reputation. An incensed Polk repudi-

ated the armistice, and the Tennesseans speculated about what the future held in store for them. Cheatham prophetically wrote that Mexico
City itself would be the eventual target of military strategists, comment-
ing that "nothing short of a thrashing at the city itself will bring them
to terms."[33]

In December, Cheatham wrote one of his relatives that the Tennesseans were growing tired of inactive camp life and that rumors of troop
movements were in the offing. He hoped the eventual destination was
Veracruz, a seaport on the Gulf, for he was convinced that its seizure
would speed the war's end. And indeed, the Bloody First was soon dispatched to join General Winfield Scott's expedition against Veracruz.
The Tennesseans first marched to Tampico, a 400-mile trek which took
from mid-December 1846 until late January of 1847. Not until March 1
did they board the steamship *Alabama* for the relatively brief journey to
Veracruz. They viewed the city several days later, and on March 9 they
participated in the first amphibious operation in American military annals. Bands played national airs while the surf boats plied to the shore
four miles below the city. The Mexicans, surprisingly, did not contest the
landing, and the operation went off smoothly. Cheatham and almost nine
thousand other Americans were safely deposited ashore. The Tennesseans formed on the left of General William Worth's division and moved
towards the city in conjunction with the rest of the army.[34]

The progress of Scott's force was impeded by stifling heat and rugged
terrain. On March 22, the first artillery pieces were brought into action,
as Worth's mortars lobbed shells into the city. The bombardment continued for several days, increasing in effectiveness as naval guns were
brought ashore to pound Veracruz's walls. As Scott tightened his grip on
the city, rumors spread that the Mexicans were assembling a strong force
to threaten the American rear. Colonel William S. Harney reported a
large body of Mexicans barricaded on a stone bridge, and portions of
the First and Second Tennessee were sent to his assistance. Cheatham
was among the men dispatched to aid Harney, and when he arrived, he
boldly suggested that Harney postpone the assault until artillery could
be brought up. Harney readily accepted Cheatham's counsel and waited
for the two artillery pieces to arrive. He then deployed Cheatham's company to the right, through thick shrubbery, to attract the attention of the
Mexicans. Cheatham and his men commenced firing on the bridge defenders as Harney brought the artillery into play. After five rounds the
Americans charged, Cheatham's company bursting from the chaparral
and reaching the bridge first. The Mexicans hastily abandoned their position and were pursued as far as the village of Madellin.[35]

Cheatham's advice to bring the artillery helped reduce casualties for the attackers, and only two men were killed in the skirmish, with nine others wounded. The action itself was probably not as important as Harney later intimated in his report. Still, the incident revealed several things about Cheatham. He felt confident enough to suggest some minor tactical arrangements to a superior and saw them work effectively. He also revealed again the eagerness for combat displayed at Monterrey. An admiring observer wrote Cheatham's youngest brother, John, that Frank "is always in the hot[t]est and thickest of the danger."[36]

Veracruz capitulated on March 29, and Scott quickly pushed his army on the road towards Mexico City. Mexican commander Santa Anna attempted to block the road at Cerro Gordo, but a brilliant flanking movement splintered the Mexicans and compelled them to retreat in disorder. Cheatham and the First Tennessee were held in reserve during the battle, though the Second Tennessee was badly cut up by three strongly fortified positions. Scott and the victorious Americans moved on to Jalapa, the site Scott selected for continuing the advance.[37]

In early May, General Scott decided to send the twelve-month volunteers home, realizing that they would grow increasingly restive as their enlistment expiration date neared. The announcement angered some of the Tennesseans, who hoped to accompany the army to the capital. Despite their disgruntlement, four thousand volunteers set off for Veracruz on May 6, and some of them vented their anger by vandalizing property along the way. Arriving near Veracruz on May 10, the Tennesseans embarked for home the next day. Less than a third of the original unit boarded the ships, the remainder having fallen to disease, wounds, or the earlier discharge at Camargo. The Blues reflected the depletion: Cheatham was one of only forty healthy men at the time of their discharge, fewer than half the number which had set out so optimistically for Mexico the previous year.[38]

The Tennesseans arrived back in Nashville in early June. Captain Cheatham disembarked with the first contingent. The city responded with a grand reception and procession. The Eagle Blue Banner was returned to the Nashville Female Academy, speeches were delivered, and the unit thereupon disbanded.[39] Most of the regimental members were content with their service. They had "seen the elephant," fought creditably, and were happy to be back in Tennessee. Not so Cheatham, who apparently found army life agreeable and wished to return to Scott's army for the final campaign. Scott had requested a number of new volunteer regiments to enlist for the duration of the war, including two from Tennessee. During the fall of 1847, Cheatham seized this opportunity for further military service and "set to work with characteristic energy" to raise one of the two regiments. Despite the grim realities of the war, which were apparent to at least the returned veterans, the new regiment was filled in less than a month. Cheatham was unanimously elected colonel of the new unit, named the Third Regiment of Tennessee Volunteers. The ten companies of the regiment arrived in Nashville around the first of October, and the men were formally mustered into service October 8.[40]

The troops sailed from Nashville at the end of October, and made the trek via Memphis and New Orleans to Veracruz. The route was familiar to Cheatham, as it was to a citizenry accustomed to seeing soldiers pass by on their way to war. Memphis residents, for instance, went about their everyday tasks and generally ignored the passage of the regiment through their city.[41] After arriving in Veracruz in mid-November 1847, the Third Tennessee was placed in a brigade with the Fifth Indiana, another volunteer regiment. Towards the end of the month, the brigade headed for Jalapa and then Mexico City. Cheatham was placed in temporary command of the brigade and received orders to convey a supply train of wagons and pack mules to Mexico City. Although the task may not have been what Cheatham desired, it was not without its dangers. Mexican guerrillas and bandits followed the column closely, eager to steal goods and dispatch unwary Americans who lagged behind. In December, four stragglers were murdered, despite the efforts of over a hundred riflemen and horsemen who formed a search party and retraced the previous day's march. In mid-month the theft of twenty pack mules sent Cheatham and fourteen other officers on a twelve-mile chase through the mountains before the animals were recaptured.[42]

An irregular diary Cheatham kept on the march consists mostly of memoranda relating to the length of each day's march, but occasionally he revealed an appreciation for the Mexican countryside. He pronounced Puebla "decidedly the cleanest and pret[t]iest city in Mexico," but he was even more enraptured by a valley which stretched some twenty miles from Puebla to San Marin. Cheatham wrote that the valley was "the richest and most beautiful [one] that was ever seen every foot of which is in a high state of cultivation." On this and a few other occasions, Frank assessed Mexico through the appreciative eyes of a farmer rather than a warrior.[43]

At Puebla, command of the brigade fell upon Brigadier-General Joseph Lane, who joined the column. After an arduous journey through the mountains, the supply train reached "the city of the Montezumas," as Cheatham styled it, on January 17, 1848. What should have been a joyful occasion became tragic when a measles outbreak immediately swept the regiment. Within a month 125 men were dead, a repetition of the heavy losses suffered by the First Tennessee in the early days of the war.

"We have certainly suffered far more than any other Regt. ever did in the same length of time," Cheatham wrote his father. The tiny number of men who were healthy enough for parade and drill work discouraged Cheatham, who concluded sadly that the spectacle "was enough to dampen the spirits of any man." Perhaps inured by his previous service, Frank related that his own health "was never better," only one day of sickness having bothered him.[44]

Of the few letters relating to Cheatham's Mexican War service which survive, one 1848 missive to his father is the most revealing. Nowhere does he comment on whether he felt the war was justified, or whether as a slaveowner he aspired to gain land suited for the spread of slavery. But he did expose what he sought in the army. He confided that the fighting was essentially over, but "if there is any honour to be had or glory to be won I am in for a chance at any price." General Lane sparked this desire when he drew Cheatham aside, divulged that he was going home, and promised that he would strive to have Frank elevated to brigadier. Cheatham was taken aback by the suggestion and found potential roadblocks. There were other qualified officers, including one from Lane's home state of Indiana. He was also startled that Lane would make the confidential offer after such a relatively short acquaintance.

As the letter progressed, Cheatham took the other tack and debated the merits of the appointment. Lane promised to use his considerable influence in Frank's behalf. Leonard could exploit his political connections in Tennessee, while Cheatham sought support from army superiors. Moreover, Frank was comfortable with the idea of being a brigadier and noted with wry humor, "I have had command of a brigade so long, that I believe that I could stand the elevation without any great *shock* to my delicate nerves." In an aside he later urged his father to see if either of two other officers applied and, if so, to lay aside letters intended for President Polk.[45] In the end, Cheatham did not win a promotion. Records indicate that General Lane took a furlough, during which time Cheatham commanded the Third and Fourth Tennessee and the Fifth Indiana, essentially a brigadier in all but name.[46]

What the episode revealed was Cheatham's intense desire for recognition, as well as a growing confidence in his military capabilities. He yearned for success, certified by a brigadier's rank, a tangible asset he could reflect upon and perhaps use advantageously after the war was over. There is more than a hint that Cheatham found his prewar pursuits insignificant and sought to find his niche in the military. There he could prove to himself and to others that he could do at least one thing well: lead men into battle. The chance would come again, but in 1848 Frank could not foresee that Mexico was a mere prelude to a far larger conflict.

A sudden chance for advancement appeared, and he tentatively grasped it.

The war ended without Cheatham making any great national mark. Peace was declared on July 4, and the Third Tennessee was mustered out at Memphis on July 24. Five days later the regiment returned to Nashville, where it was cheered by fellow citizens both at the wharf and at a reception held at the courthouse. Colonel Cheatham and members of "the best drilled and disciplined volunteer regiment in the service" were civilians again.[47]

Chapter 2

"One of the Wickedest Men I Ever Heard Speak": The 1850s and the Onset of the Civil War

Cheatham returned to Westover, but his stay in Tennessee was a short one. Like thousands of other Americans, Cheatham's adventuresome nature was roused by the discovery of gold in California. Frank journeyed to California with several companions in 1849, one of 89,000 goldseekers who poured into the region that year.[1] He eventually arrived in Stockton, located on a peninsula between two large sloughs formed by the San Joaquin River as it wound its way northwestward to join the Sacramento River. Stockton was settled in 1848 and underwent explosive growth as the forty-niners crowded into California. The expansion was abetted by Stockton's role as a major supply and transportation center for the Southern Mines area of the rich Mother Lode gold fields, a function carried out by Sacramento in the Northern Mines. Within two years of its establishment, Stockton had nearly two thousand permanent residents and a theater, with ships ever-present on the nearby river. In the process of its rapid growth the value of real estate skyrocketed with lots selling for ten or twenty times their original price.[2]

Cheatham realized that the miners would require all sorts of supplies. Foodstuffs, shovels, axes, blankets, and liquor were all items that would fetch a handsome price. Perhaps Frank felt qualified to meet these needs because of the two-year apprenticeship he had served during his adolescence in Philadelphia. In partnership with a fellow Mexican War veteran, Captain Thomas E. Ketcham, Frank operated a general merchandise store in 1849. The next year he began an even more promising venture, opening a hotel and dining establishment called the Hotel de Mexico, a name almost certainly derived from the recently concluded war. The hotel was advantageously situated on Bridge Place, "adjacent to the head of navigation," where riverboats plied their way to and from the city with passengers and cargo.[3].

Frank Cheatham was a perplexing character, with many facets to his personality. If he was a gentle humanitarian at times, as on the dark battlefield at Monterrey, where he aided his wounded comrades, there was also a darker side. According to several accounts, it surfaced in California. From his hotel base Cheatham manipulated the political life of the burgeoning city. One account describes the hotel as "the resort of gamblers and the headquarters of intriguing politicians." Another states that Cheatham "assumed the underground leadership of the city politics." Both maintain that Cheatham was flagrantly defiant of law and order, quick to brandish his revolver "on every occasion which would exalt him in the eyes of his clique."[4] The portrait is distinctly unflattering: it is that of a political boss anxious to elevate himself in the estimation of his associates. The description of Cheatham is a sordid one. He is depicted alternately as "a Southern gambler, a corrupt politician, and a cowardly leader." Not content with the political opportunities Stockton offered, Cheatham delved into statewide affairs by becoming part of the political machine which fellow Tennessean William M. Gwin fashioned after his election to the U.S. Senate from California.[5]

One recorded act best confirms the unattractive view of Cheatham. It occurred not in Stockton but in Sonora, a mining town forty-five miles to the east.[6] Cheatham was in the vicinity for some unknown reason in the summer of 1851 when a thief by the name of Jim Hill entered a mining camp near Sonora and with several accomplices robbed a store. Hill was apprehended shortly afterwards in a brothel in Sonora and taken to jail. The next morning, several Sonorans removed him from the jail and took him to the mining camp for an impromptu trial. A guilty verdict was followed by the determination to execute the thief. Hill acknowledged his guilt in the robbery but denied ever shedding blood. His plea for mercy resulted in a vote regarding his fate, and the large crowd now assembled split on the issue of Hill's sentence. In the ensuing uproar and debate, Sheriff George Work arrived, promised to deliver Hill to the proper authorities, and spirited the robber into a waiting wagon, which sped towards Sonora.

Word reached Sonora that Hill was not yet lynched, and a gong summoned citizens to a meeting. There the recollection of numerous escapes from the local jail cemented the mob's intention to execute Hill. As darkness descended, the wagon containing the sheriff and Hill entered town and crashed into a post. Sheriff Work grabbed Hill and raced for the county jail. The would-be lynchers drew pistols but did not fire, fearful of hitting Sheriff Work or their own friends. On the steps of the jail stood Cheatham, six-shooter in hand. There are several versions of what he said as Work and Hill approached. In one, Frank said simply, "Let the man go, George, or I'll shoot." Another witness wrote that Cheatham challenged Work by saying, "George, you have a pistol and I have a pistol. Yours is cocked and so is mine. Blow away. I can kill too — but let this man go!"[7] Whatever Cheatham said, his actions made Work pause, and the crowd overpowered the sheriff. Hill was seized, and within fifteen minutes was hanged from an oak tree near the jail.

The Cheatham described in these accounts is an unsavory character. Nonetheless, it would be erroneous to conclude that he was alone in his behavior. California during the Gold Rush was not a place for the faint-hearted. Bereft of many of the social and moral restraints of the East, the miners often behaved in ways they would have found inconceivable before their arrival in El Dorado. Especially in the early years, when the mining camps were often all-male enclaves, mining, gambling, and drinking were the chief preoccupations. Cheatham no doubt participated in all three pastimes. As transients, whose sole aim was to make a fortune and clear out in as short a time as possible, the miners tended to disregard legal niceties. Though the lynching of Jim Hill was a brutal act, life itself was a cheap commodity in the mining camps. Criminals routinely robbed and murdered unsuspecting miners. Arguments over claims, accusations at gambling tables, frustration at days of useless toil — all led to murders. In Stockton and Sonora, the Central Valley's dazzling summer heat frayed nerves and induced more bloodshed. Murder was such a common event that the miners and townspeople quickly became inured to it.

The violence spilled over into vigilante-style justice of the kind that cost Jim Hill his life. Scores of people were lynched in the early years of the Gold Rush. The chief attraction of lynchings was their speedy conclusion, important to men who did not like their gold-seeking delayed by legal formalities. In addition, the vigilantes thought of themselves as necessary bulwarks of order. One observer who participated with Cheatham in the Hill lynching described the vigilantes as "the most respectable portion of the community" and applauded the act by citing its deterrent value. A Californian summed up the feelings of many when he remarked, "There's nothing like lynch law, after all. It's so prompt and so effectual."[8] Seen in this light, Cheatham's actions, while still dubious, were not different from those of many of his fellow settlers. The simple fact is that the Cheatham of California was a far less restrained man than he was in faraway Nashville.

Frank, by now in his late thirties, returned to Tennessee, probably via Panama, in 1853. What prompted him to return home is unknown. Maybe it was his sparse luck at mining. He allegedly brought back only enough gold to present gold-headed canes to a number of his friends.

Perhaps his business endeavors proved less than satisfactory. He may have felt that he had had enough adventure and that it was time to settle down. Another possibility revolves around his family. Leonard Cheatham sold Westover in 1850, an act which strongly suggests another period of financial instability for the family. It is hard to imagine that Elizabeth Cheatham would have allowed her husband to sell the property of her ancestors without a protest unless something was amiss. Frank may have come home because Leonard required his assistance. It is impossible to verify this conjecture in the absence of letters from Frank's California sojourn, but it seems plausible. Ironically, shortly after his return, Frank risked his life on Nashville's Public Square by rescuing a man from a mob intent on lynching the fellow for having murdered a prominent citizen. To ascribe this act to belated remorse over the role Cheatham played in the Jim Hill affair is misguided. More likely, Cheatham felt that lynch law was acceptable in the gold fields, but not in his hometown, where justice was meted out in more conventional fashion.[9]

Most biographical sketches summarize Cheatham's activities between his return from California and the outbreak of the Civil War by blandly stating that he resumed farming. Frank Cheatham would have approved of this compressed summary, since he disingenuously represented himself as a simple farmer for the rest of his life. The farming aspect was indeed a good part of Frank's persona, but in the 1850s he made quiet inroads into local and state affairs well beyond the reach of a humble plowman. Many of the activities evolved from the military reputation Cheatham had gained in Mexico.

The first recognition of his martial talents came in the form of an appointment as major-general of Tennessee militia. Cheatham was in charge of the Second Division of state militia when the Civil War erupted. His militia duties allowed him to keep abreast of military developments in much of the state, and also provided him with a new title. He was a general at last, though the rank was acquired in a manner quite unlike he had envisioned in Mexico. In any event, he was alternately referred to as "colonel" or "general" for the rest of the decade.[10] There is little doubt that Cheatham's service in volunteer military organizations, first in the Nashville Blues and later in the state militia, influenced his actions during the Mexican and Civil wars. What is regrettable is that so little is known of this formative period in his army training. Even the date of his elevation to major-general in the militia is unknown, although it seems to have been conferred soon after he returned from California. His experience as a citizen-soldier had both drawbacks and benefits. As one associated with volunteer units in the antebellum period, Cheatham probably respected the potential of men drawn from private pursuits into army life. His own ancestors, particularly General Robertson, included such men. He and the other Tennesseans who served in Mexico shared the notion that they had performed creditably alongside the Regulars. What Cheatham may have been less cognizant of was the resentment felt by many West Point–trained men towards their volunteer counterparts. The sentiment of many professional soldiers was that the volunteers were ill-trained, troublesome, and undisciplined. A certain number of Cheatham's peers in the officer class of the Confederate States Army disparaged the talent of men like Cheatham who were not West Point graduates. Cheatham himself encountered this obstacle when Braxton Bragg became army commander in 1862.[11] The prejudice displayed by Regular army troops towards the volunteers is understandable. Men trained for a professional army career cannot have failed to regard volunteers as amateurs. The prejudice was evident in Mexico and later in the Civil War, despite the fact that both the Union and Confederate armies relied on volunteer regiments. What the professionally trained soldiers may have ignored was that combat was a remarkably democratic experience. Cheatham and his volunteers were expected to take the same risks in battle as any West Point graduate and were just as likely to wind up on the casualty rolls.

Cheatham's military acumen also attracted the attention of three Nashville newspapers in June 1857, when they proposed that the Buchanan administration name Cheatham as governor of Utah, then a territory. This rare unanimity among the papers was in response to widely circulated and sensational (if false) accounts of Utah's Mormon community. Brigham Young and his followers were depicted as religious fanatics, murderers, and hedonists, the latter charge stemming from the avowed Mormon practice of polygamy. One editorial touting Cheatham's selection that he would "in less than no time . . . oust the great apostle of Mormondom, and teach his ill-judging and unfortunate followers that the authority of the United States has to be respected." In spite of the inflamed rhetoric on Frank's behalf, the post went to a Georgian, Alfred Cumming, who eventually cultivated the respect of Brigham Young.[12]

The Buchanan administration apparently sought to placate Cheatham supporters by offering him a diplomatic post instead. At the height of the newspaper campaign to install Cheatham in Utah, he received notice of his appointment as consul to Aspinwall. Aspinwall (or Colon, as the Panamanians successfully insisted on calling it) was a newly constructed port city in north-central Panama. Founded in 1850, it served as the northern terminus of the Panama Railroad, a rail line hacked out of the jungle to link the Caribbean and the Pacific.[13] The unexpected offer caught both Cheatham and Nashville's press off guard. One newspaper wrote approvingly that the consulship was tendered because of Cheatham's "reputation as a gentleman and successful officer" who possessed "practical sense, . . . strict integrity, and fine business habits." All this blithely ignored whether Cheatham spoke the local language or knew anything of Colombian social and diplomatic mores. Another editorial complained that the governorship of Utah was "more suited to the calibre of the man than a consulship." The latter paper correctly guessed that Cheatham would decline the position in Panama, as he did less than a week after receiving the offer.[14]

Though none of the accounts indicate why Cheatham spurned the appointment, several reasons suggest themselves. If the attempt to win Frank the Utah post extended to Washington, the consulship could be construed as a way of eliminating Cheatham from contention while deflecting criticism from Cumming's imminent selection as governor. The timing of the Aspinwall offer suggests a correlation in this regard. Moreover, Aspinwall was no jewel so far as diplomatic posts went; it was a growing city, but one consisting mainly of rickety wooden buildings built on a mud flat. Heat and poor sanitation led to periodic epidemics for decades.[15] Cheatham probably knew at least some of this, since the chances are that he returned from the Gold Rush via Panama. He thus sent his regrets to the Buchanan administration and awaited more appealing enterprises closer to home.

He did not have to wait long. The Democrats in Nashville needed a candidate for the mayoral race in the fall of 1857 and settled on Cheatham as a likely choice. He was no stranger to party politics. Following in his father's footsteps, Frank was a loyal Democrat and party supporter. The previous year he had been selected to serve as president of a club designed to help elect Democrats in Middle Tennessee. Five men announced themselves as candidates for the mayoral contest, but three aspirants withdrew, reducing the race to Cheatham and Nashville attorney John A. McEwen. McEwen was a former editor, was a member of Nashville's first board of education, and was allied with the Whig and Know-Nothing parties. The Democrats relied upon Cheatham's personal popularity to sway voters, for Nashville was dominated by the Whigs and Know-Nothings. One estimate cited "an anti-Democratic majority of 500."[16]

The accord which Nashville's press demonstrated in Cheatham's behalf regarding the Utah governorship disintegrated just weeks later in the face of partisan politics. The Democratic organ strongly endorsed his election, as might have been expected, and asserted that the selection would be "a personal compliment" to Cheatham. Two other newspapers backed McEwen, one citing the Whig's superior qualifications and the other arguing that Cheatham's election would be a severe blow against

Nashville as the stronghold of Know-Nothing sentiment. Both opposition papers were careful not to criticize Cheatham personally, a gesture indicative not only of Frank's popular stature but also of an unwillingness to alienate voters who would otherwise be tempted to cast their ballots for Cheatham. The *Nashville Daily Patriot* bluntly stated that Cheatham's Democratic friends in the state legislature should help him get elected to that body, a none-too-subtle request that he abandon the mayoral contest in favor of McEwen.[17]

The editorials on behalf of each candidate do not reveal what the main issues in the election were. The two men apparently spoke to voters in different areas of the city, but their remarks and arguments were not recorded. In fact, the overridding consideration seems to have been whether the personable war hero Cheatham could garner enough opposition votes to win the election. This was an uphill fight, and when the election was concluded in late September, Cheatham fell short. Cheatham bested McEwen in five of the city's eight wards, but his slim margins in these areas were offset by the Fifth Ward, where McEwen held a 146–66 plurality. The final vote totals were 1,157 for McEwen and 1,082 for Cheatham. Seventy-five votes shy, Cheatham failed to win the one-year term as mayor.[18]

Cheatham's name disappeared from the papers in a political context, but not altogether. Frank was involved with two business arrangements that relied on the dailies for advertising and kept Cheatham's name before the public in a commercial vein. In the first of these enterprises, he was the area sales agent for a manufacturer of farm implements from 1855 through at least 1859. In advertisements from these years, Frank urged local agrarians to purchase Manny's Improved Patent Reaping and Mowing Machine, an implement which sold for $160 when it was introduced. The early sales pitches took a local tack, with a testimonial from eight Davidson and Sumner County farmers. The agriculturalists attested that the machine was a "great labor-saving" device, capable of reaping or mowing ten to fifteen acres a day. As the years elapsed the cumbersome name was shortened; it was billed as the Manny Reaper and Mower by 1859, and the advertising subtly changed. A local tie remained with the mention of the Manny implement's success at an 1857 Davidson County Agricultural Society competition, but the firm also cited the machine's triumphant performance in Louisville and Syracuse. Frank's continued role as area sales agent reflected not only his name recognition among area farmers but also his own steady involvement in agriculture.[19]

The second undertaking was a product of Cheatham's lifelong passion for horses. Frank's affinity for thoroughbreds was strongly influenced by his father, an early member of Nashville's racing establishment. Leonard not only bred horses but raced them as well. His interest extended to the Nashville Jockey Club, an organization which sponsored turf events and which Leonard headed as president in 1839. Frank emulated his father in both the breeding and racing operations, which undoubtedly aided him in becoming proprietor of the Nashville Race Track in 1860.[20] The racetrack, which was in existence from the late 1820s until 1884, was located on the Cumberland River opposite Burns Island. Annually the track proprietor publicized the start of spring and fall meets at the mile-long oval. The meets were of relatively short duration, but attracted gamblers and other spectators. In contrast to modern horse races, the antebellum variety featured several heats among the equine entrants and their jockeys. Frank was no stranger to the course, and he apparently referred to it in an earlier letter to Leonard which exhorted the elder Cheatham to bring horses up for workouts. In 1857, Frank also put up a registration fee and entered horses in two days of the spring racing season. Cheatham's stint as proprietor was short-lived, although he did oversee both thoroughbred and trotting action during his tenure.[21] Given Frank's ardent love of horses, it is reasonable to assume that he could have happily held sway at the racetrack for years. It was not to be. As the new decade unfolded, Frank Cheatham left the paddocks behind and enlisted in the greatest adventure of his century.

There are several maddening mysteries in the Cheatham story, one being to what extent Frank supported the secession of Tennessee. Two postwar sketches suggest that he broke with the Union reluctantly, but these claims are not easily verified. Surely his service in the Mexican War was cause for reflection, but stronger sentiments overrode the old allegiance. One factor was his close friendship with Tennessee governor Isham Harris, a fervent secessionist who propelled the Volunteer state out of the Union. Harris, incidentally, was in a position to promise Cheatham high rank in any state military combine. In the wake of Fort Sumter and after the secession of the Deep South states, Tennessee's position was still undecided. Lincoln's call for volunteers to suppress the rebellion reached Nashville in mid-April 1861, when Secretary of War Simon Cameron wired Harris and requested "two regiments of militia for immediate use." Governor Harris indignantly refused the request, and any hopes moderate Tennesseans may have harbored for peace soon were crushed.[22] Eventually Harris and his followers succeeded in manipulating Tennessee toward secession. In an era where loyalty often lay less with national than with state interests, Cheatham's defection of his native region for the Union would have been extremely unlikely. If any doubts or misgivings existed on Cheatham's part, Harris soon kept him busy enough that no such unwelcome thoughts intruded. Most likely Cheatham had no reservations. War had arrived, and Frank Cheatham was back in his element again.

Governor Harris deemed it important that Tennessee enter the Confederacy with an already existent military organization. To that end he formed the Provisional Army of Tennessee in the spring of 1861. Ostensibly created to dissuade any Federal invasion of the region, Harris's state force became the backbone of the Confederate Army of Tennessee after a military alliance between Tennessee and the Richmond government was finally cemented. The officers appointed to the Provisional Army reflected Tennessee politics and Harris's debt to Whig politicians who helped him win the governorship in 1857 and 1859. The two major-generals—Samuel R. Anderson and Gideon Pillow—were Democrats, but of the five brigadiers appointed, only Cheatham was a Democrat. Gideon Pillow was placed in charge of the state army. The Provisional Army was officially activated May 9, 1861, and Cheatham's appointment bore the same date.[23]

The task of organizing and outfitting the new army was a daunting one. The state militia system had been dissolved between 1859 and 1860, and though a new version had been revived in 1861, its organization was far from perfect.[24] Problems of every sort attended the new force, though manpower was not one of them. Thousands of eager recruits enlisted for service. The main problems were in deciding what to do with all the volunteers and figuring out how to supply them. Harris tapped Cheatham to help out in the latter area, appointing him as acting quartermaster-general for the Provisional Army, and Frank labored energetically in this capacity for two weeks. His actions were supervised by the Military and Financial Board, a trio of businessmen who oversaw the disbursement of $5 million in state funds on behalf of the army. The agency operated even before the army was officially announced, and their messages to Cheatham provide a glimpse of the wide array of items needed to outfit a nineteenth-century army. Cheatham was authorized to obtain cavalry saddles and other leather goods, arrange for military units to be properly uniformed, and secure sites around Nashville for encampments. He provided hand tools to an engineer, forwarded tents to Knoxville, and procured food for Nashville's burgeoning military population. These details were necessary but tiresome, and one wonders if Cheatham felt relieved when Colonel V. K. Stevenson replaced him as quartermaster in mid-May.[25]

Following the brief stint as quartermaster, Cheatham's destination was the ironically named village of Union City in western Tennessee. There he took charge of Camp Brown, a "Camp of Instruction" for the western third of the state. Union City was a small hamlet located on the Mobile

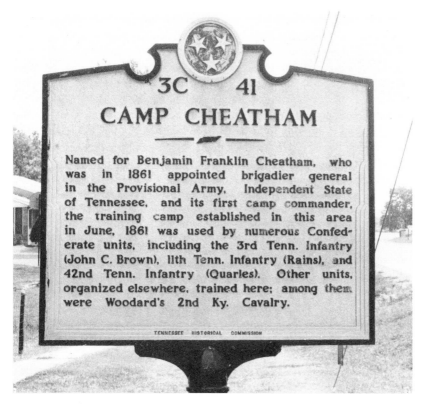

A highway marker in Robertson County indicates the wartime site of Camp Cheatham. Cheatham remained here but a short time, as he was soon dispatched to Camp Brown, in Union City. (Author's photo)

and Ohio Railroad, a line which connected Tennessee with nearby Kentucky as well as with points farther south. There was not much to the place besides the railroad station. One of the recruits who would serve throughout the war with Cheatham, John Cavanaugh of the Ninth Tennessee Regiment, wrote later that there was a general store, "an old blacksmith shop," and a building which "was called, by courtesy, a 'saloon.'" The camp itself was situated on a poplar ridge which one newly arrived volunteer described as "beautiful."[26] Despite the attractiveness of the surroundings, Cheatham faced another arduous task as men poured into Union City. The recruits appeared in all manner of dress and organization, or lack thereof. Many arrived without arms, or with unreliable flintlock muskets. Cheatham remained at Camp Brown and attempted to familiarize the new regiments with army routine. This was a laborious process and occasionally a frustrating one for both the recruits and their superiors. One officer wrote to his father, after being in camp for two weeks, "I have more to do than I had anticipated," but acknowledged that this was because "we were fresh from the woods and unacquainted with drill." Belonging to such a large concentration of men was a new experience for many of the troops. One wrote, "I am better pleased with camp life than I thought I would be but what a contrast between this and the pleasures and quietude of a home." He concluded his missive home by asking that its recipients forgive his spelling errors, "For there is so much fuss [here] a man can't keep his mind on one thing long."[27]

Cheatham was not always popular in these early months of the war and earned the enmity of "the multitudes" who were denied furloughs. Unaccustomed as yet to military discipline, men who wished to slip away for a visit to wives or sweethearts, or to check on the crops, regarded Cheatham as "unfeeling and tyran[n]ical" when he refused to release them.[28] Instead of furloughs, Cheatham made them drill incessantly as spring gave way to summer. An observant private, Joe Spence, provided a portrait of Cheatham at Camp Brown. The general, then approaching his forty-first birthday, was described as being nearly five feet nine, with dark, weatherbeaten skin, "portly looking, quite personable, pleasant and affable in his manners at all times." The description added that Cheatham wore a heavy moustache, looked like a soldier, and was "quite commanding in his appearance." Other sources indicate he possessed light blue eyes and wavy dark hair, and was known for his extraordinary physical strength. Spence's otherwise favorable assessment concluded sadly that Cheatham was "one of the wickedest men I ever heard speak." His talent for profane outbursts, already established at Union City, became legendary and continued throughout the war.[29]

As Spence sized up his commander, Governor Harris was winning re-election, which bolstered his resolve to admit Tennessee into the Confederacy. He formally tendered the Provisional Army to Jefferson Davis in June, noting that it contained twenty-two infantry regiments, a pair of cavalry regiments, and ten artillery companies. Richmond accepted the transfer later that month but did not grant all of Harris's high command a corresponding rank in the Confederate army. Harris interceded on their behalf and was partially successful in winning appointments for his supporters. He strongly urged that the Tennessee troops be led by officers from the state.[30] This ploy to have Richmond acquiesce in commissioning all of Harris's political appointees had far-reaching effects. Cheatham, who won a brigadier's rank to date from July 9, led men from Tennessee for most of the war.

Cheatham may or may not have been aware of Harris's machinations on his behalf. The weeks at Union City occupied all his energies. Well before the Provisional Army was transferred to Confederate service, units from other states were added to the numbers at Camp Brown. Cheatham wrote Gideon Pillow that there were Mississippians in camp, Kentuckians were "anxious to get in," and some Missourians wished to be discharged. Other correspondence with Pillow revolved around the specific details of the growing army's needs. Cheatham complained that he had trouble procuring supplies from Memphis, mentioned he had sent an officer there for rifles, and asked Pillow to send cartridges and cap and cartridge boxes. He sought to have a surgeon assigned to a Mississippi cavalry unit and received regular communications from an informant in Cairo, Illinois, of projected Federal troop movements. The dispatches occasionally reveal Cheatham as being exasperated. The dilapidated "saloon" described by Cavanaugh must have had competition as entrepreneurs moved near the encampment to provide the troops with liquid refreshment. "I am troubled to death with the whiskey shops in Union City," Cheatham wrote in June, and he asked permission to close the liquor establishments.[31] The tenor of the messages is of a somewhat harried man trying to impose order in a semichaotic situation.

Cheatham drilled and organized at least nine regiments during his stay at Camp Brown. This ended in late July, when he took part in an excursion into Missouri with several of his regiments. The movement into Missouri was part of a quixotic invasion scheme formulated by Gideon Pillow and General Leonidas Polk. Polk, the former Episcopal bishop of Louisiana, was in temporary command of the western theater. Polk and his subordinate envisioned a bold sweep towards St. Louis, an idyllic vision that collapsed soon after it was conceived. The army was not seasoned enough or healthy enough for such an offensive, factors that Polk soon acknowledged, although Pillow continued to support the invasion. Before the impracticability of the scheme became evident, Pillow and later Cheatham brought troops into Missouri's Bootheel via New Madrid. Cheatham and the force at New Madrid languished while Pillow vainly urged the grand offensive to Polk. Cheatham was left briefly in charge at New Madrid when Pillow went to consult with General Polk. Like Pillow, Cheatham was subjected to entreaties from others to plunge northward with his tiny army. M. Jeff Thompson, a Missouri cavalry leader, feverishly implored Cheatham to move on Cape Girardeau and close the Mississippi to navigation. Thompson added that if Cheatham did not strike quickly, "the hordes of the North" would engulf the state and snuff out the hopes of Missourians loyal to the Confederacy.[32]

The last thing Cheatham wanted to do was to head for Cape Girardeau. He and several other officers conferred with Pillow before the latter went to see Polk. They strongly opposed any movement up the Bootheel and argued that the army could be easily attacked by Union forces if Pillow persisted in his plan. Faced with this opposition, Pillow finally relented to Polk's wish that the Missouri offensive be aborted.[33] This did not mean that Pillow abandoned all hopes of leading an offensive. He merely changed targets. The new site for Pillow's projected grandeur was Kentucky, which suddenly became more appealing than the dismal swamps and forests around New Madrid. Kentucky was attempting a hopeless but game strategy of neutrality, and Pillow never considered that the state served Tennessee as a temporarily convenient buffer zone. Nor did Polk comprehend the potential danger of entering Kentucky, for he accepted Pillow's advice that Columbus, thirty miles north of Union City, be seized.

The Confederates who marched into Kentucky were not the first soldiers to violate the state's neutrality. An indignant Columbus citizen related how a Union vessel loaded with troops had halted at the town so that a Confederate flag could be torn down. The essential difference, minute as it was, was that the Federals arrived, destroyed the flag, and then went back to Cairo, Illinois. The Confederates who seized Columbus and the smaller town of Hickman obviously intended to stay. They aroused the wrath of the Kentucky legislature, as well as the state's prosecession governor, and alienated many citizens in the state.[34] The Confederates were viewed as the aggressors, offsetting whatever advantage Columbus may have provided with a public relations debacle.

Cheatham's force grabbed Hickman, a Mississippi River town just north of the Tennessee state line, in early September. On September 4, two Union gunboats steamed down the river and exchanged ineffectual artillery fire with Cheatham's batteries and a Confederate vessel. This was allegedly the first hostile engagement on the Mississippi, and the Southerners brashly claimed that they repelled the "squadron." It is more likely that the Union gunboats were on a reconnaissance mission and wound their way upriver after locating their adversaries. Two days after crossing into Kentucky, Cheatham was at Columbus. Polk considered an attack on Paducah, which Ulysses S. Grant occupied after the Confederate invasion, but after sending Cheatham twenty-five miles east to the town of Mayfield, he reconsidered and summoned the force back to Columbus.[35] There, the Southerners set to work constructing a gigantic anchor and chain which they later strung across the Mississippi to close navigation.

Thomas Connelly has suggested that Columbus was an untenable position and that the Confederate strategists blundered in not building adequate defenses on the vital inland river arteries which flowed into Tennessee. Cheatham shared this myopic view that the Mississippi was the most important river system and the one which required the bulk of Southern attention. He, Polk, and Pillow disregarded the danger inherent in a Union drive up the Cumberland or Tennessee Rivers.[36] For Cheatham it was an odd miscalculation, considering that the Cumberland flowed past Westover and was his hometown's lifeline.

Cheatham and the other officers at Columbus continued erecting fortifications and drilling their troops as summer gave way to autumn. Many Kentuckians around Columbus supported the Confederacy, but the Southerners did not trust all the inhabitants. Cheatham caused a stir when he arrived at the local branch of the Bank of Kentucky on November 1, 1861. Acting on Polk's orders, Cheatham threatened bank officials with a military takeover of the institution to prevent funds from being removed to Union lines. The bank cashier wrote a heated note to Polk, protesting the seizure and vowing not to transfer the funds to Paducah "as was contemplated."[37] Whether the bank deposits were confiscated is unknown, but the episode is symptomatic of Kentucky's divided loyalties.

Back in June, when the troops were still at Union City, one of Cheatham's men had written home that "when the time comes should it ever you will hear a good account of Brigadier General B. F. Cheatham and those under his command."[38] Not until November 7, and a week after the minor diversion at the bank, did Cheatham's troops finally get their first taste of battle. Union commander Ulysses S. Grant provided the opportunity when he collected a force of 3,000 men and sailed downriver on four transports. Two gunboats accompanied the expedition. Several miles upriver from Columbus the Federals halted, debarking on the Missouri side of the river. From their landing point the Union column marched for Belmont, an inconsequential hamlet across from Columbus which existed primarily because of a steamboat landing at the site. The alarm sounded in the Confederate camp at Columbus when Grant's movement was discovered, and Cheatham's green troops prepared themselves for battle. At first, Polk felt the Union column represented a diversion aimed at drawing attention from another attack against Columbus itself. Still, to protect the undersized garrison at Belmont, he sent Gideon Pillow across the river with four regiments.

Two of the four regiments had been organized and trained by Cheatham at Union City, and the prospect of a battle at Belmont represented a sort of commencement both for Cheatham and his men. One of the soldiers, Alfred Tyler Fielder of the Twelfth Tennessee, wrote in his diary later that Pillow's force advanced quickly to meet Grant's approaching bluecoats. Fielder recounted that when the order to fire was given, "such roar of cannon and sound of small arms never saturated my ears." For Fielder and the other participants on both sides, Belmont transformed

Alfred Tyler Fielder served in the Twelfth Tennessee Regiment, and his wartime diary is one of the best sources for information related to Cheatham and his division. Fielder was wounded twice during the war, but he survived the conflict and returned to his Dyer County home afterwards. (Tennessee State Library and Archives)

combat from an eagerly awaited possibility to an abrupt reality. Perceptions sharpened by the conflict helped soldiers to focus on certain vivid details. At one point, Fielder's company withdrew to the rear to replenish their cartridges, and when they returned to the battle line, Fielder noted how "the bullets whistled about our heads and our feet." James Rosser of the Twelfth Tennessee wrote that "the balls sing merrily over our heads" and recalled the "cannon balls, bom[b] shells, grape & canister shot playing all around thick as hail in a storm." Rosser relived the experience so completely that his diary entry, written the day after the battle, begins in past tense but then slips into the present as if he were again on the battlefield. Samuel Latta of the Thirteenth Tennessee wrote that the Yankees were posted in the woods and that the Southerners were subjected to a "perfect hail of bullets from an enemy that we could scarcely see." Although the Tennesseans tried to shield themselves by lying flat on the ground, when they returned the Union fire there was little noticeable effect. When his unit advanced, Latta was struck on the hip by a minie ball. He checked the wound, "expecting to find [his hands] covered with blood" but was "agreeably surprised" to discover that his watch fob flap had deflected the bullet. Latta was bruised, not bloodied.[39]

Pillow's and Grant's men banged away at one another for the better part of two hours, and then the Southern line suddenly collapsed. Efforts to rally the troops were unsuccessful, and Pillow's men scrambled for cover behind a low bank near the river. At this juncture, Polk decided to reinforce Pillow, convinced apparently that Columbus was safe from a rear attack. The former cleric dispatched Cheatham across the river with additional troops. Before he departed, Cheatham left instructions for his artillery leader, Melancthon Smith, to shift a battery and shell the Union troops, now exposed to fire from the Kentucky side of the river. Smith's gunners swung into action as Grant's victorious Union troops overran the Confederate camp at Belmont and proceeded to plunder it. Union officers attempted to restore order but had a difficult time as their charges busied themselves collecting souvenirs and other artifacts from the Rebel encampment. Some Confederates took advantage of this respite to creep northward along the riverbank and reorganize. Cheatham and his reinforcements steamed across to the Missouri shore and were greeted by shouts from dispirited comrades telling them not to land. Cheatham ignored the advice, and the appearance of fresh troops further emboldened some of Pillow's men who were huddled under the bank. The two generals met and together managed to rally enough of the troops for Cheatham to move upriver with a portion of the command. The aim was to strike the Federal flank, but a potential obstacle appeared less than a half mile from Cheatham's starting point, when a column of cavalrymen rode up. Cheatham hailed the mounted force and was startled when his inquiry revealed that they were from Illinois. The Tennessean cooly replied, "Oh, Illinois cavalry! All right; just stand where you are." Cheatham then cantered back to the Southern line, deluding not only the horsemen but a nearby battle line composed of Illinois and Iowa infantry. Reaching the safety of a small ravine, Cheatham hastily threw his own troops into battle formation and assailed the bewildered Federals.[40]

Soon afterwards, Cheatham rendezvoused with Polk, who ferried across the river with elements of Cheatham's brigade and another regiment. Polk urged Cheatham to continue his pursuit of the Yankees, who fled for their transports as the Southern advantage in numbers began to tell. The chase wound through river thickets and cornfields for more than two miles. With the tables turned in their behalf, the Confederates who had retreated earlier managed to regain much of their previous self-confidence. Samuel Latta of the Thirteenth Tennessee reported: "We stood behind the trees and shot them down. I saw them fall in my direction." Latta, an officer, rushed up to a fleeing Federal and "seized him by the neck," an action which convinced the Yankee to "surrender without a struggle." Latta wrote later, "The poor fellow was worried [and] frightened to death," a fairly sensible reaction considering the manner in which he was captured.[41] If Latta and his comrades had been nervous earlier, this sentiment appears to have dissipated as they pursued Grant's troops.

Cheatham's men were never able to cut off the retreating Yankees, and the protective fire of the gunboats halted the Rebels as they approached the riverbank. There, they fired upon the Union flotilla until the Yankees severed the boat lines and steamed out of range. Fortune smiled on Grant as well as Cheatham. He was the last man aboard the transports, and during the pursuit Cheatham's men had been within fifty yards of the Union general as he spurred his mount through a cornfield. While Grant and his force were not bagged, as Cheatham might have wished, their hasty retreat to the boats did provide the graycoats with a number of tangible benefits. Several accounts made note of the vast quantity of goods abandoned by the Federals as they fled. Men who a short time before were acquiring items from the Rebel camp jettisoned not only the Southern mementos but much of their own gear. The path of their retreat was strewn with arms, ammunition, blankets, knapsacks, and anything else which may have impeded their speedy flight. Cheatham's men may have been novices at war, but they were quick learners when it came to appropriating the discarded items. "I have a trophy in the shape of a nice comfortable militaire [sic] overcoat," Samuel Latta wrote to his wife, and other members of Cheatham's command were as adept as Latta in garnering equipment.[42]

Grant later claimed victory at Belmont, asserting that the raid kept Polk from sending men to reinforce M. Jeff Thompson as Union columns probed into Missouri. The Confederates denied the boast, citing that they drove Grant's men back upriver. In reality, both sides acquitted themselves well, considering the inexperience of the two contestants. Compared to later battles, Belmont was exceedingly small, and strategically it proved worthless. But it did provide a combat opportunity for both armies, and the casualties, which totalled roughly six hundred men on each side, were evidence that Yankees and Rebels alike could fight. Samuel Latta was exuberant and crowed, "The victory is complete." Alfred Tyler Fielder was somber and wept as he read two letters from his wife. The tears were probably a delayed reaction to the initial shock of battle. Fielder, Latta, and the remainder of their comrades had yearned for battle, but when it came, they quickly lost any notions about warfare's being romantic. Both men reported that they saw men who were nearby shot down. Fielder returned to the Missouri side the next day with three other members of his company to help tend to the dead and wounded of both armies. The scene sobered him and inspired this fatalistic notation in his diary: "I do not remember to have ever seen a day in my life that I felt more thankful and more willing to submit to the will of providence."[43]

Cheatham had seen men die before in distant Mexico, but at Belmont he was involved in the altogether different proposition of killing fellow Americans. It would be interesting to know what his thoughts were as Grant's expedition steamed away. Certainly the adrenalin surge prompted by the chase and his own close encounter with the Illinois cavalry would have been working on him. His official report indicates that he felt gratified by the conduct of his brigade and the other men he helped train at Union City. One wonders how much regret he felt at not being able to keep Grant from escaping, or if he harbored feelings of sadness as he inspected the casualties of both armies scattered about the field. No matter what his private thoughts were, the Confederacy as a whole celebrated the victory at Belmont. Polk, Pillow, and Cheatham were honored by a resolution of thanks the Confederate Congress passed in December.[44]

Despite Belmont's relative insignificance, it figured in a couple of peculiarities as far as Cheatham was concerned. Mark Twain included a brief description of the battle years later, in *Life on the Mississippi*. Twain supposedly heard about the action from a riverboat pilot who conveyed Confederates from Kentucky to the Missouri side during the fray. According to the pilot, Cheatham had his men strip their coats off and throw them in a pile, and then urged them on by hollering, "Follow me to victory or hell!" The phrase sounds authentic in the light of Cheatham exhortations in later battles and was typically direct. One can imagine the conflicting emotions of the men aboard the steamer with Cheatham. On the one hand was their commander, inviting them to attack in no uncertain terms, while simultaneously they heard some of Pillow's more dejected soldiers bellowing from the shore, "Go back! We are whipped!"[45]

Cheatham and several members of his command met with Grant and his staff a few days after the battle, when the Federals came downriver. The two sides exchanged prisoners, arranged to bury the Northern dead, and even agreed that the Yankees would return a black servant owned by an Arkansas officer. Cheatham and Grant renewed an acquaintance on the boats, as the two knew one another from their service under Zachary Taylor in Mexico. Several of Cheatham's obituaries noted that he was a "close friend" of Grant, but this was probably not true. Close friends were a rare commodity for U. S. Grant among his Union counterparts, much less among the opposing ranks. Nevertheless, the two men did share several qualities and were in may respects of the same temperament. These similarities would explain the mutual respect the two officers seem to have had. Both were horse enthusiasts, and after a spirited discussion Frank good-naturedly suggested that the war be settled by a horse race. Grant laughingly replied that he wished they could do so.[46]

There was also a less seemingly similarity between the two men. Rumors about both Grant's and Cheatham's affinity for liquor dogged both men for the rest of their lives. One source implies that the two men lived up to the billing during the river truce. Following the prisoner exchange, Grant invited Cheatham to the saloon of his boat. One of Cheatham's staff officers recalled that champagne corks were popping as the erstwhile combatants entered the saloon. "The table was spread and the wine was distributed to willing hands," wrote the officer, "and for one hour it was the gayest, liveliest crowd of belligerents that ever assembled." The captain of Cheatham's boat twice suggested that the Confederates should be heading back to Columbus, as daylight was fading, and the Rebels reluctantly prepared to depart. Before they did so, several toasts were made, and then Grant divulged that he wanted a button off of Cheatham's coat as a keepsake of the occasion. Cheatham replied, "Help yourself," and Grant thereupon obtained a knife and cut off a button from the bottom of Cheatham's coat. Unfortunately, he also made a hole in Cheatham's "splendid new uniform" about the same size as a "silver half dollar." Cheatham then invited members of Grant's staff to snip some buttons, and additional havoc was wreaked on the garment. Cheatham and his compatriots took leave of their hosts, and returned to their own vessel. Arriving near Columbus, Cheatham and his cohorts wisely decided to remain on the boat for the night, and delayed their report to Polk until the morning.[47]

In spite of the conviviality shared by Grant and Cheatham on the boat, perhaps the strongest link between the two was their behavior between the Mexican and Civil Wars. Grant remained in the peacetime army after the Mexican War, then resigned his commission. He knocked around, unable to make a success of farming, and wound up working in Galena, Illinois, in his father's store.[48] Cheatham's California stay did not pan out as he had hoped, and he wound up back in Nashville. At least he had the demonstrated approval of his fellow citizens, who voted for him in a mayoral race, and thought he would make a fine governor of Utah. But underlying the 1850s was the notion that Cheatham, like Grant, did not measure up to his own self-image. After all, he lost the mayoral election and the appointment as governor and had not married. As the years elapsed, the Mexican War experience must have loomed larger to Cheatham, as it did to Grant. Both men must have wondered if they would ever recapture the same sense of mission and accomplishment that they felt at Monterrey. The most striking resemblance between the two men is that the Civil War rescued them from oblivion. Both became famous, though Grant's fame far outshone Cheatham's, by excelling in a terrible business: leading men to their death.

Chapter 3

"Old Frank Is One of the Boys": Shiloh and Its Aftermath

The months surrounding New Year's Day 1862 were eventful ones for Cheatham and his fellow Confederates. Just prior to Belmont, Leonidas Polk wrote his old friend Jefferson Davis and tendered his resignation, noting the arrival of Albert Sidney Johnston to command the Western Department. Responding after the battle of Belmont, Davis refused to accept Polk's resignation and cited the success at Belmont and a continued need for Polk's services.[1] Polk remained in the military, and his continued presence was to have far-reaching consequences for Cheatham and the army's future. Shortly after Belmont, Polk was incapacitated for a month because of injuries incurred when a Dahlgren gun burst while he was standing near a river battery. His recuperation was not speeded by Gideon Pillow, who found in Polk's injury an opportunity for personal initiative in solidifying the Columbus defenses and then embarking on an offensive. When Polk refused to endorse the move, Pillow angrily fired off a long list of grievances to Richmond, along with his resignation. Pillow did not help his cause by implying that Polk was insane and unfit for command. Polk waited until the summer before replying to Pillow's charges but eventually dispatched an equally long letter depicting Pillow's inadequacies. A furious Pillow left the army. Although Pillow's military service did continue, Polk was undoubtedly pleased when his antagonist stormed out of Columbus.[2] The Polk-Pillow feud was a precursor of the many intraarmy squabbles which hampered the western army's performance throughout the war.

Cheatham became involved obliquely in the argument. Gideon Pillow's major problem was that he could not forget his leading role in the Mexican War. He was aggrieved that men who were subordinate to him in Mexico were now his equals or his superiors in the Confederate service. Cheatham was one of the former, and it apparently galled Pillow that he and Cheatham shared the same rank at Columbus. He was also vexed when Cheatham sided with Polk in arguing that an offensive was inadvisable. Frank must have let his family know that he regarded Pillow as a nuisance, for Pillow's departure from Columbus was hailed by Elizabeth Cheatham. "I hope you have had time to dry your eyes since the crying at Pillow's parting from the army," she sarcastically wrote her son. She added wryly that a Memphis correspondent would eventually be "reconciled to the great loss the War department has sustained in his resignation."[3]

While several officers thus squandered their time in quarrels, Johnston's Kentucky defense line, centered at Bowling Green, remained vulnerable. The Federals exploited the weakness in February by bringing a flotilla up the Tennessee River. The Union move forced the surrender of Fort Henry, and the scene shifted to Fort Donelson on the Cumberland River. Union gunboats and Grant's infantry were assisted by a series of Confederate errors, and Donelson's capitulation paved the way for an assault on Nashville. In a two-week span, Johnston's long Kentucky line collapsed, and much of valuable Middle Tennessee was evacuated. Cheatham and others worked to remove guns and other supplies from Columbus, which was vacated in the wake of the disaster.[4]

The army fell back via Union City and Humboldt, finally halting at Corinth, Mississippi. For Cheatham it must have been an unpleasant time. As his men passed through Union City, thoughts of the previous summer at Camp Brown surely came to mind. The high hopes of those months contrasted with the depression engendered by the sudden retreat. More personal considerations added to Cheatham's anxiety. He eventually learned that his cousin Richard B. Cheatham, mayor of Nashville, rowed across the Cumberland River when the first Federal units appeared and offered the city to the Yankees. Cheatham's family apparently remained in the city, though many other residents fled. Frank's sister Louise lived in Louisiana, and she expressed in a letter the fears her brother must have shared. "I have heard nothing of the family and try to think that nothing disagreeable will happen to them."[5]

In spite of the generally dark news during this period, Cheatham's military career received a boost when he was promoted to major-general. The promotion was due in part to the strenuous efforts of Tennessee senator Gustavus A. Henry. Henry was a former leader of the Whig party in the state and had been twice defeated for the governorship by Andrew Johnson. Regarded as a Davis supporter in the Confederate Congress, Henry wrote a letter on March 10, 1862, imploring the president to promote Cheatham. The two politicians had previously discussed the matter, and apparently Davis mentioned another possible claimant to the rank. Henry urgently pressed Davis to send Cheatham's nomination to the Senate, maintaining that Cheatham was "greatly . . . superior" to

Cheatham entered Confederate service as a brigadier and won promotion to major-general after the Battle of Belmont. (National Archives)

the other officer. Henry argued that Cheatham's "great experience" supplanted "any want of training in the schools." This was obviously intended to allay any reservations Davis may have had regarding Cheatham's lack of a West Point education. The Tennessee politician enthusiastically described Cheatham's "cool deliberate courage and gallantry" and asserted that the "appointment would create a thrill of joy in the army and impart hope [and] confidence to the people of the state." Davis knew something of Cheatham from their service together in Mexico and had described him as a "brave & zealous" officer to Polk in the fall of 1861. When the decision to promote one of the two officers was rendered, Cheatham was the winner. Senator Henry's impassioned plea had the desired effect; Cheatham's nomination and approval followed almost immediately. Cheatham's appointment was made March 14, but was backdated to March 10, the very day Henry had dispatched his letter to Davis.[6]

With the new rank came increased responsibilities. As a major-general, Cheatham commanded a division and supervised larger numbers of troops. Though the number of regiments and brigades he directed varied, in the early weeks as a divisional commander he led two brigades, one under Ohio-born Bushrod Rust Johnson, and another under William H. Stephens. Cheatham's division consisted of eight regiments and two artillery batteries. One Kentucky and one Mississippi regiment were the only non-Tennessee units, as generals often directed troops from their own state, especially in the early part of the war. This practice was exactly what Isham Harris had recommended for Tennessee troops earlier, and Davis approved of the custom, rightly figuring that Southern soldiers were more willing to be led by prominent men from their home states.[7]

Cheatham was destined for action as a divisional commander less than a month after receiving the promotion. After the fall of Fort Henry and Fort Donelson, Union troops probed up the Tennessee River. Heavy spring rains forced them to abandon a thrust into northern Mississippi, so they congregated in large numbers at Pittsburg Landing, an insignificant freight depot for goods going to Corinth. Other riverboat landings were occupied as well, including Crump's Landing and Savannah, the largest village along this stretch of the river. The Union general in charge of most of these dispersions was an Ohioan, William Tecumseh Sherman. A grizzled, red-haired graduate of West Point, Sherman occupied Pittsburg Landing in mid-March, partly because reports reached him that Cheatham was in the vicinity with a large force. If Cheatham was in the area, he was probably headed for Corinth, where troops from other parts of the West were massing. The numbers attributed to Cheatham's column ranged as high as 18,000, an absurdly exaggerated figure. Nonetheless, the reports concerned both Sherman and General Lew Wallace, destined in the future to write *Ben Hur*, who was commanding a division at Crump's Landing.

If alleged sightings of Cheatham made the Federals uneasy, the reverse was also true. As Northern forces under Grant continues to concentrate around Pittsburg Landing, anxiety among the Confederate high command grew. Albert Sidney Johnston sought to keep an eye on the expanding force, as did his military associates. These included officers such as Polk, P. G. T. Beauregard, and Braxton Bragg, who arrived from the Gulf Coast. Disquieting rumors that twenty-five to thirty thousand men under General Don Carlos Buell were on their way to link up with Grant also provoked alarm. The Southerners had one brigade, under Bushrod Johnson, at Bethel Station, over twenty miles north of Corinth, to screen any Yankee moves. Towards the end of the March, Johnson reported increasing enemy activity between Pittsburg Landing and Lew Wallace's division at Crump's Landing. Since Bethel Station was accessible from Crump's Landing via a road which cut through the hamlets of Adairsville and Purdy, Johnson feared his small force might be attacked and cut off from the main army at Corinth.

This prospect troubled Beauregard, for Bethel was on the vital Mobile and Ohio Railroad. Accordingly, he sent Cheatham northward with another brigade to bolster Johnson. Beauregard gave Cheatham elaborate instructions to guard the Mobile and Ohio and Mississippi Central rail lines. He was especially insistent that Cheatham personally make a five-mile reconnaissance of the roads leading to and from Bethel Station. Cheatham was also told to station several regiments and pieces of artillery near Purdy, closer to the Union encampment. Beauregard, perhaps mindful that Cheatham was a new divisional commander, also cautioned him not to heed false rumors and set off false alarms.[8]

Cheatham arrived at Bethel Station, superseded Bushrod Johnson, and made several troop dispositions. One of the regiments he sent out toward Purdy was the 154th Tennessee, a unit which retained its old militia designation throughout the war. Colonel Preston Smith used cavalry to scout the Union positions, interrogated three prisoners, and tried to estimate the number of Yankees clustered at Adairsville and Crump's Landing. The two sides were close to one another, Smith's troopers being only eleven miles from Wallace's outposts at Adairsville. In essence the two opposing sides startled one another, and each believed the other was about to attack. More importantly, Beauregard at Corinth interpreted Cheatham's reports concerning Federal activity as a signal that Grant and Buell were about to effect a junction. At a conference with other army officers, Beauregard suggested that the Southerners strike Grant before Buell arrived.[9]

For Albert Sidney Johnston, the suggestion was welcome. Hailed as the savior of the west when he arrived in the department, the handsome Kentuckian had presided instead over the disastrous loss of Kentucky and Middle Tennessee. Defeating Grant's army would be a way of rebutting the criticism heaped upon him for the reversals. Johnston allowed Beauregard to construct an intricate battle plan and got the army on the move back into Tennessee.

From the outset difficulties impeded the advance. Most of the forty thousand–plus troops were raw, unaccustomed yet to discipline or hard marching. With the army divided into four corps, delays and mixups slowed progress. Cheatham's division exemplified some of the problems. A dispatch from Beauregard on April 3 mystified the Tennessean. It specified that he defend Bethel and Purdy if attacked, then join Polk's main column if no assault was forthcoming. The message did not say how long he should wait at Bethel Station nor specify the number of rations his men should carry. To further complicate matters, Cheatham did not recognize the name of the road where he was supposed to rendezvous with Polk. Faced with the confusing instructions, Cheatham did not advance until April 5 and did not link up with the rest of the corps until the afternoon. Johnston and Beauregard had envisioned an attack on April 4, and that day and the next elapsed without an assault because of the delays by Cheatham and other units. A thoroughly exasperated Johnston labeled the effort "perfectly puerile," and Beauregard, convinced that the essential element of surprise had long since evaporated, conselled a withdrawal back to Corinth.[10]

Johnston debated the issue with his top officers and then overruled Beauregard's suggestion. The army was already in battle formation, the four corps arranged in successive lines. The strategy devised by Beauregard called for the Union left to by rolled up away from the Tennessee River and pinned along Owl and Snake Creeks. There, the Confederates could annihilate Grant's five divisions. With Johnston firmly resolved to fight, troublesome delays were nearly over for the Army of Mississippi. The ensuing battle of Shiloh would be their first major test. The first wave belonged to the corps of William J. Hardee, a Georgia native whose textbook on light infantry tactics was studied by officers on both sides. Hardee's men ran into the nearest Federal division and discovered that the Yankees had not entrenched themselves, as Beauregard feared. Although some Union units disintegrated as the initial shock wave struck, others began to organize and resist the long lines of gray infantry.[11]

Cheatham's division was in Polk's corps, aligned behind Hardee's and Bragg's troops. As the conflict escalated, Cheatham led his soldiers forward about a mile, the din from the battle growing louder as they advanced. Soon afterwards Polk directed Cheatham to dispatch his First Brigade to Bragg's left. Cheatham accompanied them for a half hour, but before the brigade was heavily engaged, a note arrived from Beauregard. The Creole's message ordered Cheatham to take his Second Brigade to the far right, where the firing was heaviest, and engage the enemy. The reception of this note had several ramifications for Cheatham, the main one being that he was deprived of half his force for the initial portion

of the battle. In fact, he did not supervise his First Brigade for much of
the day, Bushrod Johnson assuming that chore. This was not unusual,
but the rapid intermingling of Confederate units hurt cohesion and grew
more chaotic as the day wore on. Cheatham received Beauregard's message around 9 A.M., but even at this early hour the Rebel high command
was having trouble managing the battle. Beauregard's injunction to Cheatham indicated that the Tennessean was needed on the right but was not
at all precise as to where he could be used most advantageously or who
required his support.[12]

Cheatham led Colonel Stephens's brigade for about an hour and halted
around 10 A.M. in front of an open field. The field was owned in peacetime by farmer Joseph Duncan, and Cheatham later estimated that it was
about 300 yards wide. Cheatham's postbattle report also noted that it
was flanked by thickets on both sides, with particularly heavy undergrowth and woods to the right. Peering across the opening, Cheatham
could see that the Federals were grouped behind a fence row running along
"an abandoned road." This sunken road afforded natural protection, as
did the dense brush along the fence and in the woods. What Cheatham
surveyed was one of the clear spots in a Union line that ran in an arc
for half a mile and contained over eleven thousand blue-clad troops. These
men were mostly Midwesterners, with Iowans predominating within
Cheatham's range of vision, and represented elements of three Union divisions. Before the day was over, these Yankees would contest the Confederate attacks with such ferocity that the area they defended acquired a
nickname from the Rebels—the Hornets' Nest.[13]

Cheatham could not have foreseen in mid-morning the extent to which
the Hornets' Nest would stall the Confederate drive, but he did realize
that he needed support before he attacked. He also knew that he needed
to loosen the Yankees from their formidable position as much as possible.
To dislodge them he brought forward Melanchton Smith's Mississippi
battery. Smith got his guns unlimbered, but not without some difficulty,
as a Union battery opened up and killed a number of horses while they
were still attached to the fieldpieces and caissons. For an hour the two
sides duelled, the Mississippians doggedly shelling the Federals behind the
fencerow as the Yankee artillerists zeroed in on the Rebel guns. It took
fortitude and perseverance for Smith's gunners to keep at their task, for,
as Cheatham later conceded, the Union guns were of superior caliber
and range.[14]

The artillery sparring might have continued if Colonel Thomas Jordan,
Sidney Johnston's adjutant general, had not ridden by Cheatham's brigade.
Though a staff officer, Jordan was issuing field orders on behalf of his su-
periors and instructed Cheatham to press an attack across the opening.

Cheatham organized his three regiments, the Seventh Kentucky and the Sixth and Ninth Tennessee, in battle formation. Once his troops were properly aligned, they set out across the field, Cheatham joining his men in the assault. The command began at double-quick time and made it halfway across the field in relatively good shape. From that point well-directed Union artillery and infantry fire sliced through Cheatham's ranks. The brigade was especially staggered by "a murderous crossfire" from behind a fence and thicket on the left, and as the losses mounted, the assault lost steam. Cheatham asserted that his men halted near the center of the field and returned the fire, but confessed that he returned to his original position "after a short time."[15]

Cheatham's sortie was most successful on the right, where the Sixth Tennessee's approach was masked by the woods. The regiment burst out from the trees nearly a hundred yards from the Federal line, but they too were eventually rebuffed by concentrated Union fire. An Iowa colonel reported that Cheatham's men "men with a warm reception, and soon we repulsed him." The Confederates on the right drifted back and linked up with the survivors from Duncan Field. Cheatham reorganized his command and shifted his units to the right, so that the two Tennessee regiments were in the woods while the Kentuckians occupied the southern portion of the field. Once the realignment was complete, Cheatham's men again surged forward, but with the same result. The Federals were difficult targets, many of them lying flat on the ground, and their fire again tore through Cheatham's ranks and forced the brigade to retire. The Tennessean simply did not have enough clout to punch a hole in the Union line.[16]

The undersized force Cheatham led was one of several which assailed the aptly named Hornets' Nest. While his First Brigade operated on the Confederate left, where it helped push back two Union divisions in hard fighting, Cheatham's Second Brigade and other Rebel forces were stalled by the stout resistance they encountered. The three Union divisions they fought were commanded by Generals W. H. L. Wallace, Benjamin Prentiss, and Stephen Hurlbut. Prentiss anchored the center of the Hornets' Nest, with Wallace to his right and Hurlbut to his left. Failure to coordinate their attacks cost hundreds of Confederate lives as the Yankees stubbornly held their ground and protected the Federal army from greater disaster.[17] Cheatham's men suffered owing to the inability of the Southerners to launch a united effort. The Sixth Tennessee was particularly hard hit. The regiment boasted 851 members the previous summer at Camp Brown; nearly 500 of the men became casualties at Shiloh. Most of the losses occurred in the two attacks against the Hornets' Nest, and the unit was so depleted that it saw little action for the remainder of the battle.[18]

Cheatham halted his tired troops after the second unsuccessful attack and helped reorganize the brigade again, a task he assumed when his brigade commander withdrew from the area. Colonel Stephens had arisen prematurely from a sickbed to accompany his men into battle and was further discomfited when he was thrown from his wounded mount on the edge of Duncan Field. Exhausted by his efforts, Stephens left the field.[19] After his reorganization, Cheatham moved with his three regiments further to the right as other Confederate units were flung against the Hornets' Nest. Confusion among the Rebels continued to plague their efforts. At one point during the day, Captain William Harper of the Jefferson (Mississippi) Flying Artillery came to Cheatham and requested orders, as his battery had become separated from the division to which it was assigned. Cheatham set the battery to work against a Union unit of five guns across a field, an example of the makeshift tactical arrangements the Southerners relied upon as the battle unfolded.[20]

After his shift to the right, Cheatham was met by two officers. One was Colonel George Maney, an old friend from Nashville who had gone with Frank to Mexico as a member of the Nashville Blues. Maney led five companies of the First Tennessee Regiment, a unit which participated in the Cheat Mountain campaign in West Virginia before being transferred to the western army. Maney had but a portion of his regiment at Shiloh, as only half of his companies had obtained transportation out of Chattanooga. He had been ordered to protect the Confederate right in the vicinity of Lick Creek, but grew increasingly anxious to join the battle as it escalated. Maney's instructions from Johnston left him at liberty to abandon his surveillance if he deemed it prudent to do so, and by late morning he was headed for the fight. Eventually he found Cheatham, who placed Maney in charge of the brigade.[21]

The second officer was cavalry commander Nathan Bedford Forrest. Like Maney, Forrest left the area near Lick Creek and hurried towards the sound of battle. Forrest asked Cheatham for permission to attack, but the infantry commander hesitated. Aware that Confederate infantry had been chewed up earlier, twice in repulses involving his own brigade, Cheatham refused to give Forrest orders to attack. When Forrest persisted, Cheatham said that he could not be responsible for the actions of the cavalryman. Irritated, Forrest went forward anyway, in conjunction with a brigade of Alabama foot soldiers under Colonel Zachariah C. Deas. The targets of this foray were two Union cannons, but tangled undergrowth stalled the horsemen, and Deas's Alabamians could not break the Union line.[22]

As Forrest and Deas fell back, another wave of Rebel infantry appeared. Portions of this troop were from Cheatham's division under Maney's immediate supervision. Cheatham, perhaps stung by the encounter with Forrest, had instructed Maney to select a force for an assault. Maney collected his own five companies from the First Tennessee, then added the Ninth Tennessee and the Nineteenth Tennessee, the latter regiment from John C. Breckinridge's Reserve Corps. Maney's aggregation was shielded to some extent by the retreat of Forrest and Deas. As the Federals concentrated their fire on the latter two units, Maney's men managed to cross an open field almost unscathed. The former Nashville attorney ordered his men to lie down once they entered some protective woods, and a short time later a Union volley cracked through the dense smoke which obscured Maney's soldiers. Maney then "promptly resumed his advance," and at long last the Union line splintered on the left. "The enemy could not wait to sustain the shock," Maney reported, "but broke in disorder and fled precipitately before us." Cheatham characterized Maney's charge as "most brilliant, as it was certainly one of the most decisively successful" movements of the day.[23] Maney's success was doubly rewarding from Cheatham's perspective. Not only was the attack leader a personal friend, but his smashing of the Federal line helped compensate for the previous hours of frustration.

As Maney advanced, Cheatham dispatched the First Mississippi Cavalry to cut off the fleeing Yankees. The Mississippians arrived in time to capture a Michigan battery, as well as most of the officers and men attached to the guns.[24] After sending the cavalry forward, Cheatham collected the remainder of the Second Brigade and personally led them to catch up with Maney. He and a host of other Southerners at long last encircled the remaining defenders in the Hornets' Nest. Union General W. H. L. Wallace was mortally wounded and Prentiss surrendered, but the Yankee defenders had extracted an enormous toll in both time and lives on the Confederates. It had taken most of the day, repeated infantry assaults, and a massive artillery barrage before the Confederates were able to eliminate the Hornets' Nest. Among the Southern casualties was Albert Sidney Johnston, who bled to death when a minié ball opened an artery in his leg.[25]

As the Rebels enveloped the remaining Federals in the Hornets' Nest, preparations unfolded for one final thrust against Grant's army. Cheatham and other officers collected scattered troops and moved towards the river bank. The Tennessean shepherded a variety of commands, organization having broken down almost totally by this time.[26] Dusk approached, and with it the hostilities began to taper off. One enthusiastic private boldly asked Cheatham why the fighting was dying out. "I know my duty and understand my business," Cheatham defensively replied, "I am obeying orders."[27] The final push never materialized to any great degree, and historians have argued whether the Confederates could have inflicted more damage on Grant's army had they continued their offensive.

There were difficulties even if the Southerners had delivered their last attack, and this helps explain why it never ensued. The commands were badly intermingled, and the men were weary. Cheatham explained in a report that there was a lull because many of the regiments were out of ammunition. The Union gunboats *Lexington* and *Tyler,* which Cheatham had jousted with at Hickman and Belmont, shelled the Rebels as they neared the Tennessee River. While most of the boats' projectiles passed over the Confederate lines and crashed into the trees, the noise was un-nerving. It appears that some commands witnessed other units drawing back and then withdrew themselves. Cheatham may have followed this pattern, and his comments to the private imply that he was ordered to withdraw.[28]

Whatever the reason, Cheatham fell back from the front. For some inexplicable reason, Polk moved Cheatham all the way back to the site of the previous night's engagement, nearly three miles to the rear. Cheatham intimated that the march was made to put his men out of range of the gunboats, but he need not have gone back so far to accomplish this purpose. Polk related that Cheatham's men fell back "to obtain rations and to prepare for the work of the following day." This is not a particularly plausible explanation either, as other troops remained in their positions on the field. In any event, Cheatham's division had practically ceased to exist as a cohesive force, and not all his regiments accompanied him to the rear. The Ninth Tennessee and Seventh Kentucky are examples of this confused state. An artillery train split the Ninth Tennessee in two, so that half of the regiment went with Cheatham while the other half bedded down on the field. The colonel of the Kentucky regiment accompanied Cheatham and Polk, but his men did not. Wherever Cheatham's men were, they were subjected to a fierce thunderstorm that began late Sunday night and extended into the next morning.[29]

During the night Union reinforcements from Buell arrived, and at daybreak on April 7 the conflict was renewed. As on the previous day, Cheatham's command was fragmented and fought in different sectors of the battle. Cheatham received orders to move back towards the battle-field, a task complicated when "a stampede" of men fleeing from the front delayed his advance. When Cheatham arrived in the vicinity of Shiloh Church, he met with General Breckinridge, who told him that assistance was needed on the left. Cheatham got his men on the move, passed Shiloh Church, and then formed his command in front of a large force of Yankees threatening the Rebel flank. "My engagement here commenced almost the instant I had formed, and was for four hours the most hotly contested I ever witnessed," Cheatham later recorded. To check the Union threat, Cheatham took charge of a jumbled collection of men from his own division and other Rebel regiments. He also took an active part in the attack; Preston Smith wrote later that the soldiers "were moved forward rapidly under the lead of Major-General Cheatham." Cheatham and the other Southerners succeeded in pushing the Federals back but ultimately yielded ground themselves when additional bluecoats entered the fray.[30] By early afternoon, Cheatham was back in the vicinity where he had first collided with the enemy. Here artillery, which Cheatham lacked before, came to his aid. The Tennessean, who enjoyed dabbling with artillery, helped service one of the four guns which arrived. The cannons "did excellent execution," according to Cheatham's unintentionally expressive phrase to describe how the fieldpieces helped him maintain his position. Insistent Union pressure continued, and some of Cheatham's men began to feel fatigued. One of his regiments refused to attack the advancing Yankees until a staff officer attached to another division seized the colors and led the men forward. Still, Cheatham was instrumental in keeping his available troops together and in fighting shape. After they had been rebuffed, Cheatham rallied his troops. An officer wrote, "General Cheatham was conspicuously active in effecting the reformation, urging his troops to make a stand, and assuring them of their ability to repulse the enemy."[31]

Eventually Johnston's successor, Beauregard, ordered a retreat. Cheatham and his men fell back slowly in the direction of his previous camp and helped protect the Rebel retreat. Cheatham may have been unbowed, but his division was certainly bloodied. The Tennessean lost 1,213 of 3,801 effectives, and his officer corps was particularly victimized. Three of his top subordinates were killed, and five others were wounded. The casual language of a battle report fails to conceal the horrendous fate which befell a young aide on Cheatham's staff. Cheatham wrote, "I regret to say that young [John] Campbell, while acting as my aide-de-camp, fell dead, his entire head having been carried away by a cannon shot." Cheatham himself was hit in the shoulder, although it is impossible to ascertain exactly when the wound was sustained. Beauregard noted later that three horses had been shot out from underneath Cheatham during the battle.[32] At least one of Cheatham's men found divine justice at work on the battlefield. James I. Hall recorded that five or six officers had been ringleaders of cockfights when the regiment was at Corinth and noted that the pastime ended when all the officers were killed at Shiloh.[33]

Cheatham and his men passed their first major test in battle and conducted themselves well. Cheatham complimented his entire command but praised especially the efforts of Irishmen and Germans in several of his regiments who had fought for their adopted country.[34] Despite the valiant efforts and the heavy price, the result was still disappointing. Shiloh failed to alter appreciably the state of affairs in the west, and Cheatham's beloved Tennessee remained largely in the grasp of the Northerners.

The Confederate retreat was unimpeded by the Yankees, who made only a half-hearted effort to pursue Beauregard's army. Both sides were badly mauled at Shiloh, and no significant moves were made for a month after the battle. During May the Federals began a glacial move towards Corinth. Beauregard and his corps commanders considered the town a potential deathtrap, and the Rebels evacuated Corinth at the end of the month. Their destination was Tupelo, fifty-two miles to the south, a site that offered better defensive possibilities and an improved water supply.[35]

Beauregard supervised the movement but did not get an opportunity to revive the army once it arrived at Tupelo. The troops were scarcely in their encampments before he was replaced as army commander by General Braxton Bragg. The change in command was the handiwork of Jefferson Davis, who had carried on a bitter feud with Beauregard since Bull Run. Both Davis and Beauregard were proud, unforgiving men, and it no doubt irked Davis that one of the Confederacy's two main armies was led by an opponent. Disappointed by the defeat at Shiloh and the subsequent withdrawal from Corinth, Davis conspired to replace his adversary. An ailing Beauregard unwittingly provided Davis with the pretext he needed. Seeking relief from a nagging throat infection, the Creole left the army for a healthier clime. Davis pronounced that the absence was not properly cleared with the Richmond authorities and promptly ousted his military enemy.[36]

Such a momentous event as Beauregard's dismissal must have spawned discussion between Cheatham and the other officers. Generals were no more immune to army rumors and innuendo than the rank and file, though Cheatham's sentiments regarding the ouster were not recorded. What Cheatham could not foresee was that Beauregard's leavetaking would prove much less important than the identity of his replacement. Braxton Bragg was destined to have more impact on Cheatham's role and status with the army than any other man. To comprehend Cheatham's Civil War career, one must come to grips with Bragg, not an easy task.

The military acumen of the North Carolina native is still a source of debate among Civil War scholars. During the war he aroused intense feelings among his contemporaries. Few of his subordinates remained indifferent to Bragg, and the army eventually split into opposing camps over the issue of Bragg's leadership. A man at the storm center of one army controversy after another, Bragg was the subject of dispute even in the postwar years. Though he possessed allies both within and outside army ranks, including Jefferson Davis, Bragg's reputation suffered in part because his opponents were more prolific writers than his defenders. Historians seized upon many of the criticisms tendered by Bragg's detractors. As a result, he has become an almost despised figure, and one vilified far more than any other Southern general. Recent studies have tried to be more objective, but determining Bragg's competency in army command is still difficult.[37]

Bragg's ascent to army command in the Confederate service was relatively rapid. An 1837 West Point graduate, Bragg achieved considerable fame in the Mexican War. He resigned his U.S. Army commission in 1856 to operate a Louisiana sugar plantation. By dint of hard work he made the plantation a success and in the process became a considerably wealthy man. Records reveal that in 1860 he owned sizeable holdings in land and slaves. A reluctant secessionist, Bragg was initially assigned to command of the Gulf Coast region from Pensacola to Mobile. After building an army there, he joined the Army of the Mississippi shortly before Shiloh. He was the recipient of several speedy promotions, owing partly to his warm friendship with Jefferson Davis and partly to the South's keen need for trained officers. He was appointed and confirmed as a full general by Davis on April 12, 1862.[38]

Bragg celebrated his forty-fifth birthday shortly before Shiloh, though a beard flecked with abundant gray made him look older. Cheatham's new commander was beset by a number of recurring maladies, including boils, migraine headaches, and indigestion. One of Bragg's stronger suits was his appetite for hard work, but he often overtaxed himself. The combination of chronic illnesses and mental exhaustion tended to sour Bragg's disposition easily and caused serious problems during the war.[39] In the early months of his tenure, before he was seriously burdened by poor health, Bragg provided two qualities the army sorely needed, organization and discipline. In the weeks after Shiloh, he labored energetically to revamp the army and shape it into a reliable fighting force. His administrative efforts did improve the quality of the force at Tupelo, but to effect change he sought to eliminate officers he felt were unworthy of their positions.[40] Cheatham was one of them.

There were a variety of reasons for Bragg's hostile attitude toward Cheatham. One was Cheatham's close ties with Leonidas Polk, a man Bragg regarded as incapable of successfully filling his role as corps commander. Bragg's disdain for Polk was so strong that he once labelled the bishop "an old woman, utterly worthless." Polk nonetheless possessed powerful connections, including his own friendship with Jefferson Davis, which made it practically impossible for Bragg to remove him from the army. Bragg's dislike of Polk and Cheatham began almost immediately

General Braxton Bragg, controversial commander of the Army of Tennessee. He and Cheatham clashed on several occasions and eventually detested one another. (Library of Congress)

after he saw Polk's corps. Not impressed with the aggregation from Columbus, Bragg termed that part of the army "a mob" and was convinced that they lacked discipline. Not unnaturally, as Bragg's hostility became apparent, Polk and Cheatham grew closer together.[41]

Unable to do much about Polk, Bragg sought other quarry. At the end of June he wrote the War Department and lamented the "want of proper commanders." Citing only Hardee as a suitable major-general, Bragg snubbed the talents of both Polk and Cheatham. The latter two men were no doubt included in the ranks of "dead-weight" officers that Bragg concluded were "only encumbrances and would be better out of the way." When asked by Richmond to name the officers he wished to remove, Bragg tabbed six generals: Cheatham, John P. McCown, and George Crittenden, all major-generals; and William H. Carroll, James M. Hawes, and James H. Trapier, brigadiers.[42]

Lack of professional training was not the prime rationale for Bragg's disdain, as only Cheatham and Carroll lacked West Point degrees. This may have been a factor in Bragg's distrust of these two officers, but another, more powerful influence linked at least four of the generals. Bragg was apparently convinced that most of the six men had an overdeveloped affinity for alcohol. His suspicions helped remove Crittenden and Carroll, both of whom were arrested by Hardee, acting under Bragg's orders. The charge in both cases was drunkenness, with Carroll accused of incompetency and neglect of his regiment as well. Hawes may have liked his liquor also, since his death certificate lists "age and habits" as the reason for his demise.[43]

Though moral delinquencies were a delicate subject in the nineteenth century, there is little doubt that Cheatham drank, and sometimes to excess. Certainly Bragg thought that the Tennessean was a notorious drunkard, and Cheatham's drinking practices eventually aroused Bragg's considerable enmity. Bragg correctly believed that liquor was a potential problem within the ranks as well as in his officer corps. He nonetheless appears to have forgotten his own drinking bouts during his early years at West Point, and by the summer of 1862 Bragg acted with the fervor of a temperance advocate. Adjutant and Inspector-General Samuel Cooper tried to caution Bragg that President Davis's hands were tied in terms of removing generals once they were appointed and confirmed, but Bragg's campaign was not entirely unsuccessful. Four of the officers he listed resigned or were assigned to minor posts. Of Bragg's targeted list, only Cheatham and McCown remained with the army.[44]

Even if Cheatham had been a teetotaler, he probably would have aroused Bragg's distrust. Bragg's wife, Elise, was a devoted correspondent whose letters contained very strident opinions about army affairs. She harbored deep prejudices against troops from Tennessee, especially in the wake of the disasters at Fort Henry and Fort Donelson. She bore an especial grudge against Gideon Pillow, but regarded all Tennesseans with deep suspicion. Elise implored her husband not to trust the Tennesseans and suggested that he arrange his batteries so they could fire into the Volunteer state contingents "if they attempt to run." She added that her husband could "shame them into fighting" only by personally leading them into battle. If Elise Bragg bore considerable malice towards Tennesseans, she was overly enthusiastic about soldiers from Mississippi and Louisiana. She portrayed the latter as "our friends the *Creoles,*" and felt they were "obedient, good marksmen, habituated to exposure," with the added virtue of being "free from the besotting sin of the Confederacy, *drunkenness.*" As for the Mississippians, Elise sang the praises of her native state's soldiery by reminding her husband emphatically, "*They will never fail you.*"[45]

Toward the end of one of these diatribes, Elise interjected that her advice might be "much foolishness." In essence, she was correct about being foolish, and a different man than Braxton Bragg might have gently sloughed off her misguided notions about military life. But the Braggs had a close relationship, in part because they were so similar in temperament and outlook. His vengeance against alcohol may well have been colored by Elise's pronouncement of it as a great "sin." He also embraced her assessment of Tennesseans as fighting men. Writing to her two weeks before Shiloh, Bragg fully accepted her advice and noted: "All Tennesseans are scattered among better men in small squads, so that we can hold them in observation. I never realized the full correctness of your appreciation of them until now."[46] When he assumed command of the army, Bragg apparently retained his mistrust of Tennesseans. Since Cheatham was one of the most prominent generals associated with this state combine, he was subject to Bragg's negative scrutiny. What Bragg failed to perceive was the potentially damaging effect on army morale his suspicions would engender. Tennesseans constituted a good portion of the army at Tupelo, and it is doubtful that they would fight well for a man who questioned their dependability.

Bragg did not make a wholehearted effort to remove Cheatham during the summer. He may have been mollified by his partial success in eliminating four of the generals he considered unfit. Anyway, Cheatham was a much more difficult target. He possessed important government allies such as Governor Isham Harris, Senator Gustavus Henry, and Congressman Henry Stuart Foote. Within the army itself, Polk was likely to challenge Bragg if the army commander moved against Cheatham. A final deterrent was the solidification of a Tennessee bloc loyal to Cheatham, a phenomenon which grew in strength as the war continued. Though

Cheatham retained his command, the seeds for a Bragg-Cheatham feud were well established, and the dormant hostility between the two men would eventually flare again.

Bragg may have been further deflected from his anti-Cheatham campaign by his increased efforts to reorganize and improve the army. That endeavor occupied much of Bragg's time and attention at Tupelo. One soldier in Cheatham's division wrote, "Constant drill was our daily avocation," and added, "The health of the whole army improved materially." Tightened discipline was another element in Bragg's efforts to weld the army together but was less highly regarded by Cheatham's men. The same private who wrote approvingly of the improvement in physical well-being was unhappy with Bragg's execution of several soldiers "for being absent without leave and desertion."[47] The death penalties seemed harsh to Cheatham's troops but were necessary if Bragg's attempt to advance the effectiveness of his force was to succeed. Nonetheless, many of the Tennesseans perceived Bragg as heartless and callous, and his penchant for executing wrongdoers caused problems later.

Cheatham also stayed busy at Tupelo. Besides drilling his men for hours, he picked up on Bragg's call for improved discipline. His method in achieving that goal was suspect on one occasion at Tupelo, when an Irishman ran afoul of Cheatham. Cheatham berated the soldier with a string of curses until he ran out of breath, at which time the Irishman interjected, "Bedad, Gineral Cheatham! [If] you wasn't a gineral, you wouldn't talk to me that way." Cheatham, "always willing and anxious to accommodate any gentleman who was looking for trouble," yanked his coat off and challenged the soldier. Pointing to the coat, Cheatham angrily cried, "There lies General Cheatham, and here is Old Frank. Now pitch in." The Irishman did just that, with the unusual result that Frank "didn't get the best of the fight." Word of the encounter spread rapidly. Frank's sister Louise wrote to tease him about it, and the event was recounted in somewhat fractured fashion by a Minnesota cavalryman the next year.[48]

The episode was decidedly unmilitary but symbolic. The Tennessee troops were not horrified by the dubious display; they reveled in Cheatham's fisticuffs. The incident with the Irishman helps account for Cheatham's enormous popularity among his soldiers. "Old Frank" was a curious combination of brawler and conscientious commander. He somehow managed to walk the tightrope between revealing his humanity to his soldiers while retaining their respect. This attitude was summed up in an 1864 conversation between some of Cheatham's men and one of his prewar friends from Nashville. "Why, old Frank is one of the boys," they jovially told the woman. This easy familiarity was no doubt exaggerated for the woman's benefit, but there was underlying affection in the statement. The same soldiers evinced loyalty to Cheatham as a battlefield leader. They pledged to "go anywhere old Frank orders us, even were it in the cannon's mouth," which proved to be no exaggeration whatsoever.[49]

Cheatham was eventually so trusted by his men that they asked things of "Mars Frank" or "Old Frank" that they "hesitated to ask . . . of their regimental commanders."[50] Cheatham fit in well with his soldiers, many of whom appreciated his sometimes rough, unpolished demeanor because they were the same way. His enthusiasm for horse racing, cursing, and the occasional bottle all served to reinforce the idea that Cheatham was, in certain respects, not unlike the men he led. He may have grown up in a plantation atmosphere, but Cheatham commanded the respect of men from every social level in the Confederacy.

While Cheatham's men were delighted with his accessibility and personal characteristics, they also were the beneficiaries of his considerable talents as an administrator, an area in which not all Southern officers excelled. Numerous sources attest to his diligence and vigilance in caring for his men's needs. One postwar sketch cited Cheatham's attention to his soldiers' "care and comfort. He kept himself fully informed as to the quality of their rations, clothing and equipment." A Mississippi cavalryman who served under Cheatham at Shiloh found the Tennessean "exceedingly . . . vigilant for the welfare of his command, doing everything to promote their success and to save them from unnecessary exposure." A brigadier in Cheatham's division related how Frank's concern even extended to the animals attached to his command. Cheatham would "ride along the line of his wagon trains and observe the condition of every animal," as well as noting defects in the wagons themselves.[51] A wartime newspaper also commended Cheatham's "scrupulous attention" to the minutest details of his command in person. He inspects for himself his commissary and quarter-masters' departments, and is always acquainted with their efficiency."[52]

One of Cheatham's staff officers reported that the division was always well equipped, since "Old Frank" sent surplus good to the rear in charge of a disabled infantryman until they were needed. As in Mexico, Cheatham devoted extra attention to the sick and wounded of his command. He was particularly careful with his allotted hospital supplies, and Cheatham's preoccupation with his medical department won him the respect of his men. One colonel wrote that Cheatham "manifested as much interest in the welfare of his wounded soldiers as was exhibited by any man."[53]

While Cheatham's unreserved nature and solicitude were major factors in winning the approbation of his men, there was a third characteristic in his favor. Civil War soldiers appreciated a general who took the same risks he asked of them, and Cheatham certainly qualified in this regard. By mid-1862 his personal valor had already been demonstrated at Belmont and Shiloh, and as the war progressed, his courage would be revealed on other battlefields. Cheatham's bravery and example served as a rallying point for his men in battle. His enthusiasm carried over, and Cheatham's troops acquired a reputation as hard fighters when they followed his lead.[54]

By the summer of 1862, Cheatham had long since won over the men who grumbled against him at Camp Brown. So great was the devotion he garnered that his soldiers invariably referred to themselves as "Cheatham's division" instead of by regiment or brigade, according to one of his men.[55] Given their steadfast loyalty, it was only natural that his troops sided with Cheatham when it became evident that Braxton Bragg was antagonistic towards the Tennessean. "Old Frank" had demonstrated his leadership qualities within their sight on the battlefield and had faithfully attended to their well-being. Bragg, by contrast, seemed to be a somewhat dour and remote figure. Anti-Bragg sentiment was not overwhelming at Tupelo but surfaced later when he renewed his opposition to Cheatham. As Bragg eventually learned, when he attacked Frank Cheatham he earned the enmity of both Cheatham and an entire division.

Chapter 4

"The Most Exciting
Few Moments of My Life":
The Kentucky Campaign

Cheatham and his troops were provided a respite from camp life at Tupelo when Bragg initiated an audacious scheme which sent his army from Mississippi to Chattanooga. Prior to the movement, Bragg completed a reorganization of his army. Cheatham's division was expanded to include four brigades, the vast majority of his regiments hailing from Tennessee. His division combined with another, commanded by Alabamian Jones M. Withers, to form Polk's Right Wing.[1] The army boarded trains leaving Tupelo in late July for a circuitous route to Chattanooga. The infantry moved by railway and steamship to Mobile, thence upwards into Alabama and Georgia before entering eastern Tennessee. The move lifted the spirits of the men, one of them referring to it as a "pic-nic," as fine weather and abundant provisions contributed to their improved attitude. Ladies waved handkerchiefs and flags and provided Cheatham's men with apples, peaches, and homemade delicacies as the army progressed across the Deep South. Cheatham himself was in a good humor, especially when a Georgia woman met him and pressed for a four-day furlough for her husband, a member of the Forty-first Georgia Regiment. After "hard pleading and a good deal of amusement," Cheatham granted the request.[2]

The cavalry, artillery, and wagon train followed a somewhat different path from the infantry, and some of Cheatham's artillerists occupied themselves with less innocent diversions. John Magee of Stanford's Mississippi battery noted in his diary that some "lewd women" attracted the attention of several of his comrades at one stop. On two other occasions in Alabama he recorded that a number of officers and men got drunk. The result of the drinking sprees was that the officers "behaved very badly" and the men "wanted to fight."[3]

60   The army collected around Chattanooga throughout August, as Bragg

made preparations to invade Kentucky. The men tramped up the Sequatchie Valley towards the end of August, crossed the Cumberland Plateau at Pikeville, and advanced into Kentucky by way of Sparta, Tennessee. The heady optimism which prevailed at Chattanooga lagged somewhat in the mountains, where "extreme heat and a great scarcity of water" hindered progress. Many of Cheatham's men from west Tennessee "had never seen a mountain before" and found themselves worn out by the forced marches. The artillerists had an especially rough time pushing and pulling the fieldpieces over the inclines, and Cheatham promised to dispatch infantry to assist the battery crews and teamsters. Though the soldiers were strictly warned not to steal from farmers along the route, some of Cheatham's men complained that the rations were inadequate and that the little meat available was "not fit to eat." Near Sparta the wagon trains failed to appear, and one hungry regiment was rescued by Cheatham, who "came to our relief by buying a field of corn just in good roasting ear stage," as well as the fence enclosing the field. The money for the purchase no doubt came from back pay recently distributed. Cheatham was paid for the period March 1 to July 31, 1862, on September 2. The amount he received was $1,505, his $301 monthly salary for the five months.[4]

Cheatham's men had some misgivings at the beginning of the Kentucky campaign, but Braxton Bragg did not share them. In an exuberant letter to Elise, Bragg wrote that he hoped to redeem Kentucky and Tennessee, capture Louisville, Cincinnati, and Ohio, and drive Union General Don Carlos Buell's army across the Ohio River.[5] It was an ambitious scheme, but already an advance force of Confederates, including Preston Smith's brigade from Cheatham's division, was in Kentucky under General Edmund Kirby Smith. As the army pressed deeper into Kentucky, the men recaptured the ebullience they felt during the transfer from Tupelo to Chattanooga. Their sense of enthusiasm manifested itself in several ways, including humorous pranks. John Cavanaugh of the Ninth Tennessee recounted one incident involving two members of his company. Hugh Hamner, "a very small young man not over five feet four inches" tall, wandered up to Jim Rucker, a veritable giant of six feet seven inches. Hamner inquired, "Rucker, what kind of weather have you got up there?" Recognizing a trite query when he heard one, Rucker retaliated unerringly. He promptly spat on Hamner's hat and drolly reported, "It is raining up here, Hugh." Cavanaugh remembered that "this reply of Jim's created a loud laugh among all who heard it."[6]

This particular company had a decided flair for lowbrow humor. Earlier in the campaign, the regiment was marching near the base of Walden's Ridge in Tennessee. As they passed by a contingent of troops from another state, a soldier by the road asked, "What regiment is that?" Ned Pryor replied, "The Ninth." Not satisfied with this unrevealing answer, the stranger persisted in asking, "Ninth what?" Pryor triumphantly shot back, "Ninth Regiment, you durned galoot." Cavanaugh recalled, "Of course this raised a laugh," but confessed, "it does not take much to make a lot of soldiers laugh, especially when they are in high spirits."[7]

Even Cheatham succumbed to the relaxed atmosphere Cavanaugh described. At one site in Kentucky, a member of his command, Private Jim Heath, found the appeal of a particular apple tree too hard to resist. Heath dropped out of the column and clambered up after some of the fruit. While the private occupied himself picking the finest specimens he could reach, a mounted officer reined up and peered intently upwards. Eventually Heath glanced downward to see who the intruder was, and the sight, he later recounted, left him "mortally scared to death." The horseman was Cheatham, and Heath may well have calculated that his military career had taken an abrupt turn for the worse. On this occasion Cheatham was lenient; he broke the silence with a polite request for Heath to "drop me down a few of those fine apples." Heath happily complied, and the Tennessean rode off.[8]

The high spirits of Cheatham's men were buoyed by the progress the army made as it probed northward into Kentucky. They marched in the vicinity of the Green and Barren Rivers while Buell hurriedly abandoned Nashville and marched to Bowling Green. The Confederates arrived at Glasgow, forty miles east of Bowling Green, on September 13. Bragg halted at the village, sent two brigades to Cave City, ten miles to the northwest, and waited for telegraph lines in the area to be seized. At the same time, the rail link between Bowling Green and Louisville was destroyed. Up to this point Bragg's campaign had been conducted admirably. The bold stroke in deserting Tupelo and conceiving the invasion was paying off, as butternuts worked their way deeper into the state. Unfortunately, difficulties which Bragg could not have foreseen began to erode his confidence. One of the brigades at Cave City was led in a rash attack on a Union garrison at Munfordville and repulsed. The setback angered and distracted Bragg, who decided to move northward and subdue the fort to forestall any adverse impact on army morale. Bragg moved with the bulk of his army to Munfordville on the Green River, where Hardee's and Polk's wings encircled the Union fort. After an interminable amount of wrangling between the Southerners and the Union colonel in charge, the garrison surrendered. On September 17, the 4,000 Yankees marched out of the fort, stacked arms, and were paroled. One of Cheatham's men who witnessed the capitulation was relieved by the easy conquest, writing that he "was not hankering after any glory that morning."[9]

Cheatham was at Cave City, where he had been instructed to alert Bragg of any Union movement from Bowling Green. When Buell's army shoved northward, Cheatham was recalled to Munfordville to rejoin the Confederate force. Bragg faced a decision at Munfordville. He could attempt to draw Buell into battle by blocking the Union advance or move eastward to join Kirby Smith. His uncertainty was reflected in the marching orders Cheatham received: first northward to Bardstown, then halted, and finally back to Munfordville. In the end Bragg abandoned Munfordville and moved east, searching for Kirby Smith. One Louisiana general maintained that the barren surroundings around Munfordville made it impossible for Bragg to tarry there.[10]

Cheatham and the rest of the army shifted eastward, but the link with Kirby Smith remained elusive. As Buell's army clattered into Louisville and refitted, Bragg sought to legitimize Confederate claims to the state by having Richard Hawes inaugurated as governor at Frankfort. Hawes would replace George W. Johnson, who had been killed at Shiloh, and Bragg hoped the civil affair would lend a sheen of legality to Southern conscription acts. While the commander sought to revive the campaign, Cheatham and his men were with Polk at Bardstown. Neither general realized it immediately, but three Federal columns, commanded by Generals Alexander McCook, Thomas L. Crittenden, and Charles Gilbert, were approaching Bardstown. Buell sent another train of 22,000 troops under Joshua Sill to feint towards Frankfort. The latter arrived before Frankfort just as the inaugural ceremonies were conducted, and Hawes's gubernatorial address was punctuated by artillery fire. Bragg thought Sill represented the main portion of Buell's army and hastily ordered Polk to leave Bardstown, intending for Polk to strike the Union flank while Kirby Smith assaulted from the front. Polk, disconcerted by reports of a heavy Union concentration before Bardstown, convened his major officers on October 3 and recommended that Bragg's order to march to Frankfort be disregarded. When Cheatham and the other generals assented, Polk retreated due east to Harrodsburg.[11]

Cheatham and the rest of the army received a friendly reception upon entering the Bluegrass region. Despite being dirty and ragged, members of the division were treated "kindly and hospitably" by Harrodsburg residents. To preserve a positive image for the state's citizens, the army strictly regulated foraging, and the general attempted to enforce discipline in the ranks. Still, there were occasional violations, including some by junior officers. James Iredell Hall of the Ninth Tennessee Regiment quietly slipped out of ranks at Danville to visit Centre College, which he had attended fifteen years earlier. Hall managed to return from his unwarranted visit without being detected, but not everyone was so fortunate.

When Hall arrived back, he saw Cheatham "expostulating with one of our fellow officers, an old Centre College boy, for leaving his command without orders."[12] Although Hall and the other members of Cheatham's division encountered many area residents who were Southern sympathizers, not everyone was entranced by the Confederate presence. One member of the Shaker religious sect assessed Cheatham's men and other Rebels as looking "more like the bipeds of pandemonium than beings of this earth." Despite this unflattering appraisal, the Shakers freely provided water, meat, bread, and pies to Cheatham's men. The water was especially appreciated, as a severe autumn drought afflicted the Bluegrass. Hall wrote that the men drank water "so muddy that we could not see our faces in it" and noted that dust clouds on the turnpikes made marching almost intolerable.[13]

Buell's Union columns continued to pursue the Rebels, and the Federal commander decided to unite his separated forces at Perryville, a tiny hamlet just south of Harrodsburg. Buell's center column, under Gilbert, arrived near Perryville October 7, despite annoying clashes with a cavalry screen which protected Hardee's wing near the village. Both sides sparred for the few water holes near the town, and Confederate riflemen beat off two Union efforts to seize the water pools as evening approached. McCook's corps encamped near Perryville late in the day, and Crittenden was nearby.[14]

Bragg was still deluded in thinking that the main Federal force was aimed at Frankfort. He assumed that Buell was spread out, and therefore sent Kirby Smith to Versailles. Cheatham and Withers were ordered to join Kirby Smith, completing a partial consolidation of Confederate forces. Bragg also ordered Hardee to attack the next morning, then transfer his wing to Versailles as well. The directive worried Hardee, who felt he was confronted by more than one Union corps. The tactician wrote Bragg a letter which implored the army commander to keep his force intact and smite the Federals at Perryville. Bragg failed to heed Hardee's advice, but the missive convinced him to alter his strategy somewhat. He diverted Cheatham from the rendezvous at Versailles and sent Cheatham's division to aid Hardee. Cheatham reversed direction and moved to Perryville, with General Polk accompanying the column. Their nighttime arrival boosted Southern strength in the area to roughly 16,000 men, but Buell mustered 58,000 troops. The opposing commanders both acted under erroneous assumptions. Buell believed the entire Confederate army was in his front, while Bragg felt that only one Union corps was at Perryville.[15]

When Cheatham arrived, Hardee placed him on the left of the Rebel line, near Perryville. This line was set along a ridge behind Doctor's Creek, a sluggish tributary of Chaplin Fork of the Salt River. Doctor's Creek paralleled Chaplin Fork for several miles, and it was on the high ground near where the two streams converged that the battle of October 8 was fought. One of Cheatham's men described the "beautiful morning" which dawned, but Union General Philip Sheridan's men took advantage of the early hour to grab the water supply in Doctor's Creek. Polk, who had assumed overall command upon his arrival, sent Joseph Wheeler's cavalry out to reconnoiter. As the early morning hours elapsed, Bragg strained to hear the sound of battle crashing from the south. He listened in vain, for Polk, feeling that the Union force was larger than forecast, substituted a "defensive-offensive" posture in place of an assault. As at Bardstown, Polk summoned his ranking lieutenants to a meeting to obtain approval for his independent actions. Cheatham and the rest of the group endorsed Polk's recommendation that the size and strength of the Yankee host be ascertained before an attack was launched.[16]

An irritated Bragg rode to the scene and arrived around 10 A.M. While he surveyed the setup, McCook's corps moved into position on Gilbert's left. Bragg was determined to strike the Federals at Perryville but feared being overlapped on the right. He altered his battle formation in response to McCook's arrival, but still remained unsure that the force represented an entire corps. About an hour after Bragg reached the field, Polk ordered Cheatham to shift from the left side of the Rebel line to the right. The move was soon underway, the hot sun beating on Cheatham's men as they marched northward for more than a mile. The movement attracted sporadic artillery fire, but Cheatham's men were periodically sheltered by the undulating hills along Chaplin's Fork. When the shift was completed, Cheatham's division and a Texas cavalry unit under John A. Wharton anchored the Rebel right flank. To Cheatham's left were two divisions of Hardee's wing, one led by Simon Bolivar Buckner and the other by Patton Anderson.[17]

Though Bragg was anxious for the battle to start, another delay ensued when Polk discovered a Federal column moving on a road and waited for them to get into position. He explained to Bragg that the Union force would take him in flank if he assaulted, and Bragg withdrew to the rear after agreeing with Polk's assessment. During the lull, Cheatham arranged his three available brigades in parallel lines of battle, with an interval of roughly two hundred yards between each brigade. The brigades were commanded by Daniel Donelson, Alexander P. Stewart, and George Maney. Both Donelson and Stewart were West Point graduates. Donelson was a nephew of Andrew Jackson and had been a planter in Sumner County prior to the war. He was also a politician, having served in the Tennessee legislature. Stewart began the war organizing camps of instruction, then commanded the heavy artillery and water batteries at Belmont before winning a brigadier's rank in November 1861. Maney was an 1845 graduate of the University of Nashville, had participated in the Mexican War, and was practicing law when the war broke out. At sixty-one years of age, Donelson was by far the oldest of the trio.[18]

Before Cheatham completed his battle preparations, Bragg ordered a battery commanded by Captain William W. Carnes of Donelson's brigade to occupy an eminence and sent the Eighth and Fifty-first Tennessee Regiments along as a supporting force. Carnes opened on a Union battery situated on a ridge to his front. Carnes quickly discovered that the Yankees had rifled fieldpieces and that his own six-pounder smoothbores were no match for his Union adversaries. Apprised by Carnes that the Confederate battery was in an unequal contest, Cheatham ordered Carnes to fall back and brought up Captain Thomas Stanford's Mississippi battery from Stewart's brigade. Stanford's guns, three-inch rifled fieldpieces, enjoyed more success than Carnes had had in disrupting the Union artillerists. During the hour-and-a-half artillery engagement that resulted, Stanford compelled the Yankee gunners to change their position several times. Cheatham reported that the Federal battery finally retired, "nearly if not all of his guns having been silenced."[19]

The attack finally began around 2 P.M., when Cheatham's men moved out "as if on dress parade" and advanced three-quarters of a mile through an open field which sloped towards Doctor's Creek. Once on the western side of the creek, Cheatham deployed his command, moving Donelson straight up a bluff while he threw Stewart to Donelson's left. The two brigades found the terrain troublesome, Donelson noting later that it was impracticable to ascend the bluff in line of battle. When Donelson gained the summit, his men paused to realign their formation as two Yankee batteries opened up from several hundred yards away. Donelson was handicapped by the absence of the two regiments with Carnes's battery, and as a result he had only three regiments on hand—the Fifteenth, the Sixteenth, and the Thirty-eighth Tennessee. The Sixteenth Tennessee was on the right, and Donelson had it move in the direction of the Union battery to the north. The other two regiments were supposed to swing around and link with the Sixteenth Tennessee, but an officer on Cheatham's staff commanded the latter regiment to move forward rapidly. Colonel John Savage sent his lone regiment forward against the Federals, who were posted "near a small farm house and cornfield." Caught in a crossfire by the Union guns, Donelson's brigade suffered mounting casualties as they struggled forward. The Fifteenth and the Thirty-eighth Tennessee linked up with the Sixteenth Tennessee, and Donelson's men charged "amid yells and cheers at every step." Savage was hit by a minié ball in the leg, was bruised by a shell fragment, and had his horse shot out from underneath him. Still, the three regiments managed to shove their opponents back to the battery and into some woods. Both sides were heavily punished in the attack, but Cheatham later reported that when the Yankees gave way, their former lines were "thickly strewed with dead and wounded."[20]

Donelson's command faltered in a cornfield some one hundred yards from the vexing battery, which continued to pour out a "most terrible and destructive fire." Eventually his remaining soldiers were forced to take refuge in a small woods. As Donelson's thrust lost steam, Cheatham's Third Brigade came to the rescue. This was Maney's command, which Cheatham had pushed some distance to the right when it became apparent that Donelson and Stewart would not overlap the Federal left as intended. The brigade crossed the creek and formed under the shelter of a small ridge after Wharton's Texas cavalry drove Union skirmishers from the area. Maney placed his brigade in two lines, the first being composed of the Forty-first Georgia, the Sixth Tennessee, and the Ninth Tennessee Regiments, from right to left. In reserve were the First and the Twenty-seventh Tennessee. Ordered by Cheatham to attack and carry the eight-gun battery which had shattered Donelson, Maney faced a difficult task. These guns, posted on an eminence which dominated much of the surrounding countryside, were commanded by Yankee Lieutenant Charles C. Parsons. They were heavily supported by infantry, and the formidable force belonged to the division of Union brigadier James S. Jackson, who directed the artillery fire against Donelson's regiments.[21]

Maney's men must have heard the cannon blasts and small arms fire directed against Donelson, and two members of the Twenty-seventh Tennessee had no delusions about the reception they would meet. William Rhodes and Frank Buck came to Captain John W. Carroll and predicted that they would be killed shortly. Carroll was impressed by their forceful premonition, surely recognizing that the natural inclination of young men, even those about to enter a battle, is to resist the notion of their mortality. Even though he did not have the authority to do so, Carroll offered a pass to the two soldiers which would allow them to drop out of ranks and avoid the battle. Both refused.[22]

As Donelson's attack lost steam, Maney's men suddenly popped over their protective ridge some three hundred yards from Parsons's battery. They advanced under heavy fire as Parsons's gunners hurriedly shifted their cannons to meet this new threat. Maney's men took cover behind an old vine-covered fence as the Federals concentrated their fire on the Confederate force. The fence provided little protection. One of Maney's regimental commanders later wrote that a "storm of shell, grape, canister and Minie balls was turned loose upon us as no troops scarcely ever be-

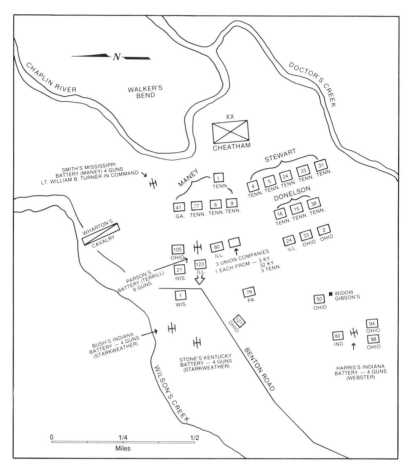

Map 1. Cheatham's Division at Perryville—October 8, 1862, about Mid-Afternoon

fore encountered. Large boughs were torn from the trees, the trees themselves shattered as if by lightning, and the ground plowed in deep furrows." Maney consulted with his adjutant, Captain Thomas Malone, who maintained that the brigade had to advance or it would be slaughtered. Maney's horse was knocked out from underneath him, but he continued on foot and quickly passed down his line to encourage his troops. Recognizing that his position behind the fence was untenable, Maney urged his men, who were lying prone on the ground, to take Parsons's guns. The exhortation inspired his soldiers, and they rose up, crossed the fence, and rushed for Parsons's battery. As if united by one impulse, the Southerners raised the Rebel yell as they surged for the guns. Four of Maney's five regiments participated in the charge. The Twenty-seventh Tennessee of the second line "lost its grip, couldn't stand still, and, despite orders, went with us to a man." Captain Malone noted that the Twenty-seventh "had been nearly wiped out at Shiloh, but the men that remained were still as game as bulldogs." That they were, but Maney's command took some losses as they raced forward. Joe Wheeler, color bearer for the Twenty-seventh Tennessee, had his right arm broken in the advance. He seized the flag in his left hand until a bullet slammed into his brain.[23]

A Rebel volley delivered delivered along the way ripped through the Yankee ranks and killed General Jackson, who was hit twice in the right breast. Maney's men charged through the battery as Parsons's infantry support melted away. The Yankees were subjected to brutal punishment whether they stayed by the guns or ran. A drummer boy in the Ninth Tennessee threw away his drum when it was shattered by a shell fragment, picked up a rifle, and crushed the skull of a Union soldier attemting to discharge one of the cannons. The Georgians and Tennesseans poured a destructive fire into the fleeing Federals. One of Cheathams' men noted that the "butchery was awful," and the expanse near the battery was littered with Yankee bodies by the time the survivors retreated. Parsons could save only one of his Napoleon twelve-pounders before Maney's men engulfed the position.[24]

While Maney's men were advancing, Cheatham had placed himself about a hundred yards to their right and checked their progress. As he rode, Cheatham "looked down the lines between the contending forces" and peered through the smoke to see Maney's men driving stubbornly forward. In an 1886 letter to *Southern Bivouac,* a Louisville-based periodical, Cheatham reminisced that Perryville was the only battle where he "found the enemy's flank sticking out in the air." The sight of Maney's brigade making headway "under the terrible storm of artillery and musketry" was so uplifting that Cheatham termed it "the most exciting few moments of my life."[25] While Maney's four infantry regiments finally wrested control of the guns, their accomplishment had been aided by their own artillery. The path to the battlefield was difficult enough for the foot soldiers, but Cheatham's artillerists belonging to Maney had to dig out a portion of the road leading up to the bluff before they could wheel their guns forward. While Maney's brigade was struggling to carry Parsons's position, Cheatham had met Lieutenant William B. Turner, who arrived with several fieldpieces. Cheatham had two howitzers placed some two hundred yards from the Federal left flank, and the fire from these Rebel guns soon shredded the infantry supporting Parsons. One of Turner's crewmen was interrupted by a voice behind him saying, "Let me try my hand at them." The soldier wheeled and found Cheatham at his shoulder. As the young artillerist stepped aside, Cheatham took over, directed the aiming and firing of the cannon, and enjoyed himself immensely. The interlude was brief, but Cheatham responded "with as much pleasure as a boy shooting at rabbits."[26]

Shortly afterwards, Cheatham rode to the captured battery. There he saw the body of General Jackson, which had fallen into the possession of the Confederates. Cheatham wrote later that he "had known [Jackson] well for years," but it is not known where the two met or to what extent they were acquainted. Cheatham had little time to ruminate on past friendships, as hard fighting remained ahead for his division. His men had few chances to recuperate from their exertions, although Stewart's brigade did come up and link with Maney after Donelson fell back to regroup. Maney and Cheatham met at the fence where the attack against Parsons had temporarily stalled, and Cheatham ordered Maney to bring his reserve regiment, the First Tennessee, into action on the right of the Rebel line. Their target was a Union battery some five hundred yards from Parsons's captured guns that was sending shot and shell into Maney's and Stewart's ranks. The First Tennessee passed through some woods and a cornfield before reaching the hilltop where the Yankee guns were situated. A Wisconsin regiment hid in the cornfield and let loose a volley before it was hurled back. Both sides suffered severely, one Wisconsin private writing to his wife later, "You cannot [imagine] the *horrors* of war no pen no tongue can begin to tell the misery that I have seen." The Southerners managed to kill most of the battery crew and horses, but even though they drove the Yankees back, the undersized force could not hold the position. A Union counterattack forced the First Tennessee to retreat to the base of the hill. They reformed, attacked again, and laid claim to the guns a second time but were again driven off. The Tennesseans fell back in some confusion and were unable to bring the guns off. A Wisconsin unit managed to capture the colors of the First Tennessee in the fierce fight for the guns.[27]

The remainder of Cheatham's main battle line stretched to the left of Maney's hard-hit First Tennessee. Stewart's five regiments formed an imposing line which had pursued the enemy after the capture of Parsons's guns. They encountered seven Federal regiments which took advantage of the cover provided by a forest and yet another cornfield to decimate Stewart's ranks. An Ohio officer reported later that it took but a few minutes for the cornfield to "be covered with rebel dead." Despite the losses, Cheatham's men relentlessly pushed forward, and as they overwhelmed this second Union line, they took four guns belonging to an Indiana artillery unit.[28] Cheatham had ridden to the far right to observe the work of the First Tennessee and employed two of his own batteries to assist in the effort. Carnes brought his guns into action against the Federal left, and Turner joined him in shelling the Union battery, which the First Tennessee had failed to carry. The combined power of Cheatham's two batteries finally compelled the Yankees to remove their fieldpieces.[29]

Donelson entered the fray as dusk approached, taking with him the two fresh regiments which had been acting as Carnes's support, as well as the Thirty-eighth Tennessee. With these three regiments he went to assist Stewart, and the added impetus of this line again managed to shove the Federals back some distance. By the time twilight neared, Cheatham's men had beaten the Union left back twelve hundred yards, compressed three Union lines into one, and shattered McCook's corps. Late in the afternoon their assault on a third Union line ground to a halt, as high casualties, exhaustion, and the onset of darkness combined to halt the carnage. Before the violence diminished, both of Jackson's brigade commanders had been mortally wounded. Throughout the afternoon, Cheatham had cooly directed the operation of his command. A chaplain remembered that Cheatham placidly smoked a pipe "through an incessant shower of shot and shell, breathing the very soul of chivalry and enthusiasm into his men." A staff officer came up at one point to warn Cheatham that a gap had formed between Buckner and his left. Minié balls "buzzed about my ears," the aide recalled, but an unperturbed Cheatham was "as calm . . . as if in a peaceful bivouac." He sent some of his men to check the Union force that probed at the opening, and the receding clatter of musketry gave evidence that they were successful.[30]

At dusk, Hardee dispatched a force under a Louisiana officer, General St. John Richardson Liddell, to assist Cheatham's fatigued soldiers. Some of Cheatham's calm reserve eroded as he rode up to Liddell and excitedly asked the Louisianan to "save the fight!" Liddell asked Cheatham to point out his line, but the Tennessean steadfastly refused to point out where Liddell should go, replying as he rode off, "No — go on and save the fight, you will find the line." Liddell fell into the area between Cheatham's and Buckner's men, saw a dark line to his front, and commenced firing. A voice cried out, "You are firing upon friends," and implored them to stop. At this juncture Polk rode up. Liddell recounted the mishap and berated Cheatham for not having accompanied him. Polk went forward to discover the identity of the force, and when he returned he told Liddell, "Every mother's son of them are Yankees," a fact he gleaned after chatting with an Indiana colonel. Liddell's men unleashed a deadly volley, then captured a large number of survivors, colors, and arms. They also took in General McCook's papers, which were sent to Bragg.[31]

Night descended on a battlefield that many of Cheatham's men considered, for the time they were in action, the most hotly contested engagement

Battle flag of the First Tennessee Regiment, captured by a Wisconsin regiment during fierce fighting at Perryville in October, 1862. The unusual color arrangement (the flag features a blue field instead of the customary red) and placement of the stars made this a distinctive banner. The Tennesseans replaced their captured flag with a near-identical one. (David A. Busch Photograph. The State Historical Society of Wisconsin. From *The Civil War: The Struggle for Tennessee* © 1985 Time-Life Books, Inc.)

of the war. Cheatham had ample reason to be proud of his command. He had been well served by both his artillery and infantry throughout the day. The veteran in Cheatham's division who described the day as "beautiful but bloody" captured the mingled sense of accomplishment and loss his comrades felt.[32] Cheatham's men had borne the brunt of the fighting, and his casualty list was correspondingly higher that those of Buckner and Anderson. The division lost 1,466 men, and all three of his engaged brigades suffered heavily. The Sixteenth Tennessee of Donelson's brigade lost 199 men, 41 of these killed. Stewart's Thirty-first Tennessee listed 100 men as casualties. Maney's brigade was the most devastated. The First Tennessee counted 179 casualties, the Forty-first Georgia 151, and the Ninth Tennessee 154, including all eight company commanders. The Twenty-seventh Tennessee paid for their impulsive charge against Parsons by losing 112 of the 210 men they carried into battle.[33] Overall, Bragg's army lost 510 dead, 2,365 wounded, and 251 captured or missing. The corresponding Union figures were 845, 2,851, and 515, with McCook's corps accounting for 672 of those killed and over 3,000 total casualties.[34]

The cold statistics fail to convey the human tragedy that accompanied the numbers. The dead and wounded of both armies were sprawled about the field, Cheatham's casualties stretching from the hill leading toward Parsons's battery all the way to their final position. Colonel Charles Mc-Daniel of the Forty-first Georgia was mortally wounded, and Lieutenant-Colonel John Patterson of the First Tennessee was killed outright. Ten other officers were wounded. Nor were the losses limited to the officer class. Among the dead were William Rhodes and Frank Buck, the two soldiers from the Twenty-seventh Tennessee who had predicted their violent demise. Dead also was diminutive Hugh Hamner, who had teased his tall comrade, Jim Rucker, back when the Confederates were driving confidently into the state. Cheatham praised his men for their achievements, claimed that he captured twelve guns and some prisoners, and noted that "never did men fall on any field fighting more gallantly."[35] Sadly enough, the bodies of many of Cheatham's dead veterans were never returned to Tennessee. As Federal burial crews took care of their dead the day after the battle, a resident of the area, Squire Henry Bottom, gathered more than four hundred Rebel dead and buried them in several pits. The greater part of these casualties were collected near the fence where Maney's brigade had been stymied before they renewed their charge against Parsons. They remain interred near the spot where they fell, few of them identified by name.[36]

It remained for Squire Bottom to bury the Confederate dead because the Southerners did not linger long enough to perform the task themselves. During the night Cheatham remained on field until 2 A.M. and accompanied his infirmary corps as its members searched the battlefield. Many of his wounded were brought to Doctor's Creek, where Cheatham had established at least one of his hospitals. The physicians attached to Cheatham's division concentrated their efforts on the wounded and won Cheatham's esteem for making the injured "as comfortable as circumstances would allow." While tending to the casualties was a top priority, Cheatham also arranged with artillery chief Melancthon Smith to appropriate some of the captured guns. Lieutenant Turner carted off several pieces, including some of Parsons's twelve-pounders, as well as ammunition, limbers, and caissons. Captain Carnes exchanged a disabled gun for a serviceable one, and Cheatham helped his artillerists chop down the remaining cannons which had to be left on the field. Cheatham explained later that every able-bodied man of the division was instructed to bring two muskets from the battleground, in the hope that transportation could be found to haul off the weapons. "As our wounded filled all our extra wagons, [the muskets] were left on the ground in a line the length of the command."[37]

In the early morning hours Cheatham rode to attend a meeting with Bragg and the other general officers. Bragg at last realized that the bulk of Buell's army was at Perryville, and the officers agreed that a withdrawal was imperative. Cheatham's men fell back from their hard-won position around daylight. Besides discarding the muskets they had harvested, Cheatham's men discovered that there were not enough wagons to bring off all the wounded. Cheatham left at least two of his surgeons behind to care for them, and one of the doctors constructed shelters of brush and cornstalks to shield the men from the sun. Cheatham later boasted that "more badly wounded men recovered than history of hospitals had ever recorded," but this opinion was written some years after the war and is not easily verified.[38]

Bragg's army fell back to Harrodsburg, where Kirby Smith united his force with the Army of the Mississippi for the first time, on October 10. Buell expected the Southerners to remain rooted at Perryville after the contest and was surprised when skirmishers reported the Confederate evacuation. Buell cautiously shadowed Bragg to Harrodsburg, and the two armies encamped nearby the night of October 11. The Kentucky campaign ground to an inglorious finale at Harrodsburg, where both armies declined the opportunity to strike the other. Buell was understandably wary, realizing that a good portion of his army had been splintered by a fraction of the Southern force. He waited in vain for Bragg to hurl the first blow. Bragg cited the approaching winter as one factor in a retreat when he met with Kirby Smith, Polk, Cheatham, and other officers at Bryantsville on October 12, but there was a more important reason. Almost everyone in the army was disappointed by the muted enthusiasm Kentuckians extended. Cheatham's brigade under Preston Smith had entered the state with Kirby Smith and received a warm welcome in towns such as Georgetown and Lexington, but this fond memory was offset by the perplexing attitude of the Kentuckians, who did little to throw off the Union yoke. General Liddell noted that the Kentuckians were friendly but hesitated to do anything "which would in any degree compromise the safety of their persons and families, or the security of their property." Liddell rationalized that the Bluegrass residents were naturally averse to having the war conducted "at their doors," but noted that that was precisely what was required to redeem the state. Bragg earned the enmity of Kirby Smith and the Kentucky elements in the army when he opted to withdraw from the state, but he squelched their protests by flinging his columns eastward to the mountains.[39]

The processsion out of Kentucky was a gloomy one. The optimism which had characterized the beginning of the invasion was gone as the Southerners entered eastern Kentucky. Cheatham was in an ugly mood, and one soldier noted that Frank "cursed and beat" a wagon train officer "for some malfeasance." The full rations gave out quickly, making the mountain trek a torturous one for the Tennesseans. Forced to march long distances with little to sustain them, their energy flagged. "The boys looked stupid," one diarist recorded at the end of a twenty-mile march.[40] The fatigue occasionally gave way to anger, "some cursing such times and some 'Old Bragg.'" All of Cheatham's troops were disheartened by the withdrawal. "The retreat out of Kentucky was one of greater trial and hardship than any march made during the war," wrote Colonel Alfred J. Vaughan of the Thirteenth Tennessee.[41] Vaughan's bleak assessment was echoed by one of the soldiers in his regiment, Thomas J. Firth, as well as other veterans of the division. Cheatham must have wondered what his men had sacrificed their lives for at Perryville. Early in the retreat, he rode by members of Company H of the Ninth Tennessee, the "Obion Avalanche." These soldiers had been among Maney's men who had overrun Parsons's battery, and they paid for the deed by losing 52 percent of the company within half an hour. As Cheatham rode by the company, he cried emotionally, "O, Avalanche, I'm your friend for life." As the retreat progressed, conditions worsened. The desolate surroundings were made even more depresssing by the presence of bushwackers, Union sympathizers who risked being hanged by Bragg when they persisted in sniping at the column. The first frost of the season, on October 18, and a five-inch snowfall near Knoxville on October 26 did little to lift the spirits of Cheatham's men.[42]

The Tennesseans who vented their anger at Bragg probably did not understand the necessity of abandoning Perryville after they had won a decided tactical victory. Nor could others make the distinction, as elements both within and outside the army showed their displeasure by criticizing the commander. A judge in Mobile wrote President Davis to disparage Bragg, while another correspondent wrote a chaplain in Cheatham's division and lamented that "we were . . . much disappointed at the result of Bragg's Ky. campaign."[43] Bragg reacted defensively and was particularly upset by Polk's open criticism. In his official report, filed shortly after the battle, Bragg lauded Hardee, Polk, Cheatham, and a number of other officers. "Nobler troops were never more gallantly led," Bragg enthused, and he allowed Cheatham's regiments to sew a pair of inverted cannons on their flags as a symbol of their valor in claiming the rival batteries. Bragg originally maintained that the country owed his top officers "a debt of gratitude," but he reassessed his favorable pronouncements when Polk and then Hardee voiced their displeasure at the results of the invasion. There is no record of Bragg's opinion regarding Cheatham during this interval, but it may be surmised that Cheatham's close alliance with Polk made him suspect in Bragg's eyes. Perhaps he felt Polk's unflattering remarks represented Cheatham's ideas as well, perhaps not. The army discord prompted Jefferson Davis to summon his friends Kirby Smith, Bragg, and Polk to Richmond, but little came of the meetings.[44]

The divisiveness in the army command remained as the army embarked on a movement into Middle Tennessee. Before the transfer, Bragg reorganized his force and renamed it the Army of Tennessee. The army consisted of two corps, one under Polk and the other led by Hardee. Cheatham's and Withers's veteran divisions constituted Polk's corps, while Hardee managed divisions under Patrick Cleburne, John McCown, and John C. Breckinridge. The Army of Tennessee moved into its new base of operations in November, passing through the great loop of the Tennessee River near Chattanooga as winter descended. Cheatham and the other officers busied themselves with transportation and supply arrangements as the army moved into Middle Tennessee. Bragg concentrated his force in the Stones River valley, thirty miles southeast of Nashville. His Army of Tennessee was one of three armies under the supervision of General Joseph E. Johnston. Johnston was given authority over a vast area, and armies under Kirby Smith in East Tennessee and John C. Pemberton in Mississippi, in addition to Bragg's forces.[45] Michael Mauzy of the Sixteenth Tennessee reported in November, when Cheatham was at Tullahoma, that a number of the men in the division were given furloughs. Mauzy was one of the lucky men from his company to enjoy a brief respite from soldiering.[46] When the men rejoined the division, they may have felt somewhat refreshed in spirit, but the bitter memories of the retreat from Kentucky were never fully erased for Cheatham's troops.

Chapter 5
Controversy at Murfreesboro

Cheatham's arrival in Tullahoma on November 5 marked the close of the rigorous Kentucky campaign for the division. The Tennessean and his men eased back into the occasionally monotonous routine of army life as they recuperated from the Kentucky excursion. The men drew pay and devoted several hours daily to dress parade drill. It was at Tullahoma that Michael Mauzy of the Sixteenth Tennessee Regiment received his furlough. Five members from each company were furloughed, with the stipulation that they spend their time in Coffee County or one of the adjoining counties. A number of Cheatham's men hailed from the area, and they took advantage of the opportunity to visit their homes before the army shifted from the Tullahoma encampment.[1] The visits were brief because the division embarked later in the month for Murfreesboro, forty-four miles to the north. The Murfreesboro area favorably impressed Cheatham's men; one of his soldiers described the region as "a rich country finely wooded." Unfortunately, the contentment Cheatham's troops manifested in their new surroundings was interrupted when a perennial foe, smallpox, broke out in several of Cheatham's units. The Thirteenth Tennessee was isolated from the remainder of its brigade when the disease appeared and was moved four miles from the other regiments. The disease was "soon checked" by the strict quarantine and vaccinations, but the regiment's commander later attested that the malady caused "the loss of some good soldiers."[2]

While some of Cheatham's troops battled disease, Cheatham took two of his brigades to divert Federal attention from a cavalry raid near Nashville. The movement was made despite the four-inch snowfall during the first week of December that impeded their progress. Cheatham took his command to within eleven miles of Nashville and skirmished briefly with a Union force before falling back to Murfreesboro. George Maney's brigade went to LaVergne, midway between Nashville and Murfreesboro, to report on Federal movements and screen any advance the Yankees might make.[3] Cheatham and the other Confederates who camped near Murfreesboro welcomed the onset of the Christmas season with a series of festivities. In mid-December Jefferson Davis undertook an inspection tour of his western armies, and during his brief stay in Murfreesboro he conferred with Bragg and other officers, met with area citizens, and reviewed elements of the army, including Cheatham's division. Davis's visit coincided with the storybook marriage of Kentucky cavalry leader John Hunt Morgan and Martha Ready, a wedding celebrated by Bishop Polk and attended by most of the leading figures of the army. Cheatham, Hardee, and Breckinridge stood by Morgan as the marital vows were exchanged.[4]

The rank and file shared the interest manifested by their superior officers in the visit by President Davis, but more immediate concerns also captured their attention. In the wake of the Kentucky campaign, some of Cheatham's units were forced to combine their rosters. Wartime attrition and the inability to replace losses led to the practice of consolidating depleted regiments. Such was the case when the Twelfth and the Forty-seventh Tennessee Regiments consolidated at Knoxville just before the army shifted to Tullahoma. The organizational changes did not always meet with the approval of Cheatham's troops, especially when officers they were accustomed to serving under were deprived of their commands. The officers considered superfluous naturally resented the consolidations, and it was not uncommon for these disgruntled men to leave the army. Colonel Tyree H. Bell and Lieutenant Colonel L. P. McMurry of the Twelfth Tennessee responded to the consolidation of their regiment and the Forty-seventh Tennessee by returning to West Tennessee on a recruiting trip. Bell and McMurry were joined by several other officers of the Twelfth who became supernumeraries after the consolidation, and it is doubtful that all of these returned to Cheatham's division. Colonel Bell did return but eventually abandoned the infantry for a cavalry assignment.[5] While the Twelfth and the Forty-seventh Tennessee were among the first of Cheatham's regiments to consolidate, as the war continued there were other such combinations. In early 1863, for instance, the First and the Twenty-seventh Tennessee consolidated, partly because the First Tennessee had several companies from the Nashville area and could not recruit from that region once it fell to the Union forces.[6]

On occasion a regiment which did not consolidate with another one was forced to merge and alter formerly separate companies within the regiment. At Murfreesboro, the Thirteenth Tennessee battled both smallpox and the "dissatisfaction" that followed the rearrangement of several companies. There were annoyances aplenty for Cheatham's soldiers, and they were not reticent about expressing their displeasure with the irritations of army life. Still, by late 1862 Cheatham's men were veterans of both battle and camp life, and they had long since discovered methods to compensate for the less thrilling aspects of soldiering. Some of these were uplifting; Alfred Tyler Fielder of the Twelfth Tennessee regularly attended religious services, and his diary is liberally sprinkled with references to the army's spiritual bent. Fielder and like-minded compatriots represented one element in the army, but not all of Cheatham's troops were similarly inclined. William J. Rogers of the Thirteenth Tennessee also kept a diary, and his entry for Christmas Day 1862 proves that typical vices continued unabated as the holiday arrived: "Eggnog was fashionable in camp and Captains, Lieutenant, and Privates was drunk and very troublesome."[7] Certainly officers higher than the captains and lieutenants Rogers referred to behaved in similar fashion. Cheatham may have been one of them.

The lingering holiday merriment faded abruptly on December 26, when George Maney reported from LaVergne that Union troops were advancing from the capital city. After advising Bragg of the movement, Maney slowly withdrew towards Murfreesboro while Bragg sought hurriedly to draw his army together along the meandering banks of Stones River. The Federal troops which threatened Bragg's army were essentially the same ones he had met in the Kentucky campaign, but they were under a new commander. General William S. Rosecrans had replaced Don Carlos Buell when the latter antagonized Abraham Lincoln and War Department officials by his sluggish pursuit of Bragg after Perryville. Rosecrans's Army of the Cumberland advanced by three routes and converged before the Confederate position. The left corps was directed by Thomas L. Crittenden, the center by George H. Thomas, and the right by Alexander M. McCook, whose troops had been so roughly handled by Cheatham's division at Perryville. Estimates of troop strength vary, but one author suggests that the Yankees mustered 44,000 men to 38,000 for the Rebels.[8]

While Bragg defended a valuable agricultural area around Murfreesboro, his decision to establish the Confederate base there was a questionable one. Five turnpikes provided ample passage for Rosecrans's army from Nashville to Murfreesboro. Worse yet, Stones River bisected the Southern line. To add to the hazards, the area around the river was a combination of open fields, dense cedar brakes, and rough limestone outcroppings. Bragg ignored or disregarded the disadvantages and resolved to defend Murfreesboro from his position along the river. As the Union force concentrated in front of Bragg's army, sharp skirmishing broke out. Near sunset on December 30, Cheatham dispatched the 154th Tennessee Regiment to bolster a battery on the left of the Rebel line. The two sides sparred with one another for some time, Cheatham's infantry helping the

Alabama and Florida artillerists repel an assault upon the guns by three Federal regiments.[9] The fighting done on Tuesday served as a prelude to a far more deadly contest the next day, when the battle for Murfreesboro erupted in earnest. The prospect of a violent New Year's Eve was apparent to soldiers on both sides, and during the night of December 30, bands from both armies played their respective national airs until one of them played "Home, Sweet Home." Soon enough all other tunes ceased, "and the bands of both armies, far as the ear could reach, joined in the refrain."[10] In one of the Civil War's incongruities, men bent on destroying one another the next day were united by the plaintive melody, and surely thoughts turned to home, whether it was in the North or South.

One wonders whether Braxton Bragg heard the song, or whether it activated any misgivings about the battle he was preparing to launch. From December 29 to December 31, Bragg had aligned his force for a massive blow against Rosecrans. McCown's division formed the Confederate left, with Cleburne stationed behind him. To McCown's right was Withers, whose division curved from the Triune Road toward the Wilkinson Pike. Cheatham formed a second line several hundred yards behind Withers, some of his regiments resting near the river bank. Only Breckinridge remained on the east side of the river.[11] Bragg's plan consisted of an intricate wheeling movement from left to right. McCown was to open the battle by forcing McCook to the northeast. Cleburne would support McCown, and then Polk would have Withers and Cheatham pound McCook and Thomas as Rebel brigades successively took up the attack. The aim was to roll up the Union right flank and pin it against Stones River.[12] An ambitious plan, Bragg's strategy required excellent coordination and timing to succeed.

Complications which would bedevil the Confederates throughout the fray began to crop up before the battle fully opened. One of McCown's brigades needed to be realigned, and Cheatham, Hardee, and McCown consulted late in the afternoon on Tuesday, December 30, to resolve the situation. Cheatham accompanied McCown and pointed out where the brigade should be repositioned. Though the troops were shifted, the placement of this aggregation caused problems the next day, and later became a source of angry dispute between McCown, Hardee, and Bragg.[13] More directly related to Cheatham was an ungainly command shuffle formulated by Polk on the eve of the battle. Worried about the broken terrain in his front, the bishop devised a means by which his divisional commanders could more easily control the action as it progressed. Cheatham led the two left brigades of Withers's division, one commanded by Colonel J. Q. Loomis and the other under Colonel Arthur M. Manigault. Cheatham also directed the two left brigades of his own division, under Maney and A. J. Vaughan, the latter in temporary command of Preston Smith's troops. Withers supervised four brigades on the right: two from his own division under Patton Anderson and James Chalmers, along with Cheatham's reserve brigades of A. P. Stewart and Daniel Donelson. Polk's basic idea was sound, as it was intended to help the divisional commanders determine when to commit reserve forces, but it also carried the potential for confusion among the brigade and regimental officers.[14]

Despite the inherent problems, the early portion of the battle went in favor of the Southerners. McCown inaugurated the assault around 6:30 A.M., and as his men shoved out along the Triune Road, they forced the startled Federals back. He erred by not wheeling properly, so that a gap formed between McCown's right and Loomis. Cleburne's supporting division fell into the opening, and gradually the extreme right of Rosecrans's army was knocked backwards in the direction of the Wilkinson Pike. Cleburne's attack stalled when the Rebel infantry on his right failed to attack as scheduled, and Union artillery began to pour in an enfilading fire. Hardee complained to Bragg that Cheatham was tardy in pressing the attack, and not until orders were dispatched by Bragg did the Tennessean bring his men into action. Cheatham's troops had expected the order to advance for some time. They had arisen quite early and then listened as the opening guns signalled the beginning of the battle. As the noise increased and swept closer, they "instantly fell into place, the men throwing their knapsacks into piles," and added fatalistic remarks such as, "You know what that means."[15]

Roughly an hour after the initial Confederate thrust, Cheatham belatedly sent Loomis forward. His Alabamians ran headlong into the left division of McCook's corps, commanded by Philip Sheridan, and a brigade from Jefferson C. Davis's division. These units were posted in a thick cedar grove less than 300 yards from Loomis's left, and concentrated Union fire shattered Loomis's soldiers as they crossed an open woods and cornfield. Cheatham described the fighting here as "extremely fierce," but Loomis's assault was doomed from the outset. All element of surprise had evaporated by the time Cheatham committed the brigade, with the result that Loomis's men were forced to retreat, which they did in some disarray. Loomis himself was wounded when struck by a sheared tree limb, and Colonel J. G. Coltart assumed command as Cheatham assisted in reforming the brigade. As Loomis's men retreated, Vaughan's Tennesseans and Texans taunted the Alabamians for their lack of success. It was the second time in the war that these Alabamians had broken off an engagement only to endure the scorn of Cheatham's men. The same thing had occurred at Shiloh, when the Alabama regiments were under

Deas, and at Murfreesboro at least one of Loomis's command was irritated by the smugness of Cheatham's soldiers. As Vaughan's troops prepared to advance, the Alabamian angrily told them, "You'll soon find it the hottest place you ever struck!"[16]

Vaughan's men soon found that the Alabamian knew whereof he spoke. As they retraced Loomis's advance up a gentle slope, they met the same galling fire from Union muskets and cannons. The Tennessee units and the Ninth Texas attacked "with great fury" and were marginally more successful than Loomis, as they drove Yankee artillerists from two guns. Still, Vaughan could not withstand a brisk fire which blistered his right flank, and he also retired as his losses mounted. Cheatham helped reorganize the brigade and sent it forward in conjunction with Coltart. Cheatham instructed Vaughan to alter his second approach somewhat to avoid the heavily wooded area in his front. This second charge was assisted by the Texans, who had not received the original order to retreat and had instead penetrated the woods, where they began to drive the Federals facing Cheatham's left. At last Cheatham's men made headway, as Vaughan and Coltart finally dislodged the Northerners from their strong position.[17]

Stones River was an exceedingly confusing action, and nowhere is the problem of pinpointing Confederate movements more evident than in regard to Manigault, the brigade to Coltart's right. According to Cheatham's published report, an entire hour elapsed before the brigade was hurled forward to support Loomis. This suggests that Manigault did not assault in unison with Loomis, as the battle plan stipulated. Nonetheless, other sources imply that Manigault did indeed follow Loomis in echelon by regiments. A rough draft of Cheatham's battle report indicates that he wrote two times in reference to Manigault's first advance (7:30 and 8:00 A.M., the latter figure appearing in the *Official Records*), with the result that it is impossible to determine when Manigault first assaulted and whether he properly supported Loomis. If the time and circumstances related to his first sally are murky, the reception he received is much clearer: his neat alignment was shredded by Union battery and infantry fire. Manigault's men filled the gaps in their ranks until they got to within fifty yards of the Union line, when a volley of musketry broke their momentum and forced them to withdraw. A second charge by Manigault's Alabamians and South Carolinians met the same fate, partly because Coltart and Vaughan had given way on the left, and soon Manigault requested Maney's assistance in breaking the Union stronghold.[18]

Sheridan drew his men back to a new line near the Giles Harding farmhouse and awaited developments. Up to this point, Cheatham's performance was extremely suspect. Not only was he late in taking up the attack, but in addition, his assault was not particularly well coordinated.

The two forward brigades did not remain linked together, and Cheatham may not have funneled in Vaughan and Maney as promptly as he should have. As it was, Loomis, Manigault, and Vaughan all suffered severe losses; Vaughan, for instance, lost a third of his force early in the engagement, while Loomis's Alabamians were chewed up so badly that they were essentially through for the rest of the day.[19] Cheatham's men had achieved some success and inflicted a heavy toll on Sheridan's defenders, but the Yankees were aligned in a new defensive position near the Wilkinson Pike and still offered stout resistance.

Cheatham's men faced obstacles when they renewed the attack. Two Union batteries were especially vexing and were partially responsible for breaking Manigault's previous charges. The two batteries were situated about six hundred yards apart, one on a ridge near the Harding farmhouse and a nearby brick kiln, and the other in a woods to the east. The batteries were advantageously placed so that when an attack was made against one, the other was able to pour in a flanking fire. Maney and Manigault determined to attack the batteries together, Maney selecting the First and the Fourth Tennessee Regiments to dash for the one near the Harding house while Manigault drove for the one in the woods.[20]

As with other developments in Cheatham's front, the venture was marked by confusion. Maney moved forward before Manigault was fully reformed, with the result that Maney's two regiments were vulnerable to the Federal fire. The Union battery near the Harding house withdrew across the Wilkinson Pike as Maney's men advanced, but the second battery remained in the woods and contested the Rebel approach. Maney's two regimental commanders, Colonel Hume R. Feild of the First Tennessee and Colonel James A. McMurry of the Fourth Tennessee, mistakenly thought the battery in the woods was a Confederate one and had their men lie down without returning fire. Probably thinking the guns belonged to Withers, Lieutenant R. Fred James of Cheatham's staff rode rapidly to within thirty yards of the guns to let the cannoneers know of the supposed error in identity. James may have discovered that the battery was a Yankee one, but as he whirled his horse a shot from a Federal infantryman struck him in the head and killed him. Feild sent another mounted officer to scout the situation, and this envoy was also fired upon, though he escaped. By this time a number of Maney's men were convinced that they were facing a hostile gun crew, and they shouted for the Confederates to fire. Still, it was not until color bearers from Maney's regiments flaunted their flags and elicited a violent response that Maney realized at last that the battery was a Union unit. To make matters worse, the Yankee battery that had retired across the Wilkinson Pike unlimbered and began shelling Maney's beleaguered soldiers.[21]

Cheatham's men attempted to protect themselves as best they could in the exposed brickyard. One reminisced later that the position "was one of the most perplexing and unfortunate in which it is possible to conceive a line to be placed." Eventually Maney's men began an irregular fire after Colonel Feild instructed his regiment to "fire on that battery, anyhow." Feild's efforts were complemented by Maney's artillery under Lieutenant Turner, who brought his four Napoleons into action from a position near the brick kiln. Thomas H. Malone, Maney's adjutant, rode to Turner and requested that he "knock to pieces that Yankee battery that is playing on our lines so." Malone added that General Maney was under the impression that the battery was a Rebel one, but Turner replied, "They are Yankees, and I've known it all the time." Turner had his guns shifted to the crest of a hill, unlimbered, and then ordered his first sergeant to set the fuses for five hundred yards. The sergeant, a preacher as well as an artilleryman, "laid his cheek along the butt of the gun and took deliberate aim, and as the gun was fired," threw himself to one side, almost upon the ground, and peered under the smoke to see the result. In a few seconds the shell exploded "right in the midst of the battery." According to Malone, the first shot "dismounted a gun, set fire to the ammunition in one of the caissons," and elicited from Turner an enthusiastic response. Ignoring the fact that he might offend his sergeant, whom he had just addressed as "Parson," Turner shouted, "Give 'em hell, G[od] d[amn] 'em!" The combined artillery and infantry fire devasted the offending battery. One of Maney's soldiers wrote later that when the smoke cleared, he could see but one horse still standing, the steed bearing a brave Union officer who refused to retreat.[22]

At this juncture, around 9 A.M., Cheatham finally decided to coordinate his attacks. Riding to Maney's line, Cheatham repositioned Manigault, who had reformed his lines for a third time, and prepared for a new assault. About the same time, he placed Vaughan to the left, while artillery units wheeled forward to assist in the effort. Seemingly frustrated by the stubborn resistance of the Federals, Cheatham decided personal leadership might provide the impetus required to dislodge Sheridan's tenacious defenders. Both Maney and Vaughan reported that Cheatham accompanied his units as they assailed the Wilkinson Pike line, with Cheatham at the head of Maney's regiments. Sam R. Watkins, a private in the First Tennessee who wrote an often-cited account of his wartime service, noted that Cheatham shouted, "Come on, boys, and follow me!" Maney's men sprinted forward at Cheatham's exhortation, moving together with the other brigades. Cheatham continued to lead the charge, prompting Watkins to recognize "the power of one man, born to command, over a multitude of men then almost routed and demoralized."[23]

Sheridan later reported that when Cheatham advanced, the "contest then became terrible," a sentiment shared by men on both sides. As Maney's men moved forward, the Union gunners with the battery in the woods tried in vain to haul their fieldpieces off. One of Cheatham's soldiers recalled that the solitary Union officer on horseback went down as Maney's line charged, as did his steed. The same observer wrote that as he passed near the abandoned Yankee cannons, he "found every man & every horse dead."[24] The Federal resistance finally crumbled in the face of Cheatham's furious assault. Cheatham was aided by Withers, who plowed into the Union flank with Patton Anderson and A. P. Stewart's brigades. Just as Withers struck, Cheatham's legions overran several gun crews on the other side of Wilkinson Pike. While Cheatham slashed with his sword, his troops broke the Union line and slaughtered the Yankees who desperately tried to hurl them back. The cost was staggering, and Sheridan wrote that there were three assaults along the Wilkinson Pike before his troops were battered back, but the second Union line melted away as McCook and Thomas shunted back through the forest to the Nashville Pike.[25]

Cheatham's efforts resulted in control of the high ground near the Harding house as well as possession of the Wilkinson Pike, but the toll extracted was horrendous. One of Vaughan's men in the Twelfth Tennessee recorded in his diary later that night that the Federal "loss was awful, ours heavy," and attributed Confederate success to God and "the justness of our cause." One of Maney's veterans in the First Tennessee wrote later that the Rebels were kept busy "killing everything in blue," but the butchery extended to both sides. The fighting was so severe that one Union battery lost ninety-five horses in a vain effort to hold their position, while one of the cedar groves in the vicinity was practically obliterated by the time the bluecoats gave way. All three of Sheridan's brigade commanders were dead by the time he pulled back, but their resistance had delayed the success of Bragg's strategy and cost Cheatham dearly.[26]

Nor was the fighting over. Cheatham dispatched Vaughan to assist Cleburne, and Withers kept pressure on Sheridan with his brigades to Cheatham's right. The din of crashing tree limbs accompanied the combat, a phenomenon, one participant wrote, that "was such as I heard no where else during the war." As Sheridan's troopers ran out of ammunition and began to withdraw, Cheatham and other Confederate officers urged their men in pursuit. The Rebels surged through the woods as the Yankees fell back. Here and there Cheatham's men captured prisoners, many of these bluecoats searching for or attending to wounded comrades. The pursuit carried them anywhere from a half to three-quarters of a mile, and as the Confederates neared the edge of the woods, they discovered

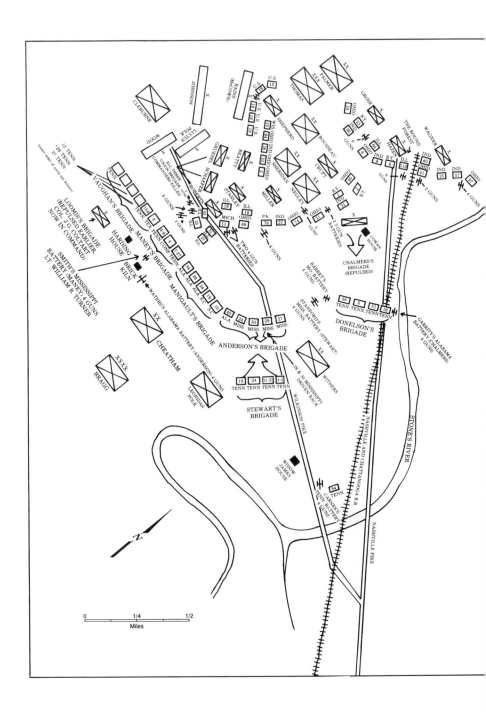

Map 2. Confederate Attack at Stones River — December 31, 1862, approximately 9:30–11:00 A.M.

a third Union line, this one resting at a strong site formed by an angle of Stones River on one side and a deep cut of the Nashville railroad on the other. Thick cedar tree clumps covered the four-acre site, which featured a sharp salient known as the Round Forest.[27]

By this time, around noon, Bragg's plan to crush Rosecrans appeared to be working. The Federal right flank had been driven three miles in some spots, and a number of Yankee units were demoralized. But the Confederate success was deceptive. The difficulties encountered in the morning sapped some of the vigor from the Rebels, and Cheatham, for example, had been forced to employ all of his reserves within the first hour of fighting. The vital Nashville turnpike had still not been seized, while the Round Forest, like the Hornets' Nest at Shiloh, became a magnet for Southern assaults.[28]

Among the first troops to aim for the salient were those under James Chalmers, Withers's right brigade commander. Chalmers was wounded in his effort, and his Mississippians recoiled after their leader was borne from the field. Up came Cheatham's men led by Daniel Donelson in support of Chalmers. "There were no finer troops in the Confederate army," an admiring Federal later wrote. A portion of Donelson's troops emerged from the woods into an open area cultivated for cotton, and as they pressed forward, they suffered dreadfully. Thirty men in the Sixteenth Tennessee were sliced down, "left dead upon the spot where they halted dressed in perfect line of battle." Massed Union artillery guns delivered a fire which "seemed to sweep every foot of ground." One of Cheatham's gunners termed it "the most terrible can[n]onading I ever witnessed," and added that Union muskets "kept up a fire equal to the falls of Niagara." A farmhouse compelled Donelson's men to break ranks, troops moving to either side of the burned dwelling, with the units on the right eventually advancing along the railroad. The punishment Donelson's men absorbed was awful. By Cheatham's tally, the Sixteenth Tennessee lost 207 of the 472 men it carried into battle. Even worse casualties were inflicted on Colonel William L. Moore's Eighth Tennessee, which clashed with Union troops in a cedar brake south of the Round Forest. Moore's men wreaked havoc, splintering two lines and capturing hundreds of prisoners, but the success was gained at a terrible price. Moore lost 306 of his 472 men before the assault ground to a halt and was eventually repulsed. Moore was not alive by the time his survivors gave way, having been hit in the heart by a minié ball.[29]

Chalmers's and Donelson's failure should have convinced the Confederates that the Union position was too formidable, but such was not the case. Cheatham did apparently worry that Rosecrans might launch a counterattack after Chalmers and Donelson were rebuffed. During the early afternoon, Cheatham "commenced forming the troops in two lines to meet any advance." The Tennessean positioned several brigades belonging to his and other Rebel divisions. A Georgia officer was told by Cheatham to move to the front, but like many of the other Confederates, his command was hesitant to attack the Round Forest. "Finding myself entirely alone with 300 men," the Georgian wrote, "it was deemed imprudent to make an unsupported attack upon the enemy."[30] While many of Cheatham's soldiers and other Rebel troops were in formation near the edge of the woods, they became targets for Federal artillery crews, who sent projectiles into the cedars. At one point the Union fire slackened when a bluecoat riding a gray horse ventured into a clearing to seek out a wounded comrade. He dismounted and was examining someone when some of Maney's pickets hollered for him to halt. The Federal them attempted to mount his horse, was fired upon by the pickets, and had his hand caught in the bridle when his steed, stung by the shot, bolted. The horse bounced the unfortunate Yankee for some distance before they parted company. The veteran in Maney's First Tennessee who recounted this story somewhat gleefully noted that the horse continued at "full speed for his friends," while the rider "crawled on his hands & feet for several hundred y[ar]ds" before rolling into the cut on the Nashville Pike.[31]

If some of Cheatham's men took delight in the discomfiture of their foe, their merriment eroded quickly enough. The Union batteries had been silent as long as the gray horse and his intrepid rider were in the way, but once horse and rider were out of danger, the gun crews again sent shells into Cheatham's ranks. The same veteran who derived such joy from the predicament of the Federal horseman was awed by the ferocity of the Union barrage and felt that "for a while it seemed all the artillery shells, canister, & solid [shot] in the universe had turned loose." Cheatham's men tried to shield themselves from the onslaught by hugging the ground, or hiding behind tree stumps and rocks "as only a scared man can do." Not all of Cheatham's men survived the heavy shelling. One of Maney's men in the First Tennessee was decapitated by a shot which carried the head, hat still attached, into a tree some twenty-five to thirty feet above the earth. The grisly sight remained visible later, when Maney's troops fell back.[32]

While Cheatham was occupied reforming troops from various brigades, Bragg and Polk persisted in hammering away at the Round Forest. Four of Breckinridge's brigades were summoned to aid Polk and fed piecemeal into the grinder. The disjointed sorties failed to force a breakthrough in the line. Confederate efforts finally tailed off at sunset, when the incessant artillery fire and musketry mercifully diminished.[33] "Thank God I have been spared to see the commencement of another year," wrote Captain Alfred Tyler Fielder of Vaughan's Twelfth Tennessee the next day. Fielder had much to be thankful for. The ground over which Cheatham and the rest of the Army of Tennessee had met the Yankees was covered with dead, wounded, supplies, and other wartime debris. Gideon Pillow rode by Vaughan's brigade early on New Year's Day 1863 and praised the troops for their accomplishments. Fielder wrote in his diary that Pillow employed a rather macabre allusion, telling Vaughan's men that they had covered "the ground thick enough with dead yankies [*sic*] if they should vegetate to bring a copious crop."[34]

Fielder might well have applied the analogy to his own regiment; the Twelfth suffered 164 casualties out of 322 combatants. Of 5,859 men in Cheatham's division listed as engaged in the battle, 1,939 were killed, wounded, or missing, a heavy 35 percent casualty rate. The brunt of Cheatham's casualty list was borne by two brigades, Donelson's and Vaughan's. The former had 691 total casualties, and when Preston Smith arrived to supersede Vaughan, he inherited a brigade with 705 men dead, wounded, or missing. Even where losses were relatively light, the manner in which they were inflicted was revealing. Hume R. Feild's First Tennessee lost the vast majority of his 83 casualties in action near the brick kiln.[35]

Despite the high casualty lists, Bragg wired Richmond that a tremendous victory had been won. When New Year's Day arrived, Bragg discovered that Rosecrans had not retreated. Withers did occupy the Round Forest salient temporarily, but it was obvious that Bragg had not crushed the Federals as he had hoped. A number of miscues caused Bragg's plan to go awry. McCown's directional error, the respective tardiness of Cheatham and Withers to attack as scheduled, and preoccupation with the Round Forest all hampered Confederate efforts. Cheatham did not seem sure of himself in the initial part of the conflict, and the brigades he led were hurt by his uncertainty. In turn, the overall Rebel operations on the field never achieved the lofty goals Bragg had established. There is strong evidence to believe that drinking contributed to Cheatham's woes early in the morning.

Several reports support the idea that Cheatham was under the influence of alcohol when the battle began. When Cheatham's men overran the Harding house, they found it was being used as a Federal hospital. An Illinois veteran who remained behind to assist his comrades revealed that the Confederates threw a provost guard around the building, and a short time later Generals Cheatham and Hardee rode up, accompanied by their staffs. The Yank was impressed with Hardee, who was "very dignified," but caustically noted that "Gen. Cheatham was more demonstrative, and answered more clearly to the character attributed to Southerners.

It was the judgement of more than one that day that he was intoxicated."
The Yankee also heard that when the body of Confederate Brigadier-
General James E. Rains was brought to the Harding house, Cheatham
"wept freely" at the sight of his slain comrade. This version of Cheatham's
behavior is supported by William J. Rogers, a soldier in the Thirteenth
Tennessee who served as part of an infirmary detail. Rogers closed his
diary entry for December 31 with a terse entry: "Cheatham drunk."[36]

A third source related that Cheatham lined Maney's and Vaughan's brigades in battle formation at one point during the morning and attempted
to encourage his men by waving his hat. As he doffed the hat, though,
Cheatham ingloriously fell off his steed. While his mortified Tennesseans
looked on in amazement, "Old Frank" sprawled on the ground, "as limp
and helpless as a bag [of] meal." The incident was recounted to General
Liddell some time later by Chaplain Charles Todd Quintard of the First
Tennessee.[37] Curiously, Bragg did not take immediate action against
Cheatham, but he used the subject of Cheatham's moral delinquency in
an acrimonious dispute during and after the war. In a postwar letter,
Bragg related that he understood Cheatham to have been so drunk all
day on December 31 that a staff officer was required to hold him on his
horse.[38]

Historians have generally accepted the charge that Cheatham was intoxicated, partly because Bragg claimed that neither Polk nor Cheatham
contested the allegation.[39] While the abundant evidence does point to
such a conclusion, it is difficult to reconcile the conflicting reports. Private Sam Watkins, who also targeted whiskey as a possible source of
Confederate woes, witnessed Cheatham wielding his sword and taking
a prominent part in the successful effort to break the Federal line along
the Wilkinson Pike.[40] His account does not jibe with the Bragg version,
or with the one in which Cheatham fell off of his horse. Both of these portray a commander who was stone drunk and seemingly insensible. Bragg's
assessment is particularly suspect, as he wrote the letter in 1873, by which
time he roundly despised Cheatham. Since both men did eventually de-
test one another, Bragg probably saw fit to place Cheatham in as poor
a light as possible. Perhaps he exaggerated Cheatham's drunkenness in
order to discredit the Tennessean. If Watkins's eyewitness account of the
charge is to be believed, and Cheatham was indeed as drunk as Bragg
maintained, his recuperative powers most have been incredible. A second
veteran wrote that he also saw Cheatham on the battlefield December
31, "riding a splendid horse and looking every inch a soldier."[41] This source
is less trustworthy, as it was written eulogistically after Cheatham's death,
but it does demonstrate that Bragg may have overstated Cheatham's intoxication. Two accounts written shortly after the battle by leaders of an

Arkansas regiment and a battalion of Georgia infantry refer to orders delivered by Cheatham.[42] It is unlikely that men in these army units, which did not belong to Cheatham's division, would respond to his commands if he was helplessly drunk.

It is almost impossible to sort out the truth or even to ascertain why Cheatham might have been drinking so early in the morning. Numerous possibilities present themselves. He could have been fortifying himself for the battle, been attempting to ward off the cold, or gotten carried away with a late-night drinking bout. Maybe he had a premonition that he would be killed in battle. Two more probable reasons are nonetheless divergent, one being that he was continuing the Yuletide celebration as the New Year approached, and the other that, with his sentimental streak, he was upset that 1863 was arriving and his family remained behind enemy lines.[43] The only facts that can be stated with certainty are that his men were poorly served by their divisional commander for the early part of the battle and suffered needless casualties until Cheatham managed to rally them for a concerted movement. And Bragg's hostility was engendered in part because Cheatham selected such an inopportune time for a drinking session.

Neither army commander pressed the other on January 1, and the day passed without a serious engagement. The next day, Bragg decided to use Breckinridge's relatively fresh division to seize a ridge on the eastern side of Stones River which threatened Polk on the other side. Without consulting Hardee, Bragg ordered Breckinridge forward, while Cheatham's artillery crews joined other Rebel units on the left in shelling the woods to provide a diversion. After a short period of success, Breckinridge's soldiers were rocked in a counterattack, and Crittenden's massed artillery tore gaping holes in their ranks. Breckinridge's two battle lines broke and hurried for the rear. An alarmed Bragg called Patton Anderson across the river to bolster Breckinridge in case the Yankees followed up their advantage. Later that evening McCown and Cleburne transferred their divisions to the eastern side of Stones River.[44]

As rain and sleet fell during the night, the river started to swell. Only Cheatham and Withers remained on the western side with their crippled divisions. While the rain continued and Stones River rose, the two generals met to discuss the situation. Fearful of being isolated, at 12:15 A.M. on January 3 they drafted a letter to Bragg stating that only three reliable brigades remained and urged Bragg to withdraw.[45] The letter went from Cheatham and Withers via Polk, who endorsed the advice tendered by his divisional commanders. Polk added, "I greatly fear the consequences of another engagement," and pointed out that "we could now perhaps get off with some safety and some credit," provided that "the affair was well managed." Awakened by a staff officer, Bragg read but part of the missives before replying succinctly to Polk: "We shall hold our own at every hazard."[46]

In the morning Bragg reversed himself. During the night captured papers were brought to headquarters, Union general Alexander McCook having been victimized in this fashion at Stones River just as he had been at Perryville. As Bragg read the papers, he became convinced that Rosecrans had an even larger force than previously estimated. A council with Hardee and Polk cemented the inclination to retreat, though it meant abandoning hundreds of wounded men in Murfreesboro.[47] Polk led the withdrawal, with Cheatham's division moving southward en route to Shelbyville in the early morning hours of January 4.[48]

The withdrawal from Murfreesboro initiated a depressing series of events for Cheatham in the early months of 1863. Not only did the retreat indicate that the army had failed to defeat decisively their Union rivals, but it also carried Cheatham farther from his hometown. Frank could not have felt heartened by the lengthening distance between himself and those Cheatham family members who remained in Nashville under Federal rule. A letter smuggled to him at the end of January from his mother was a dreary missive which could only upset him further. Elizabeth Cheatham was disturbed by the prolonged Union presence, though she was contemptuous of the Yankees she encountered "at every step in our own yard." She referred to her captors as "the very lowest set that ever carried a bayonet" but acknowledged that the Confederates were not likely to redeem Nashville, since she "knew the river could bring a power to bear on the town that would render holding it too difficult." She painted a portrait of desolation, noting that fences, trees, and homes disappeared "before the house burner and the woodman's axe."[49]

Equally distressing was the information that one of Cheatham's younger sisters, Leonora, was tremendously weakened by a long-term illness. A family favorite, Leonora did not have long to live when Elizabeth wrote her son. Her death in late February was one of two shocks the family absorbed in a short time. Leonard Cheatham, worn out by worry, his daughter's illness, and the Union occupation, died March 7, only eleven days after Leonora's death. When Frank learned of his father's death, his thoughts could only have turned to happier times. The elder Cheatham had made a vast impression on Frank's life, and surely not being on hand for his father's funeral was cause for regret. Frank's brother Felix remained in Nashville shouldering much of the burden, but he too had problems. Though he was too ill to serve in the army, being the brother of a prominent Southern general made Felix highly suspect to Union authorities.

The previous summer he had been one of several Rebel sympathizers assessed a fee imposed by Andrew Johnson to support wives and helpless children in Davidson County. The $100 assessment was payable in five days, Johnson stating at the time it was imposed that the destitute families were the result of the "unholy and nefarious rebellion."[50]

These family woes, and his own inability to alter them, may have contributed to Cheatham's drinking spree at Stones River. Even though Murfreesboro was less than thirty miles from Nashville, that was an imposing distance when Frank calculated the number of enemies who separated him from his family. How much Cheatham dwelled on such matters is unknown. As the distance between him and his family widened, he was kept occupied by the furor which attended the army shortly after the battle. The retreat was barely concluded before discord enveloped the army. Disgruntled elements of the Tennessee populace severely criticized Bragg. Among the critics were Senators Gustavus Henry and Henry Foote, while certain elements within the army joined in the campaign as well. These groups were disappointed by the Murfreesboro withdrawal and felt it fit into a recurring and depressing cycle. As at Shiloh and Perryville, Rebel forces had seemingly garnered success in the first part of the fighting at Stones River, only to end up in retreat. One of Bragg's most tormenting detractors was the *Chattanooga Daily Rebel,* which falsely observed that the decision to retreat from Murfreesboro had been made by Bragg against the wishes of his high officers.[51] The allegation angered Bragg, who read the offending article to his staff members and then drafted a circular letter to his corps and divisional commanders.

"Finding myself assailed in private and public," Bragg wrote on January 11, 1863, "it becomes necessary to save my fair name." The army commander complained that even staff officers of his generals were convinced that the withdrawal was Bragg's idea and carried out against the wishes of their superiors. Fearing the possible demoralization of his soldiers as the conflict swirled, Bragg asked his officers to report on whether they had advised the retreat. To support his position Bragg enclosed copies of the letter sent by Cheatham and Withers, as well as Polk's endorsement. Had Bragg limited his inquiry to this point, he would have spared himself a good deal of misery. But, almost as an afterthought, Bragg petulantly noted that General Kirby Smith had been called to Virginia, "it is supposed with a view to super[s]ede me." Bragg then vowed to "retire without a regret" if he discovered that "I have lost the good opinion of my Generals upon whom I have ever relied as upon a foundation of rock."[52]

The frank replies of his officers jolted Bragg. Hardee, Breckinridge, and Cleburne all responded by stating that Bragg no longer held the trust of the army and should step down. The advice echoed the recommendation of Bragg's own staff, which had reached the same conclusion in an earlier meeting.[53] Polk was then absent from the army, and Cheatham and Withers wished to consult with their corps leader before replying. Cheatham did send a short note acknowledging that he was one of the first to counsel retreat, but he gave no response regarding Bragg's offer to resign nor any indication as to the sentiment towards Bragg in Cheatham's division.[54] When Polk returned in late January, he asked Bragg exactly what it was he wanted to know: were there two questions implicit in the circular, or one, as Cheatham claimed? Thoroughly tired of unfavorable reports, and unwilling to have Polk and Cheatham slash at him as had the officers in Hardee's corps, Bragg hastened to tell Polk he was interested in but one point, the retreat. Polk then responded that his endorsement to the note from Cheatham and Withers had been "deliberately considered" and that he would tender the same advice again in similar circumstances.[55]

It is hard to believe that Cheatham failed to recognize the dual questions implicit in Bragg's circular. Hardee and his generals certainly exhibited no hesitation in recommending that Bragg resign, an indication that they indeed discovered two queries in the letter. Polk himself considered there to be two points of inquiry but did not respond on the question of Bragg's suitability as army commander because "this indication seems not to have been so clear to the mind of General Cheatham and such other of my subordinate officers as responded."[56] Polk's, Cheatham's, and Withers's lack of candor with Bragg placed Hardee and his subordinates in an embarrassing position and aroused resentment in Hardee's corps. McCown, for instance, railed that Cheatham "said one thing among the officers behind Genl. Bragg's back and wrote him a totally different thing."[57] McCown had a justifiable grievance. Cheatham almost certainly shared his fellow generals' lack of confidence in Bragg's abilities, and his silence is puzzling. Perhaps Cheatham's first thought was of self-preservation. By refusing to criticize Bragg openly, Cheatham may have hoped to escape any controversy related to his battlefield intemperance. If this was the motive for Cheatham's taciturnity, his hopes were dashed shortly after the Richmond government sustained Bragg as army commander despite the reservations of several of his high-ranking subalterns.

Bragg first sought to minimize the damage engendered by his unfortunate missive. He wrote President Davis in mid-January to explain why the army retreated and warned Davis that he would be pressured to remove Bragg. This pressure, Bragg concluded, was a sentiment attributed partially "to a temporary feeling of a part of my army—mostly new men under new officers" that was subsiding. This was a deception, as the attack on Bragg's abilities certainly extended to more officers and men than he intimated, including many veterans who had been with the army since the early part of the war. Bragg depicted himself as something of a martyr, the victim of "false reports and rumors" by "newsmongers." He also felt he was attacked "as no man ever was, probably, except yourself," the latter a passage designed to capture Davis's sympathies.[58]

Next Bragg turned to intra-army affairs. Stung by the denunciations aroused by his letter, Bragg resolved to punish those officers he considered offensive and to eliminate them from the army if possible. He also cast about for scapegoats whom he could blame as the culprits in the battle. One of his targets was Cheatham. Cheatham was responsible for Cleburne's heavy casualties by attacking later than ordered, Bragg charged, and he pointedly left Cheatham's name off the long list of officers commended in his official report of the battle. The omission touched off an uproar in Polk's corps. Cheatham's Tennesseans had anxiously awaited the issuance of Bragg's report, and when it was made public, they sided with their divisional commander. One of Polk's confidants wrote, "The Tennesseans could stand him pitching into McCown, but not Cheatham." Cheatham's backers in Congress were also incensed by Bragg's actions. A furious Cheatham threatened to resign, an eventuality he mentioned to Isham Harris. Harris conveyed the information to General Joseph E. Johnston when the latter made an inspection tour to assess the problems in Bragg's army. Johnston wrote President Davis that Governor Harris was confident that he could control Cheatham "and bring him to his senses."[59] Harris was successful in dissuading Cheatham from leaving the army, but it was obvious by now that Cheatham and his men were Bragg opponents. Cheatham may have felt betrayed by Bragg. He perhaps felt that Bragg would be more favorably disposed to him since Cheatham had refused to join in the open criticism of Bragg's martial talents.

Though Bragg was correct in asserting that Cheatham helped contribute to Cleburne's casualty lists, it is interesting to note that Bragg warmly praised Withers in his report. Historians have tended to downplay that Withers was also tardy in pressing the attack; Patton Anderson did not go forward until 9 A.M., by which time Manigault had already been repelled in his third assault of the morning. Cheatham's men suffered casualties in part because of Withers's slowness, a fact Bragg was unwilling to accept. It is natural that Bragg praised Withers, for the latter was a strong Bragg supporter and in fact published a defense of Bragg's conduct in a Mobile newspaper.[60] Nonetheless, Bragg was not exercising objectivity by the time he published his official report. Indeed, objectivity was being sacrificed by a good part of the army as the winter months dragged on.

Eventually Bragg determined to reveal Cheatham's drinking to Richmond, perhaps in part to squash the sentiment of Cheatham's soldiers, who voiced their disapproval at Bragg's version of the battle. Writing from Tullahoma on April 9, 1863, Bragg expressed surprise at Polk's Murfreesboro report, which was written March 21. In the report Polk lauded both Cheatham and Withers for "their cordial support and co-operation" during the engagement. Bragg interpreted this as undue praise for Cheatham, especially since Polk had regretfully admitted hearing of Cheatham's intoxication, an admission which confirmed Bragg's message to that effect. Polk assured Bragg that he had verbally admonished Cheatham, but in early January Bragg had insisted that Polk censure Cheatham in writing. Bragg also averred that Cheatham's dereliction was overlooked only in light "of his previous distinguished services." Polk told Bragg that the reprimand had "the desired effect." Bragg was therefore surprised and angered by Polk's complimentary remarks about Cheatham, and felt compelled to write the government and justify his omission.[61]

Secretary of War James Seddon regarded the report as "very unfortunate," as it added to the turmoil already brewing in the western army. Seddon also recommended that "a court of inquiry should I suppose be ordered," when he forwarded the report to President Davis.[62] If a court was convened, no evidence remains to prove its existence, and Cheatham continued as a divisional leader. The relations between Bragg and Cheatham were decidedly strained by the incident and deteriorated at a rapid rate.

Cheatham's angry soldiers were further alienated by Bragg's military regimen after the battle. They were particularly upset when a deserter from the division was publicly executed at Shelbyville. One soldier wrote, "Genl. Bragg should have pardoned the poor fellow and I never liked Bragg much afterwards." Sam Watkins, a more vehement critic, felt Bragg "wanted always to display his tyranny, and intimidate his privates as much as possible." A soldier in the Ninth Tennessee described the deserter as calm and self-possessed as he prepared to die, but this writer also rued the severity of military law.[63] Apparently, mutual suspicion existed between Bragg and the Tennesseans, the former distrusting the loyalty of Cheatham's men while the soldiers believed that Bragg was unappreciative of the sacrifices they had made at Murfreesboro. It is not surprising that Cheatham's men allied themselves even more closely with their divisional commander in the months after the battle, as both Cheatham and his troops turned against an army chieftain they considered oppressive.

Bragg initiated yet another quarrel in late March, when he decided to reopen controversies relating to the Kentucky campaign. The commander was perturbed by Polk's report, which failed to discuss the councils Polk convened at Bardstown and Perryville. Another circular letter was issued to brigade, division, and corps commanders, asking them of their role in the 1862 meetings, and Bragg hinted that Polk would be held responsible for disobeying orders. The reasoning was flawed; if the officers admitted that they agreed with Polk's decisions not to attack at Frankfort and Perryville, they too would be liable and could be charged with disobedience. Polk ignored the message, and Hardee made no reply. Cheatham was in no mood to assist Bragg and curtly declined to answer the circular. Other officers hedged in their replies, and the matter dragged out inconclusively through April and May.[64]

The ugly series of disputes helped speed the formation of an active opposition to Bragg that coalesced in early spring 1863. Polk and Hardee were two influential members of the opposition. Army cliques such as the Kentucky and Tennessee regiments welded against the commanding general. Cheatham was aligned with Bragg's foes, who reached into Richmond as well. Anti-Davis congressmen resented Davis's support of Bragg, criticized the administration, and jousted with Bragg supporters on the floor of the Confederate Congress. "I wish you all could get rid of Bragg—ev[e]ry body seems to hate him so," wrote Cheatham's sister Martha. Her sentiments were shared by Frank and a number of others in the army. Bragg was certainly not vilified by everyone associated with the Army of Tennessee, but his enemies were abundant and resentful. Cheatham, Polk, and the other members of the opposition exhibited a good deal of childish pride, as did Bragg and his backers. The split between pro- and anti-Bragg factions produced an atmosphere of low morale and uncertainty in the army. The quarrels within the Confederate ranks did not diminish until mid-June, when the army was forced to parry a new Federal threat.[65]

Chapter 6

"Give them hell boys!":
The Battles for Chattanooga

The bickering among the Confederates drew to a temporary close when Rosecrans, prodded by impatient Washington authorities, moved against the Southern positions. Rosecrans hoped to capture East Tennessee and aimed at a Rebel line that was thinly spread and vulnerable. Hurt by a severe food shortage, Bragg had been forced to deploy his troops across a vast front to forage for subsistence. In the seventy-mile wide cordon, Cheatham was with Polk's corps at Shelbyville, while Hardee held sway at Tullahoma. Cavalry guarded both flanks, but could not seal off heavy Union encroachments. Rosecrans began maneuvering against Bragg by feinting towards Shelbyville while he swept the bulk of his army against Hardee's advance brigades at Hoover's Gap. Bragg gathered his far-flung troops at Tullahoma, then waited as Rosecrans slogged through heavy rains. The Confederates delayed until June 30, when they abandoned Tullahoma in order to circumvent a Federal move around the rear. Despite insistent Union probes, Bragg's army managed to cross the Cumberland Mountains. Cheatham went by way of Sewanee, then crossed the Tennessee River on the way to Chattanooga. The important rail center was reached on July 8. Hardee was ordered to Mississippi and was replaced by General Daniel Harvey Hill, but Polk remained in command of his corps.[1]

Both Cheatham and Polk might have noted that the previous year had found them in Chattanooga en route to Kentucky. A year later they were in the same city, but under far different circumstances. Rosecrans's masterful campaign had forced the Southerners to yield most of the Tennessee territory that they had retained after Stones River. Cheatham's men were kept busy constructing fortifications around Chattanooga, a labor which ultimately proved to be superfluous. Many of Cheatham's men did not understand why they had abandoned so much territory and were naturally infuriated when the land ceded included their homes, farms, and towns. The withdrawal tired the soldiers, who suffered from the oppressive heat which accompanied the forced marches. The retreat also occurred at a time when news from other sectors of the Confederacy was disheartening. "We have heard that Vicksburg has certainly been surrendered to the enemy," wrote Alfred Tyler Fielder in his diary on July 9. While the report had been expected, the loss of Port Hudson and Robert E. Lee's failure at Gettysburg were additional burdens. "The news for some time has been unfavourable for the Southern cause," Fielder wrote in mid-July, and he expressed a perhaps half-hearted hope that things would improve soon. Nor was Fielder alone in being depressed. One of Cheatham's artillerists, John Euclid Magee, wrote that the men he met bemoaned and cursed the turn of events. Bragg was an especial target of Cheatham's men, although some sought to defend the commander and others opined that the War Department had ordered the shift to Chattanooga. "Most of the army believe we could have whipped them at Tullahoma," Magee noted. Magee himself did not understand why the withdrawal had been ordered, but he too was a Bragg detractor, writing, "All confidence in Genl. Bragg is lost, and I do not believe this army can win a victory under his superintendance."[2]

While the Confederates worked to fortify Chattanooga, Bragg faced a dual threat from Rosecrans and Ambrose Burnside, the former approaching from his Murfreesboro realm while the latter loomed menacingly in Kentucky. Rosecrans lurched forward in August on widely separated routes. Crittenden's corps was directed to bear upon Chattanooga from the front, while McCook and Thomas moved in via Bridgeport, Alabama. It was not long before the Yankees shuttled into the mountains of northern Georgia. They faced a formidable terrain, consisting of a series of mountains that run longitudinally. Below Chattanooga is the Raccoon-Sand Mountain chain, which hugs the Tennessee River and then broadens out at a right angle from the river, running fifty miles into the northeastern corner of Alabama. To the east is Lookout Mountain, an eminence connected to Raccoon Mountain by a low spur ridge. Lookout Mountain extends over eighty miles below Chattanooga. Chattanooga Creek flows between Lookout Mountain and the next rise to the east, Missionary Ridge. While Missionary Ridge is lower than the two previous peaks, with a general elevation of five or six hundred feet, it soars to one thousand feet in some areas. The ridge runs to the northeast and surrounds much of Chattanooga. Behind Missionary Ridge is a fourth rise, Pigeon Mountain, which begins several miles below Missionary Ridge and then links with Lookout Mountain near the Alabama border. Chickamauga Creek meanders through the valley separating Missionary Ridge and Pigeon Mountain. The geography around Chattanooga became a major factor in the campaign. It presented problems for both commanders, but particularly Bragg, who was perplexed by the task of deciding where Rosecrans was most likely to strike. Rosecrans for his part had no desire to assault the Southerners in their entrenched lines at Chattanooga, especially since the successful flank movement at Tullahoma was still fresh in his memory.

To accomplish his goal, Rosecrans sent Crittenden to the north, looping around the city, where his units might ultimately link with Burnside, who moved southward from Kentucky. Thomas forded the Tennessee River at Bridgeport, then penetrated Lookout Mountain at Steven's Gap. McCook drove through Winston's Gap at the southern terminus of Lookout Mountain and threatened to invest the Confederate positions at Chattanooga from the rear. Bragg faced a difficult decision and continued to receive conflicting intelligence reports. If he dallied too long in Chattanooga, McCook and Thomas might sever the railway to Atlanta, the lone available supply line. On the other hand, Bragg was reluctant to yield the city unless it was absolutely necessary.[3]

While Bragg wrestled with the decision, elements of Crittenden's Twenty-first Corps arrived at the Tennessee River and began an annoying artillery display. One of Cheatham's men first makes a notation of the shelling on Friday, August 21, adding that Yankee gunners managed to hit two churches and killed or wounded several women and children. Cheatham was in one of the churches that particular day, probably because it had been declared a fast day throughout the Confederacy. A passing artillery shell caused a commotion among the worshippers, but Cheatham reassured them that it was only the Confederate army taking target practice. The minister closed his eyes and resumed praying when a second shell "carried away part of the coaming from the church gable." The determined Presbyterian clergman continued to pray despite the obvious danger. Not everyone shared his faith in divine protection. When he finally concluded his prayer and turned to face the congregation, the parson discovered that everyone, Cheatham included, had quietly slipped out.[4]

The continuous Union bombardment "greatly frustrated" Chattanooga's citizens, and in the days following the original shelling many of the residents moved out of town. So did the Confederate military. After a series of conferences, Bragg decided that he was most threatened by McCook and Thomas, and he pulled out of the city. His men moved out in early September, Cheatham's men in the vanguard of the army with Polk.[5] The projected Southern destination was Rome, Georgia, but before that site was reached, Bragg attempted to snare the separated Federal corps. Two times Bragg tried to hit isolated Yankee units. The first attempt was directed against Thomas on September 11, in the area where

Lookout and Pigeon Mountains converged, forming a cul-de-sac which enclosed the eastern valley of Missionary Ridge and which was known as McLemore's Cove. Cheatham informed his troops of the Rebel plan to trap Thomas in the cove, and they made a nighttime march to reach their designated position. Bragg's ruse to snag Thomas failed when Thomas Hindman (who had replaced the ailing Jones Withers in charge of Polk's other division) delayed in making an attack from the northern end of the cove. Cheatham was in support of Hindman, but after the abortive attempt the Tennesseans were sent farther to the north, to Rock Springs Church. Bragg reinforced Cheatham with units under Hindman and W. H. T. Walker, and intended to turn on Crittenden, who was advancing from Chattanooga on several roads. Cheatham's division was deployed near two of these roads as the left of Polk's line. Bragg's initial order to attack was ignored by Polk, who worried as usual about the size and strength of the force in his front. On September 13, Cheatham's men shoved out toward Lee and Gordon's Mill and made contact with their blue-clad adversaries. Sharp skirmishing broke out between one of Cheatham's brigades under Otho Strahl and some Union forces. Nonetheless, Strahl could not induce the Yankees to pursue his men as they fell back, and when this decoying action failed, the rest of the Confederate effort petered out as well. Crittenden had withdrawn in the direction of Chattanooga, unimpeded for the most part by the bungling Confederates.[6]

Bragg was understandably disheartened by the lost opportunities and fell back to La Fayette. The soldiers with Cheatham had marched and countermarched, but despite their eagerness for a fight, they had seen little action since vacating Chattanooga. The hot weather caused problems as the Tennesseans moved in the Georgia countryside. The roads were so dusty that "frequently . . . we could not see men in the same column 25 yds. in front of us." Captain Alfred Tyler Fielder of the Twelfth Tennessee, who wrote this observation, also noted that the marches made the men sweat so profusely it seemed they "almost suffocated." Nor was their appearance enhanced by the dry conditions; Fielder wrote that as the dust settled on the soldiers, they "did not look natural." Despite the pullout from Chattanooga, the heat, and the inability to trap the Yankees, Cheatham's men remained optimistic. The prospect of coming to grips with the enemy had revitalized them. Van Buren Oldham of the Ninth Tennessee capsulized this sentiment when he wrote in mid-September, "The boys notwithstanding our retrograde are in fine spirits."[7]

While Cheatham and other troops withdrew to La Fayette, Rosecrans finally realized that the Southerners were not retreating. He used the reprieve to unite his forces and began to draw his army together along the western side of Chickamauga Creek. As the Union forces coalesced, the promise of reinforcements stirred Bragg from his three-day lethargy at La Fayette. General James Longstreet was scheduled to arrive on September 18 and 19 with two divisions from the Army of Northern Virginia. Bragg's army had been strengthened previously, if in somewhat haphazard fashion, by the accesssion of Walker and Breckinridge from Joseph E. Johnston's Mississippi army and by Simon Bolivar Buckner's contingent from East Tennessee. This concentration gave the Confederates numerical superiority over their foes, a rarity in the war, but this plus was offset by the weakness in Bragg's command structure. Problems cropped up almost inevitably, since several of the recently acquired units and commanders knew little of western personalities or topography. As Longstreet's men headed for the front, Bragg organized a five-corps system, with Polk, Longstreet, Buckner, Hill, and Walker serving as corps commanders. Cheatham's division was in Polk's corps and moved down the Chickamauga on September 18 to camp on the eastern side of the creek. While they were on the march, Bragg was busy plotting strategy. He devised a plan to roll up the Federal left flank, but fighting on September 18 was limited, due to delays and indecision. During the night Rosecrans shifted his lines to the north, so that Thomas constituted the Federal left, Crittenden the center, and McCook the right. Bragg, unaware of this development, sent out orders to activate what was now a flawed strategy.[8]

Cheatham's men were part of the cat-and-mouse game Bragg and Rosecrans had played for several days, during which time rumors of impending action swept through the command daily. The soldiers were up and stirring early on September 19, and not long after daybreak the sounds of skirmishing filtered along the creek. These were the opening strains of an exceedingly violent struggle which would shortly engulf Cheatham's division and severely test his soldiers. The battle began when Forrest's cavalry, who guarded the right flank, moved forward and stumbled into Yankee infantry. Driven back by this aggregation, Forrest notified Bragg of the fighting on the creek's western side. Bragg was mystified; there was not supposed to be a Union force that far to the north. W. H. T. Walker came to Forrest's aid with several of his brigades, but as the morning wore on, he too was forced back towards the creek and asked Bragg for assistance. Cheatham's five brigades had crossed the Chickamauga at Dalton's (or Hunt's) Ford around 7 A.M., with Cheatham supervising the movement. Cheatham's division, originally intended to act in support of Buckner, was selected by Bragg to help stem the Federal assault on the right.[9]

When Bragg's order arrived around 11 A.M., Cheatham got his men moving rapidly to the north. As Cheatham's division was moving to Walker's aid, his ragged soldiers passed by a large body of troops dressed much

The officer in this Alfred Waud sketch bears a strong likeness to Cheatham, although no notation exists which positively identifies the horseman. (Library of Congress)

better than any in Bragg's army. When Cheatham's curious men inquired what command the well-dressed Rebels belonged to, they were surprised to learn that they were from John Bell Hood's division from the Army of Northern Virginia. A captain in Cheatham's division wrote later that "this was the first intimation we had of reinforcements" from Robert E. Lee's army. Cheatham's men had little time to remark on the difference in attire between the western and eastern armies. By noon the division was in line behind Walker near the Winfrey house. Cheatham arranged his force, which contained more than six thousand men, for an attack. He placed John K. Jackson's brigade of Georgians and Mississippians to the right, Preston Smith in the center, and Marcus J. Wright on the left. Maney and Strahl were deployed as reserves behind the three lead brigades. Cheatham paused briefly to encourage his troops before their ordeal. Riding swiftly down the line, he yelled "Give them hell, boys, give them hell," an exhortation he used so frequently that it was known in the army as "Cheatham's expression." Polk accompanied Cheatham and discreetly assented in the advice, urging the soldiers to "Give them what General Cheatham says, we will pay off old chores today." With that send-off, Cheatham's brigades crashed through the dense woods and under-brush into Thomas. Jackson had not advanced more than 150 yards when his line collided with the Yankees, and shortly afterward the remainder of Cheatham's advance force was hotly engaged. The Federals recoiled as Cheatham's veterans pounded forward. The fighting was sharp and desperate, with both sides absorbing heavy casualties as Cheatham's men shoved the bluecoats back anywhere from a few hundred yards to three-quarters of a mile.[10]

Jackson's brigade succeeded in capturing three pieces of artillery and also grabbed "a large number of knapsacks" abandoned by the Yankees, but these acquisitions were made at a terrible cost. All along Cheatham's line his men pushed the Federals back to a series of breastworks they had erected the night before. Cheatham's butternuts could not pierce the works, and rapid Union fire thinned their ranks. Federal reinforcements came up to check the Rebels as Cheatham's men attempted to preserve the gains they had won. The Twenty-eighth Tennessee, one of Wright's regiments, wavered until Colonel Sidney Stanton seized the colors and urged his troops onward. The severity of the fire was evident later, when it was discovered that the flag had been pierced at least thirty times by enemy projectiles. At least Stanton retained the regimental colors. In the Fifty-first Tennessee, also in Wright's brigade, three color bearers were wounded, one mortally, and the flag was left on the field.[11] For two hours Cheatham's lead brigades and elements from all three Union corps battered one another. Cheatham's men drove the Federals along both sides of the Brotherton Road and fought valiantly against the stubborn Yankees. Jackson and Wright were hard pressed on the flanks, and Preston Smith's men struggled to establish themselves in an area owned by a farm family named Brock. Fierce fighting raged in and around Brock Field as Union reinforcements came up, and bodies of both sides littered the thickets and a ravine near the farm. It was "an awful fight the enemy disputing every inch of the ground," wrote one of Smith's soldiers. Another of Cheatham's men recorded, "The battle raged in its wildest fury—Gen. Cheatham, the glorious old hero, could be seen galloping along the lines, encouraging the troops, and giving his orders with coolness." While Cheatham strove to keep his men at their deadly task, his advance regiments began to run out of ammunition. At this juncture, Cheatham sent in his reserve brigades under Strahl and Maney to replace Smith and Jackson.[12]

The transfer was a hazardous undertaking, and Strahl's regiments were hard hit when his movement forward was not properly coordinated with Maney's. Some of his units wandered into an ambush when they attempted to close a gap that had formed between their brigade and

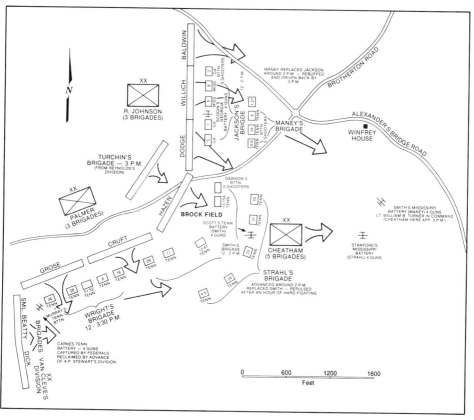

Map 3. Cheatham's Division at Chickamauga —September 19, 1863, noon–3:30 P.M.

Cheatham's right. A witness watched the Federals pour an enfilading fire into Strahl's regiments and concluded that he had never seen "so many men fall on so small space of ground." Strahl's men carried on the engagement Smith had relinquished around Brock Field, but Union pressure became more insistent. A soldier attached to Strahl's Mississippi battery under Captain Thomas Stanford wrote that the battle was a seesaw affair, "the enemy giving way very stubbornly, and sometimes making us give way." Strahl and Maney continued the destructive work begun by the two brigades they replaced, but Yankee reinforcements surged around Cheatham's unsupported flanks and hammered steadily all along his line. The roar of musketry and cannon fire reverberated through the forest. Numbers finally began to tell, and Cheatham's attack flagged only a short time after Strahl and Maney were sent forward. His men fell back from their positions and retraced their steps over the ground where they had previously advanced. The dead and wounded of both armies covered the expanse. Some of Cheatham's men could not extricate themselves. Captain W. W. Carnes's four-gun battery, stationed with Wright on the left, was captured after nearly all of their horses were slain. Worse yet, Carnes lost half his men in the process, and Cheatham later told Carnes that "it was the greatest mortality he had ever heard in one company of artillery."[13]

Cheatham's men contested the relentless Union attack until the Rebels were knocked back to either side of a battery from which they had begun their initial advance. This was First Lieutenant William B. Turner's battery of four Napoleon fieldpieces attached to Maney's brigade. These guns were the same ones Turner had received after the division overran them at Perryville, and, as at Stones River, they were employed against their original owners. Artillery could not always be used advantageously at Chickamauga, owing to the dense forests which hampered effective coordination of fire, but Cheatham's artillerists employed their guns well in the afternoon. Four of his five batteries saw extensive action during the fight. Until mid-afternoon only one of Turner's pieces had been engaged, and as Maney's foot soldiers were pushed back, this lone gun withdrew and rejoined the remainder of the battery. Maney had selected a slight rise surrounded by open woods as a favorable position for the cannons, and after nearly three hours of hard fighting, Cheatham's infantry was clustered to the left and right of Turner's battery. It was the most critical moment of the battle for Cheatham and his division. Except for an occasional sharpshooter, the infantrymen were out of ammunition and unable to contest the Yankee assault. The bluecoats sensed their advantage and raced hard for Turner's guns.[14]

Cheatham and his staff were with Turner as the shouting Yankees rushed to within a few yards of the cannons. Cheatham calmly allowed them to draw near, then ordered "Now, Lieutenant." At this command, Turner's artillerists unleashed "well-directed charges of shell and canister" which buckled the lead regiments. The Mississippians serving the guns used double charges of shell and canister to break two subsequent assaults by the determined Federals. Thrown back in disorder, the Yankees "sullenly retired out of range," but not before they suffered dreadful casualties. Turner was assisted in repelling the Federals by one of Forrest's batteries, and Captain John Scogin's Georgia battery, belonging to Jackson's brigade, also inflicted damage on the Federals.[15] Still, Turner bore the brunt of the Northern attack. One Confederate estimated that 300 dead Union soldiers were heaped before Turner's guns, and another observer heard Cheatham contend that he had "never seen artillery do such fearful execution in so short a time." A visitor from another command wrote, "Gen. Frank Cheatham's command was the greatest evidence of the terrific effect of artillery fire." Turner's cannoneers saved the division. During the engagement they fired 220 rounds of solid shot, shell, spherical case, and canister, and their effort won them praise from Cheatham and other officers. When Maney later requested that the battery be relieved, Cheatham demurred. "No, let it stay where it is," Cheatham replied, "for if it had not been for that battery, the Yankees would have been all over this country tonight."[16] Turner's success at Chickamauga belied his otherwise casual approach to army life. Turner was affectionately described as being "the best artilleryman, but the poorest drilled man in the army" by Captain Thomas Malone, one of Maney's staff officers. Whatever failings Turner manifested at drill were offset by his valuable service in battle, and Cheatham's approbation helped Turner win promotion to captain after Chickamauga.[17]

Cheatham's stout defense helped save the Confederate right, as had the earlier efforts of Forrest and Walker. If these units had broken, the Federals might have crossed the Chickamauga at Alexander's Bridge or attempted to roll up Bragg's army from the right flank. Cheatham's men were relieved when A. P. Stewart's division of Buckner's corps finally came up to help stabilize the situation. Stewart's men managed to regain Carnes's battery, and the hottest fighting shifted to the left of Cheatham as midafternoon wore on. Cheatham's men were fatigued by the long hours of combat, but their recuperation was interrupted in the late afternoon, when another attack was initiated. One diarist wrote that Cheatham "was boiling over with rage and stung to the quick, to see his division driven back for the first time in the war," and intimated that Cheatham sought another opportunity to strike the Federals before the end of the day. The Tennessean was granted his request near twilight, when his men were ordered to support Patrick Cleburne's division, which came up in support of Stewart and linked with Cheatham.[18]

The Federals were in two lines, some units having come forward to reconnoiter, and before these regiments could rejoin the main battle line, portions of Cleburne's and Cheatham's divisions attacked "with indescribable fury." Especially hard hit were the Seventy-ninth Illinois and the Seventy-seventh Pennsylvania. The Pennsylvania regiment was "lapped up like a drop of oil under a flame," losing 300 men as prisoners and the regimental colors as a brigade from Cleburne combined with Jackson's and Smith's brigades from Cheatham to surround the Federals. A deafening roar of musketry rang out when the two sides collided in the night. The Rebel advance carried for 600 yards, but breastworks and confusion checked the move. Among the Confederate casualties was Cheatham's talented brigadier, Preston Smith, who was mortally wounded when he and

Preston Smith was one of Cheatham's most dependable brigadiers before he was killed in a night attack at Chickamauga. (Library of Congress)

several staff officers rode into a detachment of troops they erroneously thought were Cleburne's. One aide, Captain Thomas King, was killed instantly by the Federal volley, and Smith died less than an hour later. Cheatham bemoaned the loss of the thirty-nine-year-old Smith, a native of Giles County, Tennessee, who had been a lawyer before the war. Cheatham eulogized Smith as being "active, energetic, and brave, with a rare fitness to command," qualities he had established early in the war with the 154th Tennessee Regiment. Smith had recovered from a wound at Shiloh in time to accompany his men in the Kentucky campaign as part of the advance force under Edmund Kirby Smith. He had been promoted to brigadier in October of 1862 but was absent during the first day of action at Stones River. In time, Smith's death was immortalized by the enemy. One of the most interesting Civil War monuments relating to Cheatham's division is that of the Seventh-seventh Pennsylvania at Chickamauga, which depicts a mortally wounded Smith on the relief carving on the face of the monument.[19]

Such magnanimity was far off in the future, and the bluecoats who killed Smith wanted to erase as many of their adversaries as possible. Colonel Alfred J. Vaughan of the Thirteenth Tennessee narrowly averted the same fate as his brigade commander, but the bullet intended for Vaughan killed staff officer John Donelson instead. Vaughan ordered men of the Twelfth Tennessee to open fire, and they dropped the Yankee who had shot the officer. Their volley also ripped through the ranks of the opposing Pennsylvanians, who hollered for the Rebels to cease firing. Shortly thereafter, Vaughan grabbed the colors of the Seventy-seventh Pennsylvania, ordered the Yankees to ground their arms, and sent the prisoners to Cheatham. The attack died out as nightfall deepened, and Cheatham's two brigades fell back and reformed. "Our men have suffered awful today and gained nothing," lamented one of Cheatham's veterans, and in his diary he wrote that the next day would bring "the hardest battle . . . ever witnessed on this continent." Chickamauga had already proved to be costly for Cheatham and his men, in large measure because they had at one time or another battled elements of six Union divisions during the day. As a chilly night descended along the Chickamauga, wounded men moaned and cried between the lines, their pleas for assistance often unanswered because it was too dangerous for anyone to go to their aid.[20]

Bragg missed an opportunity for victory on September 19 because of his disjointed attacks against Thomas. If other units had joined Walker and Cheatham earlier, Bragg might well have crushed the Federal left. As it was, Cheatham and other Confederate commands suffered heavily for minimal gains. Bragg's difficulty in managing the battle was due partially to the confusing terrain, but he also had trouble adjusting to the situation on his right. Bragg's attempt to regain control of the battle led him to implement an awkward reorganization of his army during the night. He placed Polk in command of the right wing of the army, while Longstreet was given responsibility for the left half.[21] Dawn on September 20 revealed a greatly disorganized Confederate high command. Longstreet had arrived the night before and joined his command in unfamiliar territory for the first time at daybreak. Bragg had ordered Polk to attack at daylight, but D. H. Hill never received the directive, though Cheatham and Walker had. Worse yet, the two wings of the army bunched together at a point in Cheatham's line and overlapped one another. While the sun burned off the morning mist, the tangled Rebel command glacially unraveled itself. Still unaware of battle orders, Hill made a morning inspection of his line and complained that Cheatham was situated an angle to Cleburne. Hill argued that the two divisions would jostle one another in an advance. Polk and a thoroughly harried Bragg took Cheatham's division out when the delayed movement began around 9:30 A.M. The division appeared to be out of line with A. P. Stewart as well as Cleburne, and Bragg felt a correction of the alignment would waste valuable time.[22]

During the morning and most of the afternoon, only one of Cheatham's brigades, Jackson's, was involved in the fighting between Polk and Thomas. Thomas managed to check Cleburne and other Rebel units which assailed him, chiefly because Polk insisted on sending them in piecemeal, but the Union corps commander was concerned enough to call for help from Rosecrans. Rosecrans responded by pulling units from his right and sent them to Thomas. The arrangement led to Rosecrans's undoing. Because of a mixup, an entire division was withdrawn from Crittenden's front just as Longstreet ordered his massed brigades forward. Bushrod Johnson's brigades spearheaded the drive and began the decisive assault of the battle. After two of Johnson's brigades bore into the gaping hole, the rest of Longstreet's wing moved up to exploit the quarter-mile-wide opening. Johnson and the remainder of Longstreet's units splintered the Union center, and during the afternoon McCook's and Crittenden's corps retreated up the Dry Valley Road to Chattanooga. A dazed Rosecrans was in the train of retreating Federals. Longstreet swung his half of the army to the right and ran into Thomas. Longstreet appealed for help from Polk's right wing, but Bragg, discouraged that his scheme for crushing the Yankees had not developed according to plan, replied that Polk's wing was whipped and could provide no support. Disappointed by the modification of his strategy, Bragg withdrew to the rear.[23]

Bragg was in error. Polk had worn out a portion of his command with his disjointed attacks and subsequently was unable to achieve a breakthrough, but not all of his troops were engaged. Cheatham's division, the largest such unit on the field for the Confederates, was a prime source of manpower for Polk or Longstreet to draw upon. Cheatham's men suffered somewhat from shells which burst overhead during the day, but otherwise his survivors from the previous day's fighting were rested and available for combat. Polk followed the roar of battle intently as it swung toward the north. He gathered with Cheatham and several of his other high-ranking officers around 5 P.M. to plan a renewed offensive against Thomas. As he rode up, Polk told nearby troops of the Twelfth Tennessee that "the news from every part of the field was of the most cheering character" and urged Cheatham's men to crush the remaining Federals "as between the nether and upper millstone." The Tennesseans happily complied with Polk's request. As part of a heavy force on the right, Cheatham's men prepared for a massive assault on Thomas's left and center. Maney's and Wright's brigades went into action late in the day, Wright reporting later that his men were "in the highest spirits and moved forward with an animation I have never seen surpassed." Thomas gained precious time for the rest of the Union army with his gallant defense during the afternoon but recognized that he could not resist sledgehammer blows from both Longstreet and Polk. As darkness fell Thomas ordered a withdrawal, and his corps fell back towards Chattanooga. As dusk arrived, Polk's and Longstreet's wings approached one another, trapping several hundred Yankees. At last, the Army of Tennessee had gained the decisive victory that eluded them for so long.[24]

The one Southerner unconvinced of the result was Braxton Bragg, who moodily asserted that his army was shattered. Not until the next day did he reverse his gloomy conclusion and wire Richmond that a victory had been achieved. Forrest scouted towards Chattanooga, but no infantry force pushed Rosecrans during the day. On September 22, Cheatham, accompanied by Isham Harris, moved to the base of Union-held Missionary Ridge. Cheatham considered the position "to be one of much natural strength, increased by breastworks made of stone and fallen timber," but he deployed for an attack. Maney's and Smith's brigades, the latter now commanded by Vaughan, assaulted up the hill shortly after 10 A.M. Despite the natural advantages of their defensive position, the Union troops on Missionary Ridge were "demoralized by succession of disasters, made but a feeble resistance, and fled in disorder." Cheatham mounted the rise and surveyed the panorama before him. He reported to his superiors that no troops were advancing towards him, and that the only Federals he saw were ensconced in Chattanooga's protective forts.[25] Rosecrans was indeed beaten.

Chickamauga cost both sides heavily. Union casualties exceeded 16,000 men, while the Confederates counted over 18,000 dead, wounded, and missing. Cheatham's vigilance in assembling a complete hospital proved fortunate, for he sustained high losses, mostly from the September 19 engagement. All told, his division lost 1,975 men. Jackson's Georgia regiments were weakened by their high casualty rate. The First Georgia lost nearly 43 percent of its members, while the Fifth Georgia lost 194 of 317 men engaged, nearly 55 percent of its combatants. Preston Smith was the highest-ranking casualty in the division, but other officers fell as well. The Fourth Tennessee lost its colonel, lieutenant-colonel, and major, so that a captain was the ranking regimental officer by the end of the fray. The sad statistics bore out the fierce fighting the division experienced and were reflected in each of Cheatham's brigades. The Nineteenth Tennessee of Strahl's brigade lost most of its 94 casualties within the space of a few moments, while Wright's Fifty-first and Fifty-second (Consolidated) Tennessee counted 115 of their 232 men as casualties.[26]

The battle reaffirmed Cheatham's reputation as a steady battlefield leader. He helped hold the division together during the critical fighting on September 19 and provided his men with moral support as they awaited the Federal charges against Turner's battery. Cheatham and the other Confederate forces on the right were instrumental in assisting the Longstreet breakthrough, for the insistent two-day pressure on Thomas led to the creation of the Federal gap. Chickamauga contained certain similarities to Stones River. As at Murfreesboro, Cheatham was subjected to heavy Union fire, since he attacked in a series of assaults without support. And once again, Cheatham left the Federal enemy only to encounter the opposition of Braxton Bragg.

Chickamauga was hardly over when turmoil again enveloped the inner councils of the Army of Tennessee. While his army crowned the ridges to the south and southeast of Chattanooga, Bragg attacked several of his generals and sparked a wearisome season of discontent. Bragg's initial targets were Thomas Hindman, who was held accountable for his failure to trap the Federals in McLemore's Cove, and Polk, who incurred Bragg's wrath by neglecting to launch as assault at daybreak on the second day at Chickamauga. On September 29, 1863, Bragg suspended both Polk and Hindman from their commands and ordered them to report to Atlanta.[27]

The pair departed quickly, but Polk had already allied with Longstreet in a letter-writing campaign designed to oust Bragg. Both generals solicited the aid of Robert E. Lee, while Polk wrote Jefferson Davis and pleaded for Bragg's removal. "He is not the man for the station he fills," Polk wrote, complaining that the fruits of the Chickamauga victory were being squandered. A week after the battle, Polk was incensed that "nothing of a determined character has been done or so far as I know determined upon." Polk noted that the troops were confident and in good spirits, but "they chafe under all this delay and indecision." In a second message, written after he left the army, Polk renewed his drive to have Bragg replaced. He piously defended his own actions at Chickamauga and assailed Bragg's "criminal incapacity" at letting the hard-earned triumph slip away without decisive action after the battle.[28] When Polk left, the opposition clustered around James Longstreet. The South Carolinian was especially displeased by Bragg's imperfect siege of Chattanooga and argued that the Union army could be flanked out of the city's fortifications. Bragg refused to heed the advice, so Longstreet and other subalterns stepped up their attacks against the commanding general. These included a petition to Davis which tactfully suggested that Bragg be recalled because of his ill health. Cheatham did not sign the petition, though he may have known of it, but twelve other officers did affix their names.[29] Cheatham did rally to Polk's defense when the latter requested that Cheatham clarify several points regarding Polk's whereabouts during the Chickamauga fray. The Tennessean asserted that he saw Polk on September 20 about sunrise near Turner's battery, which conflicted with Bragg's assertion that Polk was miles from the battlefield at daybreak.[30]

The Polk and Hindman arrests threatened to split the army. Bragg's chief of staff, William Whann Mackall, acknowledged that Bragg worked wholeheartedly for the cause but noted that Bragg's machinations against his generals would produce "great dissatisfaction." Mackall confided to his wife that Bragg suffered from poor judgement as well as ill health, and he worried that Bragg's leadership was flawed. Even one of Bragg's staunchest supporters, W. H. T. Walker of Georgia, felt Bragg erred by not following up the Chickamauga victory, an opinion echoed by Louisiana general St. John Richardson Liddell.[31]

Bragg later contended that the private soldiers never joined in the attacks upon his leadership, but this is untrue, particularly in Cheatham's division. One soldier in the Twelfth Tennessee wrote that Polk's banishment disheartened everyone he knew, since Polk was "very popular with the soldiers of his Corps." Captain John W. Harris, one of Vaughan's staff officers, originally felt that Bragg intended to take advantage of the Chickamauga triumph. In a letter written five days after the battle, Harris recorded how "Genl. Bragg says that we will follow the enemy through Tennessee and I have not the least doubt but that we will make our winter quarters in Middle Tenn." By mid-October, Harris was writing in a style reminiscent of General Polk. "Every one here curses Bragg," Harris wrote, "and he in turn blames & arrests Polk and Hindman for our failure to ruin the whole Federal army." Harris decried Bragg's failure to follow up

Cheatham aligned himself with Leonidas Polk, who was Cheatham's corps commander for much of the war. Polk, a cleric in the antebellum period, was killed during the Georgia campaign in 1864. (The Valentine Museum, Richmond, Virginia)

promptly on his success, charging that "we fooled around nearly one entire day in looking around Yankee hospitals, whilst the Federals were in full retreat and in the greatest confusion." If Harris's sentiments are any indication of the temperament of Cheatham's soldiers, they shared Polk's frustration as the weeks of inactivity slipped away. Harris referred to Chickamauga as "the only good thing we have had during the war and through Bragg's imbecility we have thrown it away." "I am getting very tired of Bragg as a leader," penned one of Cheatham's soldiers in the Ninth Tennessee, "he has conducted affairs so badly."[32]

A disturbed Jefferson Davis decided upon an inspection tour of the west to assess his troubled army. The executive was in the unenviable position of hearing Bragg and Polk, both men he admired and trusted, rail at the alleged inadequacies of one another. Davis met with Polk en route to the army, and the cleric again maintained that Bragg was an incompetent and should be relieved. October 9 found Davis at Bragg's headquarters. During the night, Davis convened a conference of Bragg and his four corps commanders. Longstreet, Hill, and Buckner all represented their own corps, while Cheatham was in temporary command of Polk's corps. Towards the end of the meeting, Davis solicited the views of the officers in regard to Bragg. All four were by now avowed enemies of Bragg, and one be one they recommended that Bragg be removed. The army commander sat in stony silence while Cheatham and the others tendered their advice to Davis.[33]

The current of opposition obviously ran deep, but Davis decided to sustain Bragg. In fact, within twenty-four hours of his arrival, the politician informed Bragg that he was secure. The only consideration tendered the malcontents came when Davis compelled Bragg to drop the charges against Polk, a decision Bragg acquiesced in when he learned that Polk was to swap places with Hardee in the Mississippi-Alabama department. Liddell heard Davis say that the rancor directed against Bragg was "wholly wrong and . . . would eventually be the cause of disaster to that army." Once assured of President Davis's support, Bragg rejected Liddell's sensible advice that he mend fences with his subordinates. Instead, Bragg dared the critics to send in their resignations and characterized his enemies within the army as venal and ambitious. Liddell regretted that "Longstreet, Buckner, D. H. Hill, Cleburne, Cheatham and many subordinate officers" had joined in the near-mutiny, but despaired of ever getting Bragg and his detractors to cooperate.[34]

Rumors swept through the army as the discord continued. Artillerist John Euclid Magee related that Bragg's generals voted to oust him, a reference to the meeting between Davis, Bragg, and the four corps commanders. The turmoil in the upper echelons of the army became common knowlege among the rank and file and provided a fertile source of gossip. Staff officer John W. Harris alluded to the petition calling for Bragg's head, information he may have acquired from General Vaughan. Harris stated that President Davis was "looking into matters, and trying to settle all difficulties, a paper has been signed by nearly every General Officer here asking him to remove Bragg, and very many think that it will be done, and Longstreet put in command." Harris added that he hoped the change would be made, "for it will put our troops in much better spirits." Magee complained that the army was suffering while the generals squabbled, and morale did erode as the unseemly wrangling continued. As autumn slipped away, Bragg provided more fuel for the rumor mill when he began an offensive against those who participated in the rebellion. Daniel H. Hill was charged with disobedience at Chickamauga and relieved of duty. Buckner, whom Bragg eventually blamed as the author of the petition to Davis, was notified that his Department of East Tennessee no longer existed. Reduced from corps command and consigned to a division in Cheatham's corps, the Kentuckian took a leave of absence and refused to return. Nathan Bedford Forrest left after a violent row with Bragg. Longstreet remained, but he continued to spar with Bragg. "They are having a time of it about the battle of [Chickamauga]," was Magee's rather understated comment on the furor.[35]

As Cheatham witnessed the manner in which Bragg squelched opponents, he grew increasingly uncomfortable. The long-standing enmity against Bragg still existed, but Cheatham feared that his frank views in the meeting with Davis compromised his position. Polk's absence further disconcerted the Tennessean. Polk and Cheatham made a somewhat curious alliance, for they appear to have been opposites in many regards, but apparently, this divergence actually helped weld the two men together. Cheatham admired Polk's impressive dignity and piety, while Polk indulgently envied Cheatham's exuberant, free-spirited nature. The two men shared an association akin to a father-son relationship in many regards, but what cemented the bond was their mutual distrust of Bragg. By the autumn of 1863, both officers had long since become conspirators against Bragg's authority, and as long as he served with the army, Polk faithfully screened Cheatham from Bragg's blasts. Without the bishop for protection, Cheatham felt his position in the army was untenable. On October 31 he formally requested that he "be relieved from duty with the Army of Tennessee" and asked that he be allowed "to report to the Sec[re]t[ar]y of War at Richmond."[36]

That very day one of Cheatham's veterans, Van Buren Oldham of the Ninth Tennessee, was laid up in a hospital recovering from a shell fragment wound acquired at Chickamauga. Army life was perhaps not what

Oldham had once envisioned; he noted two days earlier that he considered "the position of a private soldier in our army" to be "worse than that of a servant in peacable times." Oldham was tired of "being domineered by every 'chap in stripes'" and flirted with the idea of joining the cavalry. His mood did not appreciably improve by Halloween, when his diary became an outlet for his anger against Bragg. "He has removed Gen. Polk [and] caused Hardee to be put in his place, whom the boys can never like so well as they did the former. If he wants to lose half [his men] let him remove Cheatham." The diatribe continued the next day. Oldham wrote, "Gen. Polk was beloved by his troops and was the idol of our Div[ision]. The boys would do better fighting under him than Hardee." He concluded with a warning to Bragg, albeit one he could not deliver personally: "Should Bragg cause Cheatham to be removed half the Tennesseans will go home or [seek] some other arm of service."[37] Oldham's diary entries reflect the mood not only of the writer, but also of vast numbers of Cheatham's men. Cheatham's soldiers were devoted to both Polk and their own divisional commander. Polk's clerical mien and paternalistic nature led Cheatham's men to trust him, although some recognized his weaknesses as a military man. They also picked up on the mutual respect and affection Polk and Cheatham shared, and since they so highly esteemed Cheatham, they extended their esteem to his mentor, Polk. Cheatham's prejudices seem to have become, by extension, the prejudices of many of his veterans.[38]

Cheatham apparently took a leave of absence after submitting his resignation. Alfred Tyler Fielder makes note of Cheatham's absence on November 3, by which time the division had been sent to Sweetwater, Tennessee. Where Cheatham went after he left the army is a mystery, but Atlanta is a likely possibility. There he could commiserate with Polk and visit his sister Martha, who resided somewhere in the vicinity. A Georgian, John K. Jackson, took command of the division during Cheatham's absence. News of Cheatham's resignation spread quickly and was not confined to the Confederate ranks. By mid-November the Federals knew of the action, General Oliver Otis Howard of the Eleventh Corps reporting to his superiors twice that Cheatham was reported to have resigned. Yankee informants provided some of the news, but letters intercepted by the bluecoats also corroborated the rumors. One such letter from an unknown writer found its way in to the *Official Records*. This correspondent was more charitable to Bragg than many men in the ranks but reported that Hill, Polk, and Cheatham had all been relieved. The assessment was true in regard to Hill and Polk, if not Cheatham, and Cheatham's withdrawal did have an impact on his division, according to the writer. "It seems all the Middle Tennesseans are going to desert," wrote the soldier.[39]

Cheatham's attempt to resign created some problems in Richmond. Adjutant and Inspector-General Samuel Cooper could not think of any command to which Cheatham might be assigned "consistent with his rank," an intimation perhaps that Richmond felt Cheatham, whatever his qualities as a fighter, could not fit in with any other military department. Secretary of War James A. Seddon disapproved the application. Seddon scrawled a note on Cheatham's letter, saying, "My judgement is against relieving any valuable and experienced officer in command because of personal dissatisfaction." Appealing to Cheatham's patriotism, Seddon encouraged him to give his "full support to any commanding general placed over [him]."[40] The rejection placed Cheatham in an embarrassing position, since many of his anti-Bragg compatriots were gone.

While Cheatham and his division were apart, Bragg attacked his remaining foes in the Army of Tennessee. On November 12, he adopted a reorganization of his army which radically altered its character. Cheatham's division was ordered to serve under Hardee, but it was scarcely the outfit Cheatham led since 1862. In the reorganization Cheatham retained only six Tennessee regiments, those in the brigade led by Marcus J. Wright, an officer Bragg considered loyal. The other seventeen Tennessee regiments formerly under Cheatham's care were dispersed to other divisions. Cheatham had gotten wind of the proposal sometime in October and complained to Longstreet that the idea of being separated from his Tennesseans was abhorrent. Longstreet explained that President Davis suggested the arrangement to "prevent too much distress in the same community in case the Division should be unusually exposed in a battle." This notion had some merit, since severe losses in Cheatham's division, for instance, could lead to a heavy toll from one locale. Longstreet tried to reassure his colleague that a petition to Bragg would result in Cheatham's division remaining intact, provided he and his men were "willing to risk this distress in case of accident," and promised to assist Cheatham in keeping his Tennesseans together, but surely Longstreet knew Bragg well enough to doubt whether Bragg would provide Cheatham with any favorable consideration.[41] Cheatham had little faith in Bragg's clemency, given the bad blood between the two, and his resignation attempt was triggered in part by the impending breakup of his division.

Other army insiders recognized in the reorganization an attempt by Bragg to quell further uprisings against his authority. A South Carolinian regarded the dispersal of units from the same state as a violation of the president's earlier injunction to put men and officers from the same state together. He added that Breckinridge's and Cheatham's divisions were splintered to "break up cliques for political purposes" and to "keep down the anti-Bragg men." For all his protestations to Liddell that the soldiers were "his children," Bragg was tired of the hostile attitude toward his generalship from the Kentucky and Tennessee contingents in the army. The reorganization succeeded in rankling Cheatham's Tennesseans. Less than a month after the breakup, Van Buren Oldham of the Ninth Tennessee noted that Maney's brigade members were unhappy with their plight after they were transferred to W. H. T. Walker's division. "The boys all want to get back under Cheatham and Polk," he wrote, and Oldham's sentiments were shared by many of Cheatham's former soldiers. An officer in Oldham's regiment, James I. Hall, wrote that the transfer to Walker's division upset the soldiers because of Walker's strict discipline. Hall reported that in this Walker was a contrast to Cheatham, who some felt "was rather too lax in enforcing discipline among his men," a failing Hall thought was an underlying reason for the transfer. Cheatham's close friend and adjutant James D. Porter put the blame for the breakup squarely on Bragg's shoulders. Porter related that after Polk's departure from the army, "the men murmured, the officers resented in silence the action of the commanding general, and for this the Tennesseans were scattered."[42]

After the reorganization Cheatham retained Wright's brigade and John K. Jackson's brigade of Georgians and Mississippians. New units under his supervision included John Moore's brigade of three Alabama regiments, and several Mississippi regiments in a brigade led by Edward C. Walthall. Porter noted that Cheatham "was proud of his new command," but this assessment was made years after the war and does not convey the chagrin Cheatham felt in late 1863 when most of his beloved Tennesseans were yanked from his command. Porter more accurately caught Cheatham's mood when he described Cheatham's devotion to his old division, a devotion so strong it surpassed "the love of woman." The reorganization not only deprived Cheatham of his former regiments, but it also reduced the number of men he controlled. On October 31, the day Cheatham sent in his resignation, his division listed 5,467 men as effectives and nearly 8,000 men present. Exact figures for his new division after the November reorganization are not available, but Jackson's report for the Chattanooga campaign lists Moore's brigade at 1,205 and Walthall with 1,489 effectives. These numbers suggest that Cheatham had fewer than 5,000 effectives by late November. The reduction in brigade strength from five to four accounts for some of the lower totals. Cheatham's distinction in having the largest division at Chickamauga evaporated after Bragg's reorganization, and he was left with a considerably shrunken command.[43]

Confederates who felt demoralized by the new army organization were further deflated when it became apparent that Bragg intended to besiege Chattanooga. The inertia and monotony after Chickamauga sapped much of the elation and optimism which the soldiers exhibited immediately after the battle. Spirits dipped lower as the Rebels suffered from a lack of clothing, equipment, and rations. While Bragg attempted to starve the Yankees into submission, his own men had trouble obtaining ample foodstuffs and supplies. Captain John Harris, inspector-general on Vaughan's staff, outlined some of the difficulties in a letter he dispatched from Sweetwater, Tennessee. Writing to his mother in Memphis, he requested that his brother send some needed articles of clothing. Inflation had ravaged the buying power of the soldiers' modest wages, as evidenced in Harris's list of the going prices for certain items: "A uniform costs between five and six hundred dollars, a hat seventy-five and everything else in proportion." A pound of coffee cost ten dollars, and Harris complained that "it is an utter impossibility to buy anything here now with what pay we get."[44]

The officer's mood soured later in November, when Major Porter "of Cheatham's staff . . . brought me the very disagreeable news" that a female acquaintance in Atlanta carelessly lost a pair of boots and gloves before they could be forwarded to Harris. The loss so aggrieved him that he wrote of the woman with undisguised contempt: "I don't care whether I ever see her again or not." The frustration Harris felt was compounded by the knowledge that he would "soon need the boots and gloves badly, and there are none to be had out here." He tried to reassure his mother that all was well but admitted that provisions were low. With some humor, Harris noted that the command had "gotten fashionable lately, only having two meals a day, and if things continue to grow scarce as rapidly as they are doing . . . we soon may be induced to become still more fashionable by having only one meal per day."[45]

Harris was not alone in his plight and, indeed, was more comfortably settled than many of his compatriots, since he had a tent with a floor and a chimney, as well as blankets and some clothes sent by the family. As usual, the lowly privates suffered the most. Sam Watkins wrote that when Jefferson Davis reappeared, the inspection ritual was punctuated by the cries of men asking Davis to send food. A Mississippian on Lookout Mountain also noted the scarcity of rations, a point made evident when three crackers and two tablespoons of sugar constituted one of his daily food allotments. It is little wonder that morale eroded during late October and November as cold, rainy weather moved into the area and further dampened the men's spirits.[46]

The Union contingent in Chattanooga also confronted adversity and a paucity of rations, but their efforts to alleviate the shortcomings ultimately proved more successful than that of the Confederates. At Chattanooga the Union command also reorganized, but with little of the turbulence experienced by the Southerners. Rosecrans, McCook, and Crittenden were all removed, the latter two sent to appear before a court of inquiry. Rosecrans was replaced by George Thomas in mid-October, while Vicksburg conquerer Ulysses S. Grant took charge of all operations in the west. Grant quickly moved to break the Confederate stranglehold on Chattanooga and was initially concerned with his tenous supply line. The line hinged upon a roundabout route of some sixty miles; restoring a more direct link became Grant's first priority. War Department officials were also anxious to aid the bluecoats in Chattanooga and sent additional troops to bolster Grant's force. Two corps sent from the Army of the Potomac under Joseph Hooker arrived in October. Late that month the Federals were able to open a new supply line across the Tennessee River west of the city, effectively ending Bragg's plan to starve the Yankees out. Longstreet was the Confederate commander in charge of the area the Federals attacked, and Bragg was naturally incensed when he discovered that the bluecoats were able to seize the vital territory without much trouble. When President Davis suggested that Longstreet be dispatched against Ambrose Burnside's force at Knoxville, Bragg happily consented to the plan, obviously glad to be rid of another foe in the person of a recalcitrant Longstreet, but he weakened his army at an inopportune time. In mid-November William Tecumseh Sherman appeared, the forerunner of his army, which was on the march to Chattanooga from Mississippi.[47]

By late November, Bragg was decidedly outnumbered, with just 37,000 men to face an enemy that had roughly 80,000 troops. Grant waited until all of Sherman's force came up, then marshaled his armies for a massive blow. Sherman was given responsibility for the primary assault, which involved an attack on the northern end of Missionary Ridge, known as Tunnel Hill. Thomas was to use his Army of the Cumberland to assault the center of the Southern line on Missionary Ridge. Joseph Hooker would stage a preliminary attack against Lookout Mountain and then could be used to storm Missionary Ridge in conjunction with the other portions of Grant's host. To counter the threat, Bragg relied upon his two corps under Hardee and Breckinridge. The long Confederate defense line stretched from Missionary Ridge across to the northern tip of Lookout Mountain. Bragg's weeks of inactivity had cost him whatever psychological or material value the Chickamauga victory yielded, and allowed Grant to seize the initiative.[48]

Cheatham's temporary successor in command of the division, John K. Jackson, faced a number of difficulties throughout November. Not least among these was the fragmentation of his division. Marcus Wright's Tennessee brigade was on detached duty in Charleston, Tennessee, and would not return in time for the impending battle on Lookout Mountain.

Jackson's own brigade of Georgians and Mississippians occupied part of the valley between Lookout Mountain and Chattanooga Creek to the east, while Moore's Alabama brigade and Walthall's Mississippians were based on Lookout Mountain itself. Nominally in charge of four brigades, in reality Jackson was forced to concentrate his efforts on the two brigades belonging to Moore and Walthall. As events subsequently proved, the relationship between Jackson and his brigade commanders on Lookout Mountain was not particularly harmonious.[49]

Cheatham's absence was keenly felt as the three-day battle for Chattanooga opened on November 23, when a forward outpost manned by Rebel infantry was smothered by the Army of the Cumberland. This was the prelude to a far greater disaster the next day, when Joseph Hooker moved out against the Confederate forces on Lookout Mountain. These forces consisted of two brigades on the top of the mountain under Brigadier-Generals Edmund Pettus and John C. Brown. The other two brigades, those of Moore and Walthall, covered a long front extending from the east side of the mountain across the steep, narrow northern face and then down part of the northwestern edge of the summit. Walthall was on the left, and his troops could look forward and see Lookout Creek as it ran into the Tennessee River from the south. Moore's troops stretched across the northern base of Lookout Mountain to its eastern slope. Like Walthall, much of Moore's force was deployed on picket duty near the bottom of the mountain. The remainder of his brigade was stationed about halfway up the mountain, where farmer Robert Cravens had a home overlooking the loop of the Tennessee River at Moccasin Point. All of the Confederate forces on Lookout Mountain were under the command of Virginia-born Carter Littlepage Stevenson. Major-General Stevenson was a competent officer, but he did not take charge of the Rebel defenses on the mountain until the night of November 23. His appointment to the task came after several alterations in the Southern defenses, and Stevenson was hardly acquainted with his new responsibilities before Hooker came calling.[50]

The very night Stevenson assumed command, one of Walthall's regimental commanders suspected that the Yankees were up to something. Colonel William F. Dowd of the Twenty-fourth Mississippi heard what he thought was a large body of men on the march. Dowd was further convinced when he placed his ear to the ground and "heard the sound which no soldier of experience can mistake." Dowd's conjecture was borne out the following morning, when he saw Yankee batteries moving up in his direction and the tail end of a enemy column moving down Lookout Creek. Dowd sent word to Walthall, who also observed the Federal movement, and the Mississippians prepared to contest the Yankee advance.

Their task was complicated by the sheer size of Hooker's assaulting force, which numbered 10,000 men in three divisions. Hooker's troops forded Lookout Creek in several places and worked their way along the northwestern base of the mountain. The Federals found the going difficult, and as they struggled up the incline Walthall sought to delay their progress. Yankee batteries played on the Confederate defenders as Hooker pressured the left flank of Walthall's line. The Mississippians were in a desperate fix. Colonel Dowd recognized that it would take several hours for the Rebel forces on top of Lookout Mountain to be evacuated and felt that the entire brigade might have to be sacrificed to save the remaining troops on the summit. He ordered his soldiers in the Twenty-fourth Mississippi to take refuge "behind rocks, trees, and every cover that nature afforded," and instructed them to hold their fire until the Yankee assaulting party entered an open space in his immediate front. The Union attackers drove in Dowd's videttes and pickets so rapidly that he felt compelled to fire and was convinced that he probably killed some of his own men in the process. As the Federals reached the open ground in front of the regiments, Dowd's beleagured defenders managed to keep up a "deadly and destructive fire" which drove the Northern troops back. This repulse was repeated several times, until the Yankees managed to work their way around Dowd's flank and rear.[51]

Hooker's attackers were stung by Dowd and the remainder of Walthall's men, but they eventually managed to cut off a large portion of the Mississippians when the latter "held their position so long as to render escape impossible." Unable to locate an escape route up the rocky, timber-strewn slope, hundreds of Walthall's veterans were snared as they tried to scramble uphill. Colonel Dowd remembered Walthall's injunction to hold his position "till hell froze over," but by noon Dowd reckoned "that the ice was about five feet over it," and he withdrew beyond the Cravens house and reformed. At least he and a part of his command escaped. The left of Walthall's brigade ceased to exist when Hooker's men stormed their end of the line. As Walthall scraped the remnant of his brigade together, assistance finally arrived in the form of Moore's regiments. Moore could not see Walthall's line, owing to the persistent fog, but he moved his command to a line of trenches previously constructed some four hundred yards east of the Cravens house. He was startled to learn that the Yankees had already penetrated to this point, and Moore's Alabamians were forced to regain the lost ground. Moore faced fire from infantry in his front, while the Moccasin Point batteries continued to play on the Rebels as well. Moore reported that two Union color bearers were shot down as they tried to plant their flags on the embankment and admitted that he had never seen the Federals "fight with such daring and desperation." Moore's defense was remarkable as well, considering that his men were using weapons that had been condemned as unfit for anything other than drill and guard duty.[52]

The Confederates managed to stabilize the situation when regiments belonging to Brigadier-General Edmund Pettus wound their way down from the mountaintop in the early afternoon. Colonel Daniel R. Hundley of the Thirty-first Alabama later reminisced, "The scene presented was weird and almost indescribable." Hundley recalled "dripping leaves, the indistinct figures of men seen here and there crouching behind trees and rocks," and the "gleaming lines of fire as the two armies hurled volley after volley into the darkness." Through the mist came the rattle of bullets "above, around, everywhere." Pettus and Moore were assisted by Walthall, who rejoined the fray with the remainder of his troops, and this combined force staved off further inroads as the afternoon elapsed.[53] The resistance of the three brigades helped the Confederates retain possession of a road leading down from the mountaintop. This prevented an even greater calamity from ensuing and assured the Rebels of a means of escape.

The attack on Lookout Mountain was a Federal success nonetheless, and in its aftermath the Confederate officers argued among themselves over who was responsible for the reversal. Cheatham's replacement, John K. Jackson, bore the heaviest criticism. Walthall, Moore, and Pettus all criticized Jackson's conduct during the battle, claiming that he was generally unavailable and failed to direct the Rebel effort with any degree of competence. In fact, the three brigadiers soon dubbed Jackson "Mudwall," a sardonic play on Thomas J. "Stonewall" Jackson's nickname. Jackson naturally defended himself against his opponents, asserting that he had done as well as could be expected in view of the tremendous disparity in numbers. A fellow Georgian, W. H. T. Walker, urged Jackson to challenge his detractors to a series of duels, but fortunately this course of action was not adopted.[54] While Jackson's handling of the battle remained a bone of contention, one is left to ponder the impact of Cheatham's absence. Jackson had had no previous experience as a divisional commander, and Cheatham's advantage in this regard would no doubt have led him to take a more active role in defending the area. Still, the obstacles the Confederate forces faced were so daunting that one man was unlikely to have changed events to any great degree. Cheatham would have encountered the same difficulties as Jackson. He could not have alleviated the imposing terrain problems or done much about the numerical inferiority of the Rebel forces. He certainly could not have dispelled the thick fog which shrouded much of the action. Nor could he have redressed another problem which resulted from Bragg's reorganization of the army. This was that the main Confederate officers on the mountain were not familiar with one another. Moore, for instance, was a newcomer to the army, having been captured and exchanged at Vicksburg. Pettus and Stevenson had likewise been captured at Vicksburg. Brown, Jackson, and Walthall had served in various commands of the Army of Tennessee. Given these hurdles and the widespread distribution of the Confederate forces, it is doubtful that Cheatham could have achieved more success than Jackson and the other Confederates did.

In any event, Lookout Mountain became celebrated as the "Battle above the Clouds," a term, popularized by Northern correspondents. For years afterward, the action could ignite the tempers of participants in the Confederate ranks. Nearly two decades after the fray, Colonel Hundley of the Thirty-first Alabama published an account of the battle in a Philadelphia newspaper. His article asserted that Walthall's command was surprised by the Union assault and that the Mississippians did little to repel the enemy before most of them were swallowed by the advancing Federals. He added that the battle heated up only after Pettus sent most of his command to Walthall's aid. Walthall, enraged by Hundley's version of what transpired, began an angry correspondence with the Alabamian less than a week after the article appeared. The two men wrote a series of nine letters, each succeeding message containing more bitter remarks than its predecessor. While Hundley tried to remain cordial toward Walthall in his first two replies, the Alabamian eventually resorted to sarcasm, which in turn lapsed into sullen resentment as Walthall vigorously continued to defend his brigade. The two disputants finally turned the correspondence over the Pettus, who in late 1882 decided that Walthall and his command had indeed been defamed by Hundley's published account. Otherwise, the sorry exchange proved little more than that the wartime quarrels in the Army of Tennessee carried over well into the postwar era.[55]

Cheatham rejoined the army sometime in the early evening of November 24 and conferred with Stevenson around 8 P.M. His joy in renewing army friendships was tempered by the knowledge that he remained under Bragg's authority and that his Tennesseans were scattered. Nor was the news he received concerning his new division cheerful, especially in regard to casualties. The loss in Walthall's brigade was incredible. The Mississippian lost a total of 972 men. The vast majority of these were prisoners; 853 officers and men were listed as missing when the report was made. In the confusing, fog-shrouded action, Walthall's brigade was reduced to little more than a single regiment in numbers. Moore's losses were lighter, but the capture of many of his pickets inflated his casualty list to 254; 206 of these were men reported missing.[56]

Stevenson was in the process of bringing down the remaining troops from the mountaintop when Cheatham arrived. This task completed, the two officers met at the base of the mountain, and Cheatham formally assumed command. Bragg soon sent an order for Cheatham to withdraw the remaining Confederates from Lookout Mountain and the western side of Chattanooga Creek. Throwing skirmishers out to protect the movement, the remaining defenders filed down the mountain and began moving to Missionary Ridge. Moore's brigade did not leave until 2 A.M. on November 25. In the early morning hours, Cheatham's men trudged wearily through the valley and then up Missionary Ridge. There, they were positioned on the Confederate right, which was anchored by Cleburne's division at Tunnel Hill. To their left was Patton Anderson's division.[57]

The Confederate position, though compressed, was still a weak one. A recent study by historian James Lee McDonough pinpoints the major disadvantages and blunders which afflicted the army on Missionary Ridge. Considering the time they had occupied the area, the defensive works constructed by the Rebels were woefully inadequate. The strongest of these works consisted of a line of rifle pits near the base of the mountain. A second line was located roughly halfway up the slope, while the main line ran along the top of the ridge. This placement of the main line was in itself a mistake, as it followed the geographical crest and not a "military" one, which could have provided better opportunities to contest the Yankee assault. In Breckinridge's sector, the positioning of large numbers of men in the rifle pits could lead to problems if the pits were suddenly overrun by a heavy enemy force. And the Confederates, thinned by the dispatch of Longstreet to Knoxville, did not have an adequate force in reserve to staunch any breakthrough. Despite the addition of the survivors from Lookout Mountain, the Missionary Ridge line was vulnerable.[58]

November 25 opened with Sherman assaulting the Confederate right. Despite overwhelming superiority in numbers, the Yankees were unable to make much headway against Cleburne's force at Tunnel Hill. The fighting lasted for several hours, but Cleburne's sound troop dispositions and tactics managed to stymie Sherman's attack. At the other end of the Northern line, Hooker was even more unsuccessful and could not bring his troops into attack formation for most of the day. That left Thomas, and his assault in the center was designed to deflect attention from Sherman's effort and weaken the Rebel right flank. The Army of the Cumberland moved out around 3:30 P.M., some units operating under the assumption that they were to go no farther than the rifle pits near the base of the ridge. The Federals overran the lowest line of Confederate defenses in a number of areas, but this success was often offset by the galling fire from their adversaries higher on the summit. Fitfully the Northern soldiers began working their way up the slope, making better progress in some sectors than others. Some officers never intended to halt at the rifle pits; others did pause because they felt their instructions did not allow them the latitude to keep going. Eventually, however, Grant and Thomas were startled by the large numbers of men who charged up the slope on their own initiative.[59]

Southerners on top of Missionary Ridge who had witnessed the impressive sight of eleven Union brigades deployed in assault formation soon confronted the prospect of those brigades coming up the hill. A member of one of Cheatham's former Tennessee regiments assigned to Breckinridge reported that four double columns of the enemy advanced against his lone brigade. While the Rebels from the rifle pits and the second defensive line were captured or braved the fire from their comrades above in a dangerous return, the Yankees clambered up "like bugs, and were so thick that they were almost in each other's way."[60]

Until late in the afternoon Cheatham's men were not heavily engaged, and they were able to use the respite to regain some of the energy drained by the Lookout Mountain battle and retreat. This was fortunate, for the Union thrust pierced Patton Anderson's line scant yards to Cheatham's left, and many of Breckinridge's men retreated in hasty panic.

Cheatham recognized the danger and alertly rode to the left of his line. There, he changed Jackson's brigade front so that it was perpendicular to the original position along the ridge. Next he ordered Moore to Jackson's support. There was some momentary confusion when Jackson's men wavered and fell back as Moore was trying to get into position, but the Georgians and Mississippians in Jackson's brigade soon reformed and linked with Moore. Moore reported later, "The enemy made great efforts to drive us from the position, but failed." The determination of Cheatham's soldiers was stiffened, according to Moore, by the belief "that the safety of the right wing of the army" hinged upon their success in holding their ground.[61]

Moore's and Jackson's troops remained united as they checked the Federals, but the same cannot be said of the respective brigade commanders themselves. In his report Moore, still angered by Jackson's leadership (or lack thereof) on Lookout Mountain, slurred the Georgian once more by stating that he "did not see General Jackson or any of his staff . . . except Captain Moreno, during the engagement." Moore's criticism was highly unwarranted and somewhat ridiculous, considering that Jackson had been superseded as divisional commander when Cheatham arrived. Jackson alluded to this fact then he retorted that Moore "could have found me at all times during the engagement near the right of my line, which was on top of the ridge, while the left was down the hill. If General Moore means to reflect upon the conduct of my brigade, I am glad to say there are other witnesses who bear different testimony." One of the witnesses Jackson enlisted was Cheatham, who may have been somewhat mystified by the bickering among his subordinates. Cheatham sent a note to Jackson which reassured the Georgian that he had done his duty at Missionary Ridge. Cheatham wrote that he "saw nothing wrong in your conduct on Missionary Ridge," and added that Jackson was "always present to receive and obey my orders, as far as could be done amid the confusion of the day."[62]

While Moore's postbattle report implies that he and Jackson were able to hold the Confederate position, there is some question as to whether this is totally accurate. After the war, Cheatham and Walthall exchanged letters related to the Missionary Ridge fight, and both officers agreed that Jackson and Moore were eventually driven down the hill. At this juncture, Cheatham ordered Walthall's Mississippians to alter their position and "check the enemy." Cheatham was near Walthall when the latter received a severe wound in the foot, but Walthall's depleted brigade gallantly carried out Cheatham's directive, and the Federals were "driven back about two hundred yards to the top of a cross ridge."[63] This account is supported by the report of Brigadier—General John C. Brown, who came to Walthall's assistance with his brigade and formed on Walthall's left. Brown reported "an irregular line in our front skirmishing with the enemy, but it soon retired in broken fragments, and then we advanced," This recollection contrasts somewhat with Walthall's report, filed less than a month after the battle, which states that the Federal did not approach nearer than two hundred yards, and even then "not in very large force."[64]

Whatever the truth, by 1876 Walthall considered this effort by his brigade "perhaps the most creditable act ever performed by it," especially in light of the severe losses he had suffered the day before. The engagement did increase Walthall's casualty toll for the Chattanooga campaign. Walthall himself was incapacitated for some time by the foot injury, one of his officers was mortally wounded, and over two dozen others were either wounded or missing. All in all, the battles at Lookout Mountain and Missionary Ridge cost Cheatham's division 1,671 casualties. Of this number, 56 were killed, 371 wounded, and 1,244 were reported missing at the end of the campaign.[65]

As nightfall descended on the Chattanooga area, Cheatham took charge of coordinating the withdrawal of several Confederate units. He shepherded his own division and at least two other brigades down Missionary Ridge on the way to Chickamauga Station. Moore and Jackson led the movement, while Walthall's men abandoned their positions around 8:15 P.M.[66]

Cheatham and his troops helped Hardee's portion of the line remain intact, but the retreat from the ridge was still a depressing affair. By the time the Confederates halted at Dalton in northern Georgia, it was obvious that the damage resulting from the battles around Chattanooga was deep and pervasive. The loss of men, materiel, and territory was bad enough, but the confidence of many soldiers in the ranks was also shattered. This loss of morale was a process which began with the reorganization of the army and steadily worsened in the weeks before the Union assaults.

Not until the final weeks of the war would spirits in the Army of Tennessee dip as low as they did in the wake of the disasters at Lookout Mountain and Missionary Ridge. Word of the outcome spread rapidly. A soldier named McLean was returning to the army after a visit to Mississippi but did not rejoin his command before the Confederates were defeated. McLean was in Atlanta, but within three days he knew enough details of the defeat to convey them to an officer in Macon. McLean accurately noted that the "loss in men is not large . . . but the moral effect is terrible. The right stood its ground nobly, but the left fell back in confusion after the enemy had obtained a lodg[e]ment in the centre." McLean hoped that the Yankees would not pursue the Rebels vigorously, especially since Longstreet was retreating from Knoxville and going back to Virginia. In conclusion, McLean censured his commander by writing a damning final sentence: "From all I can learn, Bragg as usual blundered in having too long a line and putting the bulk of his forces just where the mass of the enemy *was not*."[67]

Federal prowess accomplished what Cheatham and his fellow generals were unable to achieve. Bragg, mortified by the Chattanooga debacle, wrote Richmond on November 29 and asked to be relieved.[68] The government accepted the offer the next day and placed Hardee in temporary command of the army. Bragg realized that Missionary Ridge was a disaster and reflected badly upon his leadership, but he was determined not to bear the burden of the reverse alone. He characteristically found fault with his subordinates and accused certain elements in the army of cowardice. Bragg pinned much of the blame on Breckinridge, whom he accused of being drunk from November 23 through November 27. Even as he assailed the Kentuckian, Bragg began a bitter and savage assault on Cheatham.

Bragg wrote Jefferson Davis on December 1 and admitted that the defeat at Chattanooga was "justly disparaging to me as a commander." He then proceeded to explain that he was not totally at fault and pleaded for Davis "to make other changes here, or our success is hopeless." After telling of Breckinridge's alleged intoxication, Bragg reminded Davis that

"General Hardee will assure you that Cheatham is equally dangerous," a reference to Cheatham's intemperance at Murfreesboro. Cheatham was one of the enemies Bragg had in mind when he wrote that he could "bear to be sacrificed myself, but not to see my country and my friends ruined by the vices of a few profligate men who happen to have an undue popularity." In retrospect, Bragg felt both he and Davis had "erred in the conclusion for me to retain command here after the clamor raised against me. The warfare has been carried on successfully, and the fruits are bitter."[69]

Bragg also sent a staff officer to Richmond with a report of the Chattanooga operations, and this provided another opportunity to snub Cheatham. The rough draft of this report, which eventually evolved into his official report, was compiled at Dalton soon after Bragg and the army concluded the retreat. In the first draft, Bragg originally inserted Cheatham's name once, that being a reference to November 24, when Cheatham rejoined the army. This lone notation ws eventually scratched out, probably because Bragg wanted to obliterate any reference to one of his tormentors. Bragg's report as it appears in the *Official Records* pointedly omits any mention of Cheatham and his role in the conflict at Missionary Ridge. Bragg did laud both Hardee and Walthall, and even credited Hardee with directing Walthall's change of front and counterattack. When Walthall learned of this account in the 1870s, he heatedly denied that Hardee had been responsible for the change in position, writing Cheatham that the movement was made "by your authority and in your presence."[70]

Bragg vented his anger both before and after his departure from the army. At Dalton he summoned General Liddell to chat about Liddell's request for a transfer, but most of the conversation was devoted to a tirade againt Bragg's critics. Cheatham remained a favorite target. "Here now," Bragg related, "is Cheatham, drinking in Dalton and going around shaking his head when speaking of me, 'I told you so'—but what more could be expected from a man whose occupation in Nashville before the war was to keep a drinking saloon and a stallion?" Liddell was forced to listen as Bragg complained darkly about politicians as generals, then morosely vowed to retire to private endeavors. This vow was not fulfilled, as Jefferson Davis elevated Bragg to an important post as the president's official military advisor.[71]

At the end of December, Bragg fired another salvo at Cheatham via a letter to Marcus J. Wright. In this message, written before Bragg departed from Warm Springs, Georgia, he alleged that both Cheatham and Breckinridge were drunk for five successive days around the time of the retreat from Missionary Ridge, a charge which in Cheatham's case is not substantiated by any evidence whatsoever. Bragg's antipathy towards

Cheatham and Breckinridge remained intact for the rest of his life. In an 1873 letter to an officer in Walthall's brigade, Bragg vengefully noted: "In France or Germany, either [Cheatham or Breckinridge] would have been shot in six hours. With us they pass for heroes." He characterized Cheatham and other detractors as "imbeciles, traitors, rogues, and intriguing politicians."[72]

Regrettably, there is no account which relates Cheatham's thoughts and opinions after the Missionary Ridge retreat. Given the hostile tenor of Bragg's pronouncements and the animosity between the two men, Cheatham could not have helped feeling overjoyed when Bragg left the army. He must have shared the elation expressed by W. D. Gale, one of Leonidas Polk's staff officers, who rejoiced that "Bragg is at last played out and has quit the Army of Ten[nessee]." He must have felt satisfaction, too, in knowing that he had played a key role in averting an even greater disaster at Missionary Ridge. Though he was ignored in Bragg's report, other partisans did acknowledge Cheatham's skill. Hardee in particular praised both Cheatham and Walthall. During the battle Hardee enthusiastically told Cheatham, "You saved the right of the army," as Walthall's Mississippians went into action.[73] Cheatham may have doubted the wisdom of Davis's appointing Bragg to the advisor's post, but otherwise it is difficult to imagine his feeling any remorse over Bragg's departure. The two men resented one another for months prior to the events which forced Bragg's resignation, and when Braxton Bragg left the army, Cheatham surely regarded himself as the victor in their long-standing rivalry.

Chapter 7

"This is Old Joe": From Dalton to Kennesaw Mountain

Lieutenant-General Hardee declined command of the army proffered by President Davis, and General Joseph Eggleston Johnston was appointed in mid-December to replace Bragg. Davis was unenthusiastic about the Virginia-born Johnston, but he had few other options left. Robert E. Lee did not desire a transfer to the western army, and the other logical choice, Beauregard, was also a Davis foe. Several explanations have been presented for the Davis-Johnston animosity, including one suggesting that the rift between the two men began when both were cadets at West Point. While there was almost certainly tension between the two in the antebellum period, it increased swiftly in the early months of the war, when Johnston felt aggrieved that he was not selected the ranking officer in the Confederacy. Being placed behind Samuel Cooper, Albert Sidney Johnston, and Robert E. Lee did not please Johnston in the least, and from the first year of the conflict Davis and Johnston squabbled, as did their respective supporters.[1] Bragg is the most controversial of the western commanders, but there was also, and still is, a good deal of debate regarding Johnston's martial abilities. Frank Cheatham would have come down squarely on Johnston's side. Cheatham and Johnston became firm allies, and Cheatham so admired Johnston that he named his youngest son after the Virginian.

Johnston inherited an army seriously shaken by the Missionary Ridge episode. Hardee had worked hard to refit and encourage the soldiers during his temporary stint as commander, and Johnston continued these efforts. Progress was slow, and several officers met on Christmas Eve 1863 to enlist greater aid from the Confederate government for the beleaguered Army of Tennessee. Cheatham and six other brigade or division commanders requested that John C. Breckinridge go to Richmond and exert his political skills in the Confederate Congress on the army's behalf.[2] A field return, issued four days before the generals convened, illustrates the weakened state of the force. The army had just 33,297 men listed as effectives, and Cheatham's division, hard-hit by the Lookout Mountain action, could only muster 3,799 men who fit into that category.[3]

While his lieutenants importuned Richmond for aid, Johnston collected troops at Dalton and attempted to revive morale. One of his first acts upon assuming command was to write a letter to President Davis outlining possible strategy and ways to improve the army's condition. Johnston suggested that the organization of the army prior to Bragg's breakup be reinstated, and specifically, requested that Cheatham's old division be restored. Johnston came to the conclusion after consultation with several of his officers revealed that "the West Tennesseans are . . . absolutely discontented."[4]

Johnston's observation was correct. The soldiers in Cheatham's former regiments from western Tennessee may have been the most vocal about expressing their displeasure, but his erstwhile troops from other regions were also dissatisfied. After the separation of Cheatham and his men, there was widespread disgruntlement among his former brigades. A decidedly independent group, the Tennesseans chafed at the new arrangement and occasionally questioned the orders of their new divisional commanders. Maney's men under W. H. T. Walker, for instance, defied a command during the retreat from Missionary Ridge. They watched as a brigade of Alabamians and South Carolinians under Brigadier-General States Rights Gist crossed Chickamauga Creek fully clothed and emerged from the chilly water "looking and feeling like wet dogs." When Gist ordered them to cross in the same manner, they ignored his directive. Instead, they first took time to strip and fashion their clothes into bundles, then forded the stream, and paused again on the opposite bank to don their dry uniforms. Captain James I. Hall of the Ninth Tennessee, who recorded the event, obviously took pride with his fellow Tennesseans in their commonsense approach to the situation but confessed that it was construed as a typical example of "the insubordination of the Tennessee troops" by some officers in the army.[5]

At Dalton some of Cheatham's former charges continued to agitate for the restoration of the division. Once, Cheatham was espied by several members of the Ninth Tennessee Regiment as he rode near their camp. The men intercepted Cheatham and surrounded him, some embracing him while others hugged "his old sorrel horse." As the soldiers implored Cheatham to arrange for a return to his division, Cheatham grew distraught, "cried like a child," and could only utter "Boys, I'll try."[6]

Much to the satisfaction of Cheatham and his men, the army was reorganized, and Cheatham's former Tennessee brigades were reunited in February. The act instantly lifted the spirits of the Tennesseans, who lustily cheered Cheatham as he made the rounds and visited each regiment.

Cheatham and his men idolized General Joseph E. Johnston, who took over the reins of the Army of Tennessee after the disaster at Missionary Ridge. (Library of Congress)

One private noted simply, "We were happy and so was Cheatham," while another rejoiced in the transfer back to "Old Frank," in whom the men "had every confidence." A soldier in the Sixth Tennessee regarded the re-unification of the division as "one of the sublimest occasions in the history of the war."[7] When word of the restoration was circulated, the Tennesseans "cheered and embraced each other with feeling, and when Gen. Cheatham appeared among them they gathered around him with shouts of joy. The General was very much affected and found himself unable to speak the promptings of his heart; but he took from his pocket a gold coin, and tossing it in the air, while his eyes rained tears, exclaimed 'Boys, you are as good as that!'"[8] The restoration triggered an impromptu demonstration hailing Johnston. Cheatham's soldiers marched to army headquarters with a band and called for General Johnston with a serenade. A jubilant Cheatham escorted Johnston from a back room to the front door, where he presented the Virginian in an affectionate if unmilitary manner. Cheatham placed his hand upon Johnston's bare head, patted it two or three times, then happily said, "Boys, this is Old Joe." The sobriquet stuck, and the Tennesseans heartily enjoyed the casual moment. "Old Frank"'s good-natured introduction sparked within his division a fanatical devotion to Joe Johnston that lasted throughout the war and beyond.[9]

The army settled into winter quarters as Johnston labored to increase its size. Cheatham's men constructed mud-daubed cabins to withstand the bitter cold, complete with chimneys fashioned out of clay. Camp life could be boring, but at Dalton the Tennesseans staged several diversions which broke up the monotony. Successful rabbit hunts were a source of entertainment, as well as a supplement to the regular army fare. Religious-minded veterans in the division took part in revivals, which were popular during the Dalton interlude. "A deep religious feeling seems to pervade the army," wrote Major Melancthon Smith; "nightly the 3 churches are crowded and many leave for want of room." Smith, Cheatham's chief artillerist, noted that the different denominations won new members each night. The revivals flourished in part because of the realization that the war was not going as well as it had in 1861 or 1862. Some soldiers renounced their formerly sinful ways in an effort to win God's favor for their cause, while others were more concerned with their personal salvation. Not everyone embraced the religious fervor; others took a keener interest in alcohol or sought solace in the arms of prostitutes who set up shop near the army.[10]

In spite of such disbelievers in their midst, many of Cheatham's men participated in the religious revival. Ironically, what many of them remembered most about the religious devotions was an accident which occurred the night of April 30, 1864. According to the diary of Van Buren Oldham, a tree fell among a group of soldiers attending a service, instantly killing six of the men, while four others died shortly afterwards. The tragedy occurred after some of Cheatham's men had cleared an area for devotionals. They had swept some trash against a hickory tree, then ignited the debris. The tree apparently burned at the base for some time, without anyone being aware of the development, and fell noiselessly into the kneeling soldiers. Cheatham's men were inured to battlefield deaths, but the bizarre accident deeply moved many of them. The funeral for the ten victims the next day was a solemn occasion, and the freak accident provoked religious conjectures as to whether the men had won salvation prior to their demise. The singular nature of the tragedy made it unforgettable for those who were present; at least five sources for Cheatham's division make reference to the incident.[11]

Far happier memories were generated by the many snowy days in the early part of 1864. Snowball fights gave Cheatham's men a way to burn up some of their excess energy and provided fodder for postwar nostalgia. The veterans reminisced in particular about March 22, 1864, when Cheatham's Tennesseans squared off against W. H. T. Walker's Georgians in a massive snowball battle that lasted several hours. Thousands of men participated in the fray, and though a few unfortunates had their eyes blackened, the exercise delighted spectators and contestants alike. The sham battle took on at least some of the trappings of a regular engagement when it got underway. Both sides played music, unfurled their colors, and threw skirmishers out before they advanced to the attack. The battle raged on for at least two hours, at which point the adversaries paused for a brief respite. During this interval, a messenger came to Colonel George W. Gordon of the Eleventh Tennessee and requested that he mount a horse and come to lead the Tennesseans. Gordon assented, had his black servant saddle his steed, and grabbed an improvised flag as he headed for the battlefield. When Gordon reined up in front of the Tennesseans and waved his flag (an old bandana handkerchief Gordon later termed "the largest and dirtiest one" he ever saw), his force raised "such a tremendous shout . . . that the very atmosphere seemed to quiver around us."[12]

Meanwhile, Walker's Georgians had persuaded one of their officers to mount up, and his appearance elicited an enthusiastic shout from the Georgia troops. News of the encounter had spread, and hundreds of noncombatants assembled on the surrounding hills and housetops. General officers and their staffs "mounted their horses or ascended higher elevations to witness the impending struggle." Cheatham was surely one of the observers as his Tennesseans charged the Georgians. Gordon recalled that the "air was white with whizzing and bursting balls; men were tripped up, knocked down, covered with snow, or run over." Gordon and his horse were pelted with hundreds of snowballs, but the Tennesseans managed to flank the Georgians at last, drove them from their camp, and then plundered the Georgia tents of foodstuffs recently sent from home. For a brief time the real war was forgotten; Melancthon Smith described how the struggle was carried on with "light hearts as if no more serious battle had, or ever would, engage their attention."[13]

The Tennesseans and Georgians were especially fond of one another after their epic battle (the Georgians invariably raised a cheer for "The Snowball Colonel" whenever they saw Gordon), but the same cannot be said of their respective divisional commanders. Both Cheatham and Walker had been drawn into a controversy in January, when most of the army's high command met at the request of General Hardee to discuss the manpower shortage. Cheatham was absent the night of January 2, when Patrick Cleburne read a paper which proposed that slaves be enrolled in the army. Cleburne argued that the measure would help win support from Europe while it fragmented the North. To attract the blacks, Cleburne offered a guarantee that their army service would win freedom for themselves and their families. The suggestion shocked most of the assembled officers, who hotly debated the propriety of the proposal. Among the most incensed generals were cavalry chieftain Joseph Wheeler and W. H. T. Walker. Wheeler wrote Bragg in mid-February and related that Cleburne would have been hanged "in five minutes" had he authored such a paper in Wheeler's hometown before the war. Walker was even more outraged, collecting the document and soliciting answers from officers as to their stance on the proposal. These he eventually forwarded to Jefferson Davis.[14]

Both Wheeler and Walker were convinced that Cheatham backed Cleburne's proposition, even though Cheatham had not been present at the meeting. Wheeler wrote Bragg that Thomas Hindman, Cheatham, and Hardee all approved the measure. Walker also accused Cheatham and related that Brigadier-General William Bate told him that Cheatham "had signed it or authorized Cleburne to sign it for him." Walker was even more convinced of Cheatham's complicity when he received the latter's response to his query about the proposal. Cheatham received Walker's inquiry on January 9, and the next day fired off a brusque reply. The paper was not an official (military) document, Cheatham wrote, and he concluded that that was "a sufficient excuse for declining to answer your interrogations." This reply was an evasive one, especially contrasted to the answers of men such as Bate, Carter Stevenson, Patton Anderson, and A. P. Stewart, all of whom abhorred the proposal.[15]

Major-General W. H. T. Walker implicated Cheatham as a
supporter of Patrick Cleburne's proposal to enroll slaves
in the Confederate army. A Georgian, Walker was killed
July 22, 1864, at the Battle of Atlanta. (Author's photo)

The proposal has been characterized as a triumph for the pro-Bragg faction in the army, since a majority of Cleburne's most vociferous critics were
Bragg supporters. Bragg needed little pretext to attack his old foes and readily accepted the claim that Cheatham backed Cleburne's scheme. He also
welcomed news of Cleburne's paper, since he recognized that it would erode
the influence of his detractors. "It will kill them," Bragg gleefully wrote Marcus J. Wright in February. The proposal was suppressed at the insistence of
President Davis, and word of the emancipation plan apparently did not leak
to the rank and file. In a letter to Wright in early March, Bragg concluded
that it was well to let "the abolition gentlemen subside for the present," but
warned that "they are agitators and should be watched."[16]

For Cheatham, having Bragg as an enemy was nothing new, but the relationship between Cheatham and Walker soured in the aftermath of the proposal. In fact, there are indications that the fiery Walker already resented Cheatham even before Cleburne's plan was unveiled. When Bragg left the army, Walker was both saddened and angry and blamed Bragg's fall on opponents within the army, a group which undoubtedly included Cheatham. During Hardee's short-lived stint as army commander, Cheatham filled in for Hardee as corps commander and was therefore Walker's superior. The Georgian conveyed this information to his wife in a sentence punctuated by three exclamation points, an obvious sign that Walker was outraged by Cheatham's temporary promotion.[17] Another historian has intimated that Walker disliked Cheatham partly because Cheatham's commission as major-general predated Walker's, which put Cheatham in line for promotions on the basis of seniority.[18] Indeed, letters through the summer of 1864 reveal that Walker grew increasingly irked by his failure to win a higher rank. He also felt that a long association with Johnston did not provide him with any special consideration within the army. "I feel that I am an outsider," Walker told his wife in one missive, and his resentment of Cheatham may have stemmed in part from the knowledge that Cheatham was on good terms with "Old Joe."[19] Thus, Cheatham's response to Walker's inquiry regarding the emancipation proposal was only one of several factors which drove the two generals apart. Still, it was the most obvious source of friction between the two men. Walker wrote Bragg that Cheatham's answer "did not suit me any more than Hindman's." He also confided that contact with Hardee, Cleburne, and Cheatham was so displeasing that he considered asking for a transfer.[20]

If it is easy to ascertain that Cheatham was a recipient of Bragg's, Walker's, and Wheeler's ire after the proposal, it is more difficult to sort out what his real role and motives were in the affair. Certainly his absence from the meeting is interesting. Something may have arisen which prevented his attending the conclave, but the possibility remains that Cheatham knew of Cleburne's proposal in advance and deliberately avoided the meeting. That way he might avoid being drawn into the controversy, and on some occasions Cheatham did reveal a reluctance to commit himself too openly on divisive issues. In this regard he was similar to Polk, who created controversy but had an uncanny knack for evading responsibility when things heated up. Yet, this scenario is not in keeping with Cheatham's response to Walker, which amounted to a brushoff and confirmed Walker's suspicions that Cheatham was behind Cleburne's proposal. If Cheatham indeed supported the Irishman, perhaps his loyalty was based on an appreciation of Cleburne's martial talents. Both men also shared a distrust of Bragg. Cheatham may also have accepted Cleburne's reasoning that the South was doomed unless desperate measures were taken to prevent further reversals. It is unclear to what extent he advocated Cleburne's solution. Frank was from a slaveholding family and grew up with slaves at Westover. His sister Louise regularly included information on her slaves when she wrote to Cheatham from her plantation in Louisiana.[21] If Cheatham was indeed a proponent of emancipation, he was naive in assuming that the proposal would not arouse antagonism. Such a bold suggestion could not fail to arouse intense passions in men who were committed to slavery, such as Walker and Wheeler. The entire episode came at an unfortunate time for Johnston, who scarcely needed dissension in the officer corps as he sought to revive morale. Nonetheless, the army's high command did continue their discord through the early months of 1864.

In addition to the intra-army turmoil, there was an external threat in February, when a Federal force advanced into east-central Mississippi. To counter the movement, Hardee's corps was dispatched to aid Leonidas Polk. Cheatham's men went by train to Atlanta, where they arrived February 21, then on to Demopolis, Alabama. The Tennesseans welcomed the opportunity to assist their former corps commander and decided to make the best of their winter journey. Along the way, Cheatham's troops "wrote a great many notes and threw them out to the girls that thronged the road."[22] This rather innocuous diversion gave way to a different form of merriment when the division rolled into Atlanta. W. J. Worsham of the Nineteenth Tennessee related that a number of Cheatham's men got drunk in Atlanta and chased "Mars Frank" from one street corner to another asking him to make a speech. Cheatham, himself a bit "tight," would sidestep the request by saying, "Come along, boys, you are all my boys," and move on without delivering the speech. An approving Worsham regarded Cheatham as a prime example of a "General belonging to his men and vice-versa," a view reinforced when the officer and much of his command "had a lively time in the streets of Atlanta that day."[23]

By the time the Tennesseans arrived in Demopolis, the Northerners were on a return trip to Vicksburg, having paused to burn Meridian. Though the division did not battle the Yankees, Polk was glad to see Cheatham and his men again. He eventually decided to ask Richmond to make the transfer of Cheatham and his division a permanent one. Polk advanced several arguments to help win approval for his request. Polk reasoned that he could harass the Union flank when a movement commenced against Johnston and might threaten the long Federal supply line in Tennessee. The cleric also felt that he could expand his ranks by sending some of Cheatham's men from western Tennessee out on a recruiting mission. From late February until April, the bishop entreated Jefferson Davis for Cheatham's division, even though the unit returned to Dalton around the first of March.[24] Polk had broached the subject with Johnston previously, but the latter was unenthusiastic. Johnston feared that possible losses via desertions would offset any recruiting gains and was unwilling to part with the division. Finally, Davis asked Bragg's opinion. Bragg was typically vindictive and bluntly stated that placing Cheatham's men in northern Alabama would soon result in "another large portion of them on stolen horses marauding over the countryside."[25] After this outburst the matter was dropped, and Cheatham's men remained with the Army of Tennessee for the rest of the war.

Perhaps the reason Cheatham's men remembered the snowball battle so vividly was because it represented one of the last innocent touches in a war which had long since lost its romance. The winter respite ended as warm weather appeared in April, and the war's grimmer side resurfaced. At the same time the military situation in the west changed. Grant went to Virginia as overall commander of Union armies. Sherman replaced him at Chattanooga as head of the Military Division of the Mississippi, a giant enterprise embracing three armies. Grant ordered Sherman to break Johnston's force, while offensives began simultaneouly against other Confederate sectors. This concerted policy began in May, and in the western theater the Federals enjoyed a decided edge in numbers. Sherman collected roughly 100,000 men, over half of them enrolled in the Army of the Cumberland, under George Thomas. John M. Schofield directed the Army of the Ohio, while the Army of the Tennessee was led by James M. McPherson.[26]

Johnston had far fewer men than Sherman boasted, with somewhere around 55,000 troops available. His army was divided into two corps, with Hardee's corps comprised of divisions under Cheatham, Cleburne, and Walker. Johnston's second corps was under Kentucky-born John Bell Hood, who had distinguished himself while serving in the Army of Northern Virginia. Hood won a promotion to lieutenant-general in February, and he joined the Army of Tennessee that same month.[27]

Sherman's plan was to move along the route of the vital Western and Atlantic railroad, which linked Chattanooga and Atlanta. He could use his separate armies to threaten Johnston in several places at once, or slide them around the Confederates and strike a Southern flank. All the while, Sherman intended to pressure Johnston. The Ohioan hoped to trap the Rebels or force Johnston into a fight in open ground, where the Union commander could bring his numbers to bear. Johnston for his part hoped Sherman would blunder and leave a portion of his huge force open to destruction.

When the spring campaign began, Sherman's advantage in manpower was offset to some extent by the improvement in Johnston's army. The Army of Tennessee was not strong enough to mount an offensive, in Johnston's opinion, but the Confederates had recovered a great deal from the devastating blows struck around Chattanooga the previous November. Deserters, disheartened by the army's prospects, fled in droves during December and the first part of 1864. One of Johnston's tasks was to reclaim as many of these men as possible. He dispatched officers with orders to round up as many of the absentees as possible. The army did recoup some of its former strength, as officers such as Captain Alfred Tyler Fielder of the Twelfth Tennessee managed to bring some of the runaways back to Dalton. Fielder and other officers in Cheatham's division could use the restoration of the Tennessee division as an incentive for the deserters to return, and perhaps some men did come back after they learned that "Old Frank" was again their divisional commander. Johnston's efforts at reviving morale were not confined to those who had fled the service. He furloughed the entire army using a rotation system, provided new equipment, improved rations, and restored discipline within the ranks. "General Johnston . . . has a very fine army here who are always ready for any emergency," wrote one correspondent in February, adding that "the men will now fight for revenge — I would hate to be a Yankee now [and] fall into the hands of a southern private." The writer also concluded that Johnston kept "his men under better discipline than General Bragg and he punishes them for disobedience more promptly."[28]

Cheatham's men reflected the new sense of pride that Johnston instilled within the army. A writer in the First Tennessee, Samuel Robinson, stated that "while at Dalton the Army of Tennessee was soon placed in good condition, well disciplined, and the men were better clothed and fed than they had been since the battle of Shiloh; stragglers returned, many who had been sent to the hospitals, sick or wounded, reported back for duty." Captain Henry C. Irby of the Ninth Tennessee felt the troops were "under better discipline than they had been since the battle of Perryville." Irby also wrote that as the expiration date for their enlistments neared, troops in the consolidated Sixth and Ninth Tennessee Regiment set a precedent by reenlisting for the duration of the war, a pattern which repeated itself throughout the division and the remainder of the army. This claim was challenged in the postwar period by men in Vaughan's brigade, who asserted that their brigade, not Maney's, had initiated the reenlistment drive. No matter which of Cheatham brigades was responsible, their patriotism must have gratified the high command, and particularly Cheatham. Significantly, the men often linked the restoration of Cheatham's division as one of the reasons for their improved attitude;

such was the case when Samuel Robinson noted that Johnston "soon brought every one to perfect order and discipline. Gen. Cheatham was given command of his old division, and the Tennesseans in this part of the army were again happy and contented."[29] By the time May arrived, the Yankees claimed sizeable advantages in men and materiel, but Johnston's efforts had made the Army of Tennessee a formidable foe once again.

Sherman's thrust against Johnston began the first week of May. The initial difficulty confronting the Federals was Rocky Face Ridge, a steep, twenty-mile-long summit situated to the west of Dalton. Thomas had probed half-heartedly at the ridge in February to divert attention from Sherman's Meridian campaign, but in May the Federals were determined to shove Johnston from the Dalton area. Attacking the summit directly posed a challenge, because most of the mountain was well fortified. There were openings in the ridge, including Mill Creek Gap, four miles northwest of Dalton, and Dug Gap, five miles farther south, but Sherman could expect that Johnston would defend these spots vigorously. Such was particularly the case at Mill Creek Gap, where the rail line pierced through the mountain in an area dubbed Buzzard's Roost by natives of the region. Rebels clogged culverts near the railroad and converted the creek into an artificial lake. Stiff Confederate resistance confronted George Thomas's Army of the Cumberland as it advanced along the railway.[30]

The Mill Creek Gap area was defended by the divisions of William Bate and A. P. Stewart, who occupied breastworks in the rear of the gap. Cheatham's men moved from winter quarters on May 7 and took position on the ridge. His left rested just above the railroad at Mill Creek Gap, while the rest of the line extended along Rocky Face and linked with Carter Stevenson's troops. The Federals appeared in force soon after Cheatham was established on the mountain, and his skirmish line engaged the Yankees shortly thereafter. Cheatham's men fashioned crude breastworks using rocks found on the summit, and this protection allowed them to repulse two enemy assaults on their position. Skirmishing continued, and at one point Cheatham ordered sharpshooters to drive off a Union battery. Captain James I. Hall of the Ninth Tennessee attested to the success of the sharpshooters, who were armed with deadly Whitworth rifles. "On the first fire we could see a commotion among the gunners. Next we saw them hitch their horses to the quick and before half a dozen rounds had been fired they were all in full retreat."[31] While Cheatham and the remainder of the Rebels successfully beat off Yankee attacks at the northern end of Rocky Face, the skirmishing presaged several weeks of steady contact with the enemy. The casualties from the fighting at Rocky Face were the first of many the division would suffer in the ensuing weeks.

Cheatham was compelled to dispatch portions of his command to other areas of the Rebel line threatened by Sherman. Two regiments from Strahl's brigade, the Fourth and Fifth Tennessee, were sent to reinforce some cavalry at Dug Gap. The roundabout route of ten miles, "part of it at double quick and part of it up the mountain side," thoroughly fatigued the Tennesseans, who arrived just as the Yankees tried to press their way through the gap. The two regiments deployed, poured in a heavy fire on the attackers, and compelled their withdrawal.[32]

A more significant threat emerged at Snake Creek Gap, fourteen miles south of Dalton, where a valley provided access to the town of Resaca and the nearby Oostanaula River. As Thomas and Schofield jousted with Johnston near Dalton, McPherson's Army of the Tennessee passed undetected through Snake Creek Gap on May 9. Sherman, exhilarated by McPherson's success, recognized that he could snare Johnston north of the Oostanaula, where a battle was likely to be fought on Federal terms. "I've got Joe Johnston dead!" crowed the Ohioan. He certainly had the opportunity, but about a mile west of Resaca, McPherson ran into resistance. The main force opposing him belonged to Brigadier-General James Cantey and represented the advance element of Leonidas Polk's army as it hurried from Alabama to join Johnston. Soon Cantey was reinforced by Alfred J. Vaughan's brigade from Cheatham, and McPherson was unable to capture Resaca. Daunted by the Rebel opposition, McPherson withdrew to Snake Creek Gap and camped for the night. This move allowed Johnston to rush reinforcements to the south, and Cheatham and the rest of the Army of Tennessee slipped quietly away from Rocky Face Ridge and the Dalton area.[33]

Frustrated by his inability to entrap Johnston, Sherman gathered his force to the west of Resaca and decided to strike the Confederates. Johnston successfully drew his command together, strengthened by 18,000 reinforcements from Polk's army, and awaited his enemy. Skirmishing broke out on May 13 and grew heavier as the two armies came to grips with one another. Cheatham's men arrived from Rocky Face and took position near the center of the Southern line. The Tennesseans had difficulty erecting suitable breastworks during the day, as Union artillery and rifle fire intensified. When Cheatham's skirmish line engaged their adversaries, it was evident that the months of drill around Dalton had restored the morale and confidence of the men. Johnston was impressed as he watched a portion of Vaughan's skirmish line drive some Yankees from the field and then beat off another attack by Union reinforcements. "What command is this in your front?" he asked. Vaughan proudly told the army commander, "That is the Thirteenth and One Hundred and Fifty-fourth Tennessee of my brigade, Cheatham's division." Informed that

Lieutenant-Colonel John W. Dawson was in command of the skirmish-ers, Johnston turned to Cheatham and said, "I never witnessed such a display of skill and courage, and never saw troops under such discipline and control."[34]

Despite the skill evinced by his men, the contest for Resaca cost Cheatham a number of casualties. Among the most grievous losses was Colonel Sidney Stanton of the Twenty-eighth Tennessee, who had seized his regiment's colors and rallied his men at Chickamauga. Stanton was killed, and a captain in his regiment received a terrible wound when one side of his jawbone was shot away, the ball entering his mouth. Most of the casualties were men serving on the skirmish line, but Cheatham's veterans were also subjected to punishment in areas where they did not have adequate protection. Cheatham attempted to impress upon his soldiers the necessity of building breastworks. At one point he passed along the line of the Ninth Tennessee and warned, "Boys, you'll have to stay here another day, you'd better get down in the ground as deep as you can." The soldiers who heard this pronouncement may have been fatigued, for they were not particularly conscientious about the quality of their defenses. They dug a trench in somewhat haphazard fashion and soon had cause to regret their shoddy labor, as a "fierce bombardment" of artillery and rifle fire battered in their imperfect breastworks. The troops miraculously averted serious casualties, but one man who left a knapsack and blanket outside the trench retrieved the items only to discover them "so completely riddled with bullets that he threw them both away." Not all of Cheatham's men failed to heed his advice. Members of the Fifth Tennessee worked throughout the entire night in shifts to construct solid works, prodded by the casualties they had absorbed during the daylight hours.[35]

On May 15, Hood renewed attacks against Sherman's left, and Cheatham sent Maney's brigade in the afternoon to support A. P. Stewart's division. Maney's men were in the third line but became engaged when the advance lines gave way. When the Confederates on Maney's left withdrew, Maney's brigade was compelled to fall back as well. "We came off in very bad order," one soldier noted, and some of Maney's units became disorganized as they retired through some thick woods. Stewart's men rallied, but the assault was not renewed. Maney angrily complained to Stewart that his men had been left isolated when the troops to the left of the brigade retreated. He was also anxious to renew the attack and became agitated when Stewart demurred. Stewart's reply to Maney, that he could not bear to see the brigade sacrificed, did not mollify Maney a great deal. Maney's ardor may have been inspired by two factors. He had a horse shot out from underneath him, and he apparently had fortified himself sometime during the day. "Genl. Maney felt his whisk[e]y," explained Van Buren Oldham of the Ninth Tennessee. Oldham and many of his comrades did not share Maney's enthusiasm for an engagement. "We are considered fortunate in getting out safe," Oldham wrote, and he was relieved when the brigade moved out and rejoined the remainder of Cheatham's division around midnight.[36]

The Confederates used darkness to cover their evacuation of Resaca and hurried to cross the Oostanaula, burning the bridges behind them as they withdrew southward through Calhoun. Sherman's men were not delayed significantly at the river and pursued the retreating Southerners in three columns. Johnston did not halt long at Calhoun, despite the defensive possibilities of the area, but he did devise strategy to assist his army as it retreated further south. He sent the bulk of Hardee's corps and most of the army's wagons and artillery on a good road due south to Kingston. Polk and Hood moved on a less traveled road to Cassville, some five miles east of Kingston. Johnston's main fear was that contingents from Sherman's army would move fast enough to endanger the baggage trains moving with Hardee. To impede the Union advance, Johnston ordered Cheatham's division to block the road from Calhoun some three miles above Adairsville.[37]

Adairsville was a small hamlet, its main service as a rail depot being captured by one of Cheatham's men when he termed it a "little station." As the remainder of the army moved south on May 17, Cheatham's division occupied the ground along both sides of the road from Calhoun. During the day the Tennesseans were allowed to file into the woods and rest, but were ordered to take their weapons with them. Both Cheatham and his men had to be aware of the danger inherent in their position, as Sherman's massive army struck out after Johnston. The Yankees would have liked nothing better than to slice off a part of Johnston's elusive host, especially if the slice contained a division acknowledged to be one of the finest in the Army of Tennessee.[38]

In late afternoon it began to rain, and about the same time the forward elements of Sherman's army arrived near Adairsville. Some of Cheatham's men were cooking supper, while others were just stretching out on blankets for the night, when the Yankees made their appearance. Confederate cavalry screened the Union advance, and Cheatham's men at first were "thrown into a kind of hollow square or ambuscade" to help defend the cavalry as they fell back. The Rebel horsemen fought more stubbornly once they realized that Cheatham's infantry were in support, and the Tennesseans shifted into battle line as the enemy neared. Part of Maney's brigade occupied an open field, and soon Union sharpshooters began sniping at Cheatham's men. Colonel Hume R. Feild's First and Twenty-seventh Tennessee Regiments defended an area which featured "a large octagon-shaped building with three or four smaller buildings around it." The brick house, obviously the residence of a wealthy Georgian, impressed Cheatham's men because of its unusual design and elegant furnishings. For the Yankees it represented a challenge, especially when Feild's men stationed themselves at windows from all three levels of the house and directed rifle fire at their opponents. The bluecoats moved to within a few hundred yards of Cheatham's line and also brought up artillery to shell the resisting Confederates.[39]

The cannonading which ensued unnerved some of the Tennesseans, who were acutely aware of their isolation. One disconcerted soldier was Captain William C. Flournoy, who commanded Company C of the First Tennessee. Flournoy's men occupied one of the outbuildings near the octagonal house, and when the Federal artillery opened up, the captain was convinced that his company would be annihilated. Flournoy also happened to be Feild's favorite cousin, and he sought out Feild to explain that the company's position was untenable. In spite of the family connection, Feild was implacable and remembered his own orders to hold his ground, "though it cost the entire command." He softly responded to his cousin, "William, our orders are to hold this position. Go back to your company." Flournoy complied. Nor did Feild confine his morale-boosting to members of his own family. When some of his men began running low on ammunition, Feild solicited a volunteer to retrieve some more. The volunteer was "a youth," Charles Ewing, of the First Tennessee. Aware of the danger that Ewing would face, Feild sauntered outside the house and said, "Charlie, I will stand here and draw their fire while you run."[40]

While Feild attempted to stiffen the resolve of his men, elsewhere along Cheatham's line there were troops with serious apprehensions about their immediate future. The Ninth Tennessee was posted in front of Turner's battery, and members of the regiment anticipated that the Yankees would rush for the guns. They realized that reserve forces were too far distant to be of any help and that they would have to defend Turner's guns. Turner's cannons, purchased at a terrible price at Perryville, were the pride of the division, and the infantry resolved to "save our battery." When the Federal attack failed to materialize, rumors spread that Cheatham's soldiers would launch their own attack against a Union battery. Van Buren Oldham and his compatriots found the thought of running through an open field while the Yankee gunners blasted away unappealing and were pleased when they were not directed to charge. "Happily," Oldham wrote later, "we did not become engaged although an attack was made on our right [and] left but were repulsed." Daunted perhaps by Turner's guns, the Yankees instead torched a building in front of the Confederates, and "the skirmishing was continued by its lights." As darkness deepened over the Georgia countryside, Cheatham's men debated what the next day would bring. Oldham wrote, "Some think we will fight tomorrow while others say we will continue to retreat."[41]

The soldiers remained in battle formation until midnight and could plainly hear the Federals building entrenchments. The night was extremely dark, and early on May 18 Cheatham's men began withdrawing quietly. They had suffered more casualties but had fulfilled their objective in delaying Sherman's advance. By the time of the evacuation, an entire Federal corps was in front of Cheatham. As Feild's men abandoned the octagonal house, one veteran noted sadly how warfare had scarred the handsome edifice. The exterior and many of the valuable furnishings were bullet-pocked, while blood from Feild's dead and wounded soldiers stained chairs, sofas, and carpeting. As they trudged south, the Tennesseans became scattered along the muddy roads. Drained by the constant tension and lack of sleep, bone-tired soldiers dropped out and slept along the roadside. The naps were generally of short duration, and the men soon resumed their wearying march. The confusion lessened somewhat when morning light appeared, and the men managed to move two miles below Kingston, where the division halted for a rest. The Yankees, undeterred by Cheatham's successful escape, resumed the pursuit but did not threaten the division seriously the rest of the day.[42]

At Cassville, Johnston recognized his chance to hit Sherman while the Federal army was divided. Sherman had split his force at Adairsville, sending McPherson and Thomas to the southwest after Cheatham. Schofield took the alternate route, in a southeasterly direction to Cassville, where the bulk of Johnston's army was massed. The Confederate commander planned to fall on Schofield's army while it was separated from the other Union forces. Polk would hit the Federal column from the front, while Hood would swing in from the east and crush Schofield's left. The strategy, if it went as planned, would allow the Rebels to have numerical superiority against Schofield, while Cheatham and the other units with Hardee would hold the other Federal armies back from successfully rescuing the Army of the Ohio.[43]

Johnston issued a stirring battle order on the morning of May 19 which publicized his intention to "retreat no further" and "turn on the enemy." Cheatham's men, recovered from their exertions at Adairsville, welcomed the news. Unfortunately, the plan went awry when Hood reported a large enemy force to the east. This was probably a roving band of Union cavalry, and Johnston doubted that the report was true, but Hood called off his flank movement, and eventually Johnston cancelled the attack against Schofield. The Confederates moved into a defensive position to the south and east of Cassville along a wooded ridge. The ridge commanded a broad, open valley, and Johnston felt he could use the terrain to lure Sherman into a costly assault. Hood and Polk were less confident, arguing that Federal artillery could enfilade the area where their two corps linked. At a nighttime meeting Johnston listened to their objections and reluctantly agreed to retreat to Cartersville and then cross the Etowah River.[44]

The army encamped near Allatoona for several days, where a gap through the Allatoona Mountains provided a good defensive position. Sherman refused to take the bait, abandoned his approach along the railroad, and marched his force to the south and west. His target was Dallas, a small town some fourteen miles southwest of the railroad. Johnston divined the Union commander's intentions when cavalry reported the Federal movement, and he sent his own army to counteract the move. Cheatham left camp on May 23 and marched seven miles on the Dallas Road. The next morning Cheatham's division shifted to a position near New Hope Church, a crossroads over two miles northeast of Dallas. As the day wore on, they were sent marching to the southeast but were recalled to the New Hope Church area in the afternoon and arrived around 6 P.M. Cheatham's right rested near the church, while his left occupied a ridge line covering the road into Dallas. On May 25, the Union troops appeared in force and attacked Hood's corps in the vicinity of New Hope Church. Cheatham's men were withdrawn again along the Powder Springs Road, but the next day they once more returned to New Hope Church.

Placed in between Hood's corps to the right and Polk's to the left, Cheatham's skirmish line was heavily engaged along his entire front. That night Cheatham received orders to move to the left and drive the enemy from Elsberry Ridge, a rise below New Hope Church. Members of the division were awakened at 3 A.M., marched to the left, and formed in line of battle. Strahl's and Vaughan's brigades were in front, with Maney and Wright in reserve, when the attack began at daylight. The fighting was sharp, and Vaughan was repulsed in one assault, but eventually the soldiers succeeded in driving the Federals from the ridge. Cheatham reformed his lines and connected with Bate on the left, but discovered that a three-quarter-mile gap existed on his right. When the Tennessean learned that the Federals were attempting to gain a foothold on the ridge to his right, he prolonged his line "sufficient to meet [and] check their first advance." The Yankees continued moving to Cheatham's right, and his line was in turn stretched farther and farther in that direction. By mid-afternoon Cheatham's division was extended "to the utmost," and Hardee managed to forestall additional trouble by dispatching reinforcements to complete the link between Cheatham and Polk. The skirmishing was constant throughout the day, and Cheatham's casualties mounted. The heaviest attack during the day fell on Cleburne, stationed on the right flank, but

Cheatham and other Confederate commanders were hard pressed by their Union adversaries. Even when sheltered by a hill, Cheatham's Tennesseans were in a dangerous position. Yankee shots that flew overhead ricocheted off tree branches and sometimes struck Cheatham's men. The psychological toll inflicted by the Yankee sharpshooters was summarized in a diary entry by one of Cheatham's men, who wrote, "Really there is no safety within two miles of the battle field."[45]

After Cleburne successfully fended off the Federal attack late in the day, Johnston decided the next morning to turn the Union left with a flank movement of his own. Hood's corps moved out to begin the movement, and the remainder of the army shifted to the right to cover the gap formed by Hood's absence. Cheatham's men found themselves once more near New Hope Church, where they remained, even though Hood never launched an attack. Sherman soon decided to abandon his thrust at Dallas and began moving his huge army eastward to the railroad line. Over the next several days, the two sides continued sparring, as both Sherman and Johnston slid to the east. By June 2 the other divisions assigned to Cheatham's left had been withdrawn, and the Tennesseans anchored the left end of the Rebel line. The final days of May and early ones of June found Cheatham's men continuing their familiar skirmishing with various Yankee units, as Johnston moved into a new defensive position. Cheatham's men were exhausted by their week-long ordeal. When Alfred Tyler Fielder rejoined his comrades in the Twelfth Tennessee on May 30, he discovered that they were "much fatigued, having marched, fortified and skirmished with the enemy for the last 23 days." For many of Cheatham's men, the contest for Dallas blurred into a montage of marching, erecting defenses, and sharpshooting, but some units did experience events which later seemed particularly memorable. Such was the case for members of the Sixth Tennessee Regiment, which at one point was posted in a graveyard and forced to repel several Federal assaults upon the cemetery. Soldiers in the regiment felt they were never "so suggestively situated" as on this occasion, where "they fought and died . . . amid the tombs of a generation that had not dreamed of civil war."[46]

The attrition within Cheatham's ranks begun at Rocky Face Ridge and Resaca continued unabated during the New Hope Church fighting. Unlike the previous campaigns, where the bloodletting was done in major battles, the losses in northern Georgia were inflicted at a different rate. Men died or were wounded every day, but aside from the battle of Elsberry Ridge, most of Cheatham's casualties were the result of skirmishing. The picket line was a deadly spot to be assigned, but even there, the casualties ensued in relatively random fashion. Still, weeks of constant contact with the enemy produced a long casualty list. Cheatham later reported that the New Hope Church engagements cost him 185 men killed and wounded, "among them many valuable officers." One of the latter was Colonel Jonathan J. Lamb of the Fifth Tennessee, who was mortally wounded as he directed the operations of his picket line. A lieutenant who was with Lamb recalled hearing the jubilant cry of a Yankee marksman shouting, "I hit him! I hit him!" as Lamb fell. Another casualty was Captain John Harris, Vaughan's staff officer who had so bitterly criticized the loss of some boots and gloves by a female acquaintance in Atlanta the previous November. At Elsberry Ridge, Harris was hit in the heart as he tried to coordinate a movement between Vaughan's and Strahl's brigades. The fire was too heavy to permit the Rebels to retrieve the officer's body until June 2, by which time the remains were so decomposed that Harris was buried on the field, far from his Memphis home.[47]

Cheatham withdrew from the New Hope Church area after dark on June 4 and followed Cleburne's troops southeastward to near Pine Mountain, a salient held by Bate's division. Two days later the Tennesseans fell back half a mile to cover a road to Marietta. For over a week there was a relative lull in the action as Sherman gathered his army astride the railroad. The morning of June 14, Hardee, Polk, and Johnston rode up Pine Mountain to inspect the terrain. A group coalesced around the Confederate commanders, and an alert Union artillery officer fired upon the gathering. The first shell struck a tree, which compelled the generals and men to scatter, but before Polk could reach safety, he was killed outright by a shell which mangled his body. One of Cheatham's artillery officers described the event — "a 10 [pounder] shell passing through his body breaking both arms"—a line which conveyed the gruesome nature of Polk's death as well as a grudging admiration for the chance Union shot.[48]

Historian Thomas Connelly maintains that Polk's death was a severe blow, not because Polk was an inspired corps commander, but because the army lost his experience and positive impact on morale.[49] Polk was beloved by the rank and file, and his death severed another link with the early days of the war, when the Confederates could stretch a giant chain across the Mississippi River and confidently expect it to impede the Yankees. Cheatham and many of his men had been with Polk since the start of the war, at Columbus, and they reacted sorrowfully to news of his death. Cheatham's chief of staff, James D. Porter, wrote that the men "had discovered at an early day that [Polk] was insensible to fear and was just and generous, qualities which secured for him the love and confidence of officers and men." W. J. Worsham of the Nineteenth Tennessee felt Polk's death created "a loss not to be easily filled. Gen. Polk was a brave officer, a good man and a Christian soldier." A. T. Fielder of the Twelfth Tennessee wrote that it could be "said of him that a great and good and brave man has fallen." Sam Watkins of the First Tennessee regarded Polk as "a favorite with the army," since soldiers associated with the cleric "loved and honored him," and were convinced that when Polk held a position, "we knew and felt that 'all was well.'"[50] Cheatham's own response to Polk's death is unrecorded, but surely he shared the grief of his veterans. The Union shell shattered forever the alliance forged between Cheatham and Polk, an alliance which had served them both well and which had frustrated Braxton Bragg. Curiously, Cheatham's postwar account of this period omits any reference to Polk's death, perhaps because the memory was still painful years after the event.[51]

Although Cheatham and his men mourned Polk, the war intruded on their thoughts soon afterwards. The day after Polk was killed, Sherman pushed forward past Pine Mountain, and heavier fighting resumed. Federal skirmishers pressed against Cheatham's line, and his entire division was occupied for the better part of two days. The Tennesseans fell back four miles toward Marietta, where their Yankee pursuers attempted on June 17 to dislodge Cheatham's skirmishers but were "driven back from the rifle pits." That evening the Federals made a vigorous attack on the Rebel left, and Cheatham received orders to move rapidly to support the threatened sector. Cheatham extended his line one brigade front to Cleburne's left and helped beat off an attack by Union cavalry and artillery. The next day the division shifted to within two and a half miles of Marietta and bivouacked. In the late afternoon on June 19, Cheatham dispatched Vaughan's brigade to Cleburne's assistance, and the next day the entire command went into position to Cleburne's left.[52]

Two days after Cheatham completed his shift, Johnston sent Hood from the right of the army to the far left to counter another Federal flank movement. Hood attacked Joseph Hooker's bluecoats along the Powder Springs Road but was bloodily repulsed on June 22. Despite the rebuff, Johnston's defensive position was quite formidable. The key to that position was Kennesaw Mountain, four miles west of Marietta. Two and a half miles long, Big Kennesaw rose to seven hundred feet, while connected Little Kennesaw afforded a splendid view of the approaching Union host. The mountain proper was occupied by Polk's command, temporarily led by Major-General William W. Loring. To the left of Loring was Hardee. Hardee's line was at a right angle to Loring's corps on the mountain and ran along a spur ridge which extended from the summit. Hood's corps was on the far left as the Confederate line arced back in a semicircle.[53]

Until the armies reached Kennesaw Mountain, the fighting in northern Georgia had followed a uniform pattern established early in the campaign. Sherman tested Johnston, occasionally accepted a fight, then would sidle one or more of his armies around the Rebels. Johnston conversely attempted to make Sherman pay a high price for the ground that was yielded by selecting areas well suited for defense. Up to this point in the campaign, neither commander was totally pleased with the results. Sherman had been unable to come to grips with Johnston in a decisive action, and Johnston had not successfully brought the bulk of his army against a fraction of Sherman's behemoth. At Kennesaw Mountain, Sherman opted for another strategy. He reasoned that the butternuts had weakened their line to assist Hood during the latter's June 22 fight. Sherman guessed that the weak link resided in the center, along Hardee's front, and he hoped that the success at Missionary Ridge could be duplicated by a similar assault. Incessant rain had dampened the spirits of both armies, and Sherman perhaps sought to shake his men from their lethargy with a bold gamble. The Union commander devised a two-pronged assault to strike both Loring and Hardee. The main blow was aimed at Cheatham's and Cleburne's divisions, and was left to George Thomas.[54]

Cheatham's position was vulnerable in large measure because of an angle along his line, where his right brigades under Vaughan and Maney linked. Vaughan's brigade extended from the right of Cheatham's line, where it connected with Cleburne, to the angle, and faced to the northwest. Four companies of Maney's First and Twenty-seventh (Consolidated) Tennessee Regiment were aligned in the same direction as Vaughan's troops, but the remainder of his regiments faced to the southwest as the angle bent back to the left. The line had been charted out by engineers during the night, and when Cheatham moved into position on June 19, also after dark, he discovered the presence of the salient. Cheatham later wrote that he left an interval of 150 yards to Maney's left, the distance "to a ridge running at an angle of 45° to the one occupied by Cleburne and my right." On this ridge Cheatham posted the remainder of his force, brigades under John C. Carter (who led Marcus Wright's former troops) and Otho Strahl. To protect the salient, Cheatham placed two batteries of artillery to Maney's left, so that they commanded the approach to the angle and the valley below. These eight guns were manned by Alabama and Florida artillerists under the overall direction of Major Llewellyn Hoxton. Cheatham also posted two more cannons to the right of the angle, with Lieutenant Luke E. Wright in charge, while one section of Turner's Mississippi battery was positioned to Vaughan's right.[55]

The potential weakness of the salient "cost General Cheatham nights of anxiety for its safety," as one of his veterans recounted, and the Tennessean did not confine his efforts at strengthening it to artillery placement. He also sent a force of skirmishers several hundred yards to the front and tried to control a commanding height across the valley. Cheatham recognized the importance of the rise, and when his skirmishers were shoved from the hill, they received reinforcements from Vaughan's brigade. This force too was dislodged from the ridge, and despite help from one of Maney's regiments, Cheatham's men were unable to reclaim the eminence. They instead dug rifle pits and established a strong skirmish line at the bottom of the slope below the salient. As Cheatham feared, Union artillery appeared on the crest across the valley and opened up a devastating fire. The Yankee shells fell thickest among Vaughan's troops and Colonel Hume Feild's First and Twenty-seventh Tennessee Regiment. The heavy barrage dismayed Cheatham. "I soon became satisfied that if the enemy should increase [and] continue their artillery fire that my position in the salient would become untenable," Cheatham wrote. His alternatives appeared to include either attacking once again across the valley, or withdrawing several hundred yards to eliminate the angle. Cheatham eventually decided that the Federals were trying to discover the location of any Confederate batteries and had no idea of the effect of their fire. He decided to maintain his position but was still concerned about the safety of his line. To offset further damage from the Yankee artillery, Cheatham ordered his men to strengthen the works as much as possible.[56]

The Tennesseans were kept busy obeying Cheatham's directives in the days prior to the Union attack. They constructed elaborate entrenchments, some dug so deep that men could stand straight up without being exposed to enemy fire. Strong dirt embankments were thrown up in front of the trenches, with logs placed on top and openings carved out for the marksmen. Cheatham's men felled trees to create abatis and cheveaux-de-frise and wired these together to retard Union progress. Cheatham also had the ten guns nearest the salient camouflaged with brush, and strictly forbade these masked guns from replying when Yankee batteries once again probed the Rebel fortifications. The defensive improvements allayed some of Cheatham's fears, and the Union barrages were less destructive after the works were completed. By the time Thomas received his orders to attack, Cheatham's soldiers were firmly entrenched.[57]

A bright sunrise on June 27 promised that a hot day was in store. The men in Feild's regiment ate breakfast, then arranged blankets across poles to provide a welcome bit of shade. Some withdrew to the wagons in the rear to wash their clothes, while a heavy detail was serving on the skirmish line. That left roughly 180 of Feild's men in the trenches when Cheatham came to inspect the salient. The Tennessean warned his men to expect an attack, and his prediction was confirmed when Union artillery cut loose with a bombardment that lasted, according to Cheatham, for forty minutes. The shelling ceased abruptly, and by 9 A.M. Federal troops could be seen across the valley. Feild's veterans removed the poles and blankets, and with the remainder of the troops along the angle, braced themselves for the assault. The Confederates could see seven lines of bluecoats in the distance. The Yankees marched down a hill, across the valley, and then drove in Cheatham's skirmish line, taking prisoner some of the Tennesseans who waited too long to make their escape. The Federals began to push harder as they ascended the slope, and despite the irregular terrain, they were an impressive sight as they charged.[58]

The force confronting Cheatham and Cleburne consisted of several divisions of the Army of the Cumberland, one under John Newton advancing against Vaughan's right and Cleburne, while another under Jefferson C. Davis headed for the salient. The men detailed to hit Cheatham at the angle were mostly Ohioans and Illinois troops and represented two brigades from Davis's division. The troops in these brigades, led by Colonels Daniel McCook and J. G. Mitchell, sounded a cheer as they neared Cheatham's position. Cheatham ordered his men to patiently hold their fire until the Yankees were within sixty yards. Suddenly a "yell of defiance" erupted from the Rebels, along with a murderous wave of musketry. Cheatham wrote later that the advance column was almost completely wiped out by the initial volley, "the remainder being driven in confusion into the ranks of the assaulting mass." A soldier in the First Tennessee recalled a Union officer leading the attack turned his back to the Confederates to exhort his troops. The Federal was in mid-sentence when the first Rebel volley rang out, killing the officer and "more than half the men he was leading." Both Northern and Southern sources note that the obstacles fashioned by Cheatham's troops slowed the bluecoats as they neared the works. A member of Vaughan's Eleventh Tennessee recalled that the Yankee assaulting party came up with their guns uncapped, intending to carry the defenses with their bayonets, when they encountered the dense abatis the Rebels had constructed. At this point Cheatham's troops unleashed their fire, and the Yankees "halted and staggered with considerable confusion."[59]

Despite their losses, the Union troops continued their dangerous task. Cheatham's men marveled at the perseverance of their foes. One Confederate private wrote that the bluecoats ascended to their death "as coolly as if they were automatic or wooden men," while another Southerner felt that never "did men march into the very jaws of death with a firmer tread and with more determination than did the Federals to this attack."[60] This determination was apparent to Cheatham, who was stationed with the batteries to the left of the salient. The remaining Union lines came up, prodded by their persistent officers, when Cheatham ordered his secreted guns to open up. Cheatham noted later that his cannon blasts struck the

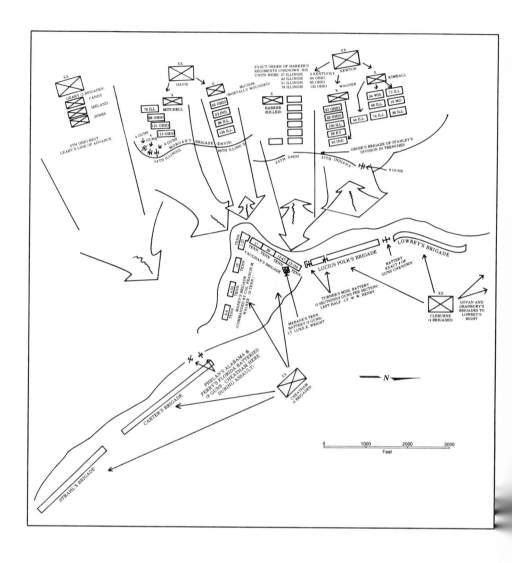

Map 4. Cheatham Hill near Kennesaw Mountain, Ga.—June 27, 1864

Union columns "from within 50 y[ar]ds of my works to their rear which was still in the valley below." Lieutenant Wright's two guns along Vaughan's front also came into action, as did the two left fieldpieces from Turner's battery. Gaping holes formed in the Union ranks, and Yankees who survived the carnage later attested to the savage impact of the shells and canister which swept the slope. "The concussion from the enemy's cannon[s] nearly unjointed my neck and the heat from them burnt my face," wrote an officer in the Third Kentucky Regiment.[61]

Colonel Mitchell's brigade was shredded by Cheatham's defenders as it struggled up the incline and was hit by the artillery fire of the eight guns to the left of the salient. As his men neared the Rebels works, Mitchell later reported, "the fire, which had before been very heavy, now became terrific," and the brigade was "subjected to an enfilading fire of artillery and musketry." According to Cheatham, when his cannons opend up, the Federal rear and center was thrown "into the utmost confusion." Artillerist Melancthon Smith believed that Cheatham's decision to keep his batteries concealed was a decisive factor in the battle. Smith wrote that the Yankees "were surprised . . . at receiving fire from these guns, which did great execution and contributed no little to the repulse."[62]

The Federal casualties were horrendous along both Cheatham's and Cleburne's fronts but were particularly bad in McCook's and Mitchell's brigades as they attacked the salient. Two Ohio regiments lost half their force, and one of these lost 153 men in twenty minutes. McCook himself was mortally wounded near the Confederate works, and the colonel who replaced him was killed five minutes later by a shot through the heart. The lead ranks of the assaulting party melted away as the Tennesseans continued their withering fire. One of McCook's Illinois regiments had nearly 60 men killed within a few moments, and the officer contingent of several Federal units was nearly extinguished. One impetuous Yankee officer leading the third line was mounted on a white horse, which attracted a heavy volley from Feild's men. "He turns his horse to the rear and is seen no more," recalled one of the Tennesseans, but the infantry pressed their attack.[63]

By sheer weight of numbers, the Yankees managed to break through in small groups to the works, where vicious combat erupted. Some of Cheatham's men swung their rifles like clubs to repel their foes, while others hurled stones at the onrushing enemy. At least twice, Yankees planted their colors on Cheatham's breastworks, and a fierce struggle ensued for control of the flags. One Union color bearer placed his standard on the works, killed a Confederate officer who grappled for the staff, then was "riddled with bullets from a dozen" Rebel guns. "The enemy were mowed down in heaps," reported a correspondent for a Southern news-

Cheatham's men repel the Federal assaults upon the "Dead Angle" in this scene, taken from a picture drawn by a Confederate participant. Note the flag of the First Tennessee Regiment, which features the inverted cannons that were placed on the banner after the unit helped overrun a Union battery at Perryville. (Dennis Kelly. Kennesaw Mountain National Battlefield Park)

paper, adding that "a few of those nearest the works, including the color bearer of the 27th Illinois, surrendered."[64]

As the Federals continued their desperate effort, Cheatham ordered men from the Sixth and Ninth Tennessee Regiment to move to the point of the angle and assist their comrades in the First and Twenty-seventh Tennessee. The reinforcements worked their way under the braces and added their firepower to that already being directed against the Yankees. The clatter of rifle and artillery fire deafened the Tennesseans, who relied on the recoil of their rifles to let them know the guns had discharged. The combination of soaring temperatures and repetitious firing overheated the muskets. An officer with the Ninth Tennessee discovered that the brisk, rapid fire clogged the rifles of his men when melted lead deposits developed, the lead "pared off from the minie ball by the grooves of our rifles." When he ordered his men to reverse their guns after shooting, "small round pellets of melted lead poured out of their gun barrels on the ground." It was impossible to miss hitting a Yankee, several of Cheatham's men later contended. One remembered that "the enemy were crowded so thickly that a shot from our men could not fail to hit somebody." When one of the companies shifted to the right, a private delayed the movement momentarily by telling his supervising officer, "Just wait, Captain, till I kill this Yankee."[65]

After Vaughan's men beat back the Federals in their front, they joined in the concentrated fire before the salient. With two brigades and his artillery, Cheatham directed a close-range fire that the Yankees could not withstand. The Federals scattered, many trampling fallen comrades in their haste to flee. Cheatham's men poured more shots into the enemy, and the "terrific cannonade" continued unabated. Some bluecoats vainly sought cover behind trees, while others established themselves under the crest of a hill fifty yards from the salient. Here they laboriously scooped up dirt and formed crude protection. Within an hour the Federals constructed a line which afforded some safety. Until then, one Ohio officer considered it "almost sure death to take your face out of the dust."[66]

As the attack petered out, Cheatham's worn defenders paused to catch their breath and inspect the damage they had inflicted. A few foolhardy soldiers were struck down when they mounted the breastworks to get a better view of their handiwork. Cheatham and his men were awestruck by the sight before them. Union casualties crowned the area in front of the hinge, which was known thereafter as "Dead Angle." Writing some years after the conflict, one of Cheatham's soldiers in the Ninth Tennessee recalled: "A frightful and disgusting scene of death and destruction was presented to our view. During all of the four years of the war I do not remember ever to have seen the ground so completely strewn with dead bodies." Captain James Hall added that the expanse in front of his regiment was "literally blue with Yankees." An officer in Vaughan's brigade recalled seeing eleven bodies clustered around a large tree and felt the vast numbers of dead "impressed us anew with the awful horrors of war."[67]

Casualty figures became a matter of dispute after the war. General Sherman placed the number of Union casualties at 3,000, but Johnston and artillerist Melancthon Smith estimated the number to be twice that. "The loss of the enemy must be great," wrote Cheatham, and he calculated that there were at least 350 slain near Dead Angle alone. The day after the assault, Union general Jefferson C. Davis tabulated the casualties for his division at 824. Of these, 131 were listed as killed, and undoubtedly some of those listed as wounded died later at Federal field hospitals. On the Confederate side, Hardee's corps lost but 206 men, with Cheatham's division counting 26 dead and 169 wounded or captured. Among the injured was Colonel Feild, who temporarily lost consciousness when a bullet grazed his head. A newspaper reported that one of Cheatham's men lost his life due to Yankee treachery. Not long after the attack was repulsed, a wounded Union soldier cried out "in great agony" for a Rebel to bring him a drink of water. One of the Tennesseans climbed upon the breastworks, and hollered to the Yankees: "I am going to take one of your wounded men a drink of water, don't shoot at me." The Confederate took his canteen to the Federal soldier, who was dying, allowed the man to drink, then started back for the Confederate lines. A dozen Federals fired at the Southern Samaritan, and he was killed instantly. Outraged by this perfidy, Cheatham's men nearest the scene unleashed a volley which allegedly killed every one of the Northerners who had fired.[68]

Despite the sordid scene described above, and as intent as both armies were on destroying one another during the attack, after the battle ended, both acknowledged the efforts of the other. An Illinois captain who felt that Union troops never "fought better than on that day" would have found that Cheatham's men agreed with the assessment.[69] A veteran with the Sixth Tennessee likened the attack to "ocean waves driven by a hurricane . . . sweeping on as if by irresistible impulse," and doubted if "any other troops on earth could have made such a charge." "The assault was brilliant," wrote an officer in the Eleventh Tennessee, and a soldier in the First Tennessee recalled that the troops "fought bravely, and it is evident that nothing but the unflinching courage of the defenders saved the place from capture." Even the *Chattanooga Daily Rebel* (being published for the time being in Griffin, Georgia), which referred to the Union victims as "unhappy wretches," conceded that "as a general thing, their charge was bold, steady and creditable."[70] The Yankees likewise respected the valiant defense made along the Southern line. One Ohioan remembered Cheatham's works as being "heavily fortified and defended with all the appliances of the most skillful engineering." Another officer admitted that the "valor displayed by the defense calls for the highest admiration . . . the staying and successfully repelling repeated attacks shows a determination only equaled by that displayed on the Federal side." Having seen large numbers of his men sacrificed in the assault, Col. Henry B. Banning of the 121st Ohio Regiment wrote, "We fought the flower of the Southern army, being Cheatham's division, of Hardee's corps."[71]

Despite the repulse, Cheatham's line was still endangered. The next two days and nights the Yankees scraped out a stronger line along the shielded crest and burrowed slowly toward Cheatham's position. Cheatham did not feel he could safely dislodge the Northerners from the ridge, especially when the Yankees dug rifle pits and commenced a "continuous and annoying fire" on his position. "The close proximity of the enemy rendered the utmost vigilance necessary," Cheatham wrote, and sleep came hard as both sides anticipated an attack. Cheatham ordered his men to be alert, and fire "at the least sound of approach," as any hesitation "would have placed a charging column in our works."[72] Cheatham's men manufactured turpentine-soaked cotton balls, which they lit and threw toward the Federal lines after dark. The balls illuminated an area temporarily and sometimes fell among the huddled Union troops. Less dangerous items were exchanged as well, the Southerners hurling "corn dodgers" while the Yankees retaliated with hardtack. Yankee ingenuity came to the fore when the Federals rigged mirrors to their gun butts. The mirrors protruded above the trenches, and enabled Union marksmen to squeeze off a round at a curious Confederate without exposing themselves. Other Yankees began tunneling toward the salient in hopes that they could plant explosives to blow it up. The Confederates apparently knew of the mine, for a paper in Atlanta revealed its existence while the army still held the Kennesaw line. The newspaper correspondent, for one, was confident that Cheatham could deal with the threat. Cheatham was depicted as "the last man to sit down quietly and wait for [the Federals] to finish a work of this description," and the paper warned that "we may expect to hear of some one being hurt should the report prove correct."[73]

Sporadic fire rang out in this atmosphere of mutual suspicion, and a particularly sharp firefight broke out the night of June 29. Cheatham's men in the salient were provoked by a sound, perhaps a shout from a Federal, and their response was a volley which rippled along the rest of the command and was taken up by Cleburne's men. Even the artillery joined in. The Yankees, for their part, were convinced that the Confederate volley presaged an attack on their line, and they returned the fire. Despite the severity of the fire, only a few of Cheatham's men were wounded during the alarm. Morning showed that the ammunition expended by the Rebels during the false alarm was not totally wasted. The action began just as the bluecoats were drawing supplies, and to the rear of their lines lay a host of dead animals and overturned wagons.[74] At least one other Confederate command was delighted by the jittery trigger fingers displayed by the Tennesseans along the Kennesaw front. Earlier in the Atlanta campaign, men from General James Cantey's Alabama brigade had been accused of wasting ammunition on lightning bugs. According to the rumors, Cantey's men were nervous, mistakenly took the firefly flashes for the flash of guns, and opened fire. Cheatham's men, never ones to shy away from a good joke, ribbed the Alabamians mercilessly. When any of the Alabama troops were in earshot, one of Cheatham's men would loudly proclaim that General Cheatham had gone to Atlanta, "to get blacking to put on the tails of the lightning bugs to keep Cant[e]y's men from wasting their ammunition." The joke was reversed after the June 29 firefight. When the Tennesseans tried to tease the Alabamians, the latter retorted that General Cheatham had indeed gone to Atlanta, "to buy candles for his babies who were afraid to stay in the dark."[75]

The night alarm followed on the heels of a rare break in the fighting. The blazing June sun had taken its toll on the unburied Federal bodies, which quickly took on what Melancthon Smith described as "a revolting appearance, as black as negroes [and] enormously swollen." Both sides agreed with Cheatham that the bodies were "becoming extremely offensive," and earlier on June 29 a truce was arranged to allow the Yankees to inter their dead. They were buried not far from the Rebel line, and as the details went about their work some of Cheatham's men tried to gauge the number of dead they found in the expanse. It was during this interval that Cheatham formed his estimate of the number of Federals killed near Dead Angle. Others in the division, including Maney and Colonel George Gordon of the Eleventh Tennessee, also attempted to calculate the Union casualty rate. Gordon finally concluded that 800 Federals had been killed, a number he reached after conversing with a Union officer during the truce.[76]

Gordon was not the only Rebel who took advantage of the burial truce, for as the grisly process went on, both armies relaxed, and the soldiers fraternized. Men who had tried to kill one another just moments before perched on their respective breastworks and chatted. Some veterans of both armies circulated between the lines and struck up conversations. Coffee and tobacco were traded. Generals Cheatham and Hindman were among those fraternizing, although Cheatham was not identifiable as a high-ranking officer. One of Cheatham's veterans recalled that Frank was "never better pleased than when passing himself off as one of the boys," and his informal attire fooled one Yankee, an Irishman, who assumed that the man before him was a private. The Federal brashly poked Cheatham in the ribs and asked "Old Frank" for a drink from his canteen. When Cheatham obliged, the Irishman felt so friendly that he tried to "put his arms around the General's neck." At this point, Colonel Horace Rice of the Twenty-ninth Tennessee felt obliged to reveal Cheatham's identity. "A forty-pound shot thrown in their midst would not have produced a greater sensation than did this announcement," recalled an eyewitness to the proceedings. "Instantly all eyes were fixed upon the old hero," added the veteran, but after their momentary astonishment a crowd of Northerners gathered and presented autograph books for Cheatham and Hindman to sign.[77]

A soldier from Illinois, Lyman S. Widney, soon afterwards wrote his parents and described the two Southern generals. "Cheatham looked very unlike [what] I supposed a Rebel Major General commanding a corps would look." Cheatham was a divisional commander, but Widney's description nonetheless caught his casual look: "He wore nothing but a rough pair of grey pants tucked under the tops of an unpolished pair of boots, a blue flannel shirt and rough felt hat completed his attire. He had neither coat or vest and was without any . . . manner to indicate his rank." A Confederate source adds that Cheatham was contentedly smoking a short pipe during the truce. Widney compiled an account of his wartime service after the conflict, and even in the postwar era he was struck by Cheatham's appearance during the truce. "He looked as if he had made his headquarters in the ditch with his men," Widney wrote, which in Cheatham's case may have been correct. Widney seems to have been more impressed with Hindman, partly because he looked appropriately dressed, with "an abundance of gold lace and cord." The Illinois veteran also recounted that Cheatham commented to the Yankees, "It is useless for you to keep up this contest. We don't expect to whip you, and you can't whip us, so you will after awhile get tired of the war and let us alone." Whether these were Cheatham's actual sentiments or false bravado for the benefit of his assembled adversaries is impossible to judge. Given the timing of his statement, which was delivered during the burial truce, Cheatham may well have meant what he said.[78]

When the armistice ended, the deadly waiting game ensued. Sherman eventually broke the deadlock by shifting one of his armies, and Johnston was compelled to abandon the Kennesaw line. Cheatham's division quietly evacuated their works the night of July 2 and headed for Atlanta.[79] The defense at Kennesaw further enhanced the reputations of both Cheatham and his men, though the reverse did not stall Sherman or daunt his

Though Cheatham donned his general's uniform for this photograph, on some occasions he was attired much more casually. During the truce after the fighting at Kennesaw Mountain, some Union soldiers assumed Cheatham was a private until a Rebel officer revealed his identity. (Eleanor S. Brockenbrough Library. The Museum of the Confederacy. Richmond, Virginia)

resolve. The fight at Dead Angle remained a popular reminiscence among Cheatham's men, and the June 27 assault is the best-documented action of Cheatham's division for the entire war. Though they left the area within a few days, Cheatham and his men bestowed a lasting name to the geographical region where they fought. Long after the last gun in the Civil War had cooled, visitors to the Kennesaw area were directed to "Cheatham Hill," where the Tennesseans had fended off the Union attacks. Today, Cheatham Hill is a part of Kennesaw Mountain National Battlefield Park and contains some of the best-preserved trenches and earthworks to be found in any Civil War park.[80]

Chapter 8

The Fight for Atlanta

Despite the glory they had won along the Kennesaw line, some of Cheatham's troops may have welcomed the withdrawal toward Marietta. The close proximity of the two forces along the Kennesaw front made it impossible to do much but stay low and avoid the enemy sharpshooters. When the deadlock ended, the respite, temporary as it may have been, was appreciated.[1] The Yankees pursued, as always, and kept in close contact with Johnston's retreating army. Cheatham's men threw up fortifications whenever they halted, kept a good many of their number on watch, and were subjected to occasional Union artillery probes.

On July 4, 1864, Cheatham's division was at Vining's Station, below Marietta, where each brigade was instructed to construct breastworks and then remain in battle formation. After superintending the building of his entrenchments, General Alfred J. Vaughan retired with several staff officers to the shade of a large oak tree. A Virginian by birth, Vaughan had graduated from the Virginia Military Academy in 1851. Before the war he had bounced around somewhat, working as a surveyor in California before settling down to farm in Mississippi. When the conflict began, Vaughan raised a company in his adopted state but could not secure arms for them. He eventually joined a Tennessee company as a captain and was soon after elected lieutenant-colonel of the Thirteenth Tennessee Regiment. He distinguished himself in a number of engagements and had never been injured despite the fact that he had had eight horses shot out from underneath him. Commissioned a brigadier to rank from the previous November, Vaughan had led Preston Smith's former brigade after the latter's death at Chickamauga. At Vining's Station, Vaughan and his staff rested and ate the "scanty rations" which were available. He was in the process of trying to light his pipe tobacco with a "sunglass" when a Federal shell tore through the air and exploded just as it struck Vaughan's foot. Colonel Beverly L. Dyer was standing above Vaughan when the shell hit, and gravel blew up and ripped nearly all his clothing off. Dyer involuntarily started to run for cover behind a tree until he realized that

166

Brigade commander Alfred J. Vaughan served with distinction in Cheatham's
division until July 1864, when a Federal shell severely wounded the
Mississippian. (Library of Congress)

he was not seriously wounded. Vaughan was not so fortunate, one foot
being blown off while the other leg bore a deep cut to the bone. Soon
surgeons from Vaughan's brigade and the rest of the division arrived to
bind up his wounds, administer morphine, and provide some medicinal
whiskey.[2]

The surgeons were not the only parties to provide liquid comfort to
Vaughan. As Vaughan related later, "In going to the hospital I passed

by Gen. Cheatham's headquarters, who, hearing that I was wounded, came out to sympathize with me, and suggested that as I was looking very pale he thought that some stimulant would do me good, and gave me a stiff drink." Vaughan, somewhat refreshed, then passed Hardee's headquarters. Hardee also commented on Vaughan's paleness and poured out a big drink. The scene was repeated at General Johnston's headquarters, and Vaughan readily accepted the apple brandy that Johnston proffered. Thus fortified, Vaughan proceeded to pass out and had no further recollection of events until he awoke the next morning in Atlanta.[3]

Vaughan's plight later took on something of a comedic air when he recounted the incident after the war, but at the time it could not have been very humorous to Cheatham or the members of Vaughan's brigade. Cheatham had lost a skilled and valuable officer, and Vaughan's men were deprived of his leadership for the rest of the war. Nevertheless, whatever ruminations Cheatham or Vaughan's men may have had about the situation were quickly interrupted. The same day that Vaughan was wounded, his brigade and Maney's troops marched for several miles in the afternoon. They halted in battle line, then waited as Cheatham threw out skirmishers to contest an alleged enemy threat. The threat failed to materialize, and the next day a long march was made to the Chattahoochee River. By this time, at least one soldier in Maney's brigade was beginning to weary of the marches and occasional skirmishes. "It seems that our Division is the cavalry for the army," complained Van Buren Oldham, "and our Brigade has all the fighting to do for our Div[ision]." Some of Maney's men took advantage of a brief interlude in the fighting to bathe in the Chattahoochee, but this pleasant diversion ended when Federal artillery came up. Soon afterward, Alfred T. Fielder wrote, the guns were "thundering away and the pickets were pecking away at each other as usual."[4]

Over the next two weeks, the division shifted position to the north and northwest of Atlanta, and Cheatham's men slipped into their familiar routines of marching and fortifying. Continual contact with the Federals generated skirmishes, but fraternization between the pickets occasionally served to arrange impromptu cease-fires. During some of these intervals the Yankees obligingly warned their Rebel counterparts when to expect a bombardment. Despite the troop movements and sporadic firefights, some of Cheatham's men managed to keep abreast of significant activity at army headquarters. One alert diarist noted on July 13 that "Gen. Bragg is here his business I know not." The *Chattanooga Daily Rebel* understood that Bragg had been sent by President Davis to bear important orders and report on the condition of the army. The newspaper correspondent was certain that Bragg's report would "be satisfactory," since the army was "in good condition, ready and willing to move upon the enemy."[5] While Bragg's reappearance with the army generated interest, what followed on the heels of his visit rocked Cheatham and his men. On July 18, word spread through the army that General Johnston had been ordered to relinquish command of the Army of Tennessee to John Bell Hood. Johnston's removal had taken place the previous evening, after Jefferson Davis weighed reports from Bragg which strongly implied that Johnston was preparing to yield Atlanta without a fight.

Davis wrestled with the decision to replace Johnston for some time, but it is apparent that the campaign in Georgia did not proceed as Davis would have liked. Davis had suggested in 1863 that an offensive be made from Dalton, and he grew increasingly irked as Johnston disregarded the advice and headed his army in the opposite direction. Hood eventually accentuated Davis's fears by directing a steady stream of correspondence to Richmond with disquieting overtones. In letters to Bragg, Davis, and Seddon, Hood intimated that Johnston had no intention of fighting and hinted that another officer might be more receptive to a forward movement. Whether Hood's correspondence was motivated more by patriotism or by personal ambition is difficult to ascertain. By mid-July, at least, Hood was positioning himself as a possible successor, perhaps with Bragg's assistance. Davis did not relish the idea of changing commanders at a critical time, but his long-standing dislike for Johnston and the latter's taciturnity regarding future plans helped allay the president's reservations. Hood's most recent biographer, Richard M. McMurry, feels Davis was justified in relieving Johnston, especially since the evacuation of Atlanta without a struggle would have carried tremendous psychological, political, and economic weight.[6]

The history of the Army of Tennessee is a litany of controversies, and Johnston's dismissal in the summer of 1864 was one of the most volatile the army endured. The decision generated heated discussion at the time, and the quarrel rages to this day. Complicating matters is the fact that each principal participant had supporters in 1864, in the postwar period, and among later historians. What is more, Davis, Hood, and Johnston all wrote memoirs after the war to justify their conduct, and how the story is presented depends to a great extent on whether a writer champions one of the three men.

Davis and Bragg may well have concluded that Johnston was unlikely to defend Atlanta, a conclusion Johnston naturally disagreed with in the postwar vendetta, but one factor they may have minimized in their deliberations was the impact on army morale if Johnston was relieved. Perhaps Davis felt that the army would follow a more offensive-minded commander such as Hood. Bragg did not always gauge the army's temperament correctly during his own stint as its head, and he may have felt that the soldiers would fight regardless of who was in charge. Even if Bragg knew that thousands of men were loyal to Johnston, he may have disregarded the information, since it contrasted with the opinion many of the same men had held of Bragg himself. In any event, one of the clear points in an otherwise muddled picture was the manner in which Cheatham's soldiers responded to Davis's decision.

Johnston's removal dismayed a large portion of the army. The *Chattanooga Daily Rebel* cautioned moderation, arguing that partisan action on behalf of either Johnston or Davis "ought to be deprecated and avoided by patriotic men," especially given the close proximity of the Northern foe. While acknowledging that Johnston "enjoys the love and confidence of the army," the paper praised Hood's military qualifications and referred to him as "one of the most successful officers in the Confederacy." As to the reasons for Johnston's removal, the paper assumed that Davis had valid motives for his actions and maintained, "When there is a difference in policy, the General must succumb to the Executive, else there could be no harmony, no responsibility, no settled policy."[7]

The sensible assessment tendered by the newspaper did little to quell the upheaval within the army. Not everyone could be as objective as the editor of the paper, and many in the army loudly decried Johnston's removal. "It was equivalent to taking from the army half of its effective force," wrote one of W. H. T. Walker's officers. Nowhere was the dismay manifested more than in Cheatham's division. Perhaps more than any other unit in the army, Cheatham's division had cause to rue Johnston's departure. The Tennesseans were loyal to Johnston in large measure because he restored the division under Cheatham, an action they overwhelmingly approved. In addition, they felt that under Johnston's stewardship the army had recovered from the low period after Missionary Ridge. They felt his strategy ceded ground but were confident that "Old Joe" knew what he was doing, "would assume the aggressive at the right time, and would be successful when he did."[8]

Several of Cheatham's soldiers enjoyed the considerable advantage of hindsight when they later recorded their reactions to Johnston's dismissal. By the end of the war, it was readily apparent that Hood's leadership had not accomplished what Davis had envisioned when he replaced Johnston. Many of Cheatham's veterans considered the campaign from Dalton to the outskirts of Atlanta to be a successful one, especially compared to Hood's bloody failures at Franklin and Nashville later in the war. Most of Cheatham's men accepted Johnston's postwar assertion that the Army of Tennessee did not have enough manpower to challenge Sherman successfully in a pitched battle or one where Sherman could bring all his numbers to bear. Some, in their quest to single out one key moment when the tide of war turned against the Confederacy, selected Johnston's dismissal as the decisive act which sealed their fate. The dismissal "produced a depressing effect upon all the Tennessee troops," wrote one, while another described Johnston as "that prince of Generals and soldiers . . . a man who always outgeneraled his opponent, [and] retained the love and confidence of his officers and men under all circumstances."[9] An officer in the Fifth Tennessee recalled that the men reacted to news of Johnston's dismissal "with sad faces and downcast eyes." They realized that his cautious policy "in the face of overwhelming numbers" would be replaced by offensives, "for which our weakness in numbers rendered us totally unprepared." According to the officer, the "excellent morale of the army was destroyed and dread of desperate fighting and consequent disaster settled down on the hearts of all."[10] In a similar vein, Captain James I. Hall described Johnston's removal as "the worst thing that could have been done." Hall touched on a recurrent theme when he described Johnston as "the only commander we had ever had in whose ability and generalship the army had unlimited confidence. I do not remember that I ever heard any order or movement of General Johnston unfavorably criti-ci[z]ed by his men."[11]

Several postwar sources refer to Hood's accession as the army's "death knell," but it is erroneous to assume that Cheatham's men waited until the end of the war to vent their displeasure at Richmond's meddling. Diaries and letters written during the war attest to the negative reaction which coursed through Cheatham's division when word of Johnston's removal was first received. Alfred Tyler Fielder of the Twelfth Tennessee wrote in his diary that "Johnston was the most popular Gen. that was ever in command of this department and his removal gives great dissatisfaction amongst the army, all appear to be sorry to part with him." In a letter written less than two weeks after the event, an officer in Strahl's brigade wrote that the announcement "caused the greatest gloom that has ever been known to pervade this army." The most vehement condemnation is to be found in a diary entry by Van Buren Oldham of the Ninth Tennessee. Oldham related that he and his comrades were "completely dumbfounded" by the news, which provoked a feeling of general unrest. He also echoed the theme which carried into the postwar period, that "the men were satisfied that their Genl. knew best and wherever he [led] they were willing to follow."[12]

Significantly, Oldham cast a critical eye at Hood, whose "fighting qualities are demonstrated by his total disregard of human sacrifice." The soldier felt that the timing of the decision could not have been worse, coming as it did on the verge of a battle. Oldham and the other members of Cheatham's division could not understand why Johnston had been re-moved. He spoke for the Tennesseans in general when he concluded that Johnston had "been the object of gross injustices" and noted darkly that "Genl. Bragg [and] Prest. Davis are alone responsible for the evil which is likely to result."[13] The dismay expressed by Oldham and his fellow Ten-nesseans may not have been universally repeated throughout the army, but thousands of men did mourn Johnston's leave-taking.

Cheatham himself shared the shock and displeasure registered by the men under his command. His journal chronicling the campaign from Dalton to Atlanta ends with Johnston's removal and Hood's accession, but Cheatham evidently intended to comment further on army opera-tions. In the last line of his journal he wrote that he could not close, "in justice to my troops and the commanding Genl., without a [comment] as to their condition when he relinquished command."[14] Historical specu-lation is a risky business, but in this case there is no doubt that Cheatham intended to praise Johnston and the manner in which the campaign was conducted. Cheatham was indebted to Johnston for reuniting him with his Tennessee regiments, an action which placed Cheatham firmly in Johnston's group of supporters. Cheatham's cordial relationship with Johnston contrasted sharply with his dealings with the two other princi-pal commanders of the army. His relations with Bragg were character-ized by mutual hatred, and in the postwar period Cheatham was at log-gerheads with Hood as well. The pro-Johnston sentiments of another high-ranking Tennessean, A. P. Stewart, are the same as Cheatham's. In an 1886 publication, Stewart described Johnston as "the only commander of that army whom both *men* and *officers* were disposed to trust and con-fide in without reserve." Stewart added that the soldiers shared a personal affection for Johnston, relied upon his judgement, and felt that when the Virginian ordered them into action it was done "to some purpose."[15]

It is almost impossible to judge the extent of demoralization within the ranks following Johnston's dismissal. Certainly many of Cheatham's men were disheartened. There are reports of soldiers weeping unashamedly when they heard the news, and Sam Watkins relates that five men on the picket line crossed over to the enemy lines from the First Tennessee Regi-ment when they learned of the situation.[16] Yet most of Cheatham's men remained with their regiments. By 1864 they were veterans, acclimated to army life. They may have idolized Johnston and regretted his depar-ture, but aside from complaining about the decision, most were as com-mitted to the war effort as ever. The Tennesseans tried to "reconcile our-selves to the change," as one correspondent related, and some tried, with a certain degree of apprehension, to divine the intentions of their new commander.[17]

That commander, John Bell Hood, was only thirty-three when he replaced Johnston. Despite his youth, he was one of the few realistic successors Davis had available. Hardee was a possibility, but had refused the post once. In addition, Bragg apparently believed that Hardee favored Johnston's strategy, which Davis interpreted as another negative factor. Polk was in his grave, and no officers with the Army of Northern Virginia were seriously discussed. Bragg was discredited, Beauregard was on the outs with Davis, and none of the Army of Tennessee's other corps or divisional commanders were given serious consideration. By a process of elimination, Davis arrived at Hood as the logical successor. Hood understood his mandate for aggressive action, a policy he exhibited in both his personal and professional life. Cheatham's new commander was a gambler; a famous anecdote relates that Hood once bet $2,500 in a poker game without holding a single pair. Personally courageous, Hood had his left arm immobilized at Gettysburg, and he was again wounded at Chickamauga, necessitating the amputation of his right leg. He expected his men to risk the same sacrifices, and at Antietam his First Texas Regiment obliged him by losing 82 percent of its members. Some of Cheatham's men, well aware of Hood's reputation for headlong fury, feared its consequences. One of Cheatham's soldiers noted sardonically that "Genl. Hood will probably teach the army other tactics than fortifying."[18]

Hood's promotion created a vacancy for command of his corps. At least one of Cheatham's acquaintances hoped that Cheatham would be selected to the post. Writing from Macon, S. R. Cockrill praised the efforts of Cheatham's division during the campaign. While harboring the hope that Cheatham would rise to corps command, Cockrill reminded Cheatham that "Genl. B[raxton] B[ragg] would make no effort for such a result." With that in mind, Cockrill warned Cheatham not to feel too disappointed if he failed to win promotion, "as it is not attributable to the want of merit."[19] Cockrill's wish came true when Hood conferred with Hardee and Stewart, then appointed Cheatham to temporary command of his former corps. Hood made the appointment, even though Cheatham "did not desire it," in part because Hardee recommended Cheatham as the best officer at Hood's disposal. Cheatham's reluctance probably stemmed from the fact that the promotion was garnered at a terrible price, Johnston's removal, and he may have regretted leaving his division when a battle was imminent. Despite his misgivings, Cheatham was persuaded to accept the temporary position, and George Maney replaced him as head of the Tennessee division.[20]

Hood was determined to strike the Federals and did not have to look far to find them. Sherman had crossed the Chattahoochee, paused to rest his troops, then began swinging his force across the north of Atlanta and to the southeast. His intention was to sever the Georgia Railroad, the line which connected Atlanta with Decatur and provided access to the Carolinas and Virginia. In the course of this movement, Sherman had to cross several waterways, including Peachtree Creek, a stream some five miles north of Atlanta which ran from east to west before joining the Chattahoochee. McPherson's Army of the Tennessee was the southern edge of Sherman's force and was astride the railroad near Stone Mountain. Schofield's center Army of the Ohio was en route to Decatur, while Thomas and the Army of the Cumberland formed the right of Sherman's combine. Thomas had perhaps the most difficult assignment, as his army had to contend with both the northern and southern branches of Peachtree Creek in order to keep contact with the other elements of Sherman's force.[21]

Johnston had planned to attack the Federals in the vicinity of Peachtree Creek, and Hood adopted the strategy as well. It was an inviting opportunity. A two-mile gap existed between Thomas and Schofield, and the former was strung out along a six-mile-wide front. On the morning of July 20, Hood met with his three corps commanders. Hood directed Cheatham, the right of the Southern army, to reconnoiter, gain an easily defensible position, then interpose his corps to block Schofield and McPherson. Hardee, the center corps, was to attack Thomas, beginning with the divisions on his right. As the action rolled to the left, A. P. Stewart's corps would join in the assault when Hardee was fully engaged. If all went well, the isolated Army of the Cumberland would be destroyed as it was compressed along the creek and pinned on the southern bank of the Chattahoochee.[22]

Bad luck plagued the plan from the outset, much of it the result of Cheatham's fumbling. As preparations for the attack were being finalized, cavalryman Joseph Wheeler warned that McPherson was advancing along the Georgia Railroad from the east at a rapid pace. To counter the threat, Hood decided to extend Cheatham one division length to the right, so that infantry would cover the railway. To keep his force connected, Hood then ordered both Hardee and Stewart to move their lines by a half division front to the right "to close the interval." Hood perhaps felt that Cheatham's inexperience in manipulating a corps would be minimized by his assignment, which was not designed to involve combat. In spite of this, Cheatham erred, moving his corps two miles to the right in search of a suitable defensive position. Cheatham's movement was a start-and-stop affair, as the corps moved, halted long enough to shift into battle position, then lurched again to the right. Cheatham was on the left of his line for at least part of the day, where his attention was riveted on skirmishing in that vicinity. He later worried that his long, tenuous line in the center would not be able to sustain itself in case of an attack. With such concerns for other portions of his line, Cheatham may not have closely supervised the divisional leaders who led the shift to the right. As it was, his corps never did extend fully to the railroad, and Cleburne's division from Hardee's corps was eventually dispatched to contest McPherson's advance.[23]

The best explanation for Cheatham's actions lies in the fact that he was a novice at handling a corps, and two of his divisional commanders were also new at their posts. It is highly likely that Cheatham was determined to avoid any mistakes which would mar his debut as a corps commander. His anxiety was heightened by the knowledge that his corps confronted both Schofield and McPherson and was the only infantry force protecting the eastern approaches to the city. Cheatham's caution is reflected in several notes he dispatched to Wheeler during the afternoon and early evening. These messages conveyed the news that Cheatham was jittery about the safety of his line and felt it was vulnerable to a Union thrust.[24]

Preoccupied with his own command, Cheatham probably did not understand the impact his movements had on the remainder of the army. He snarled the timing of the Confederate attack, because Hardee felt compelled to remain linked with Cheatham's left. This was a frustrating development, especially since the resulting march was lengthier than anything Hardee or Stewart had anticipated. A member of Vaughan's brigade wrote that they moved a mile to the right before they went into battle line, and units in Stewart's corps extended their line two miles to stay in contact with Hardee.[25] The result of the delays was that the assault was not launched as promptly as Hood desired, and the chance for success diminished as the day wore on.

Stewart attacked prematurely, in part because Hardee did not launch his assault until 4 P.M. Even then, not all of Hardee's divisions made full contact with the enemy. Cheatham's division under Maney had the best success at coming to grips with the Yankees, which was a somewhat dubious distinction, given the circumstances. Before they went into the fight, not all of the Tennesseans were confident of their prospects. One diarist related that some of the men were reluctant to abandon the comparative safety of their breastworks. The reticence some of the soldiers felt may have stemmed from fears of the anticipated reception. Their fears proved well founded when they discovered Thomas's men posted in strong works. The division advanced in two lines, Vaughan's and Carter's lead brigades in the lead, with Maney and Strahl in support. Skirmishers pressed their Union counterparts back, but as the Tennesseans neared the main Federal line, they were struck by a barrage of artillery and small arms fire. The

Rebels pressed to within less than one hundred yards of the Federal works but eventually halted and took cover behind the crest of a hill, using trees and other natural obstacles to shield themselves. The Tennesseans then exchanged fire with their adversaries for several hours as night darkened the Georgia countryside. The soldiers awaited orders to storm the works, but at 10 P.M. came a withdrawal back to the main line of trenches and breastworks.[26]

The Tennesseans managed to bring their dead and wounded off, with the bulk of the casualties concentrated in Vaughan's and Carter's lead brigades. A soldier in the Twelfth and Forty-seventh Tennessee Regiment acknowledged that "in some parts of the line our men took a good many prisoners, also killing and wounding a number," but he concluded that the contest did not yield the desired results. Captain Alfred Tyler Fielder wrote, "My opinion is we did not make it pay as the enemy fought mostly behind fortifications."[27]

Hood was not deterred by the abortive Peachtree action and withdrew into a new line of works just outside of Atlanta. On the night of July 21, he unveiled a bold plan directed against Sherman's left, under McPherson. Hood originally proposed that Hardee move with his corps via Decatur and fall upon McPherson's rear. At a second council, Hood modified the plan somewhat, owing to several potential difficulties. As Cheatham later explained, "the lateness of the hour, the distance to be travelled, and the condition of the troops" entered into the deliberations. Such considerations carried special weight for Cleburne's troops, who spent July 21 jousting with the Federals. Worn from their march and subsequent daylong fight, they needed time to disengage and fall back to Atlanta. Hardee was expected to make a night march of over fifteen miles, a distance which would be even greater for Cleburne's division. Faced with these factors, Hood apparently gave Hardee leeway to move by way of Cobb's Mill and strike the flank as well as the rear of McPherson, which would provide a shorter traveling distance for some of his units. Hood envisioned that Cheatham could take up the assault once Hardee had hammered McPherson from the rear and flank.[28]

Hood's plan had merit. McPherson's left was relatively unprotected, and as Cheatham knew from Perryville, such a situation provided opportunities for success. The major flaw in the strategy was that it failed to take into account the condition of the troops. Despite Cheatham's later contention that the high command did give thought to this aspect, Hood and his subordinates did not recognize the extent to which Hardee's men would have their endurance tested. The men in Cheatham's division under Maney had slept only three hours before they were roused on July 21 and marched through the city to the southeast of Atlanta. The march drained many of the soldiers, who became progressively more fatigued as the day wore on. Some became overheated and fell out, the day being oppressively hot, and fell by the wayside to try to sleep. This generally was an unsuccessful quest, as Federal artillery crews managed to disturb the slumber of Cheatham's worn soldiers. Those Tennesseans able to keep up with the march sometimes saw a portion of Atlanta's fortifications manned by the Georgia militia. One of Cheatham's veterans alert enough to note the presence of the state troops was not reassured by the sight, since the militia was composed of "old men & boys." By mid-afternoon the division had replaced a cavalry screen and began to dig entrenchments, a habitual practice by this stage of the campaign. The labor further weakened the men, even though they were ordered to send their entrenching tools to the wagons before the job was completed.[29]

As exhausted as the Tennesseans were, at least they did not have to fight the enemy during the day, as did their counterparts in Cleburne's division. The army commanders apparently relied on the resiliency of the men, for Maney's soldiers were awakened in the early morning hours of July 22 and sent south and then east on a forced night march. Although thousands trudged wearily on the dusty roads, others repeated the previous day's performance and fell out. One of Maney's veterans confessed that he "never saw as much straggling from our Corps since we have been moving." The logistical difficulties associated with the march completely doomed Hood's original intention to have Hardee attack at dawn, and it was not until noon that the corps was aligned for an assault.[30]

The ensuing battle of Atlanta was a fierce struggle, and Hood's hopes were ultimately thwarted more by a coincidence than by any failure on the part of his army. As the Union line tightened around the eastern approaches to Atlanta, a portion of McPherson's army was crowded out of position. These troops — one entire division and a brigade from a second division — were therefore ordered to move to the west to support McPherson's left flank. The Federal movement was under way when Hardee's men came up, and the Yankees merely halted and turned to the left (or south) to await the Rebel onslaught. Their fortuitous placement ruined Confederate hopes that Hardee would be able to shatter McPherson's rear and inspire panic in the Union army. Hardee was compelled to assault an enemy force whose presence he had not suspected and which was placed advantageously to meet his attack. Nor was that the only unforseen hurdle for Hardee's corps. Woods, dense undergrowth, and a large mill pond hampered the deployment of his troops, especially on the right of his line. Worse yet, Confederates on the left of the line soon discovered that the Federal flank facing west toward Atlanta bent back in an arc to the south. Far from being unprotected, this sector of the Yankee line was heavily fortified and protected by a double set of breastworks.[31]

Hardee's attack, when it finally got under way, ran into considerable trouble. His right divisions under Walker and Bate found themselves confronting a triple line of Union infantry. The two Rebel divisions were unable to make much headway against such stout resistance and were eventually repulsed. The Southern effort in this area was not assisted by the sudden death of Cheatham's nemesis, W. H. T. Walker. Walker was shot from his horse in the battle, killed by a Federal picket as the Georgian surveyed the terrain his troops were about to cross. While Walker's and Bate's units were roughly handled, the Confederates fared better on the left of Hardee's line. Cleburne's soldiers punched through a gap in the Federal alignment, and his skirmishers killed the talented McPherson when the Union general rode unwittingly into their range. Some of Cleburne's regiments struck the Yankee breastworks and rebounded, but insistent pressure forced the Federals to fall back along much of Cleburne's front.[32]

While the movements of three of Hardee's four divisions are easily verified, such is not the case with Cheatham's division under Maney because there are no reports by Maney or any other officer in the division in the *Official Records*. Some scholars believe that this division moved in conjunction with Cleburne, serving as a reserve force to the Irishman's division. These writers assume that the Tennesseans swung to the far left of the Rebel line and advanced west of the modern-day Flat Shoals Road. This view is corroborated by Captain Fielder of the Twelfth Tennessee, whose diary entry notes that Maney's men went into action "a few minutes" after Cleburne became engaged. In addition, one of Cleburne's brigadiers, Mark Lowrey, reported that his battle formation was disrupted by a portion of Maney's command. According to Lowrey, Maney's force was supposed to remain 300 yards to his rear, but instead moved forward and passed through Lowrey's ranks.[33]

A second, more plausible theory is that Maney was originally assigned to aid the attack on the right but shifted later because of broken terrain. Captain James Hall of the Ninth Tennessee Regiment reminisced that the division moved in battle formation "for more than a mile through a dense undergrowth of bushes and brambles. We were stopped by an impassable creek and mill pond before reaching our point of attack. Finding it impossible to go any farther, we were withdrawn and double-quicked to the extreme left." The marching and countermarching tired the soldiers, according to Hall, who recalled that Cleburne's troops "had captured the first line of the enemy's works while we had been engaged in our ineffectual movement on the right." This theory is supported by several Union reports, which imply that the Tennesseans did not assault until late in the afternoon. In fact, evidence would indicate that Maney's division did not strike the Federals until around 5 P.M., several long hours after the remainder of Hardee's corps was engaged.[34]

Determining when Maney's men first assaulted is far more confusing than ascertaining their subsequent actions on the battlefield. Once committed, the Tennesseans attacked with a ferocity which belied their weariness. Moving forward in conjunction with Cleburne's troops, Maney's men struck the breastworks from the southwest. Both Confederate and Union sources agree that the fighting which took place in and around the works was brutally violent. Maney's men must have known what was in store as they prepared to advance, for they passed by casualties from earlier fighting. One of these was a member of Cleburne's command kneeling behind a tree stump with his gun pointed at the enemy. Captain Hall and his comrades discovered that the man was dead, killed instantly by a ball which smashed through his forehead and into his brain. Accustomed to seeing battlefield deaths, Hall nonetheless was moved by the sight, mainly because of its oddity. As he recalled, it "was one of the rare instances in which I had observed that a man kept the same position after death that he had taken while living." Many of Maney's men were destined to meet the same fate just a short time after viewing the dead trooper. They began taking casualties even before they completed their alignment, and as they surged forward, the Yankees unloaded a "fierce discharge of small arms and artillery" from their works. Captain Hall remembered looking down the line of his regiment as they charged and saw men "dropping by the scores."[35]

When the Tennesseans crashed into the entrenchments, they began returning the deadly greeting which the Yankees had been doling out. A member of Vaughan's brigade (now commanded temporarily by Colonel Michael Magevney of the 154th Tennessee) recalled that two regiments leaped over the embankment, led by a color bearer of the Twelfth Tennessee, who hurtled onto the works crying, "Boys, follow the flag of your country!" These two regiments began pouring in a fire which enfiladed the Federal right flank, while another pair of regiments swung around the left flank and opened up. "The enemy commenced retreating up their works," wrote one officer, and to escape the galling fire the Union soldiers "would jump first on one side of the works and then on the other," a tactic which was futile since the Tennesseans were also on both sides. The Federals resisted bravely, firing as they retreated, but in some spots where they huddled together, Maney's men "mowed them down with awful havoc . . . filling their ditches with their dead and wounded." Occasionally squads of Union soldiers threw down their weapons and ran forward to surrender.[36]

Maney's attack compelled the Federals to withdraw several hundred yards, and they established a new line on Bald Hill, an eminence which Cleburne's men had tried unsuccessfully to reclaim the day before. One Federal officer later praised the ability of his troops to change position, since it was accomplished "under a heavy fire of musketry, and of grape and canister, and in the face of a rapidly advancing force of fresh troops, composed of probably the enemy's best fighting men — Cheatham's division." Major-General Frank Blair of the Federal Seventeenth Corps reported on the savage fighting as the contestants battled to control Bald Hill. According to Blair, Maney's Tennesseans "made a determined and resolute attack, advancing up to our breast-works on the crest of the hill, planted their flags side by side with ours, and fought hand-to-hand until it grew so dark that nothing could be seen but the flash of the guns from the opposite side of the works." Union Brigadier Mortimer Leggett, whose name later attached itself to the hill which his men defended, also noted the furious nature of the action. Leggett's report indicates that "the sword, the bayonet, and even the fist, were freely and effectively used, and the enemy repulsed with a slaughter I never before witnessed." A Confederate in the Sixth Tennessee wrote that the men "swept forward to the assault like a storm on the sea," and recalled the fighting as "a series of desperate hand-to-hand contests." Weakened by their losses, the Tennesseans were unable to break through the new Federal line on Bald (or Leggett) Hill, and the action died out sometime after nightfall.[37]

Before the day was over, the battle became a two-pronged Confederate effort which included Hood's former corps under Cheatham. Hood was with Cheatham in the morning and afternoon waiting for Hardee to initiate the fray. When the battle was joined on McPherson's left, Hood held off committing Cheatham's corps until he feared the enemy might concentrate on Hardee. Hood then ordered Cheatham forward, as he later reported, "to create a diversion." If a diversion was all he desired, Hood got a great deal more than he bargained for. Cheatham attacked with practically all the troops at his disposal and launched a full-scale assault. Hood later maintained that he ordered Cheatham to attack at 3 P.M., but many reports indicate that Southern line officers did not receive their orders to attack until around 4 P.M.[38] One of the unresolved questions about Atlanta, and one not likely to be settled at this late date, is whether Cheatham was tardy in attacking. Some modern historians have accepted the charge, and it may be true that Cheatham failed at his administrative task of getting orders to the appropriate personnel very rapidly. One alternative idea is that Hood later erred in his calculation as to when he ordered Cheatham into action.[39] In all likelihood, officers received their orders at different times and may not have always recorded the hour of attack with any great precision. Under such circumstances, it is impossible to judge whether Cheatham obeyed Hood's orders to assault with alacrity or not.

Cheatham delivered his blow with three divisions, under the respective commands of Henry D. Clayton, John C. Brown, and Carter Stevenson. Some units were ordered to keep the sun to their backs as they advanced, and at least one brigade commander felt that the instructions he received were insufficient. Colonel Abda Johnson complained that he "knew nothing of the ground over which I was to move nor of the position of the enemy or how other troops were to move or [when they would] attack." Brigade commander Arthur M. Manigault reminisced that his orders were fairly simple, at least in tone: "Move on until we found the enemy, and then to attack and drive him out of his works, which we were to hold until further orders." Clayton and Brown attacked eastward along the Georgia Railroad against the Union Fifteenth Corps. Ironically, some of Cheatham's troops had a good idea of their ultimate objective, for they had occupied works on either side of the railway roughly a mile distant until the early morning hours. The Federals occupied the works once the Southerners withdrew, reversing it in places and shifting obstructions to the western side of the trench.[40]

Cheatham's troops, subjected to ever-increasing punishment, advanced quickly through the undulating terrain. They achieved their greatest success along the railroad, pressing back an advance line before striking the main set of breastworks. Men from Manigault's two South Carolina regiments clambered up to the second floor of a house and delivered several withering volleys before the brigade bounded over the Union works. The assault broke several Ohio regiments, whose members fled before the onslaught. Continuing on, Cheatham's center division seized an unfinished dwelling and four twenty-pound guns. Cheatham's attack lost steam when Sherman massed artillery from Schofield's army and began to pound the Rebel intruders. Soon afterward, a strong Union counterattack from two directions compelled Manigault and other Confederate brigades to retire. The order to retreat dismayed some of the Southerners, who were convinced that the hard-won territory could be held. Despite their reluctance, they withdrew, abandoning the four cannons and a good number of their dead. Stevenson, operating on the right of Cheatham's corps, fared no better in his assault on Bald Hill. He achieved little success before he was driven back by Blair's Seventeenth Corps, the same organization which was soon attacked by Cleburne and Maney in the 5 P.M. assault.[41]

As night deepened, it was apparent that Hood's plan to destroy Sherman's left had been unsuccessful. One of Hardee's postwar defenders blamed Hood for failing to coordinate the attacks between Hardee and

Cheatham, a charge echoed by more recent historians as well. By not doing so, Hood allowed the Northerners to repel each Confederate corps in turn. The result, despite the obvious sacrifices made in each corps, was a high casualty list. The Federals tabulated their losses at 3,722 men, while Hood's army suffered at least 10,000 casualties. By waiting at least three hours to hurl Cheatham into action, Hood condemned his army to a disappointing outcome. The thirteen artillery pieces and eighteen stand of colors Hood claimed were evidence of his soldiers' brave efforts but were poor compensation for the devastating losses they endured.[42]

Hood may have failed to coordinate the attacks for several reasons. He apparently expected Hardee alone to break McPherson's army, then use Cheatham and Stewart to complete the victory. Hood may have been puzzled when Hardee was unable to shove McPherson's host to the northwest as planned. He never acknowledged, even in the postwar period, the pivotal role of the Union Sixteenth Corps, which was in a position unanticipated by any of the Confederate high command. Communication between Hardee and Hood was probably sporadic and unreliable. Even had the Confederates unified their efforts, there is no guarantee that they would have crumpled McPherson's army. Hardee's attack was not delivered in one blow, and some officers in Cheatham's corps apparently knew little of what was expected of them. Both corps encountered problems with the terrain; and other difficulties, including the failure of regiments and brigades to remain united, were familiar battlefield woes. Hood bears responsibility if he indeed planned to coordinate the assaults, but his subordinates, including Cheatham, may not have been able to deliver the well-timed blow Hood envisioned. The one concrete lesson that Atlanta should have taught the Confederate officers was that attacking an enemy entrenched behind breastworks was a costly proposition. Unfortunately, they seemed not to learn this point despite their heavy losses.

Cheatham's temporary appointment as corps commander ended on July 27, when Stephen Dill Lee arrived to take charge of Hood's old corps. Feelings about Lee's appointment were varied. One officer wrote that many in the army felt "General Cheatham, the rough and ready fighter," should have been promoted to permanent corps command. If Cheatham felt any disappointment at Lee's promotion, he masked his feelings when he resumed command of his division. According to one of his men, the "Tennesseans were glad to get their old commander again, the General Cheatham seemed equally as glad, for there was an affection between he and his men that was sweet to enjoy.[43]

The joy Cheatham felt when he returned to the division must have been tempered when he scanned the casualty list. Though the losses were not as severe as those in Cleburne's division, the Tennesseans nonetheless suffered heavily. Cheatham discovered that 120 of his men were dead and an additional 499 were wounded. Particularly damaging was the loss in Cheatham's officer corps. A member of Strahl's staff mourned the dead in a letter to Dr. Charles Quintard: "In walking through the hospitals on the morning after the fight, I could not restrain my tears," wrote John Henry Marsh. "Many of the noblest, and most gallant spirits in the Army of Tenn[essee] have been sent off," and Marsh rued the loss of many close friends in the officer class. At least eighteen officers were killed, including three regimental commanders.[44] The most grievous loss among the dead was Colonel Francis M. Walker of the Nineteenth Tennessee, who had commanded Maney's brigade during the assault on Dead Angle. Walker went into the Atlanta engagement knowing that he was about to be promoted to brigadier-general on the basis of his efforts at Kennesaw Mountain. Walker's imminent promotion prompted another colonel in the regiment to offer to lead the unit into action. Walker declined, remarking that he had not yet been assigned to any particular brigade. When the regiment went forward, Walker was in the forefront, and his "sword swept in glittering circles above his head" as he cheered his men onward. An observer saw Walker as he was struck by a fatal shot near the enemy works, the blow forcing him to "sink upon one knee with his head resting upon the other as if in prayer." The cruel nature of the loss was made even worse by the arrival the next day of Walker's brigadier's commission.[45]

While Colonel Walker's tragic demise was loudly lamented, the attrition rate in the division extended to both officers and the rank and file. The loss of capable leaders grew in corresponding ratio to the casualties suffered by the officer corps. The loss of such men throughout the Atlanta campaign necessitated repeated changes in command. While the men who replaced the fallen leaders were generally brave and competent, it is doubtful that they always possessed the same qualities as their wounded or deceased predecessors. Nor did the soldiers escape the consequences of the grueling campaign. From Rocky Face Ridge through the battle of Atlanta, Cheatham's division lost 259 men and officers killed, with an additional 1,476 wounded. This total represented a good share of the division's strength, especially since there was little hope of replenishing the losses through recruitment. The shrinking numbers on the divisional rolls reflected themselves in each company and regiment. In one company of the 154th Tennessee, twenty-seven of twenty-nine men were either killed or wounded between May 7 and July 22. Nine of that number were slain, and two others permanently disabled. The diminishing size of Cheatham's division was a phenomenon by no means confined to the Tennesseans. The leadership vacuum and manpower shortage was a serious problem within the remainder of the army. One symptom of the lack of capable high-ranking officers manifested itself when General W. H. T. Walker's division was broken up, and his three brigades distributed among the other divisions in Hardee's corps. The brigade under States Rights Gist was placed in Cheatham's command.[46]

Despite the difficulties, the bloodletting continued as Sherman and Hood came to grips again on July 28. Within a few days of the July 22 fight, Sherman began a vast counterclockwise shift from the eastern approaches of Atlanta to the west. His aim was to sever the last rail connection which fed into Atlanta, the Macon and Western Railroad, which tied the city with Macon and Savannah. Intelligence of the movement was received soon enough by Cheatham's men, who discovered on July 27 that the enemy was gone from their front. "We were soon scattered over the ground looking at their works [and] the effects of the battle," noted one of Cheatham's soldiers, who added that the Yankees had buried the Confederate dead in several trenches. A grisly series of exhumations apparently took place, and "several bodies were recognized and reburied by their friends."[47] Hood recognized the danger inherent in Sherman's western slide and sent General Lee out along the Lick Skillet Road to control a key intersection near a Methodist church. When Lee arrived, he found the bluecoats already in possession of the two roads, and perhaps to prove his combat mettle, he sent his corps forward in an attack. A furious action around Ezra Church failed to provide the Confederates with any advantage, and Lee wore out his units with his ill-advised sortie. Stewart came up with a portion of his command and sent Walthall's division into the fray. Walthall achieved no more success than Lee's troops had before him, and by the time the fighting diminished in the late afternoon, the Rebels suffered at least 5,000 casualties while inflicting but a fraction of that number.[48]

Alexander P. Stewart was one of the Southerners sidelined by a wound received at Ezra Church. The effects of being struck in the forehead by a spent bullet idled the corps commander for a fortnight. Once Hood learned of Stewart's injury, he summoned Cheatham to army headquarters. There, Cheatham was provided with another temporary corps assignment, this time filling in for Stewart until the latter recovered. Cheatham went to work the next morning, repositioning Stewart's corps in a new network of trenches to the left of the Lick Skillet Road. There they worked feverishly to strengthen the works, fearing that the bluecoats would assault before the fortifications were completed. The massive attack Stewart's men anticipated never came, but the Yankees still managed to make things difficult. Frequent cannonading and incessant skirmishing made late July and early August a hot time in more than one sense. The long hours of nighttime labor and the accurate fire of the Federal

Alexander P. Stewart began the war as an artillery major, and finished as a lieutenant-general. His postwar career included a stint as chancellor of the University of Mississippi. (The Valentine Museum, Richmond, Virginia)

sharpshooters took their toll. As Walthall confessed, his "brigades grew perceptibly weaker from day to day."[49]

Cheatham's men, deprived of their divisional leader only two days after their reunion, contended with the same conditions Walthall reported. There were no major engagements until the end of August, but the month offered little relief to Cheatham's veterans. During the weeks following the scrap at Ezra Church, Sherman attempted to extend his right to reach Hood's indispensable rail line. Hood countered the move by shoving his left out from the city, west of the railroad and parallel to the tracks until they curved eastward below the rail junction at East Point. By this time, the Confederates had engineered a formidable and intricate series of trenches which covered most of Atlanta. Hardee's corps moved from the area they occupied after the battle of Atlanta to the left flank near East Point. Lee held the center, while Cheatham (with Stewart's corps) and the Georgia militia filled a line which stretched across the northern part of the city. Unwilling to risk a rebuff against the works, Sherman imported siege guns from Chattanooga and began a heavy bombardment of the city.[50]

Back in early July, one correspondent in the First Tennessee Regiment had predicted with wry humor that the "peace and quietude" of Atlanta's citizens would be upset by the army's retrograde movement. His prediction came true, and Atlanta's inhabitants had their tranquility disturbed even more as Yankee artillerists began dismantling large sections of the city with their shellfire. Even before the heavy artillery was employed, one soldier in the Ninth Tennessee noted that the "few citizens left behind are woefully scared." Many of Atlanta's residents fled while an escape route was available; those who remained found themselves in a town under siege. The capricious horrors of war came home to noncombatants as well as military personnel as Sherman tightened his grip on Atlanta and sought to destroy its usefulness. According to a jounal entry by Melancthon Smith, the enemy shelling "was almost a daily occurrence" which did little damage to the soldiers but succeeded in "injuring many women & children." The army did what it could to bolster the spirits of the civilians. Cheatham's entire division, for instance, sacrificed one day's rations for "the indigent families of Atlanta" on July 26.[51]

While civilians might be expected to feel pressured by being thrust into a wartime scene, evidence suggests that Cheatham's men also began to feel the strain of their long ordeal. Some openly questioned Hood's tactics and pondered the consequences of further engagements. When the results of the fighting around Ezra Church became known, the irascible Van Buren Oldham of the Ninth Tennessee confided to his diary that "the plan Genl. Hood has adopted of charging breastworks against superior numbers will soon leave him without an army if continued as heretofore." President Davis shared Oldham's concern about the high toll in lives and warned Hood not to attack Yankee entrenchments if it could be avoided. The fact that Hood probably did not know much about Stephen D. Lee's activities may not have mattered to Oldham and his comrades, who found that their fears after Johnston's removal were being realized. They blamed Hood's aggressiveness for the losses since his accession and probably gave little consideration to assessing the strategic fix Hood was in when he took command of the army.[52]

A contributing factor in their exasperation was the miserable daily routine they were forced to endure. Cheatham's soldiers found that their lives revolved around a form of warfare which none of them could have foreseen the year before, much less at the time of their enlistment. Elements of boredom and random danger interspersed, and even the weather assumed oversize proportions when rain dampened the trenches or the Georgia heat baked the same ditches later. Lack of mobility was a restriction which irritated Cheatham's men. "It is really disagreeable here," Oldham wrote on one occasion and lamented that he and his compatriots could not go outside the trenches without being exposed to enemy fire. Soldiers on the picket line vented their frustrations by banging away at their adversaries. On one such tour of duty, Oldham fired over one hundred rounds and choked two of three rifles he employed. Sometimes the activity bolstered Southern confidence more than anything else. "It looks foolish to see men shooting when they can see nothing to shoot at," Oldham divulged, "but it is necessary to keep the enemy from crawling up." The constant racket provided a queer reassurance that the status quo was being maintained. Oldham noted that when the Rebel pickets were silent, the Yankees stepped up their own fire, as if to compensate for the diminished output of their opponents.[53]

Not everyone was as vengeful toward the bluecoats as Oldham. Periodic truces were arranged by soldiers of both armies, despite the efforts of officers on both sides to quell the practice. Stephen D. Lee was so angered by a report that some of his pickets had agreed to shoot harmlessly over the heads of the Federal videttes that he ordered artillery officers and men in the trenches "to fire upon any man, or group of men, who are discovered holding communication with the enemy." Such threats may not have ended the impromptu cease-fires, especially since the two sides shared a common language and other traits. The informal truces which Cheatham's men were party to had increased since the army left the Kennesaw line. One soldier reminisced how the pickets would chat agreeably until someone hollered, "Rats to your holes," and both sides would scurry for cover.[54]

One danger in the fraternization, as some officers realized, was the temptation in a weak moment for soldiers to desert. Desertions plagued both Confederate and Union forces throughout the war, but in the latter portion of the Atlanta campaign there was perhaps more motivation for Southerners to abandon the service than was the case with their Northern counterparts. It is difficult to evaluate the total number of deserters from any one command, especially since the topic was rarely alluded to by Confederates in the postwar period. Still, the *Official Records* provide an occasional glimpse at the practice. On August 8, for instance, Major-General David Stanley of the Union army reported that "a lieutenant and private from Vaughan's brigade, Cheatham's division, deserted and came into our lines this morning." Five days later, a captain in the Thirty-sixth Alabama entered Federal lines. On August 21, another Union officer noted that "five deserters came into our lines from Maney's and Vaughan's brigades, of Cheatham's division." On all three occasions, the deserters freely provided information regarding the placement of various Rebel units. The Alabamian also confided data on troop strength and several other topics. This captain, hailing from Lee's corps, described his regiment's members as being "greatly demoralized" and "feel[ing] that they are whipped." While one cannot place too much credence in such statements, there is a reason to believe that morale in some units did weaken after the three July battles around Atlanta. For whatever reason, some of Hood's men were psychologically broken by mid-August.[55]

The one bright point in Hood's favor during late July and August came when his cavalry managed to thwart three columns of mounted horsemen from Sherman's army when the latter struck out on raids south of Atlanta. Emboldened by the success of his cavalrymen, Hood sent four thousand troopers on an expedition against Sherman's communications. The gray riders did little damage in this respect, but Joseph Wheeler's embellished reports that he had crippled Sherman's rail connection heartened Hood. When word came that the Yankees were gone from the north and east of Atlanta, it was natural for Hood to hope that Sherman was pulling back owing to the blow delivered by Wheeler's horsemen. Other Rebels shared Hood's optimism, including some of Cheatham's men.[56]

In reality, Sherman was breaking the month-long stalemate by slipping huge numbers of troops to the west and then south for another attempt on Hood's surviving rail artery. Eventually, six of the seven Union corps took part in this massive project, and the Confederates lost contact with much of Sherman's army for several days. Deprived of half his cavalry force, which would normally have kept abreast of Sherman's movements, Hood was in the unenviable position of being forced to guess where the Federals might strike. When Rebel scouts located part of the

Union columns, Hood dispatched Hardee and Lee to Jonesboro, some thirty miles south of Atlanta. Hardee received his marching orders on the evening of August 30, and Hood placed the Georgian in overall command of the force sent to Jonesboro. Cleburne assumed command of Hardee's corps.

Cheatham's men were with Hardee, but their commander was not with them. Although A. P. Stewart reassumed control of his corps in mid-August, Cheatham immediately went on the sick list. Whatever ailment troubled him must have been fairly serious, for he was still not available for combat service over two weeks later. Cheatham would miss only three of the major battles fought by the Army of Tennessee (Lookout Mountain and Bentonville were the others), but at Jonesboro his absence proved particularly damaging. The men, although they had performed under Maney at Peachtree Creek and Atlanta, were aware that Cheatham was missing. "General Cheatham was sick and the men noted his absence," recalled a soldier in the Fifth Tennessee.[57]

Hardee's entire force did not arrive at Jonesboro until the late morning of August 31, and he was not prepared to attack until mid-afternoon. When the Confederates finally did go forward, problems with coordinating Lee's and Cleburne's movements hurt the cohesion needed for success. Maney, once again in command of Cheatham's division, went with his brigade commanders to a prebattle conference with Hardee and other officers in the army. There, they were advised of Hardee's intentions to drive back the Federals with "a vigorous attack and to force the enemy back across the Flint River."[58] The division was detailed to act as a support to Cleburne's and Bate's divisions, which formed the first line. Problems began almost as soon as the Confederates moved out. The Southern line was intended to make a wheel to the right, and as they did so, a gap widened between Bate's and Cleburne's old division, under Mark Lowrey. Maney saw the opening and sent his former brigade, under Colonel George Porter of the Sixth Tennessee, and Vaughan's brigade, led by Colonel George Gordon of the Eleventh Tennessee, to fill the breach. Maney soon met with Cleburne, and the Irishman approved of Maney's decision to send the two brigades forward. Maney was on his way to accompany the force when one of Cleburne's staff officers rode up, bearing a message for Maney to shift his entire division and assail the Yankees from the flank or the rear. It was impossible for Maney to halt the momentum of his two advance brigades, but their attack proved unsuccessful. Bate's men on the right had already fallen back by the time Maney's two brigades assaulted, and the Tennesseans never even reached the enemy works before they too were repulsed.[59]

After the setback, Maney consulted with three of his brigade commanders to discern if there was any weak spot in the Union line. All of the officers agreed that the Federal works were quite formidable and were well supported by artillery. In addition, the Rebels would be forced to cross open fields along most of Maney's line, which would leave them vulnerable to artillery and infantry fire in a charge. At this point Maney's fourth brigade (Gist's, commanded by Colonel James McCullough of the Sixteenth South Carolina) came up, after a frustrating march through timber and heavy brush. Maney placed the newcomers behind his old brigade under Porter and was preparing to attack through some woods when he received word from Cleburne to cancel the assault. Shortly afterwards, Maney learned that Lowrey was withdrawing from his left, and he too fell back, arriving at his original position around 10 P.M. Despite the late hour, the men began digging entrenchments.[60]

Maney must have arrived somewhat ahead of most of his troops, for he apparently had a rendezvous with a superior officer between 8 and 9 P.M. His report strongly implies that he was relieved from command, and his successor, Brigadier-General John C. Carter, noted that he assumed temporary command of the division around 9 P.M. Sketchy evidence suggests that Maney was assailed for not attacking as ordered and either voluntarily withdrew as divisional commander or was ousted. The only men who could compel Maney to step aside were Hardee, Lee, and Cleburne; the latter's report is missing from the *Official Records,* and neither Hardee nor Lee makes any reference to Maney's fate.[61]

While Jonesboro is the only battle of the campaign for which published reports exist from officers in Cheatham's division, it is simultaneously the most puzzling battle to decipher. Maney's relinquishing the reins to Carter is by far the most enigmatic aspect. Inferential information is to be gleaned only from Maney's and Carter's accounts in the *Official Records.* Otherwise, standard sources for Cheatham's division either ignore the Jonesboro engagement or give it sparse treatment.[62] One can only imagine Cheatham's consternation when he discovered that his old friend had run into trouble at Jonesboro. Cheatham lost his most experienced brigadier after the mysterious affair, for Maney never returned to active duty in that capacity. While he did not again lead his brigade, Maney did not abandon the service. He received approval from Hood for a leave on September 6, and a field return for September 17 indicates that Maney was still absent from the army. He had returned by September 28, for his Jonesboro report was compiled "In the Field, near Palmetto, Ga." on that date. One of the more curious aspects of Maney's situation is that he remained with the army, though it is not known in what capacity, for most of the war. He did receive a surgeon's certificate for a two-month leave in January 1865, prompted by recurring pain from

Brigadier-General George E. Maney accompanied Cheatham to Mexico and served with his old friend in the Civil War. Cheatham's favorite subordinate at the brigade level, Maney was in charge of Cheatham's division at the Battle of Jonesboro. He either resigned or was forced to relinquish his command on the night of August 31, 1864, and the remainder of Maney's Confederate career is a mystery. (Library of Congress)

a severe wound he had received on the retreat from Missionary Ridge, but Maney is listed as being paroled in North Carolina with the remnant of the Army of Tennessee later the same year.[63]

August 31 may have represented an end of sorts for Maney, but the remainder of Cheatham's men obtained no respite from danger. They were awakened in the early morning hours and moved forward to occupy a set of works vacated when Cleburne's troops had moved to the right. The troop shifts were required because Hood, still unaware of the pre-ponderance of Federals at Jonesboro, ordered Hardee to send Lee's corps back to Atlanta. Hardee complied, and his remaining corps was forced to deploy in a long, thin line as his men stretched to cover ground for-merly occupied by Lee. September 1 brought with it the promise of disas-ter for the Confederates, none of whom seemed to comprehend the size of the Federal force at Jonesboro. Three full corps confronted Hardee, with an additional three within striking distance.[64]

Most of Hardee's brigades faced to the west, but the line angled off at the northern end to form what resembled an upside-down fishhook. The tip of the hook was Gist's brigade, which Hardee ordered from the extreme left to the far right during the early afternoon hours. Once the brigade arrived, Hardee personally supervised the Georgians and South Carolinians as they carved out a defense line. "Carved out" carries a lit-eral as well as figurative allusion in this case, since Gist's men created an intricate abatis by bending small trees down, slicing along the trunks with their pocket knives, and interlacing the tops of the trees. The troops used logs and rails to erect breastworks and tried to protect an exposed area along a railroad cut by building traverses. The arduous labor stood them in good stead around 4 P.M., when the Yankees first pressed against their skirmishers. Colonel Ellison Capers of the Twenty-fourth South Carolina reported that the Federal effort was directed against the left of Gist's line, near the railroad cut. The Union troops scored a breakthrough west of the rail cut at one point, but Capers rallied his command and regained the lost ground.[65]

Such success did not attend every effort along the vulnerable Confed-erate front. At the angle, one of Cleburne's brigades under Colonel Dan-iel C. Govan rebuffed one sortie, but the bluecoats returned in force. Hit from three directions, Govan was unable to fend off the second on-slaught. He and his men attempted to fight off the Yankees pouring into the works, but Govan was captured eventually, as were several hundred of his men. The Union breach in the line threatened disaster, but it snapped shut when Vaughan's brigade under Gordon delivered a furious counterpunch. Assisted by remnants of Govan's brigade and other regi-ments from Cleburne's command, Gordon's Tennesseans drove the enemy back to the parapets and managed to hold them in check until darkness ended the battle. Near nightfall the Yankees at last were in position to lap around Hardee's flanks, but by then it was too late to exploit the opportunity.[66]

Sherman narrowly missed a chance to inflict serious damage on the Army of Tennessee's premier corps and perhaps to have eradicated it altogether. He failed because the Federals exhibited a tendency the Southerners themselves were prone to — inability to attack on schedule. Sherman enjoyed a five to one edge in manpower but could not overcome the inertia which prevented an assault from being launched earlier in the day. As it was, Cleburne was able to summon Cheatham's brigades one by one from the left to shore up the right until darkness allowed the Rebels to slip away. Gordon's brigade covered the retreat as Hardee moved down the railroad to Lovejoy's, where he erected works to stymie the pursuing enemy. Hardee at least had the consolation of escaping his predicament, but Sherman got what he wanted as well: control of Hood's last operating rail line. This forced the embattled young commander to cede Atlanta, which Hood did after destroying vast quantities of supplies which could not be transported. Explosions rent the night air as Hood prepared to abandon the city and reunite his scattered army. The Army of Tennessee coalesced again by September 4 at Lovejoy's, as Stewart and Lee managed to bring their corps to a successful junction with Hardee.[67]

Sherman learned that Hood had reunited his army and, satisfied for the moment with his considerable achievement, fell back slowly to Atlanta. He previously had wired his War Department of Atlanta's capture, and added, "Since May 5, we have been in one constant battle or skirmish, and need rest."[68] The same was true, of course, for Sherman's Confederate opponents, even more so, considering their disappointment at being unable to hold Atlanta. Cheatham rejoined his command sometime after Jonesboro, and both the general and his men had to face the stark reality that the division was a far different force than had broken camp back in Dalton. Vaughan was gone, Maney was under a cloud, and ten of Cheatham's regiments were led by different officers than was the case four months earlier. The campaign took a terrible toll in Cheatham's officer ranks, with dozens either killed or wounded. The same was true among the rank and file. An exact account is not available, but evidence suggests that Cheatham lost over 300 men killed and at least 1,500 wounded, figures which include both privates and officers. The addition of Gist's brigade boosted Cheatham's numbers to some extent but did not offset the heavy losses suffered by his Tennesseans. Those losses were further inflated when one takes into account those of Cheatham's men who deserted to the enemy.[69]

Hood moved his army westward to Palmetto, on the West Point and Atlanta Railroad, in mid-September. Ironically, the shift of his headquarters to Palmetto occurred on September 19, the first anniversary of the two-day fray at Chickamauga. One wonders if Cheatham and his men reflected back to that day, when his five brigades slammed into their opponents along either side of the Brotherton Road. The high hopes engendered by the victory along the banks of the Chickamauga had long since soured by the time Cheatham's men marched to Palmetto. Northern Georgia was gone now as well, acquired by the Federals at a considerable price, but acquired nonetheless. The loss of Atlanta and the upper portion of Georgia was the latest in a string of territorial concessions which began early in the war, when the Confederate defense line in Kentucky gave way. Cheatham and his veterans must have been frustrated by the realization that their native Tennessee was under Union control. The reversals were especially galling when Cheatham's men considered the sacrifices they had made. Back in the halcyon days of late 1861 and early 1862, several of Cheatham's regiments had mustered as many as 1,000 or more men. But no longer. By autumn of 1864, those same regiments were reduced to a few hundred hardy survivors, and attrition forced a dozen of the regiments into consolidations. This process continued at Palmetto as a result of the shrunken rosters. The remaining members of the Fifth Tennessee, for instance, were formed into two companies and placed in a regiment composed of the remnants of five once-strong regiments.[70]

Perhaps because of the worsening situation, some of Cheatham's men were losing their appetite for the war. The day after he was wounded in the July 22 engagement, Captain Fielder wrote in his diary that several of his comrades "acted badly and played out of the fight, but in hopes they will do so no more I will not expose them by inserting their names here."[71] Despite such notations and problems with desertions, Fielder and most of Cheatham's men remained committed to the cause. In some respects this may have been the result of three years of experience in the service. Over the years, Cheatham and his men had endured hardships, forged bonds of friendship, and proven themselves in battle. Nor was the war over. After the rigorous Atlanta campaign, Cheatham and his men were destined to take part in the Army of Tennessee's last offensive.

Chapter 9

"I Don't Like the Looks of This Fight": Spring Hill and Franklin

Cheatham and his men may well have regarded a visit by Jefferson Davis as something of a bad omen. The Confederate leader generally appeared during a period of turmoil, as on two prior trips to the army when he assessed the infighting between Braxton Bragg and his subordinates. When Davis arrived at Palmetto on September 25, 1864, his task was again to soothe the troubled upper echelons of the Army of Tennessee. The principal antagonists on this occasion were Hardee and Hood. The former officer had resented the latter's ascent to army command, and Hardee's confidence in Hood was not boosted by the unsuccessful clashes around Atlanta. Hood, for his part, openly blamed Hardee for the disappointing results at Peachtree Creek, Atlanta, and Jonesboro. Hood was anxious to eliminate Hardee from the army, and twice in September wrote to President Davis requesting that Hardee be replaced. The first letter, on September 13, noted that Hardee "commands the best troops of this army" and recommended that either General Richard Taylor or Cheatham supersede Hardee as corps commander. Taylor was serving in another department, and his status as Davis's brother-in-law could have led to charges of nepotism if he won the appointment. Four days later Hood dispatched another letter to Richmond, this time recommending Cheatham alone for the post. "This change will promote the efficiency of the army," Hood wrote, adding, "If Hardee is relieved Cheatham takes command by seniority of rank."[1]

Davis remained with the army for several days and listened to the charges and countercharges leveled by Hardee and Hood. He also reveiwed the troops and delivered several speeches, which were received with varying degrees of enthusiasm. One veteran of the First Tennessee Regiment wrote that Davis acknowleged that there was some dissatisfaction with the removal of Johnston in favor of Hood, but the politician explained that he "had done what I thought best for your good."[2] After conferring with his generals, Davis accepted Hood's suggestion, and on September 28 orders were read relieving Hardee from duty with the army. Cheatham took charge of Hardee's corps.[3]

Cheatham's appointment has never received the attention it deserves. Several writers have suggested that Patrick Cleburne should have been elevated to corps command. Hood's biographer, Richard M. McMurry, feels Cleburne would have been a better choice than Stephen D. Lee when the latter took over Hood's old corps in July 1864. By extension, such an argument implies that Cleburne and not Cheatham should have been summoned to fill in as a corps commander when an interim officer was needed to head Hood's and Stewart's corps during the Atlanta campaign. According to Cleburne supporters, he also deserved to win command of Hardee's corps when the Georgian left the army.[4]

No person who studies the Army of Tennessee would deny that Cleburne was a superb officer or that he commanded one of the leading combat units in the western army. Problems do develop when Cheatham suffers unduly by comparison. When A. P. Stewart was given command of Leonidas Polk's old corps, a New York newspaper commented that "Cleburne, who has been raised to the rank of major general against a great deal of opposition, is perhaps the best man in Hood's army at this time, at least possessed of more of the sterling qualities of a man and experience as a soldier." Besides its implied snub of Stewart, the article dismissed Cheatham as being "only a fighter, not a general, and a better horse jockey than either." Far too many writers have accepted this comparative assessment uncritically.[5]

There were a number of factors which worked in Cheatham's favor when the corps vacancy occurred. He was available and had previously commanded a corps on three occasions, albeit for short periods of time. He knew the workings of the army, had influential friends in the Confederate Congress, and was a proven divisional leader. The latter was a particularly significant point. While historians tend to celebrate Cleburne's division, one can claim with justification that Cheatham's Tennesseans performed just as creditably. Fighting literally side by side with Cleburne's soldiers on many battlefields, Cheatham's men acquired for themselves an enviable combat record. The Tennesseans and Cleburne's men recognized the fighting qualities of one another, and what one soldier termed a "generous rivalry" developed between the two divisions. The successes of Cleburne's division at Missionary Ridge, Ringgold, and New Hope Church were no more heroic than the efforts of Cheatham's men at Perryville, Chickamauga, or Kennesaw Mountain. Cheatham's soldiers who survived the war did not place themselves above Cleburne's veterans but did not take a back seat to them either. Cheatham's Tennesseans may have exhibited an independent streak, but if the new commander was supposed to have solid combat credentials, there was less difference between Cheatham and Cleburne than later writers have assumed.[6]

Many scholars have maintained that Cleburne remained mired at his level of command because of two circumstances: his foreign birth and his authorship of the emancipation scheme. While the latter factor undoubtedly harmed the Irishman's chances for promotion, Cheatham was also implicated in the proposal and tarnished by the ensuing controversy. What makes Cheatham's appointment really surprising is the supposition that Jefferson Davis and Hood consulted Braxton Bragg concerning changes in the army. It is inconceivable that Bragg would have boosted Cheatham for the promotion. In addition, Hood could not have been unaware of Cheatham's fervent devotion to Joe Johnston. Perhaps the most plausible answer to the appointment lies in Hood's conclusion that Cheatham's status as senior officer in the corps put him in line for the post. The Atlanta campaign took such a heavy toll in the army's officer ranks that Cheatham's longevity and date of appointment worked to his advantage. By late 1864 there were not many realistic possibilities for Hood to choose from, and Cheatham was one of the few viable choices.[7]

Cheatham's promotion necessitated several changes in his former division. His five brigades were reduced to four, as Marcus J. Wright's old brigade (led in the Atlanta campaign by John C. Carter) was broken up and its regiments distributed to other commands within the division. Carter took command of Maney's old brigade, while George W. Gordon, the "Snowball Colonel," was made a brigadier in August and took charge of Vaughan's former regiments. Strahl led the third Tennessee brigade, while States Rights Gist continued to lead his Georgia and South Carolina units. Youth was one factor which linked the four brigadiers: Gist and Strahl were thirty-three, Gordon celebrated his thirty-eighth birthday in October, and Carter was only twenty-six.

Dark-eyed, dark-haired John C. Carter was battle-hardened by late 1864, despite his relative youth. A native of Georgia, he had attended the University of Virginia before studying law in Tennessee. He was practicing law in Memphis when the war opened, and once in Confederate service Carter began working his way up the ranks. He was elected captain, and then colonel, of the Thirty-eighth Tennessee and distinguished himself in several engagements. He was recommended for promotion to brigadier by a number of Georgia and Tennessee politicians, as well as by his former brigade commander, Marcus J. Wright. One supporter argued for Carter's advancement by citing his educational attainments, and added, "His habits are unsurpassed in the army for sobriety and morality." Promoted to brigadier to rank from July 7, 1864, Carter led some of Cheatham's best troops when he assumed command of Maney's former regiments.[8]

George Washington Gordon was born in Giles County, Tennessee, and was an 1859 graduate of Nashville's Western Military Institute. A surveyor in the interval before the war, he entered Confederate ranks as a drillmaster of the Eleventh Tennessee Regiment, then worked his way up to colonel. He took a commendable part in a number of battles and was elevated to brigadier status in August 1864. Vaughan's wounding created an opening for Gordon as a brigade commander, and he stepped into the void left by the Mississippian. Gordon later enjoyed one distinction not shared by the other three brigade commanders in Cheatham's old division. He lived to a ripe old age, dying in Memphis on August 9, 1911. At the time of his death, he was commander-in-chief of the United Confederate Veterans.[9]

Otho French Strahl was one of the more interesting characters in Cheatham's division, if only because of his nativity: he was born in Ohio and attended Ohio Wesleyan University. He moved to Tennessee to study law with a friend, Daniel H. Reynolds, another Ohioan who rose to the rank of brigadier in the Confederate army. Both Reynolds and Strahl were admitted to the bar in 1858, and Strahl was practicing as an attorney in Dyersburg when the war erupted. Despite his relatively brief residence in the South, Strahl enlisted in the Fourth Tennessee Regiment. He entered Confederate service as a captain, then won successive promotions to lieutenant-colonel and colonel. He was further promoted to brigadier-general in July 1863 and assumed command of A. P. Stewart's brigade after Stewart was assigned to lead a division. Described by one veteran as "a model character," Strahl differed from his long-time commander, Cheatham, in at least one respect. It was alleged that throughout the war Strahl "was never known to use language unsuited to the presence of ladies."[10]

It is hard to imagine a more appropriate name for a Confederate general than that possessed by States Rights Gist. A South Carolinian, Gist was educated at South Carolina College and Harvard Law School. He combined a legal career with service as a militia officer in his native state and cast his lot with the South after secession. He had fought with Joe Johnston in Mississippi during the Vicksburg campaign, then had been sent to the Army of Tennessee, where he served under W. H. T. Walker. His brigade later was transferred to Cheatham's division and consisted of two Georgia and two South Carolina regiments.[11]

Replacing Cheatham as divisional commander was John Calvin Brown, a native of Giles County who had been an attorney prior to the war. He had enlisted as a private but was appointed colonel of the Third Tennessee. Captured at Fort Donelson, Brown was exchanged and was later elevated in rank to brigadier. He became a major-general in August 1864 and had led a division during the battles for Atlanta.[12] In addition to his old division under Brown, Cheatham also directed two other divisions, under William B. Bate and Cleburne.

Other matters besides reorganization of the army preoccupied the Confederates at Palmetto. The major concern facing Hood and his men was the future direction of the army. The four battles in the Atlanta area were evidence that Hood would have trouble breaking Sherman's force to any great degree, especially when one calculated the high losses since the start of the campaign. To remain at Palmetto would risk demoralization and a loss of fighting spirit. Not knowing whether Sherman intended to strike out for Alabama, the Carolinas, or some other locale was another complicating factor. After Jonesboro, Hood began to devise a plan to operate along Sherman's communications and supply lines, an undertaking which was fleshed out more completely when Hood discussed it with President Davis. In a review at Palmetto, Cheatham's men heard Davis outline the new strategy. The Confederate executive promised that the movement would "make Atlanta a perfect Moscow of defeat to the Federal army," and he held out the prospect that the Rebels would then move into Tennessee and Kentucky. The latter was probably just a notion designed to win the applause of the Tennesseans in Cheatham's command and was not seriously considered as a part of Hood's forthcoming move.[13]

Hood's plan was probably the best one the Southerners could hope to utilize at the time. By moving around to the north of Atlanta, Hood hoped to constrict Sherman's supplies coming south so tightly that the Federal commander would be unable to penetrate further into the Confederate heartland. If all went as the Confederates desired, Sherman would in fact be forced to abandon Atlanta and retrace his steps across the northern Georgia landscape for which the two armies had contended so fiercely during the spring and summer. There were a number of potential problems with Hood's strategy, especially in the area of logistics, but with his manpower pool dwindling, at least Hood could seize the initiative from his Union counterpart. The initial move in the new campaign came in late September, when the Southern army crossed the Chattahoochee. During the first week in October, Hood managed to get a portion of his army astride the Western and Atlantic Railroad, destroyed part of the tracks, and was gratified when he received reports that Sherman had also recrossed the Chattahoochee.[14]

Originally Hood intended to offer battle to Sherman north of Atlanta, but as the days passed, this resolve diminished, as did his alternative plan to fight at Gadsden, Alabama. Instead, he decided to move farther to the north and again strike the railroad above the Etowah River. By October 8, Hood was nearly seventy miles northwest of Atlanta, and within the next few days he shifted to the Dalton area. Although Sherman had cautiously shadowed Hood since the Confederates moved northward, he was unable to save a Federal garrison at Dalton from capture on October 13. In a scene reminiscent of the surrender of the Union fort at Munfordville back in the Kentucky campaign, the Yankee colonel in charge of the Dalton garrison at first refused to capitulate. Some verbal wrangling ensued, during which time the officer, Colonel Lewis Johnson of the Forty-fourth U.S. Colored Infantry, was finally convinced that resistance was hopeless. The bulk of the 800 men who staffed the garrison were black, and the sight of such men in Federal uniforms enraged the Southerners. Johnson reported later that Cleburne's men could hardly be restrained from moving "upon the 'niggers'" as he and Hood completed the surrender negotiations.[15]

When the Federals were disarmed and marched out of the garrison, many of the Southern troops insulted the blacks and threatened violence. Only the diligence of the Confederate guards saved the blacks from being attacked. Even at that, several ailing blacks were shot to death when the Rebels decided that they would impede the march. The blacks were forced to shed most of their clothing, and General Bate then sent them to tear up the railway for several miles. Johnson later decried the behavior of Bate, who abused the white Northern officers mercilessly. The Yankee officer was incredibly naive about race relations in the South if he did not realize the extent to which Confederates despised the notion of blacks serving in the Northern army. The Rebels assumed that the blacks were ex-slaves, even though some hailed from Ohio and Indiana, and Bate was contemptuous of any white man who would lead such an outfit. His disgust was common throughout Hood's army. When Sam Watkins wrote his account of the First Tennessee after the war, he reminisced gleefully: "Reader, you should have seen how that old railroad did flop over, and how the darkies did sweat, and how the perfume did fill the atmosphere." Despite his wounded sensibilities and uncomfortable position, Johnson did have enough military presence of mind to make an assessment of Hood's army. He noted the presence of several general officers, including Hood, Lee, Cleburne, Maney, and Cheatham, among others. The colonel met Cheatham personally, when the Tennessean inquired whether the white officers were willing to accept paroles which Hood had previously offered. Seeing little point in being sent to a Rebel prison camp, Johnson and his white counterparts reluctantly assented and were separated from their black charges.[16]

Cheatham and the other Southern officers were probably glad to see the Yankees leave, if for no other reason than that they consumed rations otherwise intended for Rebel stomachs. By mid-October Hood was nine miles south of La Fayette, in the same general vicinity as the army had operated the year before during the Chickamauga campaign. At this point the Texan held a conclave with his corps and division officers, after which he decided that the army had neither the numbers nor the will to engage Sherman in a pitched battle. He also made a second crucial decision: to leave Georgia and head west into Alabama. Among the men who learned of the two decisions was General P. G. T. Beauregard, nominally Hood's superior. Since leaving the army after Shiloh, Beauregard had languished outside the limelight for the past two and a half years. Perhaps to quiet the lingering criticism of Johnston's removal, President Davis met with Beauregard in early October and gave him command of the Military Division of the West, where he supervised Hood's army and Richard Taylor's Department of Alabama, Mississippi, and East Louisiana. Despite the impressive title, Beauregard basically offered advice to Hood and Taylor and had little real authority. The appointment may have satisfied Beauregard's penchant for dispensing counsel, but Hood essentially ignored the Creole on most occasions and made up his own mind on strategic policy.[17]

Such independence came to the fore after the Army of Tennessee abandoned Georgia for Alabama. During the last two weeks of October, Hood drove his army across practically the entire width of the state before he finally halted on the Tennessee River at Tuscumbia. This was enough for Sherman, who had followed Hood throughout October. The Ohioan then elected to leave Hood to George Thomas, who was directed to amass a force in Nashville to halt the Confederates. To assist Thomas, Sherman detached John Schofield's Twenty-third Corps and the Fourth Army Corps, under David S. Stanley. Schofield and Stanley took rail cars to Nashville, then were sent to screen Hood's movements along the Tennessee River. Schofield's force arrived at Pulaski, fifty miles northeast of Florence, Alabama, on November 13.[18] While Thomas was busy scraping an army together to stop Hood, Sherman resumed his interrupted advance. The infamous march to the sea began, unhindered by any sizeable body of Confederate troops. Even though Hood learned of Sherman's move back south, he was too far away to pursue the Federals through Georgia. He instead decided to invade Tennessee, which was a far cry from the original plan he and Davis had concocted at Palmetto. Still, when the Confederate authorities learned of Hood's intentions, they made no concerted effort to dissuade him from his projected movement.[19]

Beauregard had some doubts about the invasion, but soon enough he

too embraced the plan. The Creole suggested to Hood that a proclamation be drawn up for Cheatham to sign which would be distributed
within Tennessee. Beauregard apparently felt Cheatham's popularity could
sway Tennesseans into aiding the army as it advanced. The document
as envisioned by Beauregard proclaimed that Cheatham's corps was entering the state, accompanied by "the chivalrous Forrest," and exhorted
Tennesseans "to redeem themselves from the yoke of a vile oppressor" by
aiding in the disruption of Sherman's communications and supply line.[20]
The proclamation may have conveyed Beauregard's dramatic flair, but
while the army halted at Tuscumbia, Cheatham himself was occupied
with far less stirring matters. Hood remained in the Tuscumbia area
nearly three weeks, waiting for Nathan Bedford Forrest's cavalry to ride
in from western Tennessee. During that span, inclement weather set in,
and as winter arrived, many of Cheatham's men found that they lacked
adequate clothing to withstand the cold weather. Those soldiers who
were barefoot were particularly uncomfortable, and Cheatham sought a
practical solution to their problem. He ordered his shodless troops to sew
shoes out of beef hides, placing the hair around the feet and then stitch-
ing the hide together. The improvisation worked, but not without a draw-
back. One of Cheatham's surgeons noted that the shoes "did fine to walk
in but did not smell well after a day or two."[21]

After crossing the river and moving to nearby Florence, Hood got his
army on the move northward by November 19. His infantry was sent forward the next day, and one of Cheatham's veterans in the Twenty-seventh
Tennessee recalled the day they left Florence as "the coldest day I ever
felt . . . a bitter cold wind was whistling, and almost cut us in two." Fires
lined the road every few hundred yards, with groups of ill-clad soldiers
hovering around each blaze. The efforts to ward off the cold weather were
not always successful, according to one soldier, who recalled, "You could
hardly keep warm from one fire to the next."[22] The chilly climate contrasted with Hood's high hopes for the campaign. Among his goals were
to retake Nashville, continue on into Kentucky, and threaten Cincinnati.
After all this had been accomplished, Hood imagined that he might take
his army to the Virginia front, where he could rejoin his idol, Robert E.
Lee.[23]

This was an ambitious agenda, and as things turned out, unachiev-
able. Still, Hood was not alone in his optimism, although he may have
carried it to an extreme. The army advanced along three separate routes,
Cheatham's corps on the left headed for Waynesboro, Stewart on the right
towards Lawrenceburg, and Lee's corps moving on country roads between the two. For many in the ranks, Tennessee was home, and the three
Rebel columns moved swiftly despite the harsh weather. The men in

Cheatham's old division were buoyed by the prospect of returning to their homeland. Hearty cheers greeted the sight of a large sign stretched across the road denoting the state line, and as one soldier remembered, "We Tennesseans stepped more briskly on our native soil."[24] The Union force at Pulaski eventually learned of the Confederate advance, and Schofield pushed his men towards Columbia in order to forestall Hood from cutting off an avenue back to Nashville. Schofield barely managed to reach Columbia before Forrest's cavalry came up on November 24. Presently an even more dangerous force appeared, as Hood reunited his army at Mount Pleasant and marched to Columbia. Schofield managed to cross the Duck River and dig entrenchments on the northern shore, while Hood drew his army together on the opposite side. The Union general realized his danger but hoped to delay Hood in order to give Thomas time to concentrate a larger force at Nashville.[25]

On the night of November 27, Hood concocted a plan to outwit his former West Point classmate. He decided to leave Lee's corps before Columbia, where it would divert Schofield's attention by delivering an artillery barrage. Hood would then move with Cheatham's and Stewart's corps to the east, ford Duck River, and then loop around Schofield by seizing Spring Hill, a village twelve miles north of Columbia. Once stationed at Spring Hill, Hood could utilize one of two options, either bringing Schofield to bay and forcing a fight, or continuing unchecked to Nashville, where Thomas might be unprepared for an assault. It was a bold but not impracticable scheme, and Hood initiated it on November 28, when Forrest's cavalry forded the river.[26]

During the night Hood's engineers laid down a pontoon bridge. Early on November 29, Hood set his plan in motion in Cheatham's and Stewart's troops crossed the river. Schofield was also busy, sending two divisions of infantry under General Stanley towards Spring Hill, along with most of the army's supply wagons and reserve artillery. Stanley arrived at Spring Hill just in time to brush back Forrest's horsemen, who were in the process of attacking an isolated Union outpost. Stanley brought one division to the hamlet, leaving the other one on the pike from Columbia to protect Schofield's left. Stanley deployed his men skillfully in a long, sparse line. The Federal line extended from the railroad depot on the northwest to cover the eastern side of Spring Hill, then bent back southwesterly toward the Columbia turnpike. Stanley had over five thousand men at his disposal and was bolstered by much of Schofield's artillery.[27]

While Stanley raced for Spring Hill, Stephen D. Lee initiated his diversion and opened up with heavy artillery fire. Meanwhile, Hood rode at the head of Cleburne's division of Cheatham's corps through the morning and early afternoon. His route to Spring Hill was a circuitous one, but as Hood neared the village, he had opportunities to attack Stanley or attempt to entrap Schofield. Though Hood could not have known it, both opportunities were destined to slip away during a confused afternoon and evening. The lone fact that cannot be disputed is that Schofield's remaining troops escaped from Columbia along the Spring Hill pike while the Confederate army was within easy striking distance. After the depressing reality of Schofield's escape sank in, Hood lashed out at his subordinates, Cheatham in particular. Long after the war, Hood and Cheatham traded accusations concerning who was at fault at Spring Hill, and the controversy remains unresolved.[28]

Though both Cheatham and Hood related varying stories as to the sequence of events, certain facts are well accepted. Hood crossed Rutherford's Creek, a stream southeast of Spring Hill, around 3 P.M. Unaware of Stanley's exact position or strength, Hood personally led Cleburne's division across the creek, then sent it forward towards Spring Hill. Hood rode with the column for a short while, and on his return he ordered Cheatham to convey several directives to Cleburne. Cleburne was supposed to consult with Forrest, assess Union strength at the village, and attack. Hood claimed later that he also ordered Cleburne to seize the vital Columbia–Spring Hill turnpike. Cheatham was to stay at Rutherford's Creek to guide William B. Bate's division, then was to ride with it to link up with Cleburne. Hood would bear the responsibility of shepherding Cheatham's old division under John C. Brown to the other two units.[29]

The plan began to go awry soon after it was initiated. Cleburne apparently failed to communicate with Forrest for some time and thus knew little of Stanley's force or location. Second, he did not approach Spring Hill from the southeast, as Cheatham desired, but moved in a more westerly direction. Cheatham later related that Cleburne's march was more parallel to the pike than perpendicular to it, and Cheatham was never able to ascertain why Cleburne's approach veered off as it did. Before Cleburne's men reached the pike, his right brigade ran directly into a Federal brigade posted a half-mile southeast of Spring Hill. The appearance of the Union troops ignited the battle ardor of Cleburne's soldiers, and they took on their Federal opponents with customary vigor. Cleburne's men swung to the right and struck the bluecoats from the flank and rear. Soon they were close enough to their blueclad opponents to hurl oaths at the Federals and demand that they halt and surrender. Some of Cleburne's men angrily accused their adversaries of being of "Yankee canine descent," as one Federal tactfully related later. The Union troops, many of them panic-stricken recruits, eventually fell back to the outskirts and reformed. Cleburne's pursuit came to a sudden halt when his men were repulsed by artillery fire from several batteries massed near the turnpike. At this juncture the Irishman sent word to Cheatham of the fighting and told Cheatham "that he had been compelled to fall back and reform his division with a change of front." Preoccupied by now with the Union force in his front, Cleburne ignored any orders he may have had to get across the pike.[30]

Cheatham had started forward to observe Cleburne's movements but did not accompany him into battle. The Tennessean apparently watched the division until Cleburne's men disappeared over a hill, then rode back towards Rutherford's Creek. Nonetheless, he was absent from his assigned post at the creek when Bate's division came up. Bate instead met Hood, who ordered the divisional commander to support Cleburne, "move directly westward to the pike and sweep toward Columbia." Cheatham claimed that he rode up and directed Bate to move to Cleburne's left and support an attack, but this does not seem likely. Evidence suggests that Cheatham did not return from watching Cleburne's men go forward in time to meet with Bate. Bate did move towards Cleburne eventually, but in the process of doing so, he never got across the turnpike.[31]

Bate actually did make a move against the road when he sighted Union troops churning up the pike to aid Stanley. These were members of the division that Stanley had stationed on the pike earlier, with an additional brigade. Schofield himself was with this force, having decided around mid-afternoon that Hood was not going to attack at Columbia. The Union general therefore set out on the turnpike to rejoin Stanley. Apparently this advance force of Schofield's command was discovered by Bate around 6 P.M., in the vicinity of the Nathaniel Cheairs farm. Bate's men fired at the Union column from a distance of two hundred yards and prepared to assault the road. About this time Cheatham sent an order for Bate to link with Cleburne. Bate hesitated, and not until a second order arrived from Cheatham did he cancel his assault. He reluctantly pulled away from the road and groped towards Cleburne in the dark. When Bate finally did rendezvous with Cheatham and related the story about Union troops on the pike, the corps commander was unconcerned. He, like Cleburne, was devoting his attention, not to the turnpike, but to Stanley's force at Spring Hill.[32]

By now Confederate confusion was prevalent. Additional complications had arisen when Brown brought Cheatham's old division into position on Cleburne's right. Brown sent word to Cheatham that he was outflanked and complained that any attack on his part would result in "certain disaster." Cheatham's first actual view of Stanley's force apparently came when he rode to assess Brown's situation. According to Cheatham, he rendezvoused with both Brown and Cleburne. He ordered Brown to connect with Cleburne, throw back his threatened right brigade, and

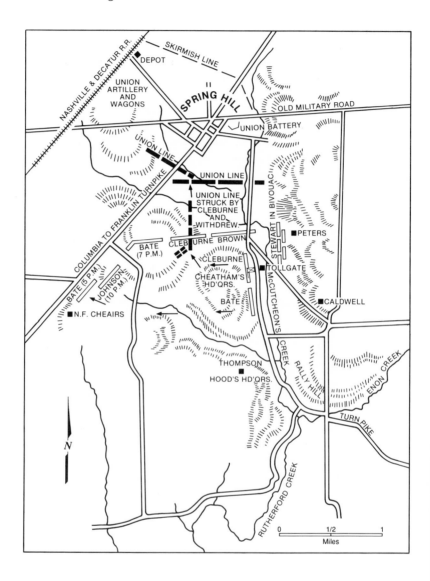

Map 5. Spring Hill, Tenn.—November 29, 1864 (based on *Louisville Courier-Journal* of December 4, 1881, and *Confederate Veteran* magazine of January 1908)

attack. Cheatham promised to escort Bate to the scene. The Rebel assault would sweep from right to left, Cleburne and Bate picking up the attack after Brown charged. As Cheatham rode to the left, he impatiently waited to hear Brown's guns signaling the start of the action. Major Joseph Vaulx, one of Cheatham's staff officers, recalled that Cheatham kept asking insistently, "Why don't we hear Brown's guns?" Increasingly perplexed by the continued silence, he rode back to meet with Brown and was probably joined by Cleburne.[33]

The attack never took place. Brown claimed that he vacillated because Stewart's corps was supposed to be advancing to his support and had not yet arrived. Some of Brown's staff officers intimated that Brown still felt uneasy about his flank and refused to advance. Cheatham later argued that he rode to meet Hood at the Absalom Thompson house, over a mile to the rear of Cheatham's headquarters, and told Hood of the planned assault. To Cheatham's astonishment, Hood ordered the Tennessean to delay any movement until the next day. Yet, other evidence indicates it was Cheatham, not Hood, who was most responsible for calling off the action. An officer on Hood's staff related seeing Cheatham with Hood after dark, "remonstrating with Gen. Hood against a night attack." This version is bolstered by Stephen D. Lee, who recounted, in a postwar letter, a rumor that "Cleburne and Cheatham consulted, and decided between themselves that no battle should be fought at night" or begun if it would run into the night.[34]

The situation worsened when Stewart was commanded by Hood to advance to Brown's support and seize the turnpike north of Spring Hill. This was in response to a message from Cheatham, via Isham Harris, that Stewart come to support Brown. After getting lost for a time, Stewart, arriving with his corps, discovered that linking with Brown would pull him hundreds of yards from the pike. Realizing that this contradicted Hood's earlier orders to cross the road north of the village, a frustrated Stewart rode to the Thompson house to confer with Hood. Daylight had long since vanished, and by the time Stewart arrived back at headquarters, Hood had retired for the night. As the two men discussed the situation, Hood apparently realized for the first time the general location of Cheatham's troops and was informed that the pike was not sealed off. Here Hood reacted curiously; he did not order Cheatham or Stewart to blockade the road, either north or south of the hamlet, and instead asked Forrest if his weary cavalry could barricade the pike. Forrest replied that he needed ammunition, but the supply wagons were still in front of Columbia with Lee. Hood thus depended on tired horsemen with a shortage of ammunition to insure that Schofield was trapped.[35]

While Cheatham's and Stewart's men went into night bivouac, the remaining Yankees evacuated Columbia and pressed northward. One Union soldier recounted that his company left Columbia after dark, then was detailed at picket duty along the pike until 10 P.M., when they were ordered to Spring Hill. Just before reaching the village at midnight, the Federals "came within plain view of Hood's army as they were in bivouac to our right, not more than a mile away." Confederate campfires glowed, and as the Yankees stole by, they could easily make out Southerners moving about and warming themselves by the fire.[36]

Evidently Hood had some inkling of this, for a barefooted private disturbed the general's slumber sometime after midnight to report that he had seen Federal infantry strung out along the road. Hood was unimpressed and merely sent one order to Cheatham to have a regiment investigate the report. In a bizarre oddity, the staff officer who wrote the message, Major A. P. Mason, contended later that he fell asleep before it was delivered. Cheatham wrote that he did indeed receive the order, around midnight, and sent word to General Edward Johnson to check the pike. Johnson had arrived in the vicinity around 9 or 10 P.M. and had moved into position to Bate's left. His division was from Lee's corps, and Johnson groused about Cheatham's command to move to the pike, feeling that Cheatham should have sent one of his own regiments. When Johnson and his contingent arrived at the pike, they found it vacant and returned to their camp. Whether Johnson's reconnaissance struck a gap in the Federal procession, or occurred after the last of the Northerners had passed, is unclear.[37]

That Schofield was not trapped became manifest in the morning, when evidence of the Union escape from Columbia was readily apparent. One of Hood's staff officers noted that the pike, in some places "no more than a narrow causeway," was littered with overturned wagons where the Yankees tried to use the road two abreast. There were also abandoned wagons and dead mules on the road. The mules in some instances may have been shot so the Southerners could not use them.[38] A Texas cavalryman later claimed that some of the havoc wreaked was the result of Confederate horsemen. According to P. B. Simmons of the Sixth Texas Cavalry, Rebel cavalry operating north of Spring Hill noticed a light shining from the pike. General L. S. Ross dismounted, then moved with an escort in the direction of the light. After he detected Yankees on the road, Ross brought up additional troopers, who "formed [a] line not over thirty yards from the pike and fired." The Texas cavalrymen also burned some wagons but could not hold the pike indefinitely. As Simmons related later, the Southerners remained until "the Yanks made it too hot for us." Forrest corroborated this story, reporting that soldiers from W. H. Jackson's division struck the road four miles north of Spring Hill around 11 P.M. on November 29. Though the Rebels had possession of the pike for awhile, they could not hold it, since the cavalrymen were not supported by infantry. No matter how the wreckage on the road originated, this conclusive proof of Schofield's escape enraged Hood. He supposedly began an acrimonious debate over the failure of the army to snare Schofield, a debate he inaugurated while sharing breakfast with several of his officers at the Cheairs home.[39]

Historians have long faced the problem of ascribing blame for the Spring Hill miscue. Part of this is because the impact of Schofield's men passing virtually under Confederate noses is dramatic indeed. Though most writers have focused on the night march along the pike, there were actually three opportunities to strike the Federals. All three were bungled; from the moment Cleburne set out for Spring Hill, a chain of errors developed which continued throughout the afternoon and night.

One chance to disrupt the Union forces came in the late afternoon, when Bate stumbled into the enemy column on the pike. A Rebel attack would have jarred at least part of Schofield's command and might have had an even greater effect if Schofield himself had been in the vicinity of the sortie. Cheatham wasted this opportunity when he insisted that Bate move towards Cleburne. His failure to investigate Bate's report more thoroughly and adapt to the circumstances reflects poorly on his judgement and grasp of the situation.

The failure to attack along the pike might have been negated if Cheatham had used his corps in an assault against Stanley, but this opportunity also went glimmering as the afternoon passed. The attack never materialized, and various explanations were set forth by the respective officers involved. The most plausible one is that Cheatham and Cleburne did consult and hesitated to begin an action which would continue after nightfall. Such an attack was reminiscent of the night assault by Cleburne's and Cheatham's divisions at Chickamauga. Both men knew the confusion and chaos which could attend such an effort. Surely both men reflected privately, and perhaps to one another, that Preston Smith had lost his life in the disorder at Chickamauga. They might also have recalled how Leonidas Polk rode unaware into a Union battle line at Perryville after darkness had descended. If so, the two officers may have been reluctant to bear such risks again at Spring Hill.

There is another reason the assault may not have begun, and which may have been an added factor in Cheatham's and Cleburne's deliberations. After the war, a number of men asserted that Cheatham covered up the mistakes of one of his subordinates at Spring Hill. James D. Porter, Cheatham's wartime chief of staff, was one of the men who put forth this suggestion. Porter may have acted as an apologist for Cheatham, but other evidence indicates that Cheatham may have indeed protected one of his subalterns. The officer in question was John C. Brown.

For years after the war, top officers in the Army of Tennessee tried to decipher what happened at Spring Hill. One of the most persistently curious was Stephen D. Lee, who wrote and talked to several of the principals involved at Spring Hill. By 1878 Lee tended to blame both Cheatham and Hood for the Spring Hill failures, but after reviewing an unpublished manuscript on the campaign, Lee revised his opinion. The manuscript was the work of a Memphis author, Judge J. P. Young, a Confederate veteran of Forrest's cavalry who studied the campaign for years. In 1902, Lee wrote General Ellison Capers and confided that the failure to attack Stanley "lays . . . on one not suspected. He was drunk and it was not Cheatham either. John C. Brown, who commanded Cheatham's old Div.— either lacked nerve on that day or was drunk (no doubt the latter)." Lee related that "Young proves this conclusively in his M.S.—Cheatham to save his friend [Brown] bore all the odium [and] even laid fault on Hood— But he was not the one to blame." The latter sentence is somewhat ambiguous, since "he" can be construed to mean Hood or Cheatham, but in the context of the previous information Cheatham is apparently the party absolved of blame.[40]

Lee was so convinced of the veracity of Judge Young's account that he repeated it to a compatriot at a United Confederate Veteran's reunion in 1903. Lee explained that Brown, extremely popular in Middle Tennessee, had been given "a great many presents of liquor" from grateful Southern sympathizers. While Brown "was not habitually intemperate," at Spring Hill he was "too much intoxicated to attend to his duties." While acknowledging that Young's version came nearly forty years after the event, Lee firmly believed the author's conclusion and felt it solved much of the mystery regarding Spring Hill.[41] Two diarists in Cheatham's old division also suggested liquor as a possible explanation for Rebel failure at Spring Hill, one writing that "rumor has it that John Barleycorn played his part in the drama." Regrettably, neither writer singled out any specific officer, but they perhaps meant their own divisional commander.[42]

If Brown was indeed drunk, he may have had difficulty assessing Stanley's force at Spring Hill or misapprehended what his orders were. He could also have been unwilling to initiate the attack as Cheatham requested. It is not totally unreasonable to assume that Cheatham eventually became aware of Brown's intoxication and knew he could rescue his friend by delaying an attack until morning, when Brown would conceivably have sobered up. Cheatham would not have been inclined to discipline his old friend, especially since Cheatham himself had been on the receiving end of Bragg's ire after his own drinking bout at Murfreesboro.

Cheatham's wartime subordinate, John C. Brown, was accused by some of stalling the Confederate attack at Spring Hill. He later won election as governor of Tennessee. (Tennessee State Library and Archives)

As with other aspects of Spring Hill, the truth of Brown's physical and mental state remains a mystery. Nevertheless, a number of Brown's subordinates and soldiers felt he squandered an opportunity in the afternoon to smite the Federals at Spring Hill.[43]

The final chance for redeeming past mistakes slipped away as the remnants of Schofield's command marched up the pike unimpeded. None of the Confederate officers seems to have paid much attention to reports of Federals on the pike. Nor, in fact, did the army, though several sources noted later that the voices of Union troops marching on the turnpike could be heard. Some Yankees apparently strayed from the road and stumbled into the Confederate encampments, but even this did not change the inertia which seems to have settled on the tired army.[44] Cheatham's own whereabouts during the night are the source of another intriguing rumor. A Union cavalry commander later heard that Cheatham whiled away the time at the home of the attractive Jessie Helen Peters, the wife of a local physician. Mrs. Peters had already engendered controversy earlier in the war, when her jealous husband killed Confederate General Earl Van Dorn. The husband was absent when Hood's army arrived near Spring Hill, so perhaps the bachelor Cheatham did avail himself of her charms. The truth of this allegation is also unclear.[45]

Why is it so difficult to sort out the truth regarding Spring Hill? One major factor was the unwillingness of any of the participants to accept blame for the many gaffes. Another was the fact that the officers generally did not record their recollections until years after the war. Hood's account of the Spring Hill affair was contained in a book published posthumously in 1880, while Cheatham delivered his version the following year. Lee did not hear of Young's manuscript and Brown's alleged intoxication until around the turn of the century. Not only did time diminish the correctness of the officer's memories, but they were also shading their writings in light of often bitter postwar accusations. The Louisville newspaper which first carried Cheatham's account, for instance, headlined the piece, "Gen. Ben. Cheatham, of Tennessee, Takes the Stand," an apt title in light of Cheatham's ability to marshal evidence on his behalf to refute Hood's narrative.[46] The intertwined friendships between Cheatham and several others, including Brown, Isham Harris, A. P. Stewart, and James D. Porter, also may have had a bearing on their recollections. It is regrettable that wartime reports are not available for more of the Confederate officers who were at Spring Hill. The absence of such reports, including any by Cheatham, is attributable to several factors. The high number of officers who were killed the next day at Franklin denied Cheatham the regimental, brigade, and divisional reports which he normally would have used to compile his own report. Casualties among his staff at Franklin also hampered Cheatham, as did the disorganization which attended the army after the battle of Nashville. The lack of reports from the 1860s severely hampers the search for the truth concerning Spring Hill. The mystery deepens when one considers the behavior of Cheatham and other Confederate officers in the postwar period. John C. Brown, for instance, allegedly wrote out a statement concerning the Spring Hill affair before his death, one which may have been different from the reply he provided Cheatham when the latter was collecting information to refute Hood's version. Apparently Brown's family refused to make the document available after Brown died in 1889.[47] There are so many inconsistencies and conflicts in the various versions concerning Spring Hill that sifting out the actual truth is impossible.

In 1894 Charles Quintard, by then a bishop in the Episcopal church, wrote to former Governor Isham Harris and inquired about the Spring Hill mystery. Harris concluded an otherwise congenial letter on a rather testy note and declined to answer Quintard's questions on the subject. "I was there and know much, if not all that occurred," Harris wrote, "and yet, I cannot fix the responsibility upon any one officer." Quintard evidently intended to write a book dealing with his Civil War experiences, and Harris suggested that the cleric omit any discussion of "the Spring Hill trouble." Harris, perhaps mindful of the harsh nature of some of his comments, softened in his final sentence: "Let's not open an old sore, and cause it to bleed again."[48]

Harris may have dissuaded Quintard from pursuing the Spring Hill affair any further, but his conclusion that more than one man blundered is correct. Brown, Cheatham, and Hood all deserve some blame. Certainly Cheatham deserves a good share of the responsibility. He displayed a disquieting resemblance to his dead mentor Polk when he failed to keep Hood apprised of the day's events. He was inflexible when Bate reported Yankees on the pike, and may have absented himself from his command during the night. There is a good possibility that he shielded a fellow officer from censure.

Yet Hood was also at fault. If Spring Hill was indeed Hood's greatest wartime opportunity to crush a Union adversary, as he later charged, he should have been more active. Hood should have personally supervised the entire operation, learned of Stanley's force, and made sure the turnpike was occupied. He should also have relieved Cheatham if the latter behaved as miserably as Hood later contended. Hood did none of these things, although his actual behavior towards Cheatham is another enigma. While the army was still at Tuscumbia, Hood had recommended to Jefferson Davis that Cheatham be promoted to the rank of lieutenant-general, a rank both Stewart and Lee already held. He also enlisted the support

After the Civil War, former army commander John Bell Hood bitterly complained that Cheatham had cost him a victory at Spring Hill. (Library of Congress)

of Isham Harris in the campaign, but the promotion was not acted upon by the Senate before the Tennessee invasion was under way. Hood maintained that after Spring Hill he withdrew the recommendation for promotion and requested Cheatham's removal, until the latter contritely acknowledged that he was to blame for the Spring Hill mistakes. After Cheatham's apology, Hood decided to retain the Tennessean, since Cheatham had learned his lesson.[49]

Correspondence in the *Official Records* confirms that Hood did withdraw his recommendation for Cheatham's promotion, asked for a replacement, and then reversed himself. Regardless of this evidence, Cheatham later dismissed much of Hood's version as pure fabrication and alleged that Hood wrote him a note absolving him from blame for not attacking at Spring Hill. Cheatham tersely added that he was not "in the habit of carrying a certificate of military character," that he attached no special value to the paper, and that he lost it sometime during the final campaign in North Carolina. He was supported in his interpretation by Isham Harris, who said Hood publicly apologized to Cheatham before Hood's own staff, though "the retraction was never so widely known as the charge." In the 1894 letter to Bishop Quintard, Harris noted that Hood censured both Cheatham and Stewart in his official report of the Tennessee campaign, yet "wrote letters to each exonerating them from all blame." James D. Porter alleged that he too saw a note from Hood which absolved Cheatham, as did another officer. Though Harris and Porter were warm personal friends of Cheatham, the evidence suggests that Hood did in fact write a brief note after the battle of Franklin which clearly stated that he did not hold Cheatham responsible for the Spring Hill fiasco. A. P. Stewart also received such a missive. Yet, for some reason, Hood continued to charge Cheatham with being the principal scapegoat for Spring Hill in communications to Richmond. Perhaps this was to deflect criticism of his own failings during the campaign.[50] In any event, Cheatham was never promoted to lieutenant-general, and much of the army apparently regarded him as the chief source of Confederate blunders at Spring Hill.

One issue shoved aside by the intra-army bickering was the extent to which Spring Hill represented a lost opportunity. Recent historians have suggested that Schofield possessed alternate routes to Spring Hill and Franklin other than the turnpike and that Stanley, supported as he was by artillery, was a more considerable foe than some postwar authorities considered him to be.[51] These are more realistic conclusions than those reached by earlier writers, who felt that Schofield or Stanley could easily have been dispatched, which may or may not have been the case.[52] These postwar accounts also portray events from the Confederate perspective and ignore the possible Union responses. Perhaps great results would have been achieved by an assault at Spring Hill; since one did not take place, we can never know.

The one element in the Spring Hill story which most writers miss is Cheatham's relative indifference to the action on the turnpike, both in 1864 and after the war. In his postwar writings, Cheatham was far less concerned with information regarding the road than he was with the assault plan against Stanley. Like Cleburne, Cheatham's appetite for combat was aroused when his forward division ran into resistance southeast of Spring Hill. From that point on, Cheatham's energies were directed towards planning an attack on the Union forces already at the village. In all likelihood he never fully understood how successful Hood's flank movement had been. Even knowing that Bate had discovered Federal troops moving on the pike did not shake Cheatham from his preoccupation with Stanley's force. Although Cheatham later admitted to Hood that a "great opportunity was lost at Spring Hill," one senses that his remorse centered more on the fact that he did not strike Stanley late in the day, rather than on the unimpeded march of Schofield's remaining troops up the road.[53] For all the attention Hood and later writers devoted to the turnpike, it was not the primary object of Cheatham's interest.

Despite the numerous conjectures about the potential for Confederate success at Spring Hill, what November 29 really demonstrated was inefficiency within the high command. Hood was adept at formulating plans which embraced flank movements reminiscent of those performed by Robert E. Lee and Stonewall Jackson earlier in the war. Unfortunately, he did not have the acumen to ensure that his strategy was carried out successfully. Some scholars feel that Hood's mental and physical powers had been dulled by the rigors of the campaign. If so, it is likely that he relied upon the judgement and leadership abilities of his subordinates to a greater extent than he would have if he had enjoyed better health. Cheatham, for his part, displayed little of the genius required to seize the initiative at Spring Hill. Cheatham's responsibilities as a corps commander were far different from those to which he was accustomed as the leader of a division. At the lower level of command, Cheatham was used to following the orders of his superiors in somewhat mechanical fashion. When he ascended to corps command, Cheatham enjoyed a greater degree of latitude, but this freedom carried with it higher risks as well. At Spring Hill he failed to deliver a heavy blow against Stanley and did not perceive that Schofield was moving up the pike. Since Cheatham operated independently for several hours, he shouldered the burden for what transpired at Spring Hill. Nonetheless, after the depressing series of events, Cheatham was unwilling to admit many of the errors which arose as he directed the Confederate effort against Stanley. In fact, he angrily charged that Hood was never man enough to bear the responsibility of failure without trying to cast it off on others. "Military operations, however well conceived, are not always successful," Cheatham wrote, "and I have had my share of failures and disappointments." He then added, "But I have never found it necessary to seek a scape-goat to bear my transgressions, nor to maintain my reputation by aspersions of my subordinates.[54]

The invective shown by both Cheatham and Hood in their postwar writings might never have been employed had the two men stayed in better contact with one another that November day. The lack of communication between the two officers constituted a prime factor in the Confederate woes around Spring Hill. While the two generals spoke to one another several times after crossing Rutherford's Creek, when Cheatham rode in advance he simultaneously cut off most contact with his commander. Despite Cheatham's protests to the contrary, what messages he did convey during the afternoon and night were sporadic and misleading. Nor was Hood very energetic about keeping abreast of the situation near the hamlet. One cannot help but feel that Cheatham was too involved with his assault preparations to bother with sending Hood detailed information, or that he wanted everything in place before he sent word of the intended attack. Hood, for his part, was probably just too tired to maintain a close eye on the situation and trusted that Cheatham would be successful. Cheatham may have been correct in his later assertion that he always obeyed Hood's orders "literally, promptly, and faithfully."[55] Still, the real disservice Cheatham performed was not that he failed to follow orders, but that he neglected to tell Hood what was going on near the village. For all of the anguish and anger which Spring Hill created, it is obvious that much of the confusion might have been averted if only Cheatham and Hood had dispatched couriers and staff officers at more frequent intervals. Certainly Cheatham should have done so, as military convention and courtesy dictated that he should have informed his superior of significant developments.

A feeling of guilt pervaded the army's high command the next morning, despite later protestations of innocence by everyone involved in the Spring Hill debacle. Cleburne felt he was a target of Hood's criticisms and was both angered and hurt. Brown told one of his staff officers that "General Hood is mad about the enemy getting away last night, and he is going to charge the blame of it on somebody. He is as wrathy as a rattlesnake this morning, striking at everything." Brown himself was given a dressing down for not pursuing the Federals the previous day. Hood took pains to emphasize that a retreating force must be attacked immediately, even "if there is but a company in advance, and if it overtakes the entire Yankee army, order the captain to attack it forthwith.[56] Cheatham cannot have escaped this dark mood, though his morning reaction to Hood's ire was not recorded. The officers were not alone in their disappointment. Once knowledge of Schofield's escape circulated, the rank and file shared the embarrassment and rage felt by their superiors. William M. Pollard of the First Tennessee related that "he was never so desperate. I wished the enemy would run upon us so that I could fight to the death-spent."[57]

Pollard's sense of despair was echoed by Hood, who brusquely sent his army after Schofield. The Union commander had continued his retreat from Spring Hill in the early morning hours, brushing aside some of Forrest's resisting cavalry in the process. Eventually he took up a line of defense at Franklin, in the Harpeth River valley. In the early afternoon Hood ascended Winstead Hill, a high rise which provided a view of the town. He saw, as did the officers clustered around him, that Schofield had his army drawn up in a bend of the Harpeth River, secure in works which had been begun in 1862. Cheatham recalled that the day was bright and clear, and as his eyes surveyed the terrain, he was struck by the open expanse confronting the Confederates. "This is the only open battlefield of the war," he reflected, "where the [A]rmy of Tennessee has met the enemy!" Cheatham "could easily see all the movements of the Federals and readily trace their line." Worried about the odds for success, especially given the unobstructed nature of the ground, Cheatham reckoned that the Southerners "would take a desperate chance if we attempted to dislodge them."[58]

Nor was Cheatham the only officer who had reservations about assaulting at Franklin. Nathan Bedford Forrest protested first, saying that he could flank Schofield from the fortifications by crossing the Harpeth above the town. Hood was not in the mood to hear of flank movements after Spring Hill and rejected the suggestion. Cheatham joined Hood and registered his own opinion. Cheatham warned: "I don't like the looks of this fight. The Federals have an excellent position, and are well fortified." Hood snapped that he preferred to fight the Yankees at Franklin rather than at Nashville, "where they have been strengthening themselves for three years and more." Already cognizant of the Texan's disappointment regarding the previous day's activities, Cheatham silently swallowed Hood's rebuke. Recognizing that Hood would not be dissuaded from his plan to attack, Cheatham turned and ordered General Bate to move his division to the left and assault the Federal flank from that direction.[59]

Cheatham arranged his troops so that Bate was on the extreme left, while Brown, with Cheatham's old division, was to the left of the Columbia turnpike, with his right resting on the road. Cleburne's line extended from the road, where his left connected with Brown, to the right of the pike. From the end of Cleburne's line, A. P. Stewart's corps stretched the Confederate line to the right. As Bate had a fairly long distance to travel, Cheatham waited some time with his two remaining divisions while Bate worked his way into position. Before moving his troops from behind Winstead Hill, Cheatham arranged with Brown and Cleburne that he would signal with a flag when the soldiers were to move out. Men in the two divisions swung into position, corrected their alignment, then faced towards Cheatham. The Tennessean delayed momentarily to see that everything was ready, "then the flag dropped, and the line moved forward steady as a clock." Cheatham spurred his horse to the top of Winstead Hill as his troops passed over the rise. James D. Porter reminisced, "It was the greatest sight I ever saw when our army marched over the hill and reached the open field at its base. Each division unfolded itself into a single line of battle with as much steadiness as if forming for dress parade."[60]

The assault preparations at Franklin remained a vivid memory for Cheatham as well as Porter. When he and Porter returned to the battlefield in 1883, at the behest of a former Federal officer writing an account for a Philadelphia newspaper, Cheatham animatedly described the action as if it had just transpired. "Don't you recall, Porter," Cheatham recalled, "that as they wheeled into line of battle in full view of the enemy, their precision and military bearing was as beautiful a sight as was ever witnessed in war?"[61] For all the awed comments the deployment later aroused, Cheatham was considerably more placid in 1883 than he was during the engagement in 1864. According to one veteran, when the soldiers started forward Cheatham was visibly upset by Hood's intention to force a fight. "It is a mistake," Cheatham cried, "and it is no comfort to me to say we are not responsible."[62]

According to Cheatham's recollections, his men moved forward in a single battle line for a mile and a half. Although most writers assume that little if any artillery was brought up at Franklin, Cheatham asserted that he had twenty-four fieldpieces which "followed the advancing troops, and occasionally dropped a shell into the Federal's line." When the Confederates approached to within a mile of the main Union line, Cheatham's troops shifted formation. Cheatham had earlier seen that the Yankees occupied a line that was short and curved, and he realized that he could easily cover it by going forward in a pattern with two brigades in the front and two in the rear of each division. In Cheatham's old division, Carter's and Gordon's brigades occupied the front line, Gordon advancing along the turnpike, while Strahl and Gist supported the lead brigades.[63]

The Southerners suffered relatively light casualties as they pressed forward, and the assault gained momentum as Cheatham's men neared an

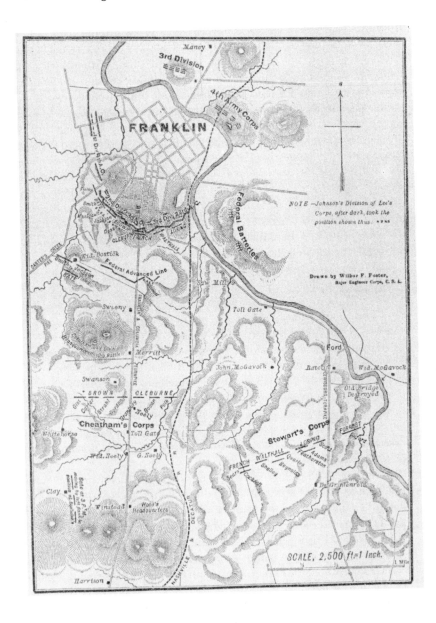

Map of the Battle of Franklin. From *Southern Bivouac* for June 1885.

advanced line several hundred yards in front of the main Federal position. Two brigades of Yankees held this area, but they were engulfed by the Confederates. At least one volley rippled through Cheatham's ranks, but his men were racing so fast by this time that they "hardly took time to return the fire, but raised the 'rebel yell' and charged at double-quick." The two Union brigades disintegrated in the face of the furious Southern assault. Some of the Yankees decided to surrender, and they threw down their arms and rushed through the advancing Rebel ranks "wherever they could find an opening." Others broke and fled for their main line, which worked to the advantage of Cheatham's onrushing troops. With soldiers of both armies intermixed in the mad dash, the bluecoats in the rear were reluctant to open fire, lest they hit their retreating comrades. Cheatham asserted that his men were within fifty yards of the Union line before the Yankees in the main line cut loose with a heavy round of fire. Even at that range the bluecoats could not help hitting some of their fellow Northerners who were still fleeing up the pike. Gordon later asserted that the "deadly fire . . . indiscriminately slew friend and foe alike." The fire grew increasingly lethal as Cheatham's men rushed forward; Gordon wrote later that it seemed as if the air was "literally filled" with "every conceivable missile used in modern warfare." The savage volleys failed to blunt the Southern charge. As the Rebels came on at a dead run, Brown, Gordon, and other officers loudly urged their men to go into the works behind the retreating Yankees.[64]

Brown's and Cleburne's men struck the Federal works before the Southern forces, partly because they had the most direct approach. But the impetuosity displayed along both sides of the road was also triggered by the long-standing rivalry between Cleburne's division and Cheatham's old unit. As Porter recalled, it was the first time that the two divisions "had met side by side in full view of each other, in an open field, with the advantages for desperate work equally balanced between them. For years each had contended for the right to wear the name of the crack division of that army, and the faces of both men and officers seemed to say, 'Here is the field upon which that right shall be decided.'"[65]

The race to win "first honors," as one Tennessean styled it, carried all the way to the Union breastworks. There, the Southerners encountered a deep ditch and obstructions along part of the line. Some of the Confederates were spent by the time they reached the Union works and fell exhausted into the ditch. Others were more energetic and fought hand-to-hand with the Yankee defenders. A number of color bearers leaped atop the fortifications and planted their flags on the parapet, a hazardous undertaking in light of the circumstances. Some paid for their intrepidity with their lives. A flag bearer with the Eleventh Tennessee toppled for-

Cheatham greatly admired the Irish-born Patrick Cleburne. The divisions led by the two generals vied for battlefield glory throughout the war, but particularly at Franklin. There, Cheatham's former division and Cleburne's regiments charged side by side along either side of the Columbia turnpike. Cleburne perished in the attack. (Library of Congress)

ward after he was shot, and his blood stained the banner as his life ebbed away. Cheatham's assault punched a hole in the Federal line along both sides of the pike, but Brown's men west of the road achieved the deepest penetration. Their momentum carried some of the Tennesseans to the rear of a handsome brick house owned by Fountain Branch Carter, who had a son, Tod, in the assaulting party. Terrific fighting swirled around the Carter house, its outbuildings, and a grove of locust trees a bit farther to the west.[66]

East of the road, Cleburne's men could not expand their initial break-through. Their attack ground to a halt near a cotton gin owned by the Carter family, and Cleburne's men suffered dreadful casualties as they were shoved back south of the main Union defense line. Cleburne himself was a victim of the incessant Yankee fire. The Irishman had realized the long odds facing the Confederate attackers, but he went into battle with wild abandon. His horse was wounded by an artillery shot, and a second steed offered by an aide was killed as Cleburne attempted to mount the animal. The divisional leader went ahead on foot, waving his cap, into the smoke which by now obscured much of the battlefield. Cleburne was shot in the left breast and fell dead some sixty yards south of the cotton gin. Years later, Cheatham could barely restrain his emotion as he described the impact of Cleburne's death. As he pointed out the spot where Cleburne's body was discovered, Cheatham noted sadly, "Here one of the best soldiers that ever drew a sword gave up his life." Cleburne's demise was the greatest loss his corps endured at Franklin, Cheatham asserted, and he described Cleburne as "a capital soldier." The Irishman's death, in Cheatham's eyes, was at least partly attributable to Hood's ac-cusations regarding the Spring Hill affair. "[Cleburne] had some unpleas-antness about Spring Hill with Hood," Cheatham explained, "and I think [he] was a little more daring than usual that day." Cheatham's account carried a certain amount of weight. As two recent historians have con-cluded, Cleburne "came to the Union lines in the manner of a private, not a division commander."[67]

Cleburne may have been Cheatham's most grievous loss, but he was by no means the only one. As the battle wore on, Cheatham's losses esca-lated at an alarming rate. Worse yet, Cheatham had little knowledge of what was happening at the front. The Tennessean was at Merrill Hill, a mile north of Hood's headquarters at Winstead Hill. Although Cheat-ham described Merrill Hill as "a sharp knob within musket range of the fight," it was still several hundred yards away from the battlefield. Ear-lier, Confederate sharpshooters had stationed themselves on the hill and picked off Union troops along the advanced line, but this activity ceased as the Confederate charge picked up steam. Merrill Hill provided Cheatham with a good vantage point from which to gauge the initial progress of the Rebel attack, but as the assault unfolded, smoke reduced Cheatham's visibility of the action. Coordinating the attack grew increasingly difficult as Cheatham's officer corps was butchered, and his staff officers and couriers alike were shot down. In Brown's division, for instance, only one staff officer escaped the battle unscathed.[68]

Cheatham could not realize, therefore, that his old division was being decimated. The members of Cheatham's command paid for their success when a Union brigade was sent to staunch the gap. This brigade, commanded by an Ohioan, Emerson Opdycke, was assisted by other bluecoats, including some of the defenders hurled back by Brown's men when the Rebels first tore through the line. Opdycke's force collided with Brown's veterans, and the impact staggered the Confederates. Incredibly fierce fighting raged in the rear of the Carter house as both sides struggled to gain the upper hand. Private Clay Barnes of the Sixth Tennessee vied with a Union soldier for control of a U.S. flag. Barnes clubbed his adversary with the butt of a rifle, then ripped the Yankee standard from its staff. Such scenes were commonplace as Brown's soldiers and Opdycke's bluecoats went at one another. Eventually the Federals forced the Rebels back, but Brown's men gave ground grudgingly. As it was, the Yankees never were able to force the Southerners completely back across the breastworks, and the Federals hastily improved and extended a second line of defense. Some of Brown's survivors, perhaps mindful of their rivalry with Cleburne's division, noted defiantly that they were the only unit able to hold some of the turf beyond the original Union line. Such tenacity served merely to make Brown's men more appealing targets. The Yankees were ultimately able to enfilade Brown's division from both the right and the left, and hundreds of men were killed and wounded as the carnage continued into the night.[69]

The severe losses in Cheatham's old division extended along both sides of the Columbia Pike. In the confusion of the initial assault, many of Gordon's men plunged into the fray east of the road, moving in conjunction with Cleburne's left brigade under Hiram Granbury. The attack in this sector withered in the face of the destructive enemy fire, and Granbury was shot in the head as he urged his men forward. The losses mounted, and eventually remnants of three brigades, including Gordon's Tennesseans, took refuge in a ditch near the turnpike. Occasional attempts to storm the works invariably resulted in failure, although the Rebels continued to launch such desperate sorties hours after the original assault had failed. After awhile, the Southerners huddled in the ditch were hit by a murderous crossfire from three directions, and a number of them saw no point in further resistance and surrendered. Among the latter was

Gordon, who had seen his brigade mangled in the terrible fighting east of the road. Aware also that he risked death if he remained in the ditch, Gordon and another soldier crawled over the parapet and gave up the fight. Years later, Gordon attributed his survival primarily to the fact that he went into battle on foot. Had he been on horseback, Gordon asserted, he would have been a ready target for the Union marksmen and would have been struck down in the initial charge.[70]

Though some of Brown's soldiers later took pride in having won a foothold in advance of any other Rebel unit, theirs was a pyrrhic victory. The three brigades of Brown's division that remained west of the turnpike became intermingled after Gist and Strahl came to the support of Carter's lead brigade. As they streamed through the opening into the area behind the Carter house, Cheatham's former command represented the high water mark of Confederate success at Franklin. Fatigue, soaring losses, and a lack of cohesion combined to check the Rebel assault after Opdycke's furious counterattack. Cheatham could not have known it at Merrill Hill, but savage combat tore the heart out of his once-proud division as afternoon lapsed into night. Casualties in Brown's brigades west of the pike were frightful and included both officers and the rank and file. General Brown himself was wounded when he was shot from his horse near nightfall. John C. Carter's brigade was cut to pieces near the locust grove, and Carter went down with a mortal wound. States Rights Gist had a horse shot out from beneath him, then was killed when a Federal minié ball pierced his heart.[71]

Otho Strahl led his brigade to near the Carter house, and portions of his command struggled to control the ground on either side of the breastworks. Strahl had gone into the fray with few illusions about what awaited his brigade; back on the slopes in front of Winstead Hill, he had foretold that the battle would be "short but desperate." Strahl's prophecy proved correct, and the brigadier found himself pinned down near the breastworks, along with most of his troops. The works were so high in some places that the Confederates were forced to stand on their dead to get off a shot, and Strahl busied himself for awhile by passing loaded guns up to those who were in a position to squeeze off a round. At some point Strahl boosted a man above the works, only to see the soldier shot down almost immediately. The scene was repeated, and when a third Rebel asked Strahl for help in crossing the parapet, the general refused, saying, "No, I have helped my last man up on the works to be shot in my hands." Strahl apparently climbed up the side of the breastworks and began to fire away at the Yankees. Private Zack Smith of the Nineteenth Tennessee, who earlier had been punished by Strahl for some act of insubordination, joined the officer on the parapet and began blazing away at the

Federals. Strahl was struck by Smith's devotion, patted the soldier on the shoulder, and said. "Go it, Zack. I will never forget you for this." As things turned out, the gratitude he displayed for Smith was one of Otho Strahl's last earthly emotions. The brigade commander was severely wounded near the works, but managed to crawl some twenty feet to turn over his command to a subordinate. As he was being borne away by his staff officers and several others, Strahl was hit again, and a third shot caught him in the head and killed him instantly. A writer remembered that Strahl's entire staff became victims of the Federal fire shortly afterwards, their bodies toppling one upon another in rapid succession.[72]

Cheatham later insisted that there was fight in the entire army at Franklin, but Stewart's corps enjoyed no more success than Cheatham's in breaking the Union line. The bluecoats were assisted by a perennial Confederate woe, inability to coordinate the timing of their assaults with any great precision, with the result that the Federals were able to rebuff one assault and then brace themselves for another one elsewhere. Stewart's men were also wrecked by concentrated fire and spent themselves in courageous but vain assaults that merely added to the already-long list of casualties. One can only imagine Cheatham's feeling of helplessness as he lingered on Merrill Hill. He must have guessed that the battle was not going well, if for no other reason than that his staff officers failed to reappear after he sent them to the front. Unable to tell Hood what was happening, Cheatham could do little except watch the flashes of gunfire off in the distance.

Lee arrived in the late afternoon with a portion of his corps from Columbia, and Hood ordered assistance sent to Cheatham. Lee located Cheatham as darkness descended, and the distraught Tennessean outlined the section of the field where he felt Edward Johnson's division could be used to the best advantage. Cheatham pointed to the Union line and said, "Yonder line of fire at the breastworks is where you are needed and wanted at once." After warning Johnson's men not to shoot into the backs of their comrades, the division was sent to the front. Johnson struck the Federals hard, but the added impetus was unable to break the entrenched Yankee position.[73]

The sustained fighting gave way to intermittent exchanges around 9 P.M., and as the turmoil subsided, Cheatham moved forward from his vantage on Merrill Hill. He later maintained that the Federals withdrew from Franklin around 11 P.M., and that he rode into the town in the early morning hours of December 1. Another source suggests that he paused for awhile as the infirmary and relief corps scoured the field for the dead and wounded. A soldier in the Nineteenth Tennessee recalled seeing Cheatham wander across the dark battlefield and peer by torchlight into the faces of the dead. Realizing for the first time the dimensions of the tragedy, Cheatham was shaken as he heard hundreds of wounded soldiers appeal for help and water. According to the soldier, as Cheatham made his somber trek, "great big tears ran down his cheeks and he sobbed like a child."[74]

Wandering around a dark battlefield searching for casualties was hardly Cheatham's responsibility as a corps commander. Yet it is hard to fault him for his behavior. When he rode up the pike from Merrill Hill, he must have been anxious to see first hand how the fighting had gone. Kept in the dark during most of the action, his nighttime investigation was the first inkling he had of the day's results. It is doubtful that a man as attached to his private soldiers as Cheatham could stifle his natural curiosity when he approached the battlefield. His familiar impulse to care for the wounded was surely his paramount concern. Besides, one can argue that losses among the field commanders and Cheatham's staff were so severe that the normal administrative routine of the corps was paralyzed by the time Cheatham rode forward. After ascertaining to some degree the extent of his loss, he did enter Franklin, perhaps to set up a command post.

Cheatham had good reason to weep during his nighttime trek, as he discovered more fully when he rode upon the field at daybreak. The Tennessean was stunned by the grisly scene that confronted him. He reminisced that the battle had raged most fiercely within a range of fifty yards to either side of the pike. Within that compressed area, Brown's and Cleburne's divisions had suffered dreadfully. "Almost under your eye, nearly all the dead, wounded and dying lay," Cheatham attested. "The dead were piled up like stacks of wheat or scattered about like sheaves of grain. You could have walked all over the field upon dead bodies without stepping upon the ground." Near the Carter house "the bodies lay in heaps," and the locust thicket west of the pike "had been mowed off by bullets, as if by a scythe." A man who counted the bodies told Cheatham that there were over 1,500 corpses in the narrow space to either side of the pike, "900 Confederate and something over 600 Union." The view was so disheartening that Cheatham later remarked, "I never saw anything like that field, and I never want to again."[75]

Hood shattered his army on the plains before Franklin. Over 6,200 of the Confederates engaged were casualties by the end of the battle, with roughly 1,750 of these killed or mortally wounded. Cheatham's officer contingent was exterminated, especially in Brown's and Cleburne's divisions. In Gist's brigade a Georgia captain was the senior officer after the fray. Cheatham could never hope to replace the experienced officers who fell, especially in light of the severe losses sustained by the lower-echelon officers. The administrative makeup of the army was also splintered by a heavy toll extracted among the staff officer ranks. One such casualty was Captain Tod Carter, serving in one of Bate's brigades, who fell wounded several hundred yards from his family home. Carter was conveyed to his home on December 1, but died shortly thereafter. Another casualty among the staff officers was Lieutenant John Henry Marsh, who had marveled at his deliverance from enemy fire at Atlanta. At Franklin, Marsh was not so fortunate; he went down near his brigade commander, Strahl, in the fighting near the breastworks. Reverend Charles Quintard was sickened when he learned of the deaths of Strahl, Marsh, and other intimate friends within the Army of Tennessee. A notation in Quintard's diary reveals his despair when the cleric learned of the unusually high losses: "How long, Lord, how long!"[76]

The depression which settled on Quintard ran throughout the army. Cheatham's sorrow at the loss of so many fellow officers was exacerbated when he pondered the equally tragic destruction visited upon his men. Vast numbers of Cheatham's "boys," as he styled them, were killed, wounded, or captured. When he rode over the battlefield, Cheatham saw the bodies of men who had served in his division since 1862, and some who had been with him since the beginning of the war. Sometimes their fate had a special poignancy, as in the case of Private J. T. Puckett of the Fourth Tennessee. Puckett lived in the vicinity of Franklin, and he had already procured a furlough from his superiors so he could visit his home. Unwilling to abandon his comrades at a critical time, Puckett jammed the furlough into his pocket and decided to "wait till after the battle." It was a fateful decision; Puckett lost his life in the fight.[77]

There were hundreds of men like J. T. Puckett who perished at Franklin, but most of the individual names have long since been forgotten. As the battle faded into history, it became harder to understand the horror which Cheatham and his men felt as they surveyed the battlefield. Even the Southerners who participated in the fight had trouble comprehending the appalling losses at Franklin. Language was inadequate to describe the carnage they witnessed, although they tried. One soldier used a poetic image: "Officers and men fell like dead leaves when forests are shaken." Sam Watkins of the First Tennessee described it as "a grand holocaust of death." William Worsham of the Nineteenth Tennessee wrote that Franklin would be remembered "as a black page in the memory of our lost cause." One soldier scanned the field and was reminded of the inscription on the sign which greeted Cheatham's soldiers as they entered the state: "Tennessee, a Grave or a Free Home." Cheatham reminisced that it "was a wonder that any man escaped alive from that storm of iron missiles." Porter summed up the tragic consequences by asserting that the

Charles Todd Quintard was chaplain of the First Tennessee Regiment, and was intimately acquainted with Cheatham. After the war, Quintard, by then Episcopal Bishop of Tennessee, officiated at Cheatham's baptism, marriage, and funeral. (Tennessee State Library and Archives)

losses in Cheatham's and Stewart's corps were "great enough to make Tennessee a land of mourning."[78]

During his 1883 visit to the battlefield, Cheatham almost apologized to the reporter at the conclusion of their tour. "It is all over now," Cheatham said, "and these are only reflections upon what might have been. I did not come here to talk [about] them, but to show you the position of our troops, and point out where we began and ended. This is the first time I have visited this battle-field since the fight took place," he continued, "and I have talked more of the events of the war to-day than during all the past fifteen years."[79] While that may be true, it is obvious that Cheatham never forgot the sight of the field at Franklin, nor did those of his Tennesseans fortunate enough to survive the engagement.

Cheatham and his veterans who made it through the war later may have had difficulty articulating what they saw after that battle, but they had no such problem when it came to placing blame for the tragedy. Years later, the haunting memory of the battlefield at Franklin kept alive a bitter resentment towards Hood that was nurtured by both Cheatham and his men. Hood contributed to this postwar enmity by asserting that his soldiers relied upon defensive maneuvers under Johnston for so long that they were incapable of assaulting boldly. They did just that in the battles around Atlanta, and it is almost inconceivable that Hood could level such an unjust charge after Franklin.[80]

Cheatham expressed a lifelong respect for the army's fighting ability and endurance, and his favorable appraisal was certainly more valid than Hood's imputation that the men lacked courage. Veterans of Cheatham's former division later questioned Hood's leadership, and some were frankly contemptuous of the Texan after Franklin. James Iredell Hall of the Ninth Tennessee sought to be objective when he acknowledged that Hood was "a gallant soldier" and hard fighter, but Hall concluded that Hood rashly sacrificed his men and was "utterly incompetent as a commander." A member of the Sixteenth Tennessee also lauded Hood's bravery but felt the army chieftain lacked prudence and discretion. Several postwar writers implied that Hood's physical disabilities impaired his ability to command, a view which has some merit.[81] Other survivors of Cheatham's command, embittered by the memory of Franklin, were less charitable to Hood. "Why was this slaughter?" wrote a veteran in the Twenty-seventh Tennessee. He and the other survivors asked themselves, "What is or could have been accomplished?" They fixed the blame squarely on Hood. The Texan had never gained the confidence of Cheatham's men after he took the reins from Johnston, and his inability to claim any decisive victories further eroded their faith in him. Their scorn for Hood often extended into the postwar era. Two veterans of the Twelfth Tennessee who wrote a brief sketch of the regiment's history summarized the sentiments of many of their comrades in the division. The authors lavishly praised Joe Johnston and criticized his successor in one telling phrase. Old Joe, the authors contended, "never drove them into a *Franklin slaughter!*"[82] It is hard not to pity Hood, who was damned for replacing Johnston and damned for not being a winner. Yet the real pity, Cheatham and his men would have asserted, was that Hood stubbornly insisted on sending his army to its doom at Franklin.

Chapter 10

Disaster at Nashville

After Franklin, Hood faced a difficult decision. A withdrawal would further dishearten the army, but a forward movement towards Nashville invited additional disaster. Despite the inherent danger, Hood opted for the latter course, after briefly tarrying at Franklin. The Texan transferred his battered command to a site several miles south of Nashville, with Cheatham's corps moving northward on December 2.[1] There are indications that Hood did not fully understand the task confronting him. Thomas had successfully amassed a large force to deal with the Confederate invaders, and Nashville by late 1864 was one of the most heavily fortified cities in America. Hood's original intention was to have volunteers storm the key works of the city, a plan he divulged to Charles Todd Quintard on November 27. Such a scheme was probably impractical even before Hood bloodied his army at Franklin. After the devastating losses there, Hood must have realized the futility of resuming the offensive. He therefore had his troops carve out a five-mile-long defense line which covered three of the seven main roads leading south from Nashville. Cheatham's corps held the right of the Southern line, Lee the center, and Stewart the left.[2] While his men erected fortifications, Hood waited for Thomas to make the first move. Perhaps he hoped that the Union commander would err and provide an opening for a Confederate counterattack. While waiting to discern what Thomas would do, Hood weakened his army by sending Bate's division and Forrest's cavalry to harass a Union garrison at Murfreesboro. That diversion deprived Cheatham of his strongest division and meant that he was forced to construct his segment of the line by using the survivors from Brown's and Cleburne's divisions. Such a development could not have pleased Cheatham.[3]

While Cheatham and his men were closer to Nashville than they had been since being shoved away from Murfreesboro nearly two years earlier, there is evidence that many of the officers and soldiers were demoralized. One of Cleburne's brigades had been left behind to convoy a supply train from Florence at the beginning of the campaign, and it rejoined the corps at Nashville on December 6. Brigadier-General James A. Smith assumed command of the division but quickly discovered that the unit was hardly the same one he had seen a few weeks earlier in Alabama. Assessing the damage inflicted at Franklin, Smith reported that he found the division "much reduced in numbers especially in officers. . . . Nor was the tone and morale such as was desirable owing to the fearful loss sustained in that battle."[4] Southern spirits dipped even lower during the second week in December, when bitterly cold weather pushed into the region. Rain turned into sleet and then snow, making life miserable for Hood's veterans. Few of the Confederates had tents or any form of shelter against the wintry blasts. Forced to sleep on the frozen ground, the Rebels also suffered from inadequate supplies of clothing. Many of them had begun the Tennessee invasion in thin, threadbare garments, and the problem was even worse after they had marched hundreds of miles into the state. A number of them were barefoot, and they left bloody tracks as the ice sliced their soles. Nowhere was the devotion of the common soldier in the Army of Tennessee more manifest than at Nashville. Faced with Federal artillery shelling as well as the inhospitable climate, Hood's men persevered in one of the most depressing military situations imaginable.[5]

Cheatham endured many of the same privations as his men, although his quarters were somewhat better than those of the average soldier. This benefit was offset by his having to deal with command problems and complications. One such woe arrived via a letter written by Brigadier-General Henry Rootes Jackson, one of Bate's subordinates. In his letter, dated December 10, Jackson violently criticized the performance of the other two brigades in the division, (Finley's and Tyler's brigades, commanded respectively by Colonel Robert Bullock and Brigadier-General Thomas Benton Smith.) Jackson believed that his own brigade had been the only one in Bate's command to engage the Federals at Franklin, and he essentially accused the remainder of the division of cowardice. Other incidents convinced Jackson of the unreliability of the other brigades, and he implored Cheatham to separate his command from Bate's division. In fact, Jackson requested a transfer from the "distressing and demoralizing scenes of the past to some new field of action." A Georgian, Jackson bitterly reminded Cheatham that the Tennessean had been instrumental in withdrawing him from a large command where he could be rendering "honorable service in defense of my own state and home." There was little Cheatham could do to alleviate Jackson's outrage, but the lack of harmony in Bate's division did not bode well for future action. As it was, Cheatham may have been left to ponder the irascibility of Jackson, who ironically had served at one time on the staff of Cheatham's intra-army foe, W. H. T. Walker.[6]

On the Union side, Thomas had his own troubles, particularly with War Department authorities who were waiting impatiently for him to strike. Among those irked with Thomas was Ulysses S. Grant, who grew increasingly vexed at Hood's continued presence in the Nashville area. Still, Thomas delayed until mid-month, when there was a break in the weather. He confided his final battle plans to his subordinates on December 14 and took aim at Hood's army. The Confederates for their part were in a precarious position, despite the return of Bate with his division. Cheatham's men on the far right were ensconced in a railway cut just east of the Nolensville Pike. From this point the Southern line extended to the west, with Lee's corps astride the familiar Franklin Pike, while Stewart's corps stretched across the Granny White Pike and bent back near the Hillsboro Pike. Despite their efforts to strengthen their defenses, the Rebels were vulnerable on both flanks. Hood simply did not have the manpower to cover as much ground as he would have liked, and the cavalry he had available could not successfully impede a vigorous Yankee attack. Thomas was aware of Hood's plight and determined to exploit the Rebel left flank.[7]

When the Federals moved out on December 15, they did so with 54,000 well-equipped and amply-fed troops. A detachment of over 5,000 men under Major-General James B. Steedman was sent to keep Cheatham at bay while Thomas directed his main effort against Stewart. The opening sequence to the battle of Nashville began around 8 A.M., as Steedman moved against Cheatham. Despite the early morning fog, Cheatham's men eventually espied Steedman's men moving eastward as they endeavored to attack Cheatham from the rear. After a half hour the Southerners discovered that the Union column was composed of black troops, who were allowed to cross the railroad cut behind Cheatham's breastworks. While this was taking place, Cheatham withdrew a portion of his command in response to the Union threat. The Yankees, oblivious to Cheatham's maneuver, shifted into battle formation and attacked. When the blacks charged the works, some of Cheatham's men about-faced while a Rebel brigade swung in behind the snared Federals. An infantryman in the brigade recalled that this was the first time that Cheatham's men had come into "contact with negro soldiers" on the battlefield. Back at Decatur many of the same Southerners had expressed their antipathy at seeing black men in Union uniforms, and at Nashville they furiously assailed the Federals. Although the blacks and their white officers eventually extricated themselves, they suffered considerable losses. The Yankees regrouped and made another assault, but it was no more successful than the previous one. When the fighting died down, one Rebel derisively noted that "all that remained on the ground were good niggers." Despite

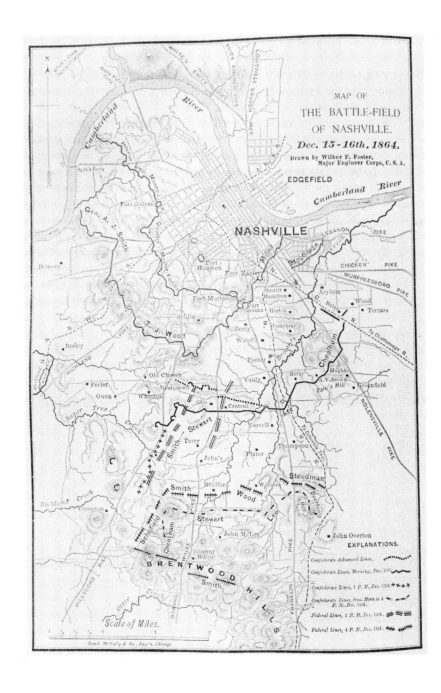

Map of the Battle of Nashville. From *Southern Bivouac* for August 1885.

the setback, Steedman and his black troops did their job by diverting attention away from the main attack and by neutralizing Cheatham for much of the day.[8]

While Cheatham occupied himself with Steedman, A. P. Stewart's troops contended with the massive pivot devised by Thomas. Stewart resisted valiantly, but he was outnumbered almost ten to one and was forced to yield ground. The heavy Union pressure finally shoved Stewart back to the vicinity of the Granny White Pike. Hood sent reinforcements, first from Lee, and then from Bate late in the afternoon. As Bate crossed the Franklin Pike, he noticed "streams of stragglers," displaced artillerymen, and horses falling back from the left. Bate quickly formed his division for battle, then discussed the situation with Cheatham when the corps commander came up. By now it was nearly dark, and Hood ordered Bate to move forward. After Bate occupied a skirt of woods pointed out by Hood, he informed Cheatham of his position and listened as the firing died out. Hood realized that he could not remain in his ruptured line and ordered a withdrawal after nightfall. Cheatham rendezvoused with Bate around 8 P.M. and led his fellow Tennessean to the new line of defense. The two generals located elements of Stewart's corps, and Cheatham told Bate that he was to move his division to the west of Stewart. The remainder of the corps would follow, with the result that Cheatham replaced Stewart as the left of the Confederate line. They fell back for over a mile and took up their positions west of the Granny White Pike. It took some time for Cheatham's soldiers to complete the move from right to left. A fire was kindled, by Cheatham's command, to help Bate and the remainder of the corps locate the general area where they were headed. Despite the blaze, Bate and the rest of Cheatham's men had some difficulty as they groped their way through the dark. Mud and marshland combined to slow their progress, and Bate found that he was unable to bring his artillery or ambulance wagons to the new line. Cheatham's men must have been weary, in light of their earlier fight with Steedman and the forced march after nightfall. They became even wearier after being ordered to construct a new set of earthworks, a task which deprived Cheatham's veterans of some needed sleep.[9]

Although there was little he could do to improve the situation, Cheatham's position was a weak one. His line extended westward to an eminence known subsequently as Shy's Hill, so named because Colonel William Shy of the Twentieth Tennessee occupied the summit, then angled sharply to the south. After running several hundred yards in this direction, the extreme left end of Cheatham's line hooked back to the east. Bate held the ground in the vicinity of Shy's Hill, while Cheatham's old division (now commanded by Mark Lowrey) continued the line to the left. Cleburne's former division, under J. A. Smith, linked with Lowrey and anchored the far left. The angle at Shy's Hill promised disaster for Cheatham the next day. Thomas knew that he had been successful with his original battle plan, and on the second day of the fray he ordered a continuation of the strategy. Once again, the Yankees sought to keep the Confederate right busy while the primary punch was delivered at the left. Having replaced Stewart, Cheatham became the main target of the Union attack forces.[10]

Cheatham was not privy to the strategy sessions which Thomas conducted, but he was aware of the vulnerability of his long line. Bate had not liked the angle along Shy's Hill from the moment he saw it, but Cheatham informed him that there was little they could do to change it. According to Cheatham, Hood's engineer had laid out the line, and Cheatham himself was not authorized to alter it.[11] The apprehensions shared by Cheatham and Bate were fully realized the next day, although it took some time for the Yankees to flex their muscle along Cheatham's front. As on the previous day, Thomas sought to divert Hood's attention away from the Southern left by launching attacks against the Rebel right. Stephen D. Lee's troops were assaulted in the morning and again around noon. Although Lee was able to fend off the Federals, Hood was apprehensive for the safety of his right flank. He withdrew Smith's division from Cheatham's left and sent it off to assist Lee, a move which further hampered Cheatham's ability to defend his portion of the line. An already attenuated left flank grew even thinner as Cheatham's units shifted to cover the area vacated by Smith.[12]

Matters grew even worse when Union batteries opened up against the Shy's Hill salient. The Federals were able to hammer the summit from three directions, and the murderous barrage increased in intensity during the afternoon. In spite of the nighttime efforts to erect suitable protection, one officer wrote that the defenses along Cheatham's front consisted mainly of "some logs and trees rolled together."[13] Such improvised breastworks were soon battered in, and Cheatham and his men were forced to take cover. Each shell directed at Cheatham's sector extracted a mental as well as physical toll. By mid-December of 1864 the characteristic esprit and resiliency of Cheatham's men had been worn thin. Nowhere was this state of affairs more prevalent than in Bate's division, even though Bate's men had not suffered at Franklin the sort of losses found in Brown's and Cleburne's divisions. They had not particularly distinguished themselves during the Murfreesboro raid, and Bate's men were unprepared for what awaited them when the bombardment tapered off late in the afternoon. Around 4 P.M. a gigantic wave of Union troops emerged from several directions against the Tennesseans. As rain steadily fell, the men atop Shy's Hill were practically obliterated, and the Confederate left gave way. Cheatham's former division under Lowrey was also affected, and a depressing scene unfolded as Cheatham watched his men break in chaotic disorder and race for the rear.[14]

The disaster widened and ultimately spread to A. P. Stewart's corps. Early in the day Hood had commanded Cheatham to fall back via the Granny White Pike in the event of a reversal, but as his men streamed down the road, they encountered another terrifying surprise. Without Forrest to harry them, James Wilson's Union cavalry easily gained Cheatham's rear and moved against the fleeing Confederates. Fresh panic gripped Cheatham's men when they smacked into Wilson's horsemen, who were armed with repeating rifles. The scared butternuts sheared off to the east and the Franklin Pike, where the scene was one of indescribable confusion. Wagons, artillery, and infantry all blended together in disorganized flight as Cheatham's and Stewart's corps disintegrated.[15]

The sudden collapse along Cheatham's front was so complete that discipline broke down almost entirely. His men had displayed their courage on many a battlefield, but at Nashville they yielded to their desire for self-preservation. The Federal onslaught triggered a stampede as Cheatham's troops scurried to the rear. The rain complicated matters for the soldiers as they fled from their adversaries. Mud clung to their shoes, and some of Cheatham's men kicked off their footwear in an attempt to gain more speed. Some of the bolder Confederates halted defiantly and fired at their pursuers, but this was not a universal reaction. In many cases the Yankees were far too close for such gestures. The color bearer of the Nineteenth Tennessee, for example, had to rip the regimental flag from its staff as Union soldiers raced after him through a cornfield. Only after he divested himself of the flagstaff was he able to outrun his pursuers.[16] As the disaster broke, Hood sent a courier to Cheatham with a request that he rally as many men as he could on a hill to the rear. The order was delivered, but things were so bad that even "Old Frank" had little luck in stemming the rout. Cheatham did manage to stop one private by his horse, but when the general turned his attention to another group of fleeing troops, the private slipped underneath Cheatham's steed and continued his getaway. Officers from several regiments tried to rally their men, but the efforts were usually futile. An observer noted that the Tennesseans "flatly refused to stop," discarding their guns and "indeed, everything that impeded their flight." Cheatham was assisted by several men in the Ninth Tennessee, who managed to form a line containing about 150 troops, but the Federal pursuit made it impossible for the Confederates to effectively reorganize. With the Yankees bearing down ever closer,

Cheatham and two other officers with him "turned their horses and gal-loped off," and the infantrymen fled once again.[17]

Not everyone escaped. All three of Bate's brigade commanders were captured, including General Henry R. Jackson, who was taken by an ex-ultant Federal private. Jackson may have rued his fate, especially in light of his complaints to Cheatham earlier in the week, but at least he did not have to bear the cruel lot of Thomas B. Smith. Smith, a young briga-dier in Bate's command, was being conducted to the rear when a vengeful Ohio colonel struck him over the head several times with a sword. The Union surgeon who attended Smith found that the Tennessean's brain was exposed and expected that he would die from the wound. The doc-tor's prognosis proved incorrect, but Smith's recovery was arguably more a burden than a blessing. As a result of the injuries he received at Nash-ville, Smith was admitted in 1876 to the state insane asylum, where he remained for the last forty-seven years of his life.[18]

Stephen D. Lee's skillful defense saved the army. After pulling his corps back to the Overton Hills, Lee managed to stave the Federals off. The onset of darkness, and confusion among the triumphant Yankees as-sisted Lee, and finally the army began sorting itself out. According to a soldier in the Fifth Tennessee, the Rebels fell back for several miles and then began to bivouac by the roadside. Men passing by continually called to find out the location of various divisions, brigades, and regiments, and eventually most were able to rejoin their proper commands. Noticeably missing from these reunions were the men in Cheatham's corps who had been killed, wounded, or captured. Most of the missing fell into the last category, but they were out of the war nonetheless. The losses, coming hard on the heels of those at Franklin, essentially destroyed the Army of Tennessee. As one of Cheatham's men related, when the march south-ward was resumed early the next morning, "it was a sad sight to see how few men formed on the colors of the different regiments." The drain in manpower was accompanied by a corresponding loss in war materiel. In their haste to escape the Union onslaught, the Southerners had aban-doned all sorts of supplies, including dozens of cannons. The survivors in Cheatham's former division particularly regretted the loss of three guns attached to Turner's Mississippi battery which were reclaimed by the Federals after being in the possession of Cheatham's gunners for over two years. One of Cheatham's staff officers later noted that the pieces had always been served "with the greatest distinction by the company of noble Mississippians who manned them."[19]

After Nashville, more than just Turner's battery could be referred to in the past tense. The combined catastrophes at Franklin and Nashville wiped out a good portion of the army, and after the second battle, it must have been obvious to Cheatham and his men that the war was lost. This depressing reality was suppressed, at least temporarily, by the struggle to escape from the Union troops who hounded the Confederate retreat. Lee continued his rear guard actions the day following the battle, while the rest of the army passed through Franklin. Cheatham's remaining troops reached the vicinity of Spring Hill that evening. Lee was wounded in the foot on December 17, and the next day Cheatham replaced Lee at the rear of the Confederate column. Forced to beat off an attack by Union cavalrymen, Cheatham crossed rain-swollen Rutherford's Creek and halted on the southern bank of the stream. He remained there much of the next day, skirmishing with the pursuing Federals, but disengaged in the afternoon and headed for Duck River.[20]

The frustration of defeat accompanied the Confederates on their retreat, and when Cheatham arrived at Duck River, the strain of the campaign almost flared into senseless violence. Cheatham had been scheduled to cross the river earlier in the day, but his fight with the Yankee horsemen had delayed his passage. When Cheatham's corps came up, they discovered that Forrest's cavalry had rejoined the army. Forrest was convinced that his cavalry was due to cross the waterway, and he stated his intentions to Cheatham. Cheatham disagreed, and he told Forrest, "I think not, sir. You are mistaken. I intend to cross now, and will thank you to move out of the way of my troops." Enraged, Forrest pulled out a pistol and spurred his horse closer to the infantry commander. He said, "If you are a better man than I am, General Cheatham, your troops can cross ahead of mine." Cheatham's men witnessed the altercation, and they reacted angrily. As tempers flared between the two commanders, muskets clicked along Cheatham's column, and his infantrymen vowed to "shoot Forrest's cavalry into the middle of Duck River in a minute" if the cavalry leader dared touch "Mars Frank." Fortunately, Stephen D. Lee alighted from a nearby ambulance and "pacified the chafing Cheatham."[21] According to one source, the two Tennesseans defused the tense moment by apologizing to one another, though reports differ as to which command then crossed the bridge.[22]

The flareup between Cheatham and Forrest was symptomatic of the stress experienced by the Confederates, but Hood vacillated over the future of the army while he was in Columbia. The army commander dabbled with the notion of staying in Tennessee and organizing a line of defense along the Duck River, a concept promoted by the Reverend Charles Todd Quintard when he met with Hood on December 18. Quintard and an officer present argued that the Tennessee troops might desert if the army abandoned the state and felt the continued presence of the

Confederates would allow Hood to claim that the campaign had been a success. Forrest reached headquarters the next day and promptly squashed Quintard's suggestion, urging Hood to withdraw from the state at once. As Hood and Forrest conversed, the sound of cannonading from the north reached their ears, and Cheatham sent word that he had repulsed the enemy's cavalry. Faced with these factors, Hood accepted Forrest's advice and made plans to evacuate the state.[23]

Forrest agreed to cover the retreat, but his horsemen had been in daily contact with the enemy for several weeks and required infantry support. To meet the requirement, Hood selected General Edward Walthall to command a rear guard composed of the remnants of eight brigades. Elements of Cheatham's former division were included in Walthall's aggregation, with the remnants from Carter's and Strahl's brigades chosen to help in the task. In truth, they could hardly be termed brigades any longer; a return dated four days before Christmas revealed that fewer than three hundred effectives were available from the two units. The other brigades at Walthall's disposal were similarly shrunken, and the Mississippian consolidated the eight brigades into four, with Colonel Hume R. Feild leading the men from Cheatham's old division.[24] Hood evidently assisted personally in the formation of the rear guard, as he met with some of Cheatham's troops and asked them to volunteer for the duty. Asserting his confidence in the Tennesseans, Hood quickly gained the assent of Cheatham's veterans. As an aside, Hood referred to the debacle at Nashville by using an analogy from his poker-playing days. "The cards were fairly dealt at Nashville, boys," Hood explained, "but they beat the game." If he was looking for commiseration, Hood chose the wrong group of men for a conversation. One of the few survivors from the Nineteenth Tennessee, James Stevenson, boldly stared up at Hood and replied, "Yes, General, the cards were fairly dealt, but they were mighty badly shuffled."[25]

Cheatham's men who acted as part of Walthall's rear guard force later looked back on this aspect of their service with inestimable pride. Given the adversity they faced, their pride was fully justified. Walthall's and Forrest's main foe was the relentless Union cavalry, but other opponents included the weather and the slow progress of the main column. The bitterly cold weather created tremendous hardships for the Confederates. Hundreds in the rear guard were shoeless. Walthall later reported that "some had no blankets and all were poorly clad for the season." Rain, sleet, and snow fell at various times during their trek. Roads became nearly impassable, and the artillery and few wagons which accompanied Walthall's command "were moved with considerable difficulty." Eventually the rear guard began to "overhaul straggling wagons belonging to the train of the main army," and they carted these off when possible, but sacrificed time in doing so. Near Pulaski, the Southerners halted and rebuffed their pursuers, and they repeated the performance the day after Christmas. On this occasion the Rebels were assisted by a dense fog which concealed their presence near Sugar Creek. Lured by an advance force into range of the Confederate infantry, the Yankee horsemen were delivered a sharp repulse. Feild's men joined with other butternuts in a charge, which netted several prisoners and nearly all the horses of one dismounted Union regiment. Stung twice by the Confederates, the blue-clad cavalry hung close to the retreating column, "but made no further demonstration." Considering the disadvantages under which they labored, the men commanded by Walthall and Forrest did a heroic job guarding the Rebel rear. The discipline and spirit they exhibited, in spite of all that had preceded the retreat, entitled members of the rear guard to the acclaim which their officers later bestowed upon them.[26]

Notwithstanding the margin of safety provided by Walthall's and Forrest's troopers, it is hard to imagine that Frank Cheatham ever spent a more miserable Christmas than he did during 1864. Whatever hopes he may have harbored about redeeming his hometown and state from Federal control were crushed. Hundreds of his men had been killed, wounded, or captured during the campaign. His friend Pat Cleburne was dead, a painful blow compounded by the loss of so many other officers within Cheatham's command. And Christmas Day brought with it no respite, as the Yankees continued to nip at the heels of the Confederate column. If there was any cause for jubilation on the holiday, it came when the Southerners managed to ford Shoal Creek and move two miles beyond to the Tennessee River. Even this accomplishment was attended by worries. The sound of fire from Union gunboats near Florence reverberated along the river, arousing fears that they would wreak havoc when the Rebels tried to cross the waterway. Cheatham supervised work crews who erected a pontoon bridge across the river, a task which took all night to complete. About sunrise on December 26, the army's trains began to cross, and by evening most of the remaining wagons and artillery were on the southern shore. Cheatham came over after nightfall, and by early the next morning the infantry began their shift to the opposite bank. Two Federal gunboats came upriver in the afternoon to within two or three miles of the bridge, but were driven off by Rebel batteries. Only after Walthall's force crossed on December 28 could the Confederates breathe a little easier, as the Union pursuit finally ground to a halt at the river.[27]

Cheatham moved with his battered corps to Tuscumbia, then on into Mississippi near Iuka before the retreat ended at Tupelo on January 13. The diminished Federal pressure may have provided Cheatham with more time to ruminate on the consequences of the invasion. His depression was readily apparent to one soldier in the Sixth Tennessee, who spotted Cheatham standing near the end of a railroad bridge as the army continued southward. The "grim old warrior . . . stood as motionless as a statue," the soldier reminisced, "his gray eyes set with a fixed and vacant look, and his countenance wearing an expression of profound melancholy." The appearance was so pained that the observer felt Cheatham's face was the saddest one he had ever seen.[28] Nor was Cheatham the only person dejected by the results of the campaign. Captain Alfred T. Fielder of the Twelfth Tennessee had been wounded at Atlanta and rejoined his regiment for the first time on December 28. Fielder was shocked by the depleted state of his unit, which he termed "a mere skeleton" of what it was the previous summer. Learning that most of his comrades were dead, wounded, or missing, while others had deserted, Fielder wrote an accurate appraisal in his diary: "Take it all [together] the army may be said to be in bad condition."[29]

The deterioration in the army was evident to noncombatants as well. Early in the retreat, a Tennessee resident described the Confederate soldiers as "the most broke down set I ever saw." Sam Watkins of the First Tennessee wrote that "citizens seemed to shrink and hide from us as we approached them."[30] Towards the end of the withdrawal, a Mississippian named Samuel Agnew noted the passage of a "good many straggling soldiers" en route for Tupelo. Agnew was visiting his uncle when one of the Rebels, "an impudent looking man," came to ask about the condition of the roads ahead. A Yankee overcoat concealed the uniform of the visitor, and Agnew inquired which command he was from. The civilian was surprised when he discovered that he was talking to General Cheatham. Basing his assessment on the brief conversation they shared, Agnew judged Cheatham as "a very energetic man, and one who is a stranger to fear." Agnew later wrote in his diary that "it was an unexpected honor" to see "so distinguished a man" as Cheatham. After learning the best route for his wagons to take, Cheatham left with two couriers and rejoined the column.[31]

Once he arrived at Tupelo, Hood at last accepted that the campaign had failed, and on January 13, 1865 he asked to be relieved. Richmond accepted the request, and General Richard Taylor was placed in temporary command. For many of Cheatham's men the war was over. Hood had earlier promised that men in regiments from West Tennessee would be furloughed after the Tennessee River was crossed, and at Tupelo the promise was fulfilled. Many of Cheatham's men took advantage of the offer and headed home. Army officials hoped that morale might rise when the soldiers visited their families and got refitted, and that absentees would eventually return to the ranks. Those with the strictest sense of duty did return to the army, but many of Cheatham's veterans recognized the futility of further resistance and stayed home.[32] For Cheatham's remaining men, orders eventually arrived that lightened the burden of defeat somewhat. Elements of the Army of Tennessee were ordered to proceed eastward, where they were to serve once more under Joseph E. Johnston.[33]

The fighting force summoned to join Johnston was hardly the same one he left behind in Georgia. A field return in January listed fewer than 17,000 officers and men present for duty. Of this number, only 12,366 were infantry privates, the backbone of the army. Enormous numbers of men were listed as sick or absent without leave. Cheatham's corps reflected the generally weakened state of the army. Losses were particularly noticeable in the officer ranks, where Cheatham and Bate were the only two generals who survived the Tennessee campaign unscathed. Chaplains outnumbered colonels by a five-to-two margin. There were fourteen surgeons, but only ten majors. The figures are shocking even when one considers that many of the soldiers in Cheatham's former regiments were on furlough. All told, fewer than 4,000 infantrymen remained present for duty in the entire corps. Of Cheatham's regiments at Tupelo, twenty-two were led by captains, one was led by a lieutenant, and a battalion of sharpshooters was commanded by a sergeant.[34]

The remnants of the once-proud Army of Tennessee left Tupelo in late January on a torturous trek to North Carolina. Cheatham escorted his men by foot, rail, and steamboat through Alabama to Augusta, Georgia, where they arrived on February 9. The next day the corps shifted across the Savannah River into South Carolina.[35] The movement of the army from Mississippi created problems for members of Cheatham's old division when their furloughs expired on February 10. They were supposed to rendezvous at West Point, Mississippi, and then move to catch up with the remainder of the corps. Apparently, not all of Cheatham's men were delighted when they learned that the main army had moved out almost two weeks earlier. Several dozen men in the Fifth Tennessee reached Corinth and decided to return to Tennessee, figuring perhaps that rejoining the corps would entail more aggravation than anything else. Others in the division eventually joined Forrest's cavalry for the last portion of the war. The most loyal and duty-bound decided to brave the journey and set out on "Old Frank's" trail. Like the main force that preceded them, these soldiers discovered that the Confederate transportation system was in disarray. Rail transit was often unreliable, dangerous, or totally nonexistent. Some of Cheatham's troops wound up walking vast distances in their quest to catch up with the main army. Thirteen veterans from a company in the Ninth Tennessee, for instance, tramped across portions of six states before they reunited with Cheatham in North Carolina. One of the few times they were able to travel by rail occurred in Alabama, where they hopped aboard a freight train. The conductor thereupon asked them for tickets or money. The Tennesseans replied that they did not have either, and the conductor threatened to forcibly remove them from the train. One of the soldiers, an Irishman named John Cavanaugh, acted as spokesman for his comrades and replied, "You will have one grand old time putting us off this train." The conductor wisely reconsidered his stance, and Cavanaugh and the other twelve soldiers rode to Mobile on the freight car.[36]

While Cheatham made somewhat better time than his former divisional members, he too encountered problems during the trip. One obstacle presented itself when the corps passed through Georgia. Some of the other state combines resented the furloughs that had been provided to West Tennessee and Mississippi regiments, and their members began to abandon the army. Cheatham's Georgia regiments melted away as soldiers anxious for the safety of their families left to check on conditions after Sherman's march. Cheatham requested an interview with a Georgia colonel, Charles Olmstead, to inquire about the desertions. Olmstead explained that he could round up most of the men if Cheatham would authorize a trip wherein the Georgian could visit several towns and appeal to his soldiers. As the interview concluded, Cheatham gave his permission for Olmstead's foray through the state. By this time the Georgian had ascertained that Cheatham was under the influence of liquor, and the colonel was unimpressed by Cheatham's behavior. According to Olmstead, Cheatham handed over the necessary orders "with a gravity that was ludicrous," and solemnly intoned, "Colonel, you go and bring these men back and if you want anybody shot just wink your eye." Olmstead had been aware of Cheatham's reputation for personal bravery and success in combat but left convinced that the Tennessean's rumored penchant for hard drinking was also deserved.[37]

If Cheatham had been required to rationalize this intemperance, he might have cited the rapid disintegration of the Confederacy as an excuse. The Federals occupied most of the South, with Sherman moving northward for a possible junction with Grant in Virginia. The woeful lack of equipment and clothing for his own men must also have troubled Cheatham. Although new Enfield rifles were provided to at least a portion of Cheatham's command in Georgia, many of his soldiers remained destitute of shoes and other apparel.[38] As Grant squeezed Richmond in a vise, Joseph Johnston marshaled his forces for one last effort against

Sherman. He struck in North Carolina at Bentonville on March 19 and temporarily checked the Union advance. Bate led his own division and Cleburne's former regiments at Bentonville, but neither Cheatham nor his old division were present, owing to a week-long delay in the rail yards at Salisbury. Cheatham's "detention at Salisbury," according to one of his aides, Major Henry Hampton, "was occasioned by a difference in the gauge of the railroad tracks, which necessitated a change of cars, and a scarcity of rolling stock." The slowness in reaching the remainder of the army upset Cheatham, and his patience gave way as his force was attempting to leave Salisbury. At one point a fully loaded troop train stood idle on the tracks, preventing other locomotives and cars from moving forward. Cheatham yelled for the conductor of the train and asked why he had not gotten under way. The conductor, attired in a splendid uniform, haughtily replied that he was "running that part of the business, sir." He had no sooner finished the response when a frustrated Cheatham landed a hook to the rail official's head that decked the conductor into a mud pile. One veteran gleefully recounted that the conductor "was up and had his train moving before he took time to shake off the mud."[39]

Knocking the conductor down may have soothed Cheatham's frazzled nerves, but it is doubtful if his presence or that of his men would have materially have altered the course of events at Bentonville. As it was, Johnston withdrew the day following Cheatham's arrival across the Neuse River in a vain hope to link with Robert E. Lee.[40] Johnston halted for two weeks near Smithfield, where he was stationed when Lee surrendered at Appomattox. As Lee was capitulating, Johnston completed a massive reorganization of his army. There were few men, but a super-abundance of generals, so Cheatham was reduced from corps command. He returned to his old role as divisional commander and was placed in a makeshift corps under Hardee. Cheatham led 2,000 natives of his home state in Carolina, as well as the remnants of Gist's Georgians and South Carolinians. Cheatham's force in North Carolina was a mere skeleton of the powerful command it once had been. The First Tennessee had once totaled 1,200 men; in North Carolina only 125 were left. Only 64 soldiers remained in the Nineteenth Tennessee, which had numbered over 1,000 in 1861. Of 1,300 men once on the rolls of the Fifth Tennessee, just 30 were at Smithfield. But 40 remained in the Ninth Tennessee. Three regiments together mustered only 50 men, with a colonel as the lone remaining field officer. In one company of the 154th Tennessee, only one soldier answered the roll, and he was disabled. The private bravely pledged to follow Cheatham "to the end," but such devotion could not dispel the tremendous disparity in numbers between the two opposing forces. Over three dozen Tennessee regiments were compacted into four such units during the army reorganization. One of the few similarities to brighter days was Cheatham's presence as divisional leader.[41]

Troubled by the outcome of the Tennessee campaign and the dark prospects confronting them, Cheatham's men cornered their beloved general for a speech. Cheatham replied that under normal circumstances he might be cashiered for what he was about to tell them, but he knew that he could be forthright and still count on the loyalty of his veterans. He was plainly embarrassed by the notion of making a speech but acceded to the request with a simple and straightforward talk. "Boys," he began, "I have gained great reputation as a fighter, but the credit belongs to you, not to me." At this several of the Tennesseans nodded approvingly and remarked, "D[am]n if old Frank can't beat 'em all speaking." Cheatham added, "We have been in many tight places, but none where you ever failed me or failed your country. How many brave men have fallen, your decimated ranks attest." Cheatham praised the valor of his troops and illustrated his point by citing statistics which stated that no more than 8,000 men had been in the division when it was at its peak. Yet the records revealed that the divisional casualties totaled over 13,000 killed and wounded, offering grim evidence that a great many of his men had "been wounded several times." Cheatham then confided that Johnston and Sherman were negotiating for the army's surrender. After advising his men to return home and become loyal citizens, Cheatham faltered, his eyes glistened, and "tears ran down the faces of his veterans." "The effect was appalling," one veteran recalled, "the soldiers walked quietly away without a word, except to reassure their commander that he might continue to depend upon them under all circumstances."[42]

With the collapse of Lee's army and the bulk of the Confederacy in ruins, it must have been apparent that the end was in sight for Johnston's Army of Tennessee. Some welcomed the thought. Captain Alfred Fielder of the Twelfth Tennessee, still nursing wounds he received at Atlanta, spent some time convalescing at the home of an old friend. Although Fielder described confirmation of Lee's surrender as "a gloomy day for the Confederacy," he was ready for the conflict to be over. In his diary entry for April 22, 1865, Fielder wrote that rumors of a peace treaty created a "general joy" activated by thoughts of home and a reunion with loved ones. James Brown Ritchey, a soldier in the Sixteenth Tennessee, echoed Fielder's sentiments. According to Ritchey, the Rebels were "anxious for peace," but feared that the peace terms they would be forced to accept would "be very humiliating." Ritchey and the other soldiers in Cheatham's command were forced in 1865 to accept that the war was lost, a notion which many of them had never seriously considered earlier. Ritchey represented the feelings of many of his comrades when he wrote,

"Yes, if our cause is wrong I pray God to pardon us. We have ever believed that it was right and have always acted accordingly."[43]

Surrender negotiations between Johnston and Sherman continued for a week and a half, but final terms were accepted by the Confederates on April 26. When word spread that "Old Joe" had surrendered the army, the news elicited various reactions. Carroll Henderson Clark of the Sixteenth Tennessee reported that "all was quiet in the line [and] many brave boys shed tears." Clark summed up the feelings of Cheatham's entire command when he admitted to having mixed feelings about the capitulation. Clark sighed when he looked at his ragged uniform and empty haversack, and he wrote in his diary, "I was glad and sorry too. Glad the war was over and sad we had to give it up." A soldier in the Fifth Tennessee wrote that some men "raved and swore that they would never submit to it. Some paced back and forth like caged lions." Still others buried their faces in their hands and wept.[44] Some Rebels who had followed Cheatham throughout the war used the occasion to garner some souvenir of their service. His cavalry escort of Georgians took Cheatham's blue and white headquarters flag, ripped it into shreds and divided it among themselves as a memento "of the Division [and] its gallant commander."[45]

The army had long suffered internal discord, and Cheatham was involved in one last squabble in the waning days of the war. Each soldier present in late April received slightly over one dollar, with the stipulation that commanders were expected to draw pay only for men then in camp. When Cheatham saw a field return for North Carolina General Robert Hoke, he complained that Hoke drew more money than he should have. Hardee ended this quarrel by accepting Hoke's return. The amount of money was relatively insignificant, and none of the accounts left by Cheatham's men allude to his challenge of Hoke's return. Some of his soldiers did offer General Johnston the silver dollar they all received as a token of their esteem, but Johnston graciously declined the offer.[46] The army remained together after the surrender, and drills and inspections occupied the men until arrangements could be made for the trip home. Cheatham surrendered with 3,003 officers and men in his division. Paroles were received the first part of May; then Cheatham's division left Greensboro and marched westward. At Salisbury, Cheatham drew up his division for a final inspection; he wished to go south for a time and did not accompany his men on the return to Tennessee. The scene was poignant indeed. Tears coursed down Cheatham's face as he passed down the line and shook hands with each of his remaining veterans. Overcome with emotion, Cheatham could only occasionally utter a farewell as his devoted Tennesseans wept unashamedly.[47] The comradeship of four years was a difficult tie to break, but after a last sad glance, Cheatham and

his men separated. The war was over, and the process of picking up interrupted private lives began.

As Cheatham admitted in the presurrender speech to his men, he was
widely known. The fame he had coveted long ago in Mexico was now
his in abundant measure. The Civil War was the highlight of Cheatham's
life, as it was for most of the men who participated in it. Cheatham's war
record with the Army of Tennessee was a generally favorable one, but
there are factors which tarnished its brilliance. As time passed, he became most remembered for his role at Spring Hill and the resulting controversy with Hood, which overshadowed more positive moments in his
career. Just as damaging was the notion that he drank to excess and was
unfit for command. This allegation is rooted in large measure in Bragg's
assertion that Cheatham was a habitual drunkard. Cheatham did have
lapses where alcohol was concerned and drank too much on occasion,
but Bragg probably overstated the case. There are four documented cases
involving Cheatham and drinking during the war years: with Grant after
Belmont, at Murfreesboro, in Atlanta in 1864, and during the interview
with Olmstead. None of these reflects creditably on Cheatham, but
Cheatham seems to have shared the tendencies with his more famous opponent, Ulysses S. Grant, who fell off the wagon on a number of occasions during the war. Cheatham, like Grant, succumbed to drinking spells,
but he was probably not a perpetual drunkard. Historians who have considered him a chronic inebriate rely almost totally on Bragg's charges,
and Braxton Bragg so despised Cheatham by 1864 that he magnified all
of Cheatham's defects. It is highly unlikely that Cheatham could have retained command if he had been an alcoholic, no matter how powerful
his civil and military allies. Nor is it reasonable to assume that Cheatham's veterans would have held in high regard a man whose judgement
was routinely clouded by liquor. While it is true that prodigious amounts
of alcohol were consumed during the war and that Cheatham appreciated good whiskey, the evidence to convict him as a drunkard is not
convincing.[48]

Cheatham's tenacious obstinacy in dealing with Bragg and Hood also
detracted from his reputation. The Army of Tennessee contained fighting
men the equal of any Robert E. Lee possessed, but unfortunately, the
army high command fought among themselves as much as they did against
the Federals. Cheatham and Bragg were particularly at loggerheads. Each
wound up detesting the other. Various reasons existed for the enmity, but
Bragg's distrust appears to have begun as early as the spring of 1862. After
a while Bragg deliberately goaded both Cheatham and his patron, Leonidas Polk. The resulting hostility between Bragg and Cheatham is not sur-

prising, though it did hinder army cohesiveness. For his own part, Cheatham was not completely innocent of wrongdoing. As time went on, he exhibited the overly sensitive pride which characterized many Southerners of his era. Eventually, he and Polk so disregarded Bragg's importance as head of the army that they participated in a near-mutiny against his authority. While personality conflicts are a common aspect of war, Cheatham and others who rebelled against Bragg helped split the army into two factions. The officers seemingly never considered the adverse impact this might have on operations in the field. Nor did the hostility cease when the final guns sounded; Bragg and Cheatham carried hatred for one another to their respective graves.

Cheatham seems to have directed open scorn against Hood only after the war, when Hood made Cheatham the scapegoat for Spring Hill in his book. Given Cheatham's devotion to Joe Johnston, he served Hood well, and not until after the Spring Hill affair was there any sign of a break between the two officers. The postwar enmity between Hood and Cheatham probably does not accurately represent the working arrangement between the two men during Hood's tenure as army chieftain. Hood's willingness in the autumn of 1864 to recommend that Cheatham be promoted to the rank of lieutenant-general is evidence that he respected Cheatham's efforts and abilities throughout the Atlanta campaign.

It is impossible to discern to what extent Cheatham was hampered by the lack of a West Point education. At least part of Bragg's difficulty with Cheatham centered on Cheatham's lack of professional training. Some of Cheatham's colleagues who were schooled at West Point made spectacular advances in grade through the war. A prime example is A. P. Stewart, who was a major of artillery at Columbus early in the war and wound up as a lieutenant-general leading a corps by late June of 1864. Stewart was a gallant officer who deserved his promotions, but there is little doubt that his 1842 graduation from West Point aided his Confederate career. By contrast, Cheatham's Mexican War and militia activities were less impressive to Confederate authorities, who had themselves been educated at West Point. Cheatham himself may not have felt so handicapped and probably regarded his Mexican War service as an educational experience which no classroom could provide. In any event, he did employ some lessons from the Mexican War to his advantage in the later conflict. One of these was Cheatham's appreciation for the role artillery could serve, and he utilized his knowledge well on a number of battlefields.

Cheatham was at his best as a divisional leader; the intricacies of corps command eluded him. He was not a tactician or a strategist, though Hood should have accepted Cheatham's advice not to attack at Franklin. His role as divisional commander called for little in the way of strategy anyway. Throughout most of the war Cheatham's main function was to carry out the wishes of his superiors, a task he generally fulfilled. Cheatham's strongest virtue was his ability to inspire unrelenting loyalty from his troops. One is struck by the depth of the affection his men exhibited. This high regard was generated by Cheatham's personality, demeanor, and genuine solicitude for his soldiers. The combination of respect and familiarity that "Old Frank" evoked helped make him an effective military commander. Moreover, he never forgot that his personal success was dependent upon the efforts of his soldiers in battle. The bond between Cheatham and his men was also cemented by the Tennessean's repeated examples of personal bravery, for Southerners in the ranks appreciated a general who took the same risks that he asked them to accept. A famed Union rival, William T. Sherman, caught the essence of the relationship between a high-ranking officer and his troops: "There is a soul to an army as well as to the individual man," Sherman wrote in his memoirs, "and no general can accomplish the full work of his army unless he commands the soul of his men, as well as their bodies and legs."[49] Sherman was not writing specifically of his Confederate foes, but the analogy applied to Cheatham and his division. Few generals so captured the collective "soul" of his command as did Frank Cheatham.

The survivors of Cheatham's division later looked back on their Civil War experiences with justifiable pride. They recalled Perryville, where they almost singlehandedly mangled the left wing of an opposing army. Another favorite reminiscence was their celebrated defense at Kennesaw Mountain, where they shattered the assaulting mass brought against them. Other memories intruded as well: the freezing nights along Stones River, the rumble of Lieutenant Turner's guns at Chickamauga, skinny-dipping in the Chattahoochee during a brief respite in the Atlanta campaign. Sadder thoughts reflected on the disaster at Missionary Ridge, the carnage at Franklin, and the panic at Nashville. Cheatham's men were aware that they were a hard-hitting combat unit, a notion shared by both Confederate and Union observers, and they were confident that history would give them their due. Much of their inspiration came from their commander, and they were beneficiaries of Cheatham's administrative and battlefield talents. The link between Cheatham and his men was strengthened by their common background. Dominated by Tennesseans for almost the entire war, Cheatham's division possessed a special character based on state pride. The tie forged between Cheatham and his soldiers was attributable largely to this kinship and shared association with the Volunteer state. The Tennesseans were often individualistic but loved and respected Cheatham since he was one of their own. Cheatham welded the division together by comprehending the devotion his men felt for their home state, and the force of his personality bound them even tighter. The results were impressive, as even Jefferson Davis attested. Lauding their valor during one of his inspection trips, Davis told the assembled veterans that their exploits had made Cheatham's Tennessee division "a household word all over the Confederacy."[50]

Chapter 11
The Postwar Years

Most of Cheatham's former troops arrived back in Tennessee shortly after receiving their paroles, but Cheatham did not return to the state until mid-July.[1] Confronted with the necessity of resuming a peacetime existence, Cheatham and his men discovered that the state was in a far different situation than it had been in in 1861. Cheatham's old acquaintance Andrew Johnson was in the White House after having served as military governor and senator. Johnson's successor as governor was William G. "Parson" Brownlow, a former Methodist preacher and newspaper publisher who regarded all Confederates with undisguised contempt. This East Tennessee native led a group of state Radicals who dominated the political arena for the immediate postwar years. It was a difficult era for men who had supported seccession and the Confederacy. Brownlow's partisan government alienated many in the state and led to the creation of a rival coalition of Conservative Unionists and former Confederates, who were heartened by President Johnson's moderate approach to Reconstruction. Cheatham helped the opposition to Brownlow coalesce when he wrote a conciliatory letter to a meeting of Conservative Unionists in February 1866.[2] Nonetheless, the Radical governor retained a firm grip on Tennessee political affairs.

Other Confederate officers shared Cheatham's difficulty in adjusting to a new order. In the fall of 1866, A. P. Stewart wrote to Cheatham from Lebanon, Tennessee, requesting that any cotton Cheatham might grow be sold in New Orleans through a company Stewart founded. In the course of the missive, Stewart lamented the political and social gains acquired by the freed slaves. The possible "perpetual disfranchisement of all rebels" also troubled Stewart, who did summon enough humor to ask if Cheatham was "reconstructed yet, or like myself, still out in the cold?" Stewart left no doubt of his antipathy to Radical Reconstruction by pointedly using Confederate stationery and envelope to convey his message.[3]

Cheatham had little control over political matters, but in personal affairs he could more easily guide his destiny. Early in 1866 Cheatham asked his old friend Charles Todd Quintard to baptize him. Quintard, by now the Episcopal bishop of Tennessee, happily complied.[4] The former army chaplain was back in Nashville less than two months later to officiate at Cheatham's wedding. The woman who ended Frank's bachelor days was Anna Bell Robertson, the daughter of Abner Baldwin and Harriet Bell Robertson. The A. B. Robertsons hailed from the Carolinas originally and were not related to the Robertsons in Cheatham's lineage. Still, Cheatham apparently knew the family before the Civil War, as Abner Baldin Robertson was a successful shoe merchant in antebellum Nashville. There was a military connection as well, for one of Anna's brothers, Abbott Lawrence, served on Cheatham's staff throughout the war.[5] An attractive, dark-haired woman, Anna at twenty-seven years of age was marrying a man eighteen years older. The wedding was a gala social event and provided former Confederates with a cause for celebration in an otherwise bleak period. One of Cheatham's acquaintances wrote that the wedding "eclipses everything in this country. It will vie in pageantry the marital ceremonies of oriental customs." While not quite that extravagant, the ceremony was fairly elaborate. Anna was attended by seven bridesmaids, while Frank asked members of his wartime staff to serve as attendants. Guests included Confederate generals Samuel Read Anderson, William Bate, Simon Bolivar Buckner, and 1860 presidential candidate John Bell. At least one local newspaper applauded the union. The *Nashville Union and American* ran an account of the marriage ceremony on the editorial page and wished "our valued friend and his accomplished bride a long life of uninterrupted pleasure."[6]

Cheatham and his new bride soon moved to a farm in Coffee County near the small hamlets of Noah and Beech Grove. The farm had been previously owned by Anna's parents, and Abner Robertson made it possible for Cheatham to resume farming. Fortune smiled more than once on Frank Cheatham during his lifetime, but perhaps no more so than in his selection of Anna Bell Robertson as a helpmate. Anna's letters to her new mother-in-law Elizabeth Cheatham chronicled the early months of the marriage and were charming epistles of a couple in love. The messages detailed the transition from city to country living, with news of Frank's building chicken coops, raising hogs, and good-naturedly demanding his buttermilk after a day in the fields. Also recorded were humorous incidents as Anna and the "General," as she termed him, bantered back and forth. When Anna suggested that Frank should also write his mother, Cheatham retorted that the family correspondence was her responsibility and teased her, saying, "What is the use of having a wife if she can't wait on him?" "Did you ever hear such a speech for a man not two months a husband!" Anna wrote in mock indignation. A later missive recounted

Anna Bell Robertson was the sister of one of Cheatham's wartime aides. She and
Cheatham wed in 1866, and their marriage produced five children. (Virginia
Cheatham Van Ness)

how Frank sat near his wife and tried to see how close he could "puff the
smoke from his pipe" to Anna's eyes, and nicknamed her "little goosie." "Oh,
I can tell you I have spoiled him," Anna laughingly wrote. It was easy for
Frank and his family to surrender their affections to this delightful woman,
and from all accounts their union was a joyous and fulfilling one.[7]

Anna's sense of humor complemented her husband's, and Frank Cheatham remained as irrepressible in the postwar years as he had been earlier in life. Even the death of his favorite wartime steed failed to blunt Cheatham's flair for comedy. According to local legend, Cheatham buried the horse "with full military honors" underneath an elm tree.[8] In addition to lighter moments, there was hard work on the farm, and Cheatham's lifelong interest in agriculture paid dividends in Coffee County, where he acquired a reputation as a progressive farmer. His crop-rotation methods and horse-breeding operations were emulated by area farmers. Cheatham also brought in new livestock, introducing "the Poland China and the Essex breed of hogs to the section." Anna provided a riotous portrait of Cheatham with the swine. He separated one group of black pigs from their compatriots in the field and paid them special attention. The pigs soon learned to expect his visits at feeding time and when they heard his voice would "run squealing after him." Anna registered the reaction after one of the pampered pigs was stolen: "I do not believe he and Father would have made as many lamentations if the finest horse on the place had been taken." Hogs occupied much of Cheatham's time, but farm records indicate that he also owned horses, sheep, and cattle. Crops cultivated on the property included corn, wheat, potatoes, oats, and turnips, and the work load required the help of hired hands, including some blacks.[9]

The farm and other diversions captured most of Cheatham's attention, but periodically the Civil War intruded upon him in a new fashion, via the mail. Letters arrived for him at the post office in Beech Grove (now Beechgrove), many of them seeking his recollections of particular wartime events. Thus Joseph Johnston wrote in 1867, imploring Cheatham to write a history of his Tennesseans and requesting information on the Georgia campaign. Cheatham evidently began an account of the campaign, using information he solicited from former artillery officer Melancthon Smith to assist in his writing, but it appears that he did not forward a final draft to Johnston. Perhaps he intended to finish, but his resolve flagged before it was completed. Johnston would almost certainly have used any Cheatham writings to his advantage in a bitter postwar feud with John Bell Hood. Nor was Johnston alone in drafting partisan documents. Leonidas Polk's widow wrote in 1869 to garner some data on the Kentucky campaign, and Polk's son later requested additional information. Other correspondents eventually included a number of Union veterans who also desired Cheatham's assistance in their writings.[10]

There are several plausible explanations for Cheatham's inability to complete the manuscript Johnston desired. Farm chores occupied most of Cheatham's attention and prevented him from devoting more hours to the document that Johnston had requested. The demands on Cheatham's time grew even more intense after May 1867, when the first child was born to Frank and Anna. Named Benjamin Franklin after his father, this new arrival was the first of five Cheatham children.[11]

Another reason for Cheatham's refusal to complete an account of his Civil War service is that it was not as important as other concerns. In the months following Johnston's request, Cheatham found himself preoccupied with political conditions in Tennessee. Specifically, Cheatham and other former Confederate officers grew steadily angrier at their disfranchisement. Their bitterness was shared by other Confederate veterans, who quickly transformed the Ku Klux Klan from a social group to a mechanism for intimidating blacks and Republicans.

Parson Brownlow sought to protect his supporters by creating a loyal militia which would counteract Klan violence. The prospect of escalating tensions within the state alarmed both the Conservative Unionists and the former high-ranking Confederates. On July 31, 1868, Cheatham was in Nashville with Bushrod Johnson and his old friend George Maney. The trio held a conference with the military committee of the state legislature and attempted to deter passage of the militia law. The next day, Cheatham, Johnson, and Maney, joined by ten other ex-Confederate generals (including Bate, Brown, Forrest, and Pillow), presented a memorial to the legislature. Cheatham admitted that the group was "perfectly powerless" but nonetheless intended to proffer some advice to the legislators. Cheatham failed to state that thousands of veterans who served in his division and in units under the other officers would in large measure abide by their advice.[12]

The memorial repudiated Brownlow's allegation that the Rebel generals were seeking to overthrow the state government and maintained that a militia force would increase rather than curb violence. They denied that any secret organization existed that was inclined to use rash and lawless actions, a fairly duplicitous statement on the part of some, considering that Nathan Bedford Forrest was probably the Grand Wizard of the Ku Klux Klan. The generals did promise to use whatever influence they wielded to uphold the law. One friend of Cheatham applauded his efforts in opposing Brownlow, writing that Cheatham's service was worth more than "all the sulking that has been done since the war." Despite the generally moderate tone of the entreaty, Brownlow, predictably, ignored the counsel of Cheatham and his compatriots. The Tennessee State Guards were organized, and stiff penalties were directed against suspected Klan members.[13] It was a turbulent time in Tennessee. Sometime during this period one of Cheatham's nieces heard that Governor Brownlow was determined to arrest and imprison her uncle. Frightened, she burned many of Cheatham's military documents and papers in a stove before he returned to Coffee County.[14]

The severity of Brownlow's administration collapsed after 1869, when the fiery Parson went to Washington as a U.S. senator. Brownlow's successor, DeWitt D. Senter, promptly began to eliminate voting restrictions on former Confederates. Senter's actions heralded a new era in Tennessee politics. A constitutional convention was held in 1870, and the next year Cheatham's former subordinate John C. Brown was elected governor.[15] Brown's election inaugurated a period where antebellum Whigs and Democrats vied for postwar control of the state. As one of the latter group, Cheatham was an attractive potential candidate, especially given his general popularity. Cheatham ventured into politics in 1872 by announcing his intention to challenge Brown, a Whig before the war, for the governorship. This was a short-lived candidacy, as the state nominating convention refused Cheatham's request to postpone their meeting date. Unable to marshal support in the month before the convention, Cheatham dropped out of the running.[16]

Unable to prevent Brown's renomination, Cheatham quickly found another political opening. Congress sanctioned the election of a tenth representative from Tennessee, this slot to be filled after a state-wide race. Cheatham's name was put forward by several supporters at a May 1872 convention which endorsed Brown's reelection, although Cheatham himself was not present. A friend of Andrew Johnson was opposed to acquiescing in Cheatham's selection until the former president was consulted, and Democratic officials agreed to reconvene in August. In the interval between, Johnson and his supporters pondered whether to challenge Cheatham for the Democratic nomination. Cheatham and Johnson had been well acquainted before the war. Cheatham had helped mediate a dispute between Johnson and a political associate in 1855; and in 1859 Johnson, then serving in the U.S. Senate, had joined eight other Tennesseans in requesting that Cheatham be considered as an agent for the War Department in the purchase of mules and horses for the army. The Civil War split the two men, and the prospect of Johnson running against Cheatham boded ill for Democratic unity.[17]

Cheatham recognized the danger posed by Johnson's possible candidacy and attempted to forestall it by meeting with Johnson in Greeneville prior to the August convention. There, the former president evasively refused to divulge his plans until he arrived in Nashville. Cheatham still hoped to avert a challenge from Johnson in the capital, but two intermediaries from the Cheatham camp were rebuffed by Johnson aides before the convention opened. Cheatham supporters controlled the August convention, which nominated Frank as the Democratic candidate for the congressional seat. Ordinarily, Cheatham would have swept to victory, even though the Republicans nominated a strong condidate, Horace Maynard, a Radical who was a political ally of Parson Brownlow. The election, however, turned out to be anything but ordinary, for Andrew Johnson refused to abide by the results of the convention and launched an independent campaign. Johnson apparently hestitated before committing himself to this course. Cheatham partisans later claimed that Johnson pledged not to oppose the results of the convention, a view supported by Johnson's own secretary, a former officer in Cheatham's division, who maintained that Johnson was concentrating on a Senate race in 1875 when associates convinced him to enter the 1872 contest against Cheatham and Maynard.[18]

Cheatham and his political allies had fervently hoped that Johnson would accept the results of the convention and permit Cheatham to run uncontested. When this hope evaporated, Cheatham resolved to follow Johnson and engage him in debate. Other Democrats sought to convince Johnson supporters that his candidacy promised disaster. Most of the Democratic newspapers backed Cheatham and excoriated Johnson. A typical editorial thundered that Johnson, " though claiming to be a Democrat," was "an open disorganizer of the party . . . and would willingly sacrifice every Democratic candidate in the state" if it advanced his own interests.[19] This was one of the opening salvos in what proved to be an extremely rancorous campaign. Johnson eventually implicated Cheatham as a member of a secessionist ring which took Tennessee out of the Union, a group which included Bate, Isham Harris, and others. The Confederacy was "an attempt to violate the Constitution," Johnson reminded followers, and he obviously detested the idea of a steady succession of former Confederate generals winning political office. A paper supporting Johnson summarized his views by stating, "We do not wish to be under marching orders to military generals" or unrepentant Confederates. Alluding to happier times when Cheatham had supported Johnson for office, the paper suggested that Cheatham withdraw from the race.[20]

Cheatham's supporters retaliated by printing letters and addresses boosting his candidacy. He was described as "an intelligent farmer" who was not a professional politician yet always kept up "a lively interest in public affairs." The backers felt Cheatham's attributes qualified him for Congress, where "he would labor in the interest of peace and for the general welfare." Somewhat less bland were the violent attacks leveled at Johnson by Cheatham partisans. They denounced Johnson's record as wartime governor, his assistance in getting Brownlow installed as a successor, and a variety of other acts which branded him as "anti-southern." An open letter by Cheatham was published in which Cheatham disclaimed any great aspirations for office while he simultaneously blasted Johnson as despotic and disreputable. Personal sentiment entered into the message when Cheatham alluded to Johnson's forced extraction of cash from Southern sympathizers, including Frank's brother Felix during his tenure as wartime governor.[21]

Cheatham was irritated not only by Johnson's candidacy, but by the necessity of being away from home while his family was expanding. Patton Robertson Cheatham had been born in 1869, and a third son, Joseph Johnston, made his appearance in February 1872. The separation from Anna disturbed Frank, and letters to her reveal a certain ambivalence about the campaign. Shortly after Johnson revealed his intentions, Frank wrote his wife to declare, "I wish I was out of this business but I see no chance now." Cheatham obviously wanted to win the election, but the obstacles daunted him. "I am now satisfied that I would gladly withdraw if I could," he wrote before beginning a speaking tour, but "my friends have decreed that we should entertain no such proposition." The tour itself dismayed Cheatham. "I have all the time dreaded the canvas," he confided to Anna, but "the die is cast and the race must be made."[22]

Whatever Cheatham's reservations, the 1872 campaign was a topic long afterwards discussed in Tennessee political circles. All three candidates participated in a three-cornered debate which opened in mid-September in Chattanooga and worked its way across the state. Some of Cheatham's qualms centered on the fact, which he himself admitted, that he was an abysmal public speaker. This failing did not enhance his chances in an age of great oratory, for he typically found himself speaking for long periods—an hour in McMinnville, forty-five minutes in Paris. He grew hoarse after addressing 12,000 persons in Nashville. Despite these efforts, he could not match Johnson's and Maynard's more polished styles, and speechmaking remained an agonizing aspect of the campaign for him. When he took to the rostrum, Cheatham attempted to deflect Johnson's criticism of secessionists. Cheatham defended his wartime service, while maintaining that he was reconciled to the South's defeat: "Let the dead issues go, let the dead past bury its dead," he reasoned. On one occasion he drew laughter from a crowd in Memphis by asserting that the South had been "badly whipped," adding that no one "had a better right to . . . make that acknowledgement than I have." Cheatham also accused Johnson of trying to drive a wedge between ex-Confederate generals and their former soldiers by depicting the officers as wealthy men and political manipulators. Cheatham naturally denied both charges. He also added, rather lamely, that after nearly three decades of political service Johnson should step aside. The three men canvassed the state for over a month, trading accusations and criticisms, and Cheatham welcomed the end of

the tiresome campaign. "How glad I am at the prospect of this thing coming to a close," he wrote Anna.[23]

A Nashville newspaper prophesied that Cheatham would beat Maynard by 10,000 votes and Johnson by 30,000, but this was not to be.[24] The
split between Johnson and Cheatham shattered the Democratic Party and
allowed Maynard to win the November election. The Republican tallied
80,822 votes, Cheatham 63,976, and Johnson 37,902. "Behold the beauties
of disorganization," a Democratic organ bitterly concluded.[25] Maynard
won the coveted Congressional seat, but Johnson felt vindicated in reducing Cheatham "to the ranks" and breaking up the Confederate political
machine. Cheatham ran well in Middle and West Tennessee and would
almost assuredly have defeated Maynard in a two-man race. A relative
in Arkansas tried to console Elizabeth Cheatham, writing that Congress
was a "den of scoundrels," and that election to the House of Representatives would have tarnished Frank's wartime laurels. "It was . . . very grati-
fying that he got a larger vote than that old demagog[ue] Johnson," the
kinsman added, but it is doubtful that this provided Frank much solace.[26]
Defeated for the second time in a political contest, Cheatham never again
ran for public office.

Cheatham's inability to win the 1872 election and his subsequent refusal to enter other political races help explain why he slipped into relative anonymity in the decades following. Compared to the political successes of many of his wartime comrades, Cheatham's postwar career was
relatively undistinguished. John C. Brown and William Bate were each
elected governor of Tennessee. Bate and Isham Harris won terms in the
U.S. Senate, and Edward C. Walthall served over a decade as a senator
from Mississippi.[27] These men were Redeemers, leaders of the Democratic
party who wrested control of Southern state governments after the demise of Radical Reconstruction. Cheatham was a Redeemer but did not
embody the C. Vann Woodward concept of them as industrialists who
embraced Yankee capitalism. Brown's association with railroad development was more indicative of this stance than was Cheatham's return to
agriculture, though both men were Redeemers.[28]

Despite his electoral setback, Cheatham retained a lifelong interest in
politics. But instead of actively seeking office, he waited for opportunities to come his way which would not entail an election process. One such
opportunity presented itself during Ulysses S. Grant's administration,
when Grant offered Cheatham a federal civil service post. Cheatham felt
he could not in good conscience accept the offer, despite his regard for
Grant, because his close ties to the Democratic party would have been
ruptured by acceptance.[29] Cheatham's rejection of Grant's offer was a
fairly common response among the Southern officers Grant tried to culti-

vate, but there were exceptions. George Maney was one of the latter. Cheatham's former brigadier became a Republican and served in several diplomatic posts during the 1880s and 1890s.[30]

For Cheatham, a more acceptable alternative eventually presented itself. In 1874 Cheatham's wartime chief of staff, James D. Porter, was elected governor. Like John C. Brown, his gubernatorial predecessor, Porter was an antebellum Whig who became involved in railroad ventures after the war. Although he differed from Cheatham in his antebellum political affiliation and postwar enterprises, Porter selected Cheatham to serve as superintendent of state prisons. The appointment reflected Porter's and Cheatham's close personal ties, as the majority of Porter's other officials were former Whigs. Cheatham remained in the post during Porter's two terms in office, serving as superintendent from 1875 through 1879.[31]

In this position, Cheatham held sway over a penal system which controlled as many as 1,200 prisoners. Black males constituted the bulk of the convict population, outnumbering their white counterparts by a two-to-one margin. A few dozen women were inmates as well, with the same preponderance of black to whites. There was no distinction made between adult and juvenile offenders; records indicate that at least two ten-year-olds were incarcerated during Cheatham's tenure.[32] Some of the prisoners resided in the central state penitentiary, an imposing if antiquated institution spread over a five-acre site at the corner of Church and West Carroll streets in Nashville. The penitentiary was unable to accommodate all of the convicted lawbreakers, with the result that hundreds of prisoners were scattered about the state on work details. When Cheatham took office, he inherited a system by which Tennessee leased convict labor to a contracting firm, Cherry, O'Connor and Company, which in turn utilized the prisoners for tasks such as farming, railroad construction, and coal mining.[33]

The convict lease system was by no means confined to Tennessee. The hiring out of convict labor prevailed in one form or another throughout the entire South by 1880. Tennessee first adopted the system in 1866, during Governor Brownlow's administration. The operation of the prison had cost the state an average of $15,000 per year from 1833 to 1865, and a heavy postwar debt focused attention on various cost-cutting measures. According to Brownlow and other advocates, leasing the convict labor supply would allow the prison system to pay its own way, or at least reduce the annual average expenditure required by the state. The same intent remained even after Brownlow's years in office. When Tennessee signed its second lease in 1871, one of the stipulations was that the lessees were obligated to pay the state $30,00 each of the five years that the lease remained in effect. To sweeten the deal, the contracting firm was also re-

Cheatham's wartime chief of staff, James D. Porter, was elected governor of
Tennessee and appointed Cheatham superintendent of the state prison in the
1870s. (Tennessee State Library and Archives)

quired to furnish food, clothing, medical supplies, tobacco, and other incidental items to the prisoners. They also paid the salaries of the guards, although prison officials retained the power to hire and dismiss personnel.[34]

Despite the alleged advantages, convict leasing proved something of a headache for Cheatham. Trouble ensued partly because the lease encompassed not only the labor of the convicts but also the penitentiary buildings, equipment, material, and supplies. Aside from the direction provided by a few upper-echelon officials such as Cheatham and the local wardens, the arrangement essentially stripped control of the penal system from the state and deposited it with the lessees. Another area of concern for Cheatham was the number of escapes that occurred when the lessees sublet the prison labor to such concerns as farmers and the railroads. Nearly two hundred convicts escaped within a two-year period between December 1874 and December 1, 1876, a trend which infuriated Cheatham. Cheatham reported that he "used every precaution to employ good men for guard duty" but acknowledged that some escapes were the result of negligence. In such cases Cheatham's "only remedy" was to fire the offending guard "and employ another."[35]

Another by-product of the convict lease system was that it forced Cheatham to travel a great deal. By law he was required to visit the branch prisons every two months, and having prisoners scattered about the state kept Cheatham on the road for extended periods. In the course of his travels he inspected sites literally all across Tennessee, as convicts were used in areas ranging from East Tennessee to Memphis, where 150 prisoners labored on a farm nine miles below the city. Occasionally Cheatham visited the prison sites once a month, and during the first half of his stint as superintendent he traveled over fifteen thousand miles. Eventually Cheatham headed more frequently for East Tennessee, as the lessees, seeking to curb the number of escapes, shifted the prisoners from the railroads to the coal mines. Prison camps established near the mines provided more security than was possible along the railroads, and by 1878 the bulk of the prisoners assigned to work details outside of Nashville were employed by four coal mines.[36]

It was the intent of both the state and the industrial concerns involved that the prisoners work long and hard hours, and the intent was fully realized in the mines. Coal mining proved to be both torturous and dangerous for the convicts. Prison reports indicate that prisoners often died from injuries received in the mines, with specific blame attached to mishaps such as earthslides and explosions in the mine tunnels. Occasionally a convict received a reprieve, but shattered health was apparently the main criterion in such cases. One such instance surfaced in 1878, when a physician at the Battle Creek Mines wrote Cheatham and requested that a fifty-year-old prisoner be removed to the Nashville penitentiary. The doctor cited the convict's heart disease, which made it impossible to "work him according to the laws of the State under hard labor in the mines."[37]

The inherent brutality of the convict lease system was readily apparent to the hapless prisoners who toiled in the mines, but not many Tennesseans shared their qualms. One who did was Governor Porter, who voiced his objections to the system in an 1877 message to the General Assembly. That Cheatham found fault with the system as well is a likelihood; it is unlikely that Porter would have criticized the leasing practice without consulting Cheatham first. Governor Porter's attack was based partly on humanitarian motives, but he noted other factors, such as the high number of escapes and the competition between convict labor and free workers in the state. Despite his opposition, Porter realized that he was in a dilemma. According to the politician, the average Tennessean favored convict leasing because it allowed the prison system to function without a tax burden being placed on the citizenry. As a result, Porter was forced to advertise for a new lease because he saw no alternative to the convict lease system then in effect. Three bids materialized, including one from Nathan Bedford Forrest, but none was deemed acceptable. Cherry, O'Connor and Company retained its lease for an additional eight months, and not until August 1, 1877 was there a new contracting firm, that of A. M. Shook, who began a six-year lease, having agreed to pay $70,500 per year to the state. Otherwise little changed, and lawbreakers continued working in the coal mines.[38]

Altering the convict lease system was one of two major crusades Cheatham and Porter embarked upon to improve the penal system. Their other goal was to build a new state penitentiary. Porter took up this theme repeatedly in addresses to the legislature, pointing out that the penitentiary was "wholly inadequate" to meet the needs of the inmates. Opened in 1831, the penitentiary originally included two wings, each with 112 cells, and a main building used for officers and guard quarters. In 1858 a third wing added 120 more cells, but by the time Cheatham took office, the prison could not accommodate the large number of offenders sent to Nashville. When first erected, the penitentiary had been outside the city limits, but eventually Nashville expanded and surrounded the prison grounds. Porter regarded the penitentiary as a stumbling block in his efforts to improve Nashville and recommended that it be removed to a site below the city, preferably on the Cumberland River. Among the many defects Porter noted was that the prison had no sewerage and poor ventilation, which rendered it an unhealthful place to reside, especially during the summer. Porter also felt that the hospital arrangement was unsatisfactory, due to space limitations, and he hoped that a new facility could provide separate areas for females and juveniles. Cheatham heartily endorsed Porter's recommendation that the prison be removed. He learned firsthand of the prison's deficiencies during his term as superintendent. Patchwork improvements were necessary while Cheatham held office, including the building of a plank fence around two wings so that contraband such as whiskey could not be smuggled to inmates from persons just outside the prison. New boilers were added when inspections revealed that the old ones were hazardous, and tin roofs were installed over the main building and the foundry. Confronted with such problems, Cheatham argued that a new prison with modern workshops could bring $25,000 to $30,000 more to the state each year than was being realized under the convict lease system. Porter recommended that the new penitentiary be funded from revenue provided by A. M. Shook under his lease, plus the sale of the old property, and Cheatham urged that the new facility "be built from the latest models for comfort and convenience."[39]

Despite the lobbying efforts of both Governor Porter and Cheatham, they achieved no concrete progress in their drive to relocate the state prison during Porter's administration. In fact, the legislature did not authorize the construction of a new penitentiary until the 1890s, long after Cheatham's death. Ironically, the state prison eventually was built on land once occupied by Westover, Cheatham's childhood plantation home. Unable to secure legislative support for either of his major prison reforms, Porter nonetheless helped set in motion the bureaucratic process which resulted in a new penitentiary opening in 1898 and the end of the convict lease system, which also occurred in the 1890s.[40] Porter was genuinely concerned about the state prison, visited the facility, and apparently relied to a great extent on the advice and observations of Cheatham. Cheatham for his part strived to improve the prison and to ensure that the prisoners were being treated humanely. This was sometimes a difficult process, given the power of the lessees, but Cheatham did institute some modest reforms, most of which benefited the inmates confined to the central state penitentiary. His first act upon assuming the superintendency was to abolish the use of the lash for offenses, a previously commonplace punishment. Otherwise, he and his assistants attempted to boost morale, circulating among the inmates and seeking to convince them that "they were not entirely friendless." In an 1879 address, Porter cited the management of the penitentiary as one of the highlights of his administration, claiming that kindness and humane treatment had markedly improved the climate at the prison. According to an account later written by Porter, Cheatham occupied the superintendent's post "in the most acceptable manner." Porter claimed that Cheatham "inspired the convicts to a new life by the practice of human and friendly acts . . . and made them cheerful and ready to perform their tasks without an overseer."[41]

At the end of Porter's four-year tenure, Cheatham also left the superintendent's office. He returned to Coffee County, no longer burdened by such numerous details as applications for pardons, salaries, inspections, and other tasks associated with his superintendency. The last two additions to his family arrived, one while he was still in office. After bearing three sons, Anna gave birth to two daughters. Medora was born in 1878 and Alice in 1880. By the time Alice was born, Cheatham had returned to farming as his full-time occupation. He may have been wealthy in one sense, in that he was surrounded by a loving family, but in practical terms he was less fortunate. While the Cheatham's were financially comfortable in Coffee County from the standpoint of having an adequate amount of land to farm, Frank never amassed a fortune as did some of his former Confederate colleagues. There are indications that he did engage in one postwar attempt to enrich himself, but it proved unsuccessful. In 1877, while Cheatham was superintendent, he and father-in-law Abner B. Robertson invested several hundred dollars in stock in a company which hoped to construct a road. The company, the Murfreesboro, Manchester and Winchester Turnpike, employed Cheatham as president, probably for his name value and potential for attracting investors. Cheatham could not have devoted a great deal of attention to the firm, given his official duties and extensive travel while superintendent, and his partners apparently had a falling out with him over the issuance of some stock. An 1878 letter from two of his partners was written in a somewhat threatening tone, and it is obvious that the venture was not mutually satisfactory. Cheatham's involvement with the company was short-lived, probably less than a year, and the project certainly did not provide a financial windfall.[42]

The birth of three Cheatham children in the span between 1872 and 1880 contrasted sharply with the increasing death toll of former Confederate generals in the same interval. Braxton Bragg fell dead in Galveston, Texas, in the autumn of 1876. Cheatham traveled the next year to Memphis for the funeral of Nathan Bedford Forrest, a journey which must have evoked memories of an earlier trip to see Pat Cleburne's remains transferred back to Arkansas. In 1878 Cheatham's state rival Gideon Pillow died near Helena, Arkansas, while John Bell Hood passed away during an 1879 yellow fever epidemic in New Orleans.[43]

These intimations of his own mortality seem to have spurred Cheatham into ruminating more on the war years, a habit shared by many of his contemporaries. The Civil War receded farther back into the past, but the conflict dominated the conversations and letters of many men who survived the experience. Cheatham's extant messages reveal that he was no exception to this trend. Even correspondence not originally written to convey Civil War reminiscences managed to contain such references. Such was the case with a letter Cheatham received during his stint as prison superintendent which asked him to arrange improved rations for a Mississippi-born inmate. As an aside, the writer revealed that he was a former surgeon in States Rights Gist's command who had examined three hundred Union prisoners at Corinth in 1865 when ordered to do so by Cheatham.[44] Cheatham himself referred to the Civil War era on a number of occasions. He exchanged letters with Edward C. Walthall regarding the battle of Missionary Ridge, tried to get information from Hood about losses in the Tennessee campaign, and supplied data about the Atlanta campaign to one of Hardee's former staff officers. He also wrote to Marcus J. Wright and forwarded photographs of himself and Patrick Cleburne. Wright was then engaged in the process of collecting documents from his former colleagues for the federal government and for use in his own historical writings.[45]

Cheatham's heightened interest in the war years was abetted by his participation in one of the frequent postwar literary quarrels relating to Confederate campaigns and personalities. He was not directly involved in any of these disputes until 1881, a year after John Bell Hood's book *Advance and Retreat* was posthumously published. Cheatham was stung by the narrative, which repeated Hood's allegations that Cheatham failed at Spring Hill. Hood's accusations were bolstered by an article written by Captain W. O. Dodd, president of the Louisville branch of the Southern Historical Society. After examining the evidence related to the Spring Hill affair, Dodd concluded that "the principal fault is at the door of General Cheatham." Cheatham first penned a response to Hood and Dodd, then ventured to Louisville, at the invitation of the historical society, to defend himself. A large crowd of ex-Confederates and Federals convened at an opera house to hear Cheatham's version of the Spring Hill affair. There, he attempted to refute Hood's charges and cited evidence on his own behalf, including letters from Bate, Brown, and Stewart. James D. Porter helped Cheatham in his defense, obtaining a letter from another staff officer which verified that Hood had cleared Cheatham of any censure for the Spring Hill miscues. Isham G. Harris also wrote Porter and averred that Hood had written Cheatham a message absolving him of wrongdoing. The *Louisville Courier-Journal* reproduced Cheatham's entire address, and it also appeared in a number of other publications, most notably an 1881 issue of the *Southern Historical Society Papers*. The newspaper accepted Cheatham's version of the campaign, but in reality it contains inaccuracies and is confusing in some aspects. This is hardly surprising, given that the account was not written until seventeen years after the event and that Cheatham shaded his version in light of Hood's previously published work.[46]

Cheatham was obviously aroused by the attacks on his conduct at Spring Hill, and his attempts at vindication were waged on several fronts. In addition to his article and address, both of which were uncharacteristic endeavors, Cheatham welcomed allies in his historical skirmish with Hood. One such ally was David Ward Sanders, a former major on the staff of Major-General Samuel G. French, of A. P. Stewart's corps. Sanders wrote an account of the Tennessee campaign which exonerated Cheatham, and he vigorously defended Cheatham against Hood's charges. Sanders lived in Louisville after the war, where he practiced law, and he presented his views in many of the same forums Cheatham later employed. He delivered an address before the Louisville branch of the Southern Historical Society, and his account also appeared in the *Courier-Journal*. There was intense interest in Sanders's narrative; the proprietor of the *Courier-Journal* stated that 250,000 copies of the supplement containing Sanders's account were sent out-of-state. Two hundred thousand of these copies were dispatched to Tennessee, where Cheatham undoubtedly learned of Sanders's article. Cheatham traveled from Coffee County to Louisville and spent several days with Sanders, a gesture made primarily to thank Sanders "for giving a correct history of the movement of the Confederate troops at Spring Hill."[47] Whatever Cheatham's failings in the Tennessee campaign, he carried into the postwar years a fierce belief that he was not responsible for the errors at Spring Hill. In this regard he was not unlike his old tormentors Bragg and Hood, who could never accept the responsibility that they seriously erred at critical times.

The Spring Hill controversy elicited one of the few published accounts from Cheatham's own pen relative to his Civil War service. He might have written more fully had not former governor Porter been asked to contribute a volume on Tennessee's role in the war to editor Clement A. Evans's "Confederate Military History" series. If ever Cheatham considered fulfilling Joe Johnston's 1867 request for a history of his Confederate career, Porter's volume provided a convenient remedy. Cheatham could rest assured that Porter would treat his war record in complimentary fashion, defend him against detractors, and provide the essential details relating to Cheatham as a division and corps commander. As a consequence, Cheatham never felt compelled to write a more complete account of his Confederate service.

James D. Porter and Cheatham were united in ventures beyond that of Porter's historical undertaking. In fact, the two men shared interests in the early 1880s that ranged from the founding of Nashville, to the Civil

First Regiment Tennessee

VOLUNTEERS, C. S. A.

Mingo Flats,
Cheat Mountain,
Brady's Gate,
Sewell Mountain,
Bath, Va.,
Hancock, Md.,
Romney, Va.,
Shiloh,
Perryville,
Murfreesboro,
Morgan's Mill,
Chickamauga,
Missionary Ridge,
Cat Creek,
Rocky Face,
Ressaca,
Adairsville,
Cassville,
New Hope Church,
Dallas,
Kennesaw Mountain,
Smyrna Camp Ground,
Peach Tree Creek,
Latham's Farm,
Atlanta,
Lovejoy S.,
Jonesboro,
Dalton,
Spring Hill,
Franklin,
Nashville,
Sugar Creek,
Bentonville,
Greensboro.

(*Facing page*): The strong link between Cheatham and his wartime chief of staff, James D. Porter, continued into the postwar period. Railroad president Porter allowed Cheatham free passage on his line. (University of the South)

(*Left*) Cheatham's likeness appeared on a ribbon worn by veterans of the First Tennessee regiment during a reunion in October 1883. The ribbon also listed the regiment's wartime engagements. (University of the South)

War era, to state politics. The first of these interests was displayed in participation in planning a Nashville celebration hailing the arrival of Cheatham's ancestor, James D. Robertson, and the subsequent progress of the city. The Nashville Centennial evolved into a month-long series of events from late April through May 1880. Planning for the occasion began two year earlier, and Cheatham served as one of the officers on a Centennial commission. Porter helped organize the commission during the latter part of his second gubernatorial term, and Cheatham at one point requested that Porter appoint a former colonel in the Federal army to the body. The Nashville Centennial included a procession, orations, military display and competitive drill, and the unveiling of an equestrian statue of Andrew Jackson. Elizabeth Cheatham lived long enough to know of the celebration in her grandfather's honor, and her own grandson, Benjamin Franklin Cheatham, Jr., celebrated his thirteenth birthday by escorting a former member of Leonidas Polk's staff to the capitol for the ceremonies.[48]

The Civil War connection continued in a variety of ways, one occurring in 1883, when Porter and Cheatham attended the initial reunion of George Maney's First Tennessee Regiment. Held on the twenty-first anniversary of the battle of Perryville, the reunion featured music, a luncheon, and several speakers, including Cheatham, Maney, and Porter. Over two hundred survivors joined Cheatham and his wartime subordinates in reminiscing nostalgically about their regimental adventures. Those attending the affair expressed regret that Colonel Hume R. Feild and Bishop Quintard were unable to be present, but otherwise, the reunion was judged a grand success. There were some obvious physical changes in the appearance of some of the former Confederates; one former private was overheard to say, "Four years of war and twenty years of wear and tear." Conversations covered everything from wartime incidents to children and grandchildren. The reunion was so pleasant that a committee was formed to ensure that it became an annual event.[49]

If the Centennial and regimental reunion represented Cheatham's ties to the past, more contemporary concerns also captured his attention. Indicative of Cheatham's continued political interest was his eventual involvement in Tennessee's most volatile issue in the 1870s and 1880s, the state debt. Like several other Southern states, Tennessee was saddled with a large debt by the time the Redeemers gained control of state and national offices. Tennessee's debt was incurred mostly for railroad construction, during both the antebellum and postwar periods. Parson Brownlow's administration added to the debt by funding such items as the General Assembly meetings and militia activities. By the end of the 1860s the total indebtedness had ballooned to over $39 million. The hefty amount angered a number of Tennesseans, including Andrew Johnson, but in the first years of Redeemer control the state retired a sizeable portion of the debt. The efforts towards completely eliminating the debt included the Funding Act of 1873, by which the state allowed the debt to be converted into bonds bearing 6 percent interest.[50]

Continued retirement of the debt foundered in the wake of the 1873 depression, when some Democrats launched a campaign to reduce the amount of the indebtedness. These men argued that a large part of the debt was fraudulent, especially the portion incurred during the Brownlow regime. Known as "low-taxers," these men directed criticism at the Funding Act of 1873 and proposed both a delay in the debt settlement and a reduction in the amount owed. Their opponents, called state-credit men, regarded payment of the debt as vital to Tennessee's credit rating and by extension its economic progress. The low-taxers naturally dubbed their opponents with the derisive label "high-taxers."[51]

Among the Democrats firmly in line with the state-credit faction were Brown, Harris, Bate, and Porter. Cheatham was a member of the group as well. During Porter's two terms as governor, the state was jarred by the aftermath of the Depression of 1873. As tax revenue lagged, the state was unable to meet its financial obligations to bondholders. Tennessee defaulted on interest payments in both July 1875 and January 1876, signaling the end of Porter's efforts to discharge the debt on a dollar-for-dollar basis. Faced with a growing schism in the Democratic ranks, the Redeemer coalition attempted to craft some compromise solution which would satisfy both the bondholders and the low-taxers. Porter and the worried bondholders tried to arrange a number of financial schemes, including two 1877 proposals by Porter that the debt be funded at either sixty cents or fifty cents on the dollar at 6 percent interest (60–6 and 50–6), but none satisfied the rebellious low-taxers.[52]

The split in the Democratic ranks widened in the late 1870s, when the state-credit faction's proposal that the debt be funded at fifty cents at 4 percent interest (50–4) was rejected by discontented voters. By 1880 the debt issue had so severely shattered the Democrats that the convention to select a gubernatorial candidate was split into two opposing forces. The sides were so sullen that only an invitation to Cheatham to sit on the dais met with their mutual approval. Cheatham was at least close to the action, which presently erupted when the low-taxers walked out and selected their own candidate. The rift in the Democratic ranks doomed the party in the 1880 race, with the result that Republican Alvin Hawkins won the gubernatorial contest.[53]

Democratic discord remained so intense that the Republicans and the state-credit wing of the Democratic party engineered yet another proposal to retire the debt. This took the form of a legislative act which would fund the debt at full value with bonds carrying only 3 percent interest (100–3) for ninety-nine years. The law aroused further antipathy from the low-tax elements, who were victorious when the Tennessee Supreme Court ruled the 100–3 act unconstitutional. Confronted with the prospect of continued Republican success due to Democratic infighting, former governor Isham Harris and some other state-credit leaders opted for compromise with the low-taxers. Cheatham was a delegate to the 1882 Democratic convention which endorsed Willian Bate for governor and accepted in the platform a reduction in the state debt.[54]

While many state-credit partisans accepted the expediency of Harris's rapprochement with the low-taxers, others decried the shift in tactics which paved the way for a settlement at fifty cents on the dollar at 3 percent interest. Former partners in the state-credit alliance found themselves at odds in 1882, and one faction walked out of the Bate convention to nominate their own candidate. Among the bolters was Cheatham, who headed a delegation of six Coffee County representatives to the dissident convention in July. Upon his arrival Cheatham was selected as chairman of the proceedings.[55]

Cheatham offered a typical disclaimer as to his qualifications, in this case citing his ignorance of parliamentary procedure. "I know how to manage a plow," he said, and with this half-apology out of the way, he offered his personal opinion on the debt issue. In his speech Cheatham revealed that he had followed the course of other state-credit leaders as the controversy unfolded. In the early years of Redeemer control he had favored settling the debt dollar-for-dollar at 6 percent interest. When this became impractical, he favored settlement at 60–6, then 50–4, then 100–3, and most recently at sixty cents on the dollar with a sliding interest scale (60–3–4–5–6). Cheatham confessed that he was in an awkward predicament, especially considering his warm friendship with Bate. The two men had been comrades ever since their service together in the Mexican War. Despite his personal ties with Bate, Cheatham drew applause when he concluded, "I like the man, but I don't like the platform upon which he stands, and therefore I cannot vote for it or him."[56]

The extreme state-credit delegates Cheatham addressed were eventually known by the title Sky Blues. The term was used sarcastically at first by opponents to suggest that Cheatham and his compatriots loftily protected the interests of the bondholders at the expense of the working man and taxpayers. The nickname eventually became a badge of honor and was adopted by the dissidents themselves. In the course of their deliberations, the Sky Blues nominated Columbia attorney Joseph H. Fussell for governor. Fussell was a former captain in Forrest's cavalry who was serving as a state district attorney at the time of his nomination. The convention which nominated Fussell advocated a debt settlement at 60–6, espoused a limited amount of railroad regulation, and decried repeal of the Four-Mile law, "which prohibited the sale of liquor within four miles of a chartered school outside an incorporated town."[57] Fussell was a firm temperance advocate, and there is a certain delicious irony in Cheatham's chairing a convention which tabbed a prohibitionist as a gubernatorial prospect.

It is obvious that Cheatham was unwilling to accept compromise with the low-taxers, but his motivations for joining the Sky Blues are far less clear. In doing so, he turned his back on close personal and political allies such as Isham Harris and Bate. His defection was also the very act which he had witnessed Andrew Johnson perform in 1872 and which had cost Cheatham a congressional seat. Surely he recognized the inherent dangers in a split party. All Cheatham had to do was recall the campaign literature circulated in his behalf in 1872, which conveyed dire but prophetic warnings against such a rift.

Nor does Cheatham fit into the general pattern of Sky Blue leaders, who, according to Roger Hart, were men of high social standing, "educated, genteel professional men, who lived in large towns." Cheatham undoubtedly enjoyed social prestige in postwar Tennessee, but he was one of only two farmers in a group of twenty-five Sky Blues whose occupations are identifiable. The general profile of Sky Blues as wealthy professionals who "stood to gain from increasing urban prosperity" does not include Cheatham, as he was tied to rural environs and was not at all wealthy.[58]

Several possible explanations for Cheatham's membership in the Sky Blues exist, though he never delineated his exact motives in the address to the Fussell convention. One is that his limited business experience as a farm manager, merchant, and salesman convinced him of the necessity to discharge debt obligations faithfully. His reference to his personal honesty in his speech may indicate his belief that a state also was required to act in good faith with creditors. His role as state prison superintendent brought him into contact with Northern and English financial concerns, with the result that he may have regarded preservation of the state credit rating as vital to continued economic progress. Perhaps he foresaw the need for Tennessee's agricultural base to be complemented by industry financed by out-of-state investors. The strongest likelihood is that Cheatham followed the lead of James D. Porter, also a Sky Blue. In his address, Cheatham admitted having supported Porter's proposals at settling the debt while Porter was in the statehouse. And though Cheatham was indebted to Isham Harris for advancement in the Confederate army, his ties to Porter were stronger and more immediate. Not only had the two men formed a tight wartime bond, but they had also faithfully supported one another in postwar politics. Cheatham's interests in postwar Tennessee were intimately bound to Porter, and his steadfast loyalty and gratitude towards Porter were manifested when they bolted the Bate convention together.

Despite Cheatham's large following and the social influence exerted by other Sky Blues, the Fussell candidacy was an abject failure. Bate rolled to victory, polling 120,637 votes to 93,168 for the incumbent Hawkins. A Greenback candidate was more successful than Fussell, who garnered only 4,814 votes and rarely captured more than 100 votes in any county.[59] The hapless performance indicates that Cheatham, Porter, and other Sky Blues, while respected men, were out of tune with the rank and file of the Democratic party. Once the Fussell campaign was crushed, Bate, Harris, and other triumphant Democrats carved out a debt reduction and settlement. The incendiary debt issue faded into the background, as Cheatham and his fellow Sky Blues were unable to impede the process further.

The debt issue represents Cheatham's last major involvement in statewide politics. However, he was not yet out of the public eye altogether, and the election of Democratic candidate Grover Cleveland to the presidency in 1884 opened one last avenue for appointive office. Cheatham was one of a host of Southern Democrats rewarded for their party loyalty by the disbursement of federal patronage jobs. Cheatham's prize was the postmastership of Nashville, to which he was appointed in October 1885. There are indications that Cheatham maneuvered to obtain the position. His desire to return to Nashville may have been influenced by Abner B. Robertson, who moved to the city from Coffee County in the early 1870s and was a partner in a wholesale grocery trade. According to one source, misfortunes attended Robertson's firm and spurred Cheatham into leaving the farm for his hometown. While sources do not indicate just what aid Abner Robertson sought from his son-in-law, he may have desired Cheatham's moral support during a rough period. There is no indication that Robertson expected Cheatham to take over the grocery or involve himself directly in the operations of the firm. Once he arrived, Cheatham quietly lobbied for the postmastership. He enlisted the support of Hampton J. Cheney, a former adjutant on John C. Brown's staff, in an effort to win the appointment. When the campaign succeeded, Cheatham secured a position at the post office for Cheney, who later became postmaster himself. The appointment brought the Cheatham family to full circle in Nashville municipal affairs, though the post office was a far larger enterprise than it had been when Leonard Cheatham served as postmaster in the 1840s. The location had changed several times since those early days when Frank assisted his father, the amount of mail handled was much greater, and carrier delivery had been instituted after the Civil War.[60]

Cheatham's appointment was for four years, but in reality he was a dying man by the time he became postmaster. The previous year he had begun telling friends that death was beckoning, and this grim pronouncement was accompanied by a change in demeanor. He "was grave, rarely ever indulging in a joke with old friends," a radical personality shift almost assuredly the result of arteriosclerosis, or hardening of the arteries. Despite worsening health, Cheatham threw himself into his new duties. He spent long hours at the post office, supervising the various departments and remaining until the last evening mail was sent to the depot. This arduous routine continued for ten months, but in August 1886 he became too ill to keep up with the work load. In an effort to recuperate, Cheatham traveled to a Tullahoma springs resort, but at the springs his condition deteriorated. He was brought back to Nashville and conveyed to his brother Felix's home in late August.[61]

It became apparent that Cheatham could not survive very long, and the family convened for a death watch. Bishop Quintard visited Cheatham on August 28 and "found him extremely ill." Three days later Quintard returned and gave Frank and his eldest son communion. Though he was able to sit on the veranda during the early days of his confinement and could move about, Cheatham's condition steadily declined. In late August and early September the family watched his strength erode. He lapsed occasionally into delirium. As with so many of his contemporaries, Cheatham was back on the battlefield in his last hours. The sound of a wagon passing in the street apparently transported him back into the Civil War. "There go the troops, bring me my horse. I am going to the front," was a widely circulated quotation from his final hours. The end came around 1:20 A.M. on September 4, while Anna and his two brothers were rearranging Frank as he reclined in a chair. Frank's last words were to Anna and expressed concern for the five children, after which he slipped quietly away.[62]

Cheatham's death had been anticipated for several days, and immediately, plans for an elaborate funeral took shape. Several committees were formed to finalize the preparations. Governor Bate, George Maney, and several of Cheatham's former aides coordinated the efforts of former Confederate soldiers, while industrialist Arthur S. Colyar chaired a citizen's committee. What resulted was the largest most imposing funeral in Nashville's history up to that time, and perhaps the largest ever. The death and funeral arrangements dominated the front page of the *Nashville Daily American* for three days. The paper reported the reflections of Cheatham's friends and acquaintances, printed laudatory letters and editorials, and

recorded the minutest trivia regarding Cheatham's obsequies. Nor was
Nashville along in mourning his demise; meetings were held in honor of
Cheatham's memory in Clarksville, Tullahoma, Jackson, and other sites
across the state.[63]

Cheatham's remains were removed from Felix's home and taken to the
Senate chamber of the state capitol. A military honor guard stood watch
over the bier. Floral decorations filled the room. In the day-and-half period
when Cheatham's body was displayed, between ten thousand and fifteen
thousand persons filed past the casket. Nashvillians of all classes and
colors were represented. A Memphis paper reported that of the hundreds
of black mourners, "many . . . were old family servants." Others who came
to pay their last respects included a small delegation of men who served
with Cheatham in Mexico. Naturally, hundreds of Cheatham's Confederate
veterans came. Many paused by the casket "as tears silently streamed down
their face."[64] Federal soldiers turned out in large numbers as well, several
relating that they appreciated Cheatham's warm friendship and acceptance after the war. One recalled an incident shortly after the war, when
Cheatham was asked the propriety of decorating Union soldiers' graves
in Tennessee. "I helped kill 'em when there was a reason for it," Cheatham
had replied, "and now I am equally willing to spread flowers on their
graves when there is a reason for it."[65] The decorations reflected Cheatham's divided military loyalties as well. Though he was buried in a Confederate battle flag, persons who viewed the casket could see only the
American flag which was wound around the lower end of the coffin and
a pillar supporting it.

At 2 P.M. on September 6 church bells began to toll throughout the
city. Shops closed and business was suspended. Thousands turned out
to watch the funeral procession make its way to the First Presbyterian
Church, where, twenty years before, Bishop Quintard had married Anna
and Frank. Quintard was on hand again, this time to conduct the Episcopal funeral service for his old friend. At its conclusion, the funeral participants made their way to Mount Olivet Cemetery. The procession
featured the survivors, political dignitaries, veterans of both armies, military companies, and musicians. It stretched over a mile in length. At
Mount Olivet more prayers were read, and a former staff officer made
a short, emotion-filled speech. A farewell hymn and an artillery salute
concluded the rites.

Frank Cheatham always regarded himself as a simple man, and he
would perhaps have objected to this extensive funeral ceremony. But the
funeral, more than any other event, proved the singular popularity and
esteem which Cheatham enjoyed in Nashville and accross the state. He
had the uncanny knack of making friends wherever he went and was al-

ways attracting new admirers. One mourner, a former Federal soldier, described Cheatham as "the most popular man I ever knew in my life. I have never heard a word against him from rich or poor, white or black."[66] An estimated twenty-five to thirty thousand people took part in or witnessed Cheatham's funeral procession, and the cortege included whites, blacks, former comrades and foes, and people from every social class.

But while Frank occupied a special place in Tennessee hearts during his lifetime, his fame dipped as succeeding generations arrived. Charisma and popularity are not always easily explained, and the reputation of a man like Cheatham can be eclipsed once his contemporaries pass away. Few of the mourners at Mount Olivet would have guessed it, but as Cheatham's remains were lowered into the grave, the subtle transition from fame to relative obscurity had begun.

Epilogue

Despite his enormous popularity, Frank Cheatham had been unable to acquire financial security for his family by the time of his death. An effort to assist his survivors began almost immediately, when prominent Nashvillians began a concerted effort to have Anna appointed postmistress to succeed her husband. As funeral preparations for General Cheatham unfolded, a simultaneous petition drive was launched on Anna's behalf. The petitions bore several thousand signatures by the time they were forwarded to Washington, accompanied by letters and telegrams supporting the cause. The outpouring of public sentiment convinced postal authorities in the capital to grant the request, and Anna became postmistress a few weeks following her husband's death.[1]

Anna also received a four-year appointment, but like her husband, she was destined to die before her term expired. In fact, she survived Frank by less than a year and a half, dying in Nashville on January 14, 1888. The cause of death was consumption, or tuberculosis, which she had contracted some years earlier while nursing one of her brothers, William Robertson, through a prolonged illness. Her health impaired, Anna at one point spent a winter in Florida because of her malady. She spent a portion of her last days attempting to secure a home in Nashville for her children, and she succeeded in this quest. Arrangements were also made to have a sister, Hattie Robertson, come and take charge of the household. Still, Anna's death at age forty-nine must have been a serious blow to the family, especially since the two daughters were only nine and seven. Frank Jr. was named executor of the estate, and at age twenty he assumed much of the responsibility for raising his younger siblings.[2]

The Cheatham children went on to lead productive lives. Frank Jr. was especially prominent and imitated his father's military drive at an early age. During a speech delivered in 1932 at the dedication of Stones River National Military Park, Frank Jr. reminisced that he had exercised his first military command as a boy in Coffee County, drilling his "city cousins and the darky boys on the place with broomstick guns." Educated at

Sewanee Military Academy and the University of the South, he followed in his father's footsteps and volunteered for military service against a foreign rival. The rival in his case was Spain, and Frank Jr. entered as a major in the First Tennessee Infantry. Sent to the Philippines, the regiment saw action against Filipino insurgents before it was mustered out in October 1899. Unwilling to abandon the service while fighting continued, Cheatham and other Tennesseans who remained behind formed a battalion which became the core of the Thirty-seventh U.S. Volunteer Infantry Regiment. Cheatham won a promotion to colonel, and he and his comrades fought in the Philippines for two more years before they were mustered out in 1901.[3]

When his volunteer regiment disbanded, Cheatham entered the regular army as a captain in the Quartermaster Corps. He remained with this branch of the service for nearly thirty years, although he served in a combat capacity as a colonel of an infantry unit which saw heavy fighting in the final months of World War I. Cheatham's quartermaster duties took him to sites as diverse as Manila, Indianapolis, San Francisco, Washington, D.C., and Honolulu. In 1926 he was appointed quartermaster general for four years. During that period he oversaw projects such as construction of housing and airfields for the newly established Army Air Corps, studies dealing with methods of supply, and landscaping at Arlington National Cemetery. The Lee mansion at Arlington was restored and the Tomb of the Unknown Soldier was built during Cheatham's tenure as well. Cheatham retired in 1930, but two years later he became the first resident superintendent of Stratford Hall, the Virginia birthplace of Richard Henry Lee, Francis Lightfoot Lee, and Robert E. Lee. As superintendent, Cheatham worked to restore the gardens, fields, livestock, and manual arts to their former colonial style. He also farmed the large Stratford plantation, a tradition which continues to this day.[4]

Frank Jr. married Mary Denman of San Francisco in December 1901, and they had three children, two sons and a daughter. An expert horseman in the mold of his father and paternal grandfather, Cheatham also maintained the family's traditional allegiance to the Democratic party. He died in Denver in late 1944 and was buried at Arlington National Cemetery.[5]

Cheatham's second son, Patton Robertson, followed Frank Jr.'s lead in some respects, most noticeably in his education at the University of the South and his service as an officer in the First Tennessee Regiment during the Philippines campaign. He differed from his elder brother by returning to civilian life, where he was involved in Nashville business affairs as an underwriter and broker. He eventually formed a partnership and opened a brokerage house in the city. The lone Cheatham offspring who

General and Mrs. Cheatham's children from a photograph in the December 1895 issue of *Confederate Veteran* magazine. *Seated,* Joseph Johnston, Benjamin Franklin, Jr.; *standing* Alice, Patton Robertson, and Medora. Patton was the only one of the five who never married; he died in 1914 after visiting his eldest brother Frank in Hawaii.

never married, Patton came down with pneumonia after a trip to see his elder brother in Hawaii. The illness proved fatal, and Patton died in a San Francisco hospital in March 1914. His remains were returned to Nashville for burial.[6]

The last son, Joseph Johnston, was educated in Nashville. He was an officer in the Tennessee National Guard in the 1890s, as was Frank Jr., and worked in the post office for several years after his parents died. In 1894 he entered the U. S. Navy as an assistant paymaster and launched a career which spanned more than four decades. Johnston spent the bulk of his time in the pay and supply departments, and his military assignments carried him to a variety of locales. This Cheatham served at various times aboard ships, at several naval yards, and in the capital, and he was a member of an American naval mission to Brazil in 1922. In 1929 he was commissioned a rear admiral and appointed paymaster general of the Navy, as well as chief of the Bureau of Supplies and Accounts. He retired in 1936. Johnston apparently had his father's ability to win friends: he was praised in a biographical sketch for his "charming personality" and for his "charity, unfailing courtesy and great kindness," which "endeared him to all who knew him." Johnston married twice; his first wife died in 1922, and he remarried in 1934. He had two daughters by his first wife, Alice. Johnston died in Kalispell, Montana, in September 1942 and was interred at Arlington.[7]

Frank and Anna's two daughters were reared by their brothers and Aunt Hattie (or Tattie) in Nashville. Medora, the eldest daughter, was the longest-lived of the Cheatham progeny, dying in March 1969 at the age of ninety. She graduated from the Nashville College for Young Ladies and was married in 1917 to Telfair Hodgson. Hodgson, the son of a vice-chancellor at the University of the South, eventually became treasurer of the school as well as a bank president in Sewanee. He and Meodra were important figures in the Tennessee town and belonged to various civic and social organizations. Medora was active in the Daughters of the Confederacy, and historians who conversed with her found her to be a stout defender of her father's war record. Efforts to draw her out on any of Frank's alleged inadequacies, such as his drinking habits, proved profitless. Medora retained possession of the remaining Cheatham papers, probably because the travel demands made upon her brothers in the military made it more expedient for her to keep them. The papers were copied in 1958 by scholars at the Southern Historical Collection on the campus of the University of North Carolina at Chapel Hill. She later donated the papers to the Tennessee State Library and Archives. Medora was survived by one daughter.[8]

Alice, the youngest Cheatham child, was reared and educated in Nashville. Alice possessed "a bright mind and unusual artistic talent," and her family name secured her a prominent spot in Nashville society. Both Medora and Alice attended Confederate reunions during their youth, where "they were the recipients of many honors from the veterans." Alice married Thomas H. Malone, Jr., in 1904. Alice's "delicate constitution" suffered after she contracted a disease, probably tuberculosis, about the same time that she married. In fact, an obituary states that she was "brought home from her wedding trip . . . [as] an invalid." The remaining two years of her life were spent in a vain effort to regain her health. She journeyed to Asheville, North Carolina, where Aunt Hattie lived after raising the Cheatham children, but her condition failed to improve in the mountain climate. Alice visited specialists in New York, spent one summer at the Malone country place near Nashville, and passed her last three months in El Paso. She died in November 1906, just two days shy of her twenty-sixth birthday. Her body was returned to Nashville for burial, and she and Patton are the only two Cheatham children buried at Mount Olivet. Alice was interred in the Malone family section, while Patton rests next to his parents in the Cheatham family plot.[9]

A visit to the Cheatham graves at Mount Olivet Cemetery can be vaguely unsettling to one who is aware of the prominence of the family in life. A circle of fading, weather-beaten gravestones, some just inscribed with initials, mark the final resting places of many of Frank Cheatham's relatives. A large cross used to denote the burial spot of Frank's sister, Alice, and that of her husband. Several years ago the cross cracked off its pedestal and toppled into the grass, where weeds have all but obscured it. A few feet away, tall grass grows around the rectangular headstones which mark Frank's, Anna's, and Patton's graves.

The size of Frank's headstone is deceiving, at least if one has expectations that a grave marker should somehow provide an index of that person's prominence while alive. But Cheatham's modest tombstone may be appropriate relative to his status in this century. He hardly belongs to the first rank of Confederate heroes, men such as Robert E. Lee, Jefferson Davis, and Stonewall Jackson. Nor, in fact, would his contemporaries have rated him there, though they assumed that Cheatham's historical reputation was far more secure than it proved to be. The closest tangible evidence of Cheatham's fame is to be found in a statue in Nashville's Centennial Park. The sculptured figure atop the pedestal is that of a seated Confederate soldier, holding his cap in his left hand and his rifle in his right. The statue was erected in 1903 to celebrate the valor of the common Confederate soldier. A large plaque attached to one side of the monument's base lists over five hundred names, the roster of the group

A simple headstone markes Cheatham's final resting place. (Author's photo)

which paid for the statue: Frank Cheatham Bivouac Number 1, Association of Confederate Soldiers. The Nashville-based organization was also
known as Camp Number 35, United Confederate Veterans.

Frank Cheatham's name remained in the public eye as long as the
veteran's group bearing his name was in existence, but a subtle process
whereby Cheatham's reputation diminished was under way long before
the Centennial Park statue was unveiled. In the decades after the Civil
War, the reality of the South's grinding defeat eventually transformed itself into the "Lost Cause." The "Lost Cause" mentality embraced a number of different images, but at least one component was a near-sacred
belief that the South had fought for a noble cause. The South's ultimate
defeat was not caused by any moral superiority on the part of the North:
on the contrary, only the latter's immense superiority in numbers had
overwhelmed the valiant Confederates. As time elapsed, a mythology
of sorts arose around the Confederacy and enshrined it in Southern
memories.

Even the Confederate soldiers who fought the war succumbed to this
alluring vision. One need only thumb through the pages of the postwar
periodical *Confederate Veteran* to catch a glimpse of the process. At annual
reunions of the United Confederate Veterans, the aging soldiers dressed
in resplendent gray uniforms that were much better finery than most of
them had worn during the actual conflict. They attended the dedication

One of the few extant reminders of Frank Cheatham may be found in this
Confederate monument, located in Nashville's Centennial Park. Dedicated in
1909, the statue was erected after fund-raising drives by the Frank Cheatham
Bivouac, United Confederate Veterans, and a chapter of the United Daughters
of the Confederacy. Members of the Cheatham Bivouac were listed on a large
metal plaque affixed to the base of the monument. (Author's photo)

ceremonies at Confederate monuments which sprouted up across the region, such as the Cheatham Bivouac statue or the massive Tennessee monument which dominates the horizon at Mount Olivet Cemetery. They bought lithographs and prints bearing the likeness of favorite Confederate heroes, such as Robert E. Lee. They wrote eloquent eulogies when old comrades passed away and nostalgically recounted incidents they remembered from the war years. In many respects, what the former Confederates did was a natural process; most individuals looking back on the past tend to gloss over the rough moments and embellish the good ones.

Still, the "Lost Cause" mentality ultimately distorted much of the reality of the war years. The veterans and their heirs would have loathed a writer who had the temerity to write of Confederate deserters, or gambling in camp, or prostitutes who followed the armies. To do so would have broken the code, a code which granted virtually every Confederate veteran an exalted status in Southern lore. So strong was this belief that it extended long after most of the actual veterans had died. Veneration of the "Lost Cause" was adopted by persons born long after the Confederacy itself died, and it remains alive today in certain sectors.

The career of an officer like Frank Cheatham presented some difficulties to adherents of the "Lost Cause." There were elements in Cheatham's makeup that Southerners could extol. They could celebrate his generosity, friendly nature, his concern for his troops, and especially his boldness in combat. And yet, if one dug too deep, there were other, negative elements in Cheatham's life that would have to be accepted. That Cheatham sometimes drank. That he loved horse races and was not averse to gambling. That he was profane, sometimes spectacularly so. Taken together, these indicate that Frank Cheatham was eminently human, but they also mitigated against him winning too high a place in the pantheon of Confederate heros. One does not visualize Robert E. Lee exorting his men by bellowing, "Give them hell, boys, give them hell!" A pious Stonewall Jackson would not have frequented a poker game. Inebriation is not a state normally associated with Jefferson Davis.

Paradoxically, had Cheatham been killed in action, he would almost certainly have fared better in the historical realm. The image of Patrick Cleburne disappearing on the smoke-shrouded plain at Franklin has an undeniable romantic quality, though anyone who has studied that battle should be horrified by what actually transpired. Frank Cheatham survived. He went home, accepted that the war was over, and got on with life. Cheatham was certainly colorful on occasion, but there is little romance in an account of his life.

One is left to ponder what Cheatham and his men would have thought of his marginal place in Confederate history. At least he was fortunate enough to enjoy the esteem of his men — in fact, that of most Tennesseans — during his lifetime. Perhaps Frank Cheatham was best summed up by Reverend M. B. DeWitt, a chaplain for the Eighth Tennessee Infantry during the war. Cheatham encountered DeWitt one day in Nashville, years after the war was over, and the two had a cordial reunion. The encounter led DeWitt to write later, "Dear old Frank! He had his faults, but we boys loved him."[10] This sentiment is not inscribed on his tombstone, but surely General Cheatham would have approved of DeWitt's statement as a fitting epitaph.

Notes

Abbreviations

BFC / Benjamin Franklin Cheatham
CMH: Tenn. / James D. Porter. *Confederate Military History: Tennessee.* Ed. Clement A. Evans. Atlanta, 1899.
Connelly, *AG* / Thomas L. Connelly. *Autumn of Glory: The Army of Tennessee, 1862–1865.* Baton Rouge, 1971.
Connelly, *AH* / Thomas L. Connelly. *Army of the Heartland: The Army of Tennessee, 1861–1862.* Baton Rouge, 1967.
CV / *Confederate Veteran*
Duke / Duke University, Durham, N.C.
Harvard / Houghton Library, Harvard University
Lindsley, *MAT* / John Berrien Lindsley, ed. *The Military Annals of Tennessee: Confederate.* Nashville, 1886.
NA / National Archives, Washington, D.C.
OR / *The War of the Rebellion: A Compilation of the Official Records of the Union and Confederate Armies.* 128 vols. Washington, D.C., 1880–1901. (Series 1 unless otherwise indicated.)
Tenn. CW / Civil War Centennial Commission. *Tennesseans in the Civil War.* 2 vols. Nashville, 1964. (Vol. 1 unless otherwise indicated.)
THS / Tennessee Historical Society
TSLA / Tennessee State Library and Archives, Nashville
UNC / Southern Historical Collection, University of North Carolina at Chapel Hill

Chapter 1

1. Joseph E. Johnston to BFC, Nov. 14, 1867, Benjamin Franklin Cheatham Papers, TSLA.
2. Alice C. H. Parker (granddaughter of BFC) to author, Mar. 1982; *The National Cyclopedia of American Biography,* 37 vols. (New York, 1892–1951; reprint ed., Ann Arbor, 1967), 31:34; Frederick Adams Virkus, ed., *The Compendium of American Genealogy: The Standard Genealogical Encyclopedia of the First Families of America,* 7 vols. (Chicago, 1925–42, 6:697; Nell Marion Nugent, *Cavaliers and Pioneers: Abstracts of Virginia Land Patents and Grants,* vol. 3, *1692–1739* (Richmond, 1979), 292, 373.
3. Robert M. McBride and Dan M. Robinson, *Biographical Directory of the Tennessee General Assembly* ed. Robert M. McBride, vol. 1, *1796–1861* (Nashville, **289**

1975), 136–39; Herbert Weaver and others, eds., *Correspondence of James K. Polk*, vol. 3, *1835–1836* (Nashville, 1975), 151, 181; LeRoy P. Graf and Ralph W. Haskins, eds., *The Papers of Andrew Johnson*, vol. 2, *1852–1857* (Knoxville, 1970), 216. Cheatham County, situated to the northwest of Nashville's Davidson County, is sometimes claimed to have been named for Frank Cheatham. It was actually named for Edward Saunders Cheatham, who was president of the Tennessee State Senate when the county was formed. See Joseph Nathan Kane, *The American Counties* (New York, 1960), 60, and E. S. Cheatham's portrait in the Cheatham County Courthouse, Ashland City.

4. Marcus J. Wright, "A Sketch of the Life and Character of Gen. Benjamin F. Cheatham of Tennessee," unidentified and undated newspaper clipping in the Marcus J. Wright papers, UNC, hereafter cited as Wright, "Cheatham Sketch," UNC; Mary Hardin McCown and Inez E. Burns, *Soldiers of the War of 1812 Buried in Tennessee* (Johnson City, Tenn., 1959), 21; Weaver, *Correspondence of James K. Polk*, 3:167, 208 (editor's quote), 259; W. W. Clayton, *History of Davidson County, Tennessee* (Philadelphia, 1880; reprint ed., Nashville, 1971), 89; Charles Sellers, *James K. Polk, Continentalist, 1843–1846* (Princeton, 1966), 32; Timothy D. Johnson, "Benjamin Franklin Cheatham: The Making of a Confederate General" (M.A. thesis, Univ. of Alabama, 1982), 28; David C. Roller and Robert W. Twyman, eds., *The Encyclopedia of Southern History* (Baton Rouge, 1979), 877 (Nashville Convention).

5. BFC to Leonard Pope Cheatham, Feb. 14, 1848, Cheatham Papers, TSLA; [Garden Study Club of Nashville], *History of Homes and Gardens in Tennessee* (Nashville, 1936), 193; James Douglas Anderson, *Making the American Thoroughbred, Especially in Tennessee, 1800–1845* (Norwood, Mass., 1916), 120.

6. Wright, "Cheatham Sketch," UNC; Parker to author, Mar. 1982; Virkus, *The Compendium of American Geneology*, 6:697; Martha [Cheatham] Blackie to Anson Nelson, in THS Miscellaneous Files, 1688–1951, TSLA (microfilm) (Eliz. Cheatham quote); Roller and Twyman, *Encyclopedia of Southern History*, 1189.

7. [Garden Study Club], *Homes and Gardens in Tennessee*, 193; [May Winston] Caldwell, *Historical and Beautiful Country Homes near Nashville, Tennessee* (Nashville, 1911), n.p..

8. Sarah Foster Kelley; *Children of Nashville . . . Lineages from James Robertson* (Nashville, 1973), 99–100, 138–39; William Curry Harllee, *Kinfolks: A Genealogical and Biographical Record*, 3 vols. (New Orleans, 1934–37), 3:2471, 2483.

9. Parker to author, Mar. 1982; Harllee, *Kinfolks*, 3:2485; Kelley, *Children of Nashville*, 99–102.

10. Wright, "Cheatham Sketch," UNC.

11. Davidson County General Index to Deeds, 1784–1871 (unfinished WPA typescript, Nashville, 1942), 131, TSLA; Davidson County Tax Records for 1829 (typescript) 15, TSLA; Johnson, "The Making of a Confederate General," 5 (quote).

12. Wright, "Cheatham Sketch," UNC; C. A. Cross, "Life and Work of Professor Nathaniel Cross," THS Misc. Files, TSLA; receipt from Cross to Leonard Cheatham, 1834, Cheatham Papers, TSLA; *Nashville Daily American*, Jan. 23, 1893.

13. Wright, "Cheatham Sketch," UNC; Harllee, *Kinfolks*, 3:2485; Middle Tennessee Land Grants (microfilm), TSLA. Leonard Cheatham was granted vast land holdings in Wayne, Lewis, and Hardin Counties.

14. Ilene J. Cornwell, "Devon Farm," *Tennessee Historical Quarterly* (Summer 1975), 117; Thomas A. Head, *Campaigns and Battles of the Sixteenth Regiment, Tennessee Volunteers* (Nashville, 1885), 313; "Major General B. F. Cheatham: A Sketch

of His Military Career," unidentified and undated newspaper clipping in the M. J. Solomons Scrapbook, 1861–65, Duke. The clipping is obviously from a wartime newspaper and may be an 1863 article from the *Chattanooga Rebel*, for one of Cheatham's sisters wrote from Atlanta that his biography in the *Rebel* was "very good. . . . I think the *Rebel* wants to make you a Lieut. Gen." Martha Blackie to BFC, Mar. 30, 1863, Cheatham Papers, TSLA.

15. Sellers, *James K. Polk*, 408, 416–21; Cheatham clipping, Solomons Scrapbook, Duke; Clayton, *History of Davidson County*, 181.

16. [John Blount Robertson], *Reminiscences of a Campaign in Mexico by a Member of "The Bloody First"* (Nashville, 1849), 59–61 (quote); Robert Selph Henry, *The Story of the Mexican War* (New York, 1850), 84; Turner J. Fakes, Jr., "Memphis and the Mexican War," *West Tennessee Historical Society Papers*, 2 (1948): 122.

17. Clayton, *History of Davidson County*, 165; Robertson, *The Bloody First*, 63; First Tennessee Infantry File, Mexican War, NA.

18. Robertson, *The Bloody First*, 64–65, 68–69; Clayton, *History of Davidson County*, 165. The state of Tennessee provided some initial financial support. Cheatham, for instance, was advanced $120 by the state for the early portion of his service. See First Tennessee Infantry File, NA.

19. Robertson, *The Bloody First*, 70 (quote), 71.

20. Ibid., 74–80; James Law McLaughlin to father, July 1846, McLaughlin Family Papers, TSLA.

21. BFC to Fe[lix] Cheatham, Sept. 5, 1846, Cheatham Papers, TSLA; Robertson, *The Bloody First*, 87–89, 108–10; Henry, *The Story of the Mexican War*, 139; K. Jack Bauer, *The Mexican War, 1846–1848* (New York, 1974), 88–89.

22. BFC to Felix Cheatham, Sept. 5, 1846, and "Muster Roll, First Tennessee Regt. Vol. Infantry," both in Cheatham Papers, TSLA; Robertson, *The Bloody First*, 111; James Law McLaughlin to father, Sept. 1, 1846, McLaughlin Family Papers, TSLA; Henry, *The Story of the Mexican War*, 139.

23. Maurice Matloff, gen. ed., *American Military History*, (Washington, 1969), 168–69; Henry, *The Story of the Mexican War*, 145–46; Bauer, *The Mexican War*, 93; Justin H. Smith, *The War with Mexico*, 2 vols. (New York, 1919; reprint ed., Gloucester, Mass., 1963), 1:230–34.

24. Robertson, *The Bloody First*, 125, 129; Smith, *The War with Mexico*, 1:249, 502; BFC to Louise Cheatham, Oct. 6, 1846, Cheatham Papers, TSLA.

25. Smith, *The War with Mexico*, 1:232–33, 249; Robertson, *The Bloody First*, 127–28; Henry, *The Story of the Mexican War*, 145; Alfred Hoyt Bill, *Rehearsal for Conflict* (New York, 1947), 144–46.

26. Matloff, *American Military History*, 169; Robertson, *The Bloody First*, 129, 137–38, 164–65; Bauer, *The Mexican War*, 95; T. Harry Williams, ed., *The History of American Wars: From Colonial Times to World War I* (New York, 1981), 172.

27. The best account of the Tennesseans during their attack on La Teneria is found in Robertson, *The Bloody First*, 137–41. See also Smith, *The War with Mexico*, 1:249–53.

28. Robertson, *The Bloody First*, 140 (Cheatham exhorting his men to follow); BFC to Medora Riggs, Oct. 16, 1846 (account of ball grazing his back).

29. Robertson, *The Bloody First*, 145–46; Smith, *The War with Mexico*, 1:255; Williams, *History of American Wars*, 172; Bauer, *The Mexican War*, 99–100.

30. BFC to Louise Cheatham, Oct. 6, 1846 (criticizes Taylor, homesickness among troops, BFC's illness); "Muster Rolls/Field Returns"; BFC to Medora Riggs, Oct. 16, 1846 (laments losses), all in Cheatham Papers, TSLA; Robertson,

The Bloody First, 164–65. Fever and other ailments afflicted Cheatham at regular intervals for several months in late 1846. See BFC to Medora Riggs, Dec. 14, 1846, Cheatham-Hodgson Papers, University of the South, Sewanee, Tenn.

31. BFC to Medora Riggs, Oct. 16, 1846, Cheatham Papers, TSLA; Robertson, *The Bloody First*, 172–73.

32. BFC to Louise Cheatham, Oct. 6, 1846, and to Medora Riggs, Oct. 16, 1846, Cheatham Papers, TSLA.

33. BFC to Medora Riggs, Oct. 16, 1846, Cheatham Papers, TSLA.

34. BFC to Aunt Fanny, Dec. 4, 1846, Cheatham Papers, TSLA; Bauer, *The Mexican War*, 239–44; "Field Return," Mar. 1847, First Regiment Tennessee Volunteers, THS Misc. Files, TSLA; A. Heiman, "Concise Description of the Services of Tenn. Volunteers Commanded by Col. W. B. Campbell in the War with Mexico in 1846 & 7," THS Misc. Files, TSLA.

35. Heiman, "Concise Description," THS Misc. Files, TSLA; Robertson, *The Bloody First*, 225–30 (siege of Veracruz) and 231–32 (Cheatham and Harney attack Mexicans on bridge).

36. Robertson, *The Bloody First*, 230–32; Bauer, *The Mexican War*, 251; Heiman, "Concise Description," THS Misc. Files, TSLA; J[ohn] Wooldridge, ed., *History of Nashville, Tennessee* (Nashville, 1890), 178–79; W. F. Smart to John Cheatham, May 3, 1847, Cheatham Papers, TSLA.

37. Bauer, *The Mexican War*, 261–68.

38. Ibid., 270; Robertson, *The Bloody First*, 274–79; "Field Return," Apr. 30, 1847, Cheatham Papers, TSLA.

39. Wooldridge, *History of Nashville*, 179.

40. BFC, 1847–1848 Diary, Cheatham Papers, TSLA; Third Tennessee Infantry File, Mexican War, NA; Clayton, *History of Davidson County*, 166; Wooldridge, *History of Nashville*, 179–80.

41. BFC, 1847–48 Diary, Cheatham Papers, TSLA; Fakes, "Memphis and the Mexican War," 140.

42. Clayton, *History of Davidson County*, 166; Wooldridge, *History of Nashville*, 180; BFC, 1847–48 Diary, Cheatham Papers, TSLA.

43. BFC, 1847–48 Diary, Cheatham Papers, TSLA. The diary is not only sparse in details but also seems to be misdated in regard to some of the months, making it difficult for the reader to decipher exactly when some of the events occurred.

44. Ibid.; BFC to Leonard Cheatham, Feb. 14, 1848, Cheatham Papers, TSLA.

45. BFC to Leonard Cheatham, Feb. 14, 1848, Cheatham Papers, TSLA. General Lane may have boosted Cheatham for the promotion because one of his subordinates, Col. J. H. Lane of the Third Indiana, was resentful of the commander. The two Lanes, who were not related, had a fist fight in full view of Colonel Lane's Indiana regiment on Feb. 20, 1847; see Bauer, *The Mexican War*, 227.

46. Third Tennessee Infantry File, Mexican War, National Archives.

47. Third Tennessee Infantry File, NA; Wooldridge, *History of Nashville*, 180; Clayton, *History of Davidson County*, 166 (last quote).

Chapter 2

1. Wright, "Cheatham Sketch," UNC; J. S. Holliday, *The World Rushed In: The California Gold Rush Experience* (New York, 1981), 297.

2. David Lavender, *California: Land of New Beginnings* (New York, 1972), 169; Raymond W. Hillman (curator of history, Haggin Museum, Stockton, Calif.) to author, Apr. 19, 1983; Edward Gould Buffum, *Six Months in the Gold Mines: From a Journal of Three Years' Residence in Upper and Lower California, 1847-8-9* (Philadelphia, 1880; reprint ed., Ann Arbor, 1966), 155.

3. V. Covert Martin, *Stockton Album through the Years* (Stockton, 1959), 25, 106; George Henry Tinkham, *History of Stockton* (San Francisco, 1880), 188; Hillman to author, Apr. 19, 1983.

4. Tinkham, *History of Stockton,* 188 (description of hotel and charge that BFC brandished revolver); Martin, *Stockton Album,* 106 (leadership in city politics, BFC defiant of law and order, had "a quick pistol.")

5. Tinkham, *History of Stockton,* 188 (quote); Johnson, "The Making of a Confederate General," 25-26 (BFC and Gwin).

6. Accounts of the Hill lynching are found in [Herbert O. Lang?], *History of Tuolumne County* (San Francisco, 1882; reprint ed., Sonora, 1960), 76-79, 398; Dale Morgan, ed., *Three Years in California: William Perkins' Journal of Life at Sonora, 1849-1852* (Berkeley, 1964), 231-35; Enos Christman, *One Man's Gold: The Letters and Journals of a Forty-Niner* ed. Florence M. Christman (New York, 1930), 188-194.

7. Lang, *History of Tuolumne County,* 79 (first version of BFC-Sheriff Work encounter); Christman, *One Man's Gold,* 193 (second version).

8. The prevalence of violence in California during the Gold Rush era is covered in Morgan, *William Perkins' Journal,* 234-37; Holliday, *The World Rushed In,* 336-37; Kevin Starr, *Americans and the California Dream, 1850-1915* (New York, 1973), 55-56. Quotes cited are from Morgan, *William Perkins' Journal,* 235 (lynching participant) and Lavender, *California,* 219 (Californian).

9. Wright, "Cheatham Sketch," UNC; *Nashville Weekly American,* Sept. 8, 1886; Manuscript Guides, Cheatham Papers, UNC and TSLA. Leonard Cheatham sold the Westover property to Mark R. Cockrill, who grew sheep on the estate and won a gold medal in 1856 in London "for the finest wool produced in the world." Cockrill's son and two subsequent owners possessed the property. Cockrill became so identified with the estate that Robertson's Bend of the Cumberland River now appears as Cockrill's Bend on maps, although Robertson Island remains named for the original owner. The mansion was standing as late as 1936, by which time the property was owned by the state of Tennessee. The building is no longer in existence, and the Tennessee State Penitentiary now occupies a portion of the original Westover estate. See Caldwell, *Country Homes near Nashville,* n.p., and [Garden Study Club], *Homes and Gardens in Tennessee,* 193.

10. Manuscript Guides, Cheatham Papers, UNC and TSLA; Silas Emmett Lucas, *Goodspeed's History of Tennessee* (Nashville, 1887), 518; Cheatham clipping, Solomons Scrapbook, Duke.

11. For a brief but useful review of the hostility evinced by West Point graduates to volunteers in Mexico, see Timothy D. Johnson, "Benjamin Franklin Cheatham: The Early Years," *Tennessee Historical Quarterly* (Fall 1983), 268-69. The Bragg-Cheatham feud is covered elsewhere in this volume.

12. Roy B. West, Jr., *Kingdom of the Saints: The Story of Brigham Young and the Mormons* (New York, 1957), 220-28, 234, 266, 268; *Nashville Union and American,* June 5, 1857; *Nashville Daily Gazette,* June 7, 1857; *Nashville Republican Banner,* June 7, 1857.

13. *Nashville Daily Gazette,* June 7, 1857; David McCullough, *The Path between the Seas: The Creation of the Panama Canal, 1870-1914* (New York, 1977), 35. William H. Aspinwall was one of three Americans who pushed the railroad project. The effort to have his surname stand as the city's name was less successful than the rail line itself, which generated handsome profits as mail and passengers crossed the Isthmus of Panama. See McCullough, 35-36.

14. *Nashville Union and American,* June 7, 1857; *Nashville Republican Banner,* June 7, 1857. See also *Nashville Daily Gazette,* June 13, 1857.

15. John and Mavis Biesanz, *The People of Panama* (New York, 1955), 8, 37; McCullough, *Path between the Seas,* 175, 452-53.

16. *Nashville Daily Patriot,* Sept. 16, 1857; Herschel Gower and Jack Allen, eds., *Pen and Sword: The Life and Journals of Randal W. McGavock* (Nashville, 1959), 325, 257-59; *Nashville Union and American,* Sept. 17, 1857 (quote).

17. *Nashville Union and American,* Sept. 17, 1857 (quote); *Nashville Republican Banner,* Sept. 25, 1857; *Nashville Daily Patriot,* Sept. 24 and 25, 1857.

18. *Nashville Daily Patriot,* Sept. 25 and 28, 1857.

19. *Nashville Union and American,* May 12, 1855; *Nashville Daily Patriot,* May 13, 1858, and May 18, 1859.

20. Anderson, *Making the American Thoroughbred,* 137-40; *Nashville Union,* May 16, 1843; *Nashville Union and American,* May 29, 1860.

21. BFC to Leonard Pope Cheatham, June 23 (no year), Cheatham Papers, TSLA; *Nashville Daily Patriot,* May 29 and 30, 1857; *Nashville Union and American,* Sept. 2, 1860. The Nashville Race Track was seemingly well appointed to accommodate horse enthusiasts. An 1880 description noted that the facility contained 225 acres and two tracks, one each for running and trotting. Both were 40 feet wide and a mile in length and asserted to be "the softest track in the United States." An earlier, 1831 description cited the presence of a large mansion house, a dining room, a stage, a judges' stand, stables, and stalls. Cheatham was apparently proprietor before the second course, for trotting, was built. See Charles Edwin Robert, ed., *Nashville City Guide Book* (Nashville, 1880), 40-41; Anderson, *Making the American Thoroughbred,* 132.

22. Head, *Sixteenth Tennessee,* 315; *Memphis Avalanche,* Sept. 5, 1886; Simon Cameron to Gov. Isham Harris (telegram), Apr. 15, 1861, and Harris to Cameron, Apr. 15, 1861, both in THS Misc. Files, TSLA. It is hard to establish how much regret Cheatham felt in taking up arms against the United States. Two accounts by his intimate friend James D. Porter are contradictory. The first, which appears in the *Sixteenth Tennessee* volumes, states that "he deeply regretted the necessity that forced upon him a choice of evils," and implies that he broke somewhat reluctantly from the Union. The second account maintains that at the outbreak of war, Cheatham "espoused heartily the cause of the South," and makes no reference to misgivings; see *CMH: Tenn.,* 302.

23. Connelly, *AH,* 25, 37; Cheatham's appointment as Second Brigadier General in the Provisional Force of Tennessee, to rank from May 9, 1861, in Cheatham Papers, TSLA.

24. *Tenn. CW,* 309.

25. Dillard Jacobs, "Outfitting the Provisional Force of Tennessee," *Tennessee Historical Quarterly* (Fall 1981), 257-58, 269; Military and Financial Board Records, Isham Green Harris Papers, TSLA; Dillard Jacobs to author, Feb. 11, 1983.

26. Lucas, *Goodspeed's History of Tennessee,* 536; John Johnston, "Civil War Reminiscences, 1861-1865" (typescript), Confederate Collection, TSLA, 14; John Cava-

naugh, *Historical Sketch of the Obion Avalanche, Company H, Ninth Tennessee Infantry* (Union city, Tenn., 1922), 33–34; S. T. Williams to uncle, Aug. 30, 1861, Confederate Collection, TSLA. Before he departed for Union City, Cheatham temporarily commanded a camp named in his honor in Robertson County. Several regiments organized or trained at Camp Cheatham, but Frank's tenure there could not have extended for more than a few weeks in June 1861. See Tennessee Historical Commission, *Tennessee Historical Markers* (Nashville, 1980), III.

27. *Tenn. CW,* 185, 187, 199, 219, 245; James Iredell Hall, "A History of Company 'C' 9th Tenn. Regt. from its Organization 1861 until the Surrender 1865," 1:41–43, James Iredell Hall Papers, Southern Historical Collection, UNC (hereafter cited as "Ninth Tennessee"); Capt. J. T. Winfrey to Samuel Winfrey, June 18, 1861, letter on display at the Tennessee State Museum, Nashville (officer's quote); S. T. Williams to uncle, Aug. 30, 1861, TSLA Confederate Collection, (recruit's quote). James Iredell Hall's account of his wartime service, written in two ledger books, is one of the finest sources on Cheatham's division, and on the Ninth Tennessee Regiment in particular. Hall was a native of Tipton County, a graduate of Kentucky's Centre College, and enlisted in the army to keep watch over a number of young men from his school, the Mountain Academy. In a letter to his daughters, he also provided a view of Camp Brown at night: "Some of the boys sing, some holler, some bark like dogs, some crow like chickens and one whistles so much like a mocking bird that you would think it was a bird indeed." Hall to Misses Jesse and Mary E. Hall, Hall Papers, UNC.

28. Joe Spence Diary, 1861–1862, Confederate Collection, TSLA.

29. Ibid. (quotes); Edward A. Pollard, *The Early Life, Campaigns, and Public Services of Robert E. Lee; With a Record of the Campaigns and Heroic Deeds of his Companions in Arms* (New York, 1871), 721; Wright, "Cheatham Sketch," UNC.

30. Isham Harris to Jefferson Davis, July 2, 1861, Dearborn Papers, Harvard; *OR,* 4:372–73, 375–76; ibid., ser. 4, 1:417, 474–75, 527–28; Connelly, *AH,* 35–37, 42.

31. BFC to Gideon Pillow, June 20 and July 2, 1861, both in John C. Breckinridge Collection, Chicago Historical Society; BFC to Pillow, June 7, June 20, June 30, and July 18, 1861, all in the Ferdinand Julius Dreer Collection, Confederate Generals, Historical Society of Pennsylvania.

32. Connelly, *AH,* 48–49; *OR,* 3:613–14; M. Jeff Thompson to BFC, Aug. 24, 1861, Simon Gratz Collection, Historical Society of Pennsylvania.

33. *OR,* 3:678, 683–84; 4:396.

34. *OR,* 3:685–86; 4:183, 185–86; Connelly, *AH,* 52–54.

35. James Caswell Edenton Diary, Sept. 4, 1861 (typescript), Confederate Collection, TSLA; Cheatham clipping, Solomons Scrapbook, Duke; *OR,* 3:152. The two Union gunboats were the *Lexington* and the *Tyler.* They sparred with a Confederate vessel, the *Jackson,* and were fired upon by artillery serviced by Cheatham and other gunners. The Solomons sketch erroneously indicates that the fight took place on Sept. 3 rather than Sept. 4, and mistakenly refers to the *Tyler* as the *Conestoga.*

36. *OR,* 52, pt. 2: 223; Connelly, *AH,* 54.

37. *OR,* 52, pt. 2: 193.

38. Capt. J. T. Winfrey to Samuel Winfrey, June 18, 1861, Tenn. State Museum.

39. BFC's Report of the Battle of Belmont (microfilm copy), Cheatham Papers, Southern Historical Collection, UNC; *OR,* 3:307–9, 343–46, 348–49, 352, 356;

Capt. Alfred Tyler Fielder Diary, Nov. 7, 1861, THS Collection, TSLA; James N. Rosser Diary, Nov. 8, 1861, and Samuel Latta to Mary Latta, Nov. 8, 1861, both in Confederate Collection, TSLA. Alfred Tyler Fielder enlisted in the army in June of 1861, and served throughout the war. His diary constitutes a prime source on Cheatham and his command. Fielder's account is particularly noteworthy because of his involvement with Cheatham from the very beginning of the war, at Camp Brown in Union City, until the surrender in North Carolina in 1865. The diary not only provides information on Cheatham; it also chronicles the maturation of Cheatham's men from peacetime citizens to hardened veterans. Fielder rose from his initial rank of private to captain and was wounded twice. After the war he returned to his Dyer County home, served one term in the state legislature, and died in 1896. The diary was donated to the Tennessee Historical Society in 1941.

40. Samuel Latta to Mary Latta, Nov. 8, 1861, TSLA; BFC's Belmont Report, Cheatham Papers, TSLA; Pollard, *Robert E. Lee,* 719–20 (quote); Ben LaBree, ed., *Camp Fires of the Confederacy* (Louisville, 1898), 120.

41. Fielder Diary, Nov. 7, 1861, TSLA; Samuel Latta to Mary Latta, Nov. 8, 1861, TSLA.

42. William S. McFeely, *Grant: A Biography* (New York, 1981), 93; Fielder Diary, Nov. 7, 1861, TSLA; Joseph Myrick to mother and father, Nov. 9, [18]61, Confederate Collection, TSLA; Thomas J. Firth Memoirs, Confederate Collection, TSLA; Samuel Latta to Mary Latta, Nov. 8, 1861, TSLA.

43. McFeely, *Grant,* 93; Samuel Latta to Mary Latta, Nov. 8, 1861, TSLA; Fielder Diary, Nov. 8, 1861, TSLA.

44. *OR,* 3:270, 312.

45. Mark Twain, *Life on the Mississippi* (New York, 1883), 205–6.

46. *OR,* ser. 2, 1:516, 530; *New York Times,* Sept. 5, 1886; *Memphis Avalanche,* Sept. 5, 1886; William M. Polk, *Leonidas Polk: Bishop and General,* 2 vols. (New York, 1893), 2:47.

47. The rollicking account of Cheatham and Grant fraternizing after Belmont was contained in a letter from BFC's friend and wartime chief of staff, James D. Porter, to Col. John S. Mosby on Feb. 16, 1910. A copy of the letter was forwarded to *Confederate Veteran* magazine. See "Col. Mosby Prizes Tribute by Gov. Porter to Gen. Grant," *CV* (May 1910), 202–3.

48. McFeely, *Grant,* 42, 52–56, 58–66.

Chapter 3

1. Leonidas Polk to Jefferson Davis, Nov. 6, 1861, Dearborn Papers, Harvard; Davis to Polk, Nov. 12, 1861, in *OR,* 4:539.

2. *OR,* 3:313–24; Connelly, *AH,* 104–5.

3. *OR,* 3:667; Elizabeth Cheatham to BFC, Jan. 7, 1862, Cheatham Papers, TSLA.

4. Thomas L. Connelly, *Civil War Tennessee: Battles and Leaders* (Knoxville, 1979), 24, 26, 28; Cheatham clipping, Solomons Scrapbook, Duke.

5. Cheatham clipping, Solomons Scrapbook, Duke; "Ninth Tennessee," 1:48, Hall Papers, UNC; Louise [Chapman] to BFC, Mar. 2, 1862, Cheatham Papers, TSLA.

6. G. A. Henry to Jefferson Daivs, March 10, 1862, NA; Cheatham's appoint-

ment as major-general, to rank from Mar. 10, 1862, dated Mar. 14, 1862, Cheatham Papers, TSLA; Ezra Warner and W. Buck Yearns, *Biographical Register of the Confederate Congress* (Baton Rouge, 1975), 116-17; Johnson, "The Making of a Confederate General," 35 (Davis quote).

7. *OR,* 10, pt. 1: 382 (BFC's divisional organization); ibid., ser. 4, 1:527-28 (Harris's recommendation).

8. *OR,* 10, pt. 1: 9-10, pt. 2: 40, 360, 366-68; James Lee McDonough, *Shiloh: In Hell before Night* (Knoxville, 1977), 41-42, 44-46; Wiley Sword, *Shiloh: Bloody April* (New York, 1974), 9-10, 88, 90-91, 93.

9. *OR,* 10, pt. 1: 385, 400; ibid., pt. 2: 374-75; Preston Smith to Maj. C. G. Rogers, April 2, 1862, and BFC to Maj. (Geo. Williamson?), both in Cheatham's Service File, NA; Sword, *Shiloh,* 94-98; McDonough, *Shiloh,* 69.

10. *OR,* 52, pt. 2: 296-97; Sword, *Shiloh,* 104-6; Connelly, *AH,* 155-57.

11. Connelly, *AH,* 156-57; McDonough, *Shiloh,* 80-81.

12. *OR,* 10, pt. 1: 438.

13. Ibid., 438 (quote); O. Edward Cunningham, "Shiloh and the Western Campaign of 1862" (Ph.D. diss., Louisiana State University, 1966), 337.

14. *OR,* 10, pt. 1: 438 (BFC account of artillery duel), and 414 (data on Confederate batteries engaged at Shiloh).

15. Ibid., 438 (both BFC quotes).

16. George A. Reaves (chief, Interpretation and Resources Management, Shiloh National Military Park) to author, Aug. 24, 1983 (info on BFC troop movements); OR, 10, pt. 1, 438-39 (BFC account), 150-53 (Iowa colonel's quote, 151), 281; Cunningham, "Shiloh," 330, 337-39.

17. Reaves to author, Aug. 24, 1983; *OR,* 10, pt. 1: 444-51, 278.

18. *Tenn. CW,* 186-87; *OR,* 10, pt. 1: 439, 454.

19. *OR,* 10, pt. 1: 453.

20. Ibid., 472, 475-79, 609-10.

21. *Tenn. CW,* 172-73; *OR,* 10, pt. 1: 439, 454; "The First Regiment of Tennessee Volunteers," unsigned, undated sketch in Charles Todd Quintard Papers, Duke.

22. Gilbert Vincent Rambaut, "Forrest at Shiloh" (Paper read to the Confederate Historical Association of Memphis, Jan. 14, 1896, reprinted in Memphis *Commercial Appeal,* Jan. 19, 1896), as cited in Robert Selph Henry, *"First with the Most" Forrest* (Indianapolis, 1944), 77.

23. *OR,* 10, pt. 1: 439, 442 (BFC quote), 455 (Maney quote); "First Tennessee," Quintard Papers, Duke.

24. *OR,* 10, pt. 1: 410, 439, 459-60; J. G. Deupree, "Reminiscences of Service with the First Mississippi Cavalry," *Publications of the Mississippi Historical Society* (1903), 91, 98.

25. *OR,* 10, pt. 1: 439 (BFC account), 387 (Johnston's death); Sword, *Shiloh,* 304-7 (general account of Hornets' Nest surrender).

26. *Or,* 10, pt. 1: 418, 423, 425, 439-40.

27. Johnston, "Civil War Reminiscences," 25, TSLA.

28. *OR,* 10, pt. 1: 410, 440, 455, 467.

29. *OR,* 10, pt. 1: 410-11 (Polk quote), 440, 452, 458; *Tenn. CW,* 193; McDonough, *Shiloh,* 198.

30. *OR,* 10, pt. 1: 411, 440-41.

31. Ibid., 441, 501.

32. Ibid., 441, 395. Beauregard's report included an enclosure that has a higher casualty figure for Cheatham's division, with 195 dead, 1,020 wounded, and

16 missing, for a total of 1,231. Many of Cheatham's officers who were hit were in his First Brigade, which fought primarily against the divisions of William T. Sherman and John A. McClernand on the Rebel left during the Apr. 6 engagement. Here Col. A. K. Blythe and Lt.-Col. D. L. Herron were killed leading the Mississippi Battalion. Tennesseans Preston Smith, R. C. Tyler, Bushrod Johnson, Marcus J. Wright, and Marshall T. Polk were wounded. On Apr. 7, the Seventh Kentucky's Col. Charles Wickliffe rejoined his unit and was mortally wounded leading a charge. As for Cheatham's shoulder wound, circumstantial evidence implies that it occurred late Apr. 6 or the next day. See Edward A. Pollard, *Southern History of the War,* 2 vols. (Richmond, 1862-63; reprint ed., Freeport, N.Y., 1969), 1:305; "Personne," quoted in *Charleston Daily Courier,* Apr. 22, 1862, as cited in James M. Merrill, "'Nothing to Eat but Raw Bacon': Letters from a War Correspondent, 1862," *Tennessee Historical Quarterly* (June 1958), 147; Deupree, "First Mississippi Cavalry," 90; *OR,* 10, pt. 1: 389.

33. "Ninth Tennessee," 1:48 Hall Papers, UNC.
34. *OR,* 10, pt. 1: 441.
35. Connelly, *AH,* 175-77.
36. Ibid., 179-81.
37. Postwar defenses of Bragg may be found in Don Seitz, *Braxton Bragg: General of the Confederacy* (Columbia, S.C., 1924), and L. H. Stout, *Reminiscences of General Braxton Bragg* (Hattiesburg, Miss., 1942). William M. Polk's two-volume defense of his father, published in 1893, contains examples of the often violent condemnations of Bragg which appeared in the postwar years. Anti-Bragg references appear in a number of sources written by men who served under Cheatham and are cited on occasion in this volume. For more objective and recent accounts, refer to Grady McWhiney, *Braxton Bragg and Confederate Defeat,* Vol. 1, *Field Command* (New York, 1969), and Thomas Connelly's two volumes on the Army of Tennessee.
38. Ezra Warner, *Generals in Gray: Lives of the Confederate Commanders* (Baton Rouge, 1959), 30; McWhiney, *Bragg,* 141-44, 253.
39. Richard Taylor, *Destruction and Reconstruction: Personal Experiences of the Late War* (New York, 1900), 100; McWhiney, *Bragg,* 94, 178-79, 388-89; Connelly, *AG,* 70-72.
40. McWhiney, *Bragg,* 264-66.
41. Ibid., 275-76; Connelly, *AH,* 223; Taylor, *Destruction and Reconstruction,* 100; *OR,* 10, pt. 1: 11-12, and 17, pt. 2: 658, 663.
42. *OR,* 17, pt. 2: 627-28, 673.
43. *OR,* 10, pt. 2: 379; Ezra Warner, Correspondence and Research Files, Chicago Historical Society.
44. *OR,* 17, pt. 2: 654-55; McWhiney, *Bragg,* 12-13; Warner, *Generals in Gray,* 44-45, 65-66, 128-29, 199-200, 310.
45. Elise Bragg to Braxton Bragg, Feb. 15 and Mar. 12, 1862, both in Braxton Bragg Letters, Barker Texas History Center, University of Texas, Austin.
46. Braxton Bragg to Elise Bragg, Mar. 20,[1862], Braxton Bragg Papers, Duke.
47. John Euclid Magee Diary, 1861-1863, 18, Duke. Magee was an artillerist in Cheatham's division, and his handwritten diary is an excellent source of material on Cheatham for the period covering June 1862 to mid-Oct. 1863.
48. *CV* (Nov. 1898), 522; Louise Chapman to BFC, Feb. 4, 1863, Cheatham Papers, TSLA; Eugene Marshall Papers, Duke. Marshall was a Union horse-

man who learned of the incident from some Rebel deserters in Nov. 1863. Marshall recorded Cheatham's first name as Bill and wrote that Cheatham took off a saber and stuck the point of it in the ground to indicate that he was temporarily ceding his officer status. The deserters said that Cheatham was a "gambler [and] blackleg before the war," and was "very popular with the soldiers."

49. Mrs. Irby Morgan, *How It Was: Four Years among the Rebels* (Nashville, 1892), 85, 97.

50. *CV* (January 1894), 1.

51. Wright, "Cheatham Sketch," UNC; Deupree, "First Mississippi Cavalry," 90; Head, *Sixteenth Tennessee,* 317.

52. Cheatham clipping, Solomons Scrapbook, Duke.

53. Head, *Sixteenth Tennessee,* 316–17; *Nashville Union and American,* Oct. 31, 1872.

54. Pollard, *Robert E. Lee,* 721; Wright, "Cheatham Sketch," UNC; Cheatham clipping, Solomons Scrapbook, Duke; S. R. Cockrill to Cheatham, July 19, 1864, Cheatham Papers, TSLA; Bishop Charles Todd Quintard to Polk G. Johnson, n.d., Quintard Papers, Duke. The last item is a rough draft of a eulogistic letter by Quintard that appeared in an 1888 issue of the *Southern Historical Society Papers.* See Quintard, "B. F. Cheatham, Major-General C.S.A.: A Tribute to His Memory," *SHSP* (1888), 334–54.

55. Head, *Sixteenth Tennessee,* 317.

Chapter 4

1. "Organization of the Right Wing A[rmy] of the M[ississippi]," n.d., in Quintard Papers, Duke. This return, from the spring or summer of 1862, places five brigades in Cheatham's division. By the time the Confederates invaded Kentucky, he was down to four brigades. The Forty-first Georgia and Ninth Texas Regiments were transferred to one of Cheatham's other brigades under George Maney from the fifth brigade, which was broken up.

2. Oliver P. Tucker Memoir, 1862–1865, 3–4, Confederate Collection, TSLA; "Ninth Tennessee," 1:53–54, Hall Papers, UNC; Fielder Diary, July 25–30, 1862, TSLA (furlough quote, July 29).

3. Magee Diary, 18–26, Duke.

4. "Ninth Tennessee," 1: 54, Hall Papers, UNC (first, second, and fourth quotes); Magee Diary, 27–29, Duke (third quote); Michael Mauzy Diary, July 22–Aug. 26, 1862, Confederate Collection, TSLA; "The Confederate States of America, Offiicer's Pay Account," Sept. 6, 1862, in Cheatham's Service File, NA.

5. Braxton Bragg to Elise Bragg, Sept. 2, 1862, Dearborn Papers, Harvard.

6. Cavanaugh, *Obion Avalanche,* 26.

7. Ibid., 40.

8. Bell Irvin Wiley, *The Life of Johnny Reb: The Common Soldier of the Confederacy* (Indianapolis, 1943), 240.

9. *OR,* 16, pt. 1: 968–89; J. Stoddard Johnston, *Confederate Military History: Kentucky,* ed. Clement A. Evans (Atlanta, 1899), 128; J. S. Johnston, "Bragg's Ky. Campaign," Josiah Stoddard Johnston Papers, 1833–1913, Filson Club Historical Society, Louisville, Ky.; "Ninth Tennessee," 1:55, Hall Papers, UNC (quote).

10. *OR,* 16, pt. 2: 825, 848; Grady McWhiney, "Controversy in Kentucky: Braxton Bragg's Campaign of 1862," *Civil War History* (Mar. 1960), 21–22; St. John

Richardson Liddell, "Record of the Civil War" (hereafter cited as Liddell Record), in Daniel Chevilette Govan Papers, Southern Historical Collection, UNC.

11. *OR,* 16, pt. 1: 1024–25, 1091, 1098–1102; ibid., pt. 2: 897–98; Johnston, "Bragg's Ky. Campaign," Johnston Papers, Filson Club.

12. "Ninth Tennessee," 1:57–58, Hall Papers, UNC.

13. F. Gerald Ham, "The Shaker Village of Pleasant Hill, Kentucky, and the Battle of Perryville," pamphlet in Filson Club; "Ninth Tennessee," 1:56, Hall Papers, UNC.

14. C[harles] C. Gilbert, "Bragg's Invasion of Kentucky," *Southern Bivouac* (Dec. 1885), 432.

15. *OR,* 16, pt. 1: 1024–25, 1096, 1098–99; Johnston, "Bragg's Ky. Campaign," Johnston Papers, Filson Club; William J. Hardee, "Official Report of the Battle of Perryville, 1 December 1862," Hardee Papers, John C. Breckinridge Collection, Chicago Historical Society; Joseph H. Parks, *General Leonidas Polk C.S.A.: The Fighting Bishop* (Baton Rouge, 1962), 268–69.

16. *OR,* 16, pt. 1: 1109–10; Johnston, "Bragg's Ky. Campaign," Johnston Papers, Filson Club; Magee Diary, 39, Duke.

17. Maj. Genl. B. F. Cheatham, "Report of the Engagement near Perryville, Ky.," filed Nov. 19, 1862 (hereafter cited as BFC's Perryville Report), in Joseph P. Palmer Collection of Braxton Bragg Papers, Western Reserve Historical Society, Cleveland; B. F. Cheatham, "The Battle of Perryville," *Southern Bivouac* (Apr. 1886), 704; Thomas R. Hooper Diary, Oct. 8, 1862 (photocopy of original diary), Stones River National Military Park; Magee Diary, 39–40, Duke; Judge L. B. McFarland, "Maney's Brigade at the Battle of Perryville," *CV (Dec.* 1922), 467; Johnston, "Bragg's Ky. Campaign," Johnston Papers, Filson Club. Cheatham's account for the *Southern Bivouac* appeared in a "Comment and Criticism" section of the periodical and was written in response to a series of articles penned by Union officer Charles C. Gilbert pertaining to the campaign.

18. Brig. Genl. Daniel S. Donelson, "Report of the part taken in the Battle of Perryville by the 1st Brigade, 1st Div[ision,] R[igh]t W[in]g Army of the Miss.," filed Oct. 26, 1862 (hereafter cited as Donelson's Perryville Report), Palmer Collection of Bragg Papers, Western Reserve; BFC's Perryville Report, Western Reserve; Hooper Diary, Oct. 8, 1862, Stones River National Military Park; Warner, *Generals in Gray,* 74–75, 210, 293–94.

19. BFC's and Donelson's Perryville Reports, Western Reserve.

20. Johnston, "Bragg's Ky. Campaign," Johnston Papers, Filson Club (dress parade quote); Cheatham, "The Battle of Perryville," 704; Head, *Sixteenth Tennessee,* 95–97; *OR,* 16, pt. 1: 1060, 1065, 1144; Donelson's (farmhouse, cheers and yells quotes) and BFC's (dead and wounded quote) Perryville Reports, Western Reserve.

21. *OR,* 16, pt. 1: 1060, 1063–65 (quote, 1065), 1111, 1113–18; BFC's Perryville Report, Western Reserve.

22. John W. Carroll, *Autobiography and Reminiscences by John W. Carroll (Henderson, Tenn., n.d.),* 24.

23. The assault on Parsons and the subsequent capture of the battery remained among the most vividly remembered moments of the war for the men in Cheatham's division and was well-documented afterwards. See Cheatham, "The Battle of Perryville," 705; BFC's and Donelson's Perryville Reports, Western Reserve; "First Regiment of Tennessee Volunteers," unsigned, undated

sketch in Quintard Papers, Duke; "Ninth Tennessee," 1:60, Hall Papers, UNC; Hooper Diary, Oct. 8, 1862, Stones River NMP; McFarland, "Maney's Brigade at Perryville," 467-68 (quotes re Twenty-Seventh Tennessee); *OR*, 16, pt. 1: 1111, 1113-18 (regimental officer's quote, 1118); Carroll Henderson Clark Diary, 25, Confederate Collection, TSLA; Marcus B. Toney, *The Privations of a Private* (Nashville, 1905), 42-44.

24. McFarland, "Maney's Brigade at Perryville," 468-69 (quote, 468); "Ninth Tennessee," 1: 60, Hall Papers, UNC.

25. Cheatham, "The Battle of Perryville," 705.

26. BFC's Perryville Report, Western Reserve; Cheatham, "The Battle of Perryville," 705; McFarland, "Maney's Brigade at Perryville," 467-68; W. H. Smith, "Melanchton Smith's Battery," *CV* (Nov. 1904), 539 (quotes).

27. Cheatham, "The Battle of Perryville," 705 (Cheatham quote); BFC's Perryville Report, Western Reserve; Dr. Charles W. Miles, Sr., "Col. Hume R. Feild," *CV* (Sept. 1921), 325; Sam R. Watkins, *"Co. Aytch," Maury Grays, First Tennessee Regiment; or, A Side Show of the Big Show* (Chattanooga, 1900; reprint ed., Dayton, Ohio, 1982), 53; Charles W. Carr to wife, Oct. 10, 1862, Charles W. Carr Letters, Chicago Historical Society (Wisconsin private's quote); *OR*, 16, pt. 1: 1111, 1118, 1155-56; Toney, *Privations of a Private*, 43-44.

28. BFC's and Donelson's Perryville Reports, Western Reserve; *OR*, 16, pt. 1: 1060-61, 1067 (Ohio officer's quote), 1116.

29. BFC's Perryville Report, Western Reserve; Cheatham, "The Battle of Perryville," 705; *OR*, 16, pt. 1: 1157.

30. Donelson's Perryville Report, Western Reserve; Quintard to Johnson, n.d., Quintard Papers, Duke; Johnston, "Bragg's Ky. Campaign," Johnston Papers, Filson Club.

31. Liddell Record, Govan Papers, UNC (quotes); Hardee's Perryville Report, Hardee Papers, Breckinridge Collection, Chicago Historical Society.

32. Magee Diary, 39, Duke.

33. BFC's Perryville Report, Western Reserve; *OR*, 16, pt. 1: 1108, 1116-17.

34. *OR*, 16, pt. 1: 1033-36, 1112.

35. Carroll, *Autobiography*, 24; Cavanaugh, *Obion Avalanche*, 26; BFC's Perryville Report, Western Reserve (quote).

36. Kenneth A. Hafendorfer, *Perryville: Battle for Kentucky* (Utica, Ky., 1981), 378.

37. Cheatham, "The Battle of Perryville," 705 (both quotes); BFC's Perryville Report, Western Reserve; Mauzy Diary, Oct. 8, 1862, TSLA: OR, 16, pt. 1: 1157.

38. Cheatham, "The Battle of Perryville," 705 (quote); Watkins, *Co. Aytch*, 54; William S. Speer, *Sketches of Prominent Tennesseans* (Nashville, 1888), 297.

39. *OR*, 16, pt. 1: 1093; Liddell Record, Govan Papers, UNC (quotes); "Memoranda of Facts Bearing on Bragg's Ky. Campaign," in Edmund Kirby Smith Papers, Southern Historical Collection, UNC; Connelly, *AH*, 270, 273-77. Preston Smith commanded Cheatham's detached brigade which entered Kentucky with Kirby Smith, and these troops took part in the Confederate victory at Richmond on August 30, 1862. For accounts of the friendly reception they received in the Bluegrass region, see the Alfred Tyler Fielder Diary, Aug. 30-Sept. 8, 1862, TSLA, and William J. Rogers Diary, Roy Black Papers, Southern Historical Collection, UNC. Smith's brigade was not engaged with the remainder of the division at Perryville; see Smith's Perryville report, filed Oct. 22, 1862, in Palmer Collection of Bragg Papers, Western Reserve.

40. Magee Diary, 41–45, Duke (BFC and wagon train officer quote, 41–42); Fielder Diary, Oct. 14–15, 17–20, 1862, TSLA (second quote);
41. "Maj. Joseph B. Cumming Recollections," Southern Historical Collection, UNC; A[lfred] J[efferson] Vaughan, *Personal Record of the Thirteenth Regiment, Tennessee Infantry* (Memphis, 1897), 23.
42. Firth Memoirs, 6, TSLA; Cavanaugh, *Obion Avalanche,* 49 (quote); Watkins, *Co. Aytch,* 57–58; Mauzy Diary, entries for Oct. 9, 15, 18, 20, and 26, 1862, TSLA.
43. Judge E. S. Dargan to Jefferson Davis, Nov. 7, 1862, Jefferson Davis Papers, Duke; Fras. T. Shibling (?) to Dr. C. T. Quintard, Nov. 8, 1862, Quintard Papers, Duke.
44. *OR,* 16, pt. 1: 1088 (quotes); Connelly, *AG,* 20–23.
45. *OR,* 20, pt. 2: 411–12, 417–18, 423–24.
46. Mauzy Diary, Nov. 5, 1862, TSLA.

Chapter 5

1. Mauzy Diary, Nov. 5, 1862, Confederate Collection, TSLA; Rogers Diary, Nov. 5, 1862, Roy Black Papers, Southern Historical Collection, UNC. Portions of this chapter first were published, in somewhat altered fashion, as an article in the *Tennessee Historical Quarterly.* See Christopher Losson, "Major-General Benjamin Franklin Cheatham and the Battle of Stone's River," *THQ* (Fall 1982), 278–92.
2. Rogers Diary, entries for late November–early December, UNC (first quote); Vaughan, *Thirteenth Tennessee,* 24 (second and third quotes).
3. Fielder Diary, Dec. 5–9, 1862, TSLA; Samuel Seay, "A Private at Stones River," *Southern Bivouac* (Aug. 1885), 157.
4. Fielder Diary, Dec. 14, 1862, TSLA; Rogers Diary, Dec. 13, 1862, UNC; Basil Duke, *A History of Morgan's Cavalry* (New York, 1906; reprint ed., Bloomington, 1960), 321–22.
5. Fielder Diary, Dec. 20, 21, and 24, 1862, TSLA; *Tenn. CW,* 199–200.
6. Seay, "A Private at Stones River," 156; *Tenn. CW,* 173, 232.
7. Fielder Diary, Nov. 9, Dec. 28, 1862, TSLA; Rogers Diary, Dec. 20 and 25, 1862, UNC. These two entries in A. T. Fielder's diary represent but a small portion of Fielder's comments on religious matters in the army.
8. *OR,* 20, pt. 1: 733–34; L.E.D., "Part Taken by 1st Tenn. Regt. at Battle [of] Murfreesboro," Quintard Papers, Duke; James Lee McDonough, *Stones River: Bloody Winter in Tennessee* (Knoxville, 1980), 38, 66–69.
9. *OR,* 20, pt. 1: 705–6, 743, 748.
10. Seay, "A Private at Stones River," 158.
11. *OR,* 20, pt. 1: 705, 754, 773, 911, 916. The Triune Road referred to by Cheatham and others is the same as the Franklin Pike, Triune being situated between Franklin and Murfreesboro.
12. Draft of General Bragg's Official Report of the Battle of Murfreesboro, Feb. 23, 1863, Palmer Collection, Western Reserve; *OR,* 20, pt. 1: 706; Cheatham's Report of the Battle of Murfreesboro, Cheatham Papers, TSLA. The last item is apparently a first draft of the report which appears in the *OR.* Pages 3–9 of the draft are in the Cheatham Papers, TSLA, and contain some variations from the published report.
13. *OR,* 20, pt. 1: 774, 918–19, 922.

14. Ibid., 689, 754.
15. Ibid., 774–75, 846; Bragg's Murfreesboro Report, Western Reserve; Hardee's Murfreesboro Report (typed copy), William J. Hardee Papers, Alabama Dept. of Archives and History; Seay, "A Private at Stones River," 158.
16. BFC's Murfreesboro Report, Cheatham Papers, TSLA; *OR*, 20, pt. 1: 687, 706, 754; Alexander F. Stevenson, *The Battle of Stone's River* (Boston, 1884), 48–51; McDonough, *Stones River*, 98–99.
17. BFC's Murfreesboro Report, Cheatham Papers, TSLA; *OR*, 20, pt. 1: 687, 706, 744, 746, 750, 756.
18. *OR*, 20, pt. 1: 706; BFC's Murfreesboro Report, Cheatham Papers, TSLA; *OR*, 20, pt. 1: 348, 687, 734–35; Alexander F. Stevenson, *The Battle of Stone's River* (Boston, 1884), 48–51; McDonough, *Stones River*, 98–99; Arthur Middleton Manigault, *A Carolinian Goes to War: The Civil War Narrative of Arthur Middleton Manigault*, ed. R. Lockwood Tower (Columbia, S.C., 1983), 56–57. In the last work Manigault was somewhat critical of Maney for not advancing to his aid more promptly.
19. *OR*, 20, pt. 1: 687, 709, 745; "First Tennessee at Murfreesboro," Quintard Papers, Duke. The latter source is the only one that I have seen which gives Giles as the first name of the Harding farmhouse owner; in other sources, the building is invariably referred to as simply the Harding house.
20. BFC's Murfreesboro Report, Cheatham Papers, TSLA; *OR*, 20, pt. 1: 349, 352–56, 734–41.
21. "First Tennessee at Murfreesboro, Quintard Papers, Duke; Thomas H. Malone, *Memoir of Thomas H. Malone* (Nashville, 1928), 146–47; Watkins, *Co. Aytch*, 66–67; *OR*, 20, pt. 1: 349, 352–56, 687–88, 734–42. Lt. R. F. James was killed not far from his widowed mother's farm. One gets the impression that Cheatham did not fully understand the confusion surrounding the two batteries, even after he received his subordinates' reports. He seems to have mistakenly regarded the battery which retired across the pike as the one whose identity was in question. He also avers that Manigault assaulted a battery and was repulsed, a claim bolstered by Withers's report. See Cheatham's battle report in Cheatham Papers, TSLA, and *OR*, 706–7, 755, which imply that Manigault was repelled in three assaults before the Wilkinson Pike was seized.
22. Seay, "A Private at Stones River," 158–59 (first two quotes); *OR*, pt. 1: 706, 735, 742; Malone, *Memoir* (story and quotes of Turner and his battery in action); "First Tennessee at Murfreesboro," Quintard Papers, Duke (lone officer left).
23. BFC's Murfreesboro Report, Cheatham Papers, TSLA; *OR*, 20, pt. 1: 706–7, 735, 744; Watkins, *Co Aytch*, 67.
24. *OR*, 20, pt. 1: 349 (Sheridan quote); "First Tennessee at Murfreesboro," Quintard Papers, Duke (Union officer downed quote).
25. *OR*, 20, pt. 1: 349 (Sheridan reference to three assaults); 706–7, 735, 738, 740, 744, 755 (all Confederate accounts); Watkins, *Co. Aytch*, 67; Fielder Diary, Dec. 31, 1862, TSLA; Col. W. D. Smith, *Battle of Stone's River, Tennessee* (Washington, D.C., 1932), 38–39. Col. Smith's account, compiled for the Historical Section of the Army War College, was not published commercially; the copy cited is in the collections at Stones River NMP.
26. Fielder Diary, Dec. 31, 1862, TSLA (Twelfth Tennessean's quote); "First Tennessee at Murfreesboro," Quintard Papers, Duke (quote by Maney's veteran); *OR*, 20, pt. 1: 348–50 (Sheridan's brigade commanders killed), 354 (95 horses slain).

27. BFC's Murfreesboro Report, Cheatham Papers, TSLA; "Cumming Recollections," UNC (crashing tree limbs quote); Fielder Diary, Dec. 31, 1862, TSLA; "First Tennessee at Murfreesboro," Quintard Papers, Duke.

28. "Battle of Murfreesboro: A Graphic Account," unsigned, undated account in Johnston Papers, Filson Club; Stevenson, *Stone's River*, 102–3; Connelly, *AG*, 55–56.

29. BFC's Murfreesboro Report, Cheatham Papers, TSLA; Stevenson, *Stone's River*, 105–8 ("no finer troops" quote, 106); "Cumming Recollections," UNC ("sweep every foot of ground" quote); *OR*, 20, pt. 1: 707–22 (thirty men "left dead" quote, 717); Magee Diary, 55–56, Duke (cannonading, musketry compared to Niagara Falls quotes); Alfred Pirtle, "Donelson's Charge at Stone River," *Southern Bivouac* (May 1887), 769–70; Dr. W. J. Worsham, *The Old Nineteenth Tennessee Regiment, C.S.A: June 1861–April 1865* (Knoxville, 1902), 71–72.

30. BFC's Murfreesboro Report, Cheatham Papers, TSLA (Cheatham quote); "First Tennessee at Murfreesboro," Quintard Papers, Duke; *OR*, 20, pt. 1: 941 (Georgia officer's quote).

31. "First Tennessee at Murfreesboro," Quintard Papers, Duke.

32. Ibid.

33. Bragg's Murfreesboro Report, Western Reserve; *OR*, 20, pt. 1: 690–91; "Battle of Murfreesboro," Johnston Papers, Filson Club.

34. Fielder Diary, Jan. 1, 1863, TSLA.

35. "Recapitulation of Casualties 1st Divison PCAT," Cheatham Papers, TSLA; *OR*, 20, pt. 1: 676–77, 709, 737.

36. L. G. Bennett and W[illia]m M. Haigh, *History of the Thirty-Sixth Regiment Illinois Volunteers* (Aurora, Ill., 1876), 348; Rogers Diary, Dec. 31, 1862, Black Papers, UNC. Cheatham was no doubt acquainted with Rains, a Nashville native killed while leading his men against a Union battery. See Warner, *Generals in Gray*, 250–51.

37. John Johnston to John Trotwood Moore (Tennessee State Archivist), June 9, 1927, Gideon Johnson Pillow Collection, TSLA; Nathaniel C. Hughes, *Liddell's Record* (Dayton, Ohio, 1985), 119. Johnston maintained that the incident was related by an eyewitness, an unnamed lieutenant in the Sixth Tennessee. Johnston was of the same unit, but apparently did not see the event. Johnston's avowed purpose in writing Moore was to laud Pillow, who he felt should have received more credit than Cheatham for the Confederate success at Belmont. He also seems to have believed that Pillow's Civil War reputation was undeservedly low. These factors, as well as the late date of the letter (sixty-plus years after the war), are offset by Quintard's account and the reliability of Johnston's reminiscences, also on file in the TSLA.

38. Braxton Bragg to Maj. E. T. Sykes, Feb. 8, 1873, J. F. H. Claiborne Papers, Southern Historical Collection, UNC.

39. Braxton Bragg to Gen. Samuel Cooper (adjutant and inspector-general), Apr. 9, 1863, Palmer Collection, Western Reserve.

40. Watkins, *Co. Aytch*, 67–68.

41. *Nashville Daily American*, Sept. 7, 1886 (quote).

42. *OR*, 20, pt. 1: 862 (Arkansas officer's quote), 941 (Georgia officer's quote).

43. Another theory is that Cheatham was an alcoholic, an issue addressed later in this volume. While Cheatham was apprently intoxicated at Stones River, the notion of him as a drunkard is too closely based on Bragg's charges to be accurately verified. Bragg was anything but impartial where Cheatham was concerned (and vice versa).

44. Bragg's Murfreesboro Report, Western Reserve; Magee Diary, 57–58, Duke.
45. BFC and Jones M. Withers to Bragg, Jan. 3, 1863, Cheatham Papers, TSLA. The original letter stated that only three brigades were trustworthy, but Cheatham and Withers corrected the wording to read "divisions" on Mar. 21, 1863; see *OR*, 20, pt. 1: 702.
46. Polk to Bragg, Jan. 3, 1863, Cheatham Papers, TSLA; Bragg's reply, inserted at the bottom of Polk's letter.
47. Bragg's Murfreesboro Report, Western Reserve; Bragg to Jefferson Davis, Jan. 17, 1863, Harry L. and Mary K. Dalton Collection of Jefferson Davis Papers, Duke.
48. BFC's Murfreesboro Report, Cheatham Papers, TSLA; Fielder Diary, Jan. 4, 1863, TSLA.
49. Elizabeth Cheatham to BFC, Jan. 25, 1863, Cheatham Papers, TSLA.
50. Ibid.; Harllee, *Kinfolks,* 3:2484–86; Louise [Chapman] to BFC, March 23, 1863, Cheatham Papers, TSLA; *Nashville Daily Union,* Aug. 20, 1863; *Nashville Daily American,* Jan. 23, 1893; Graf and Haskins, *The Papers of Andrew Johnson,* vol. 5, *1861–1862* (Knoxville, 1979), 623–35; Parker to author, March 1982. Leonora (sometimes referred to as Leo or Laeo) was not quite 32 when she died. Leonard Pope Cheatham was 70, and his cause of death was "exhaustion," according to records in an Interment Book, 1855–91, Mount Olivet Cemetery Records, TSLA.
51. *Chattanooga Daily Rebel,* Jan. 6, 1863; Bragg to Jefferson Davis, Jan. 17, 1863, Dalton Collection, Duke.
52. Bragg to BFC, Jan. 11, 1863, Cheatham Papers, TSLA.
53. Patrick Cleburne to Bragg, Jan. 13, 1863, Bragg Papers, Duke; *OR*, 20, pt. 1: 682–84.
54. *OR*, 20, pt. 1: 701–2.
55. Polk to Bragg, Jan. 30, 1863, Dearborn Papers, Harvard; *OR*, 20, pt. 1: 701 (Bragg to Polk, Jan. 30, 1863) and 702 (Polk to Bragg, Jan. 31, 1863).
56. Ibid.
57. Gideon Pillow to Maj. [Wm. Clare], Mar. 9, 1863, Palmer Collection, Western Reserve.
58. Bragg to Davis, Jan. 17, 1863, Dalton Collection, Duke.
59. Bragg's Murfreesboro Report, Western Reserve; W. D. Gale to Leonidas Polk, March 27, 1863, Polk Collection, University of the South; Joseph E. Johnston to Jefferson Davis, Feb. 3, 1863, Johnston Papers, Duke.
60. Bragg's Murfreesboro Report, Western Reserve; *OR*, 20, pt. 1: 755, 763; Pillow to Maj. Clare, March 9, 1863, Palmer Collection, Western Reserve.
61. Bragg to Samuel Cooper, Apr. 9, 1863, Palmer Collection, Western Reserve.
62. Ibid. Seddon's remarks were written on a sheet attached to Bragg's letter.
63. Clark Diary, 30, TSLA; Watkins, *Co. Aytch,* 73–74; Van Buren Oldham Diary, 1863–1864, entry for June 12, 1863, Confederate Collection, TSLA. Oldham served in the Ninth Tennessee, and his diary contains a number of interesting observations covering the period from the spring of 1863 to late July 1864. Unfortunately, his tiny handwriting makes the diary all but indecipherable in certain passages.
64. *OR*, 16, pt. 1: 1097–1107.
65. Thomas Connelly and Archer Jones, *The Politics of Command: Factions and Ideas in Confederate Strategy* (Baton Rouge, 1973), 67; Martha [Blackie] to BFC, Mar. 30, 1863, Cheatham Papers, TSLA: Gale to Polk, Mar. 27, 1863, Polk Collection, University of the South.

Chapter 6

1. *OR*, 23, pt. 2: 369, 383; Gilbert C. Kniffin, "Manoeuvring Bragg Out of Tennessee," in *Battles and Leaders of the Civil War*, ed. Robert Underwood Johnson and Clarence Clough Buel, 4 vols. (1887–88; reprint ed., New York, 1956), vol. 3, *Retreat from Gettysburg*, 635–37; Fielder Diary, July 2–8, 1863, TSLA.
2. Fielder Diary, July 9 and 15, 1863, TSLA; Magee Diary, 90–91, Duke.
3. Colonel E. T. Wells, "The Campaign and Battle of Chickamauga," *United Service: A Monthly Review of Military and Naval Affairs*, n.s. (Sept. 1896), 206–7; Connelly, *AG*, 141–46; Chickamauga-Chattanooga Map, Cheatham Papers, TSLA.
4. Fielder Diary, Aug. 21, 1863, TSLA; Howard J. Popowski, "Opportunity: Clash at Dug Gap," *Civil War Times Illustrated* (June 1983), 16 (church story and quote).
5. Fielder Diary, Aug. 22–23, 1863, Sept. 7, 1863, TSLA.
6. Bragg's Chickamauga Report, Claiborne Papers, UNC; *OR*, 30, pt. 2: 27–31, 43–45; W. D. Gale to wife, Sept. 14, 1863, Gale-Polk Papers, UNC; Magee Diary, 101–3, Duke; Fielder Diary, Sept. 11–17, 1863, TSLA.
7. Magee Diary, 101–2, Duke; Fielder Diary, Sept. 11, 1863, TSLA; Oldham Diary, Sept. 15, 1863, TSLA.
8. Connelly, *AG*, 148–50, 193–97; Fielder Diary, Sept. 18, 1863, TSLA.
9. *OR*, 30, pt. 2: 77, 240, 524; Fielder Diary, Sept. 19, 1863, TSLA; Simon Bolivar Buckner's Chickamauga Report, Simon Bolivar Buckner Papers, Huntington Library, San Marino, Calif.; Bragg's Chickamauga Report, Claiborne Papers, UNC; "Cumming Recollections," 46, UNC; W. W. Carnes, "Chickamauga," *Southern Historical Society Papers* (1896), 398.
10. *OR*, 30, pt. 2: 77–78, 82–83; "Cumming Recollections," 46, UNC (first quote); Clark Diary, 34–35, TSLA; Worsham, *Nineteenth Tennessee*, 88–89 ("Give them hell" quote, Polk's quote); John B. Gordon, *Reminiscences of the Civil War* (New York, 1904), 79 (reference to "Cheatham's expression"). Cheatham's advice to "Give them hell!" appears in accounts of Perryville, Stones River, and Chickamauga, and Polk reportedly approved of the sentiment on several occasions, including both days at Chickamauga.
11. *OR*, 30, pt. 2: 78–79, 83–84, 118–19, 127, 129.
12. Topographical Map of Chickamauga Battlefield, U.S. Geological Survey, Department of the Interior, 1934; Joseph C. McElroy, *Chickamauga: Record of the Ohio Chickamauga and Chattanooga National Park Commission* (Cincinnati, 1896), 61, 104, 106; Clark Diary, 35, TSLA; Fielder Diary, Sept. 19, 1863, TSLA (first quote); Magee Diary, 104, Duke (second quote); *OR*, 30, pt. 2: 78, 94, 130.
13. *OR*, 30, pt. 2: 78, 94, 118–19, 130–31; Magee Diary, 104, Duke (first two quotes); Carnes, "Chickamauga," 399–400; W. W. Carnes to "My dear General," Oct. 22, 1893, James William Eldridge Papers, Huntington Library (Carnes quote).
14. *OR*, 30, pt. 2: 78, 95–96, 105, 107.
15. *CMH: Tenn.*, 97 (Cheatham quote); *OR*, 30, pt. 2: 78–79 ("well-directed charges" quote, 78), 95–96, 105, 107 ("sullenly retired" quote).
16. *CMH: Tenn.*, 97 (estimate of Union dead); Smith, "Melancthon Smith's Battery," 532 (BFC's "such fearful execution" and "No, let it stay" quotes); William Henry Harder Diary, 78, TSLA ("terrific effect of artillery fire" quote); *OR*, 30, pt. 2: 78–79, 95–96, 105 (number, type of rounds fired), 107.
17. McFarland, "Maney's Brigade at Perryville," 467–68 (quote); *CMH: Tenn.*, 96–97.
18. *OR*, 30, pt. 1: 555–60; pt. 2: 79, 108; Carnes, "Chickamauga," 400; Magee Diary, 105, Duke ("boiling over with rage" quote).
19. Wells, "Battle of Chickamauga," 223–24 (first two quotes); *OR*, 30, pt. 2: 79

(BFC's report of attack, quote eulogizing Smith), 107–8; Carnes, "Chicka-mauga," 400; W. D. Gale to wife, Sept. 21, 1863, Gale-Polk Papers, UNC; Ma-gee Diary, 105, Duke; J. W. Harris to mother, Sept. 25, 1863, Confederate Col-lection, TSLA. For information on Preston Smith, see Warner, *Generals in Gray*, 283.

20. *OR*, 30, pt. 2: 108, 112–13; Magee Diary, 105, Duke (both quotes); Carnes, "Chickamauga," 399 (lists six Union divisions arrayed against Cheatham); Fielder Diary, Sept. 19, 1863, TSLA; McElroy, *Record of the Ohio Commission*, 22, 24, 39, 44, 64–65; Clark Diary, 35, TSLA (wounded men left unattended).

21. Connelly, *AG*, 208.

22. *OR*, 30, pt. 2: 52–53, 57–63, 79, 141; Hal Bridges, *Lee's Maverick General: Daniel Harvey Hill* (New York, 1961), 206–7, 210–12, 215–18.

23. James Longstreet, *From Manassas to Appomattox: Memoirs of the Civil War in America* (Philadelphia, 1896), 448–50, 452; *OR*, 30, pt. 2: 458–60.

24. Longstreet, *From Manassas to Appomattox*, 455–56; *OR*, 30, pt. 2: 80, 96–97, 120 (Wright quote); Fielder Diary, Sept. 20, 1863, TSLA (Twelfth Tennessee quote); "Cumming Recollections," 47, UNC; Clark Diary, 36, TSLA; Carnes, "Chicka-mauga," 405; Watkins, *Co. Aytch*, 96.

25. Bragg to Gen. S. Cooper, Sept. 21, 1863 (telegram), Claiborne Papers, UNC; Fielder Diary, Sept. 22, 1863, TSLA; *OR*, 30, pt. 2: 80 (both quotes), 97, 113; pt. 4; 691–92; Liddell Record, Govan Papers, UNC.

26. *OR*, 30, pt. 2: 86, 100, 129, 134–35; Johnson and Buel, *Battles and Leaders*, 3:673–74.

27. *OR*, 30, pt. 2: 54–56; Bragg to Sykes, Feb. 8, 1873, Claiborne Papers, UNC.

28. Polk to Davis, [Sept. 27, 1863], Dearborn Papers, Harvard; Polk to Davis, Oct. 6, 1863, Leonidas Polk Papers, Duke; *OR*, 30, pt. 2: 69 (Polk letter to Lee).

29. Longstreet, *From Manassas to Appomattox*, 461–62; *OR*, 30, pt. 2: 65–66; Con-nelly and Jones, *The Politics of Command*, 70.

30. *OR*, 30, pt. 2: 63; Bragg to Sykes, Feb. 8, 1873, Claiborne Papers, UNC.

31. W. W. Mackall to wife, Sept. 29, 1863, W. W. Mackall Papers, UNC; W. H. T. Walker to wife, Sept. 30, 1863, William Henry Talbot Walker Papers, Duke; Liddell Record, Govan Papers, UNC.

32. Bragg to Marcus J. Wright, Dec. 14, 1863, Wright Papers, UNC; Fielder Diary, Oct. 2, 1863, TSLA (first quote); J. W. Harris to mother, Sept. 25, 1863, and J. W. Harris to George Harris, Oct. 13, 1863, both in Confederate Collec-tion, TSLA (Harris quotes); Oldham Diary, Oct. 31, 1863, TSLA (last quote).

33. Longstreet, *From Manassas to Appomattox*, 465–66; Parks, *Leonidas Polk*, 349–50. Jefferson Davis later related that he was surprised to read a statement by Cheatham that indicated Davis had solicited the opinions of the officers re-garding Bragg. He also stated that he could not recollect to what extent Cheatham assented in Longstreet's desire to have a new commander. Despite these statements, it appears probable that it was Davis himself who initiated the subject of Bragg's leadership and sought the views of the generals. Cheat-ham, for one, was convinced that his honest views with President Davis com-promised his position in the army when Davis sustained Bragg. See James Lee McDonough, *Chattanooga: A Death Grip on the Confederacy* (Knoxville, 1984), 36.

34. *OR*, 30, pt. 2: 70; Mackall to wife, Oct. 1, 10, and 12, 1863, all in Mackall Let-ters, UNC; Lafayette McLaws to wife, Oct. 14, 1863, Lafayette McLaws Letters, UNC; Liddell Record, Govan Papers, UNC (Liddell quotes); Bragg to Wright, Dec. 14, 1863, Wright Papers, UNC.

35. Magee Diary, III, Duke; J. W. Harris to George Harris, Oct. 13, 1863, TSLA; *OR*, 30, pt. 2: 148-50; George W. Brent (Bragg's adjutant-general) to Buckner, Oct. 20, 1863, and Brent to BFC and Buckner, Oct. 27, 1863, both in Buckner Papers, Huntington Library; Connelly, *AG*, 252-53.

36. BFC to Brent, Oct. 31, 1863, Cheatham Papers, TSLA.

37. Oldham Diary, Oct. 29 and 31 and Nov. 1, 1863, TSLA.

38. Oldham Diary, Oct. 31 and Nov. 1, 1863, TSLA; Fielder Diary, Oct. 2, 1863, and June 14, 1864; Watkins, *Co. Aytch*, 139; *CMH: Tenn.*, 131.

39. Fielder Diary, Nov. 3, 1863, TSLA; *OR*, 31, pt. 3: 164, 192, 209 (quote).

40. J. A. Seddon to BFC, Nov. 17, 1863, Cheatham Papers, TSLA. Cooper's remarks are on the same sheet as Seddon's, which is attached to BFC's resignation letter. Seddon's adjutant-general, H. L. Clay, returned the reply via Bragg on Nov. 21, and a notation on the sheet shows that it was received at the Department of Tennessee's headquarters on Dec. 4, 1863. Cheatham was gone most of November, but returned to the army on the night of Nov. 24, which suggests that he received word that his resignation request had been denied sometime during the third week of November.

41. James Longstreet to BFC, Oct. 21, 1863, Cheatham Papers, TSLA; *OR*, 31, pt. 2: 658-60.

42. Richard I. Manning to mother, Jan. 17, 1864, Richard Irvine Manning Letters, South Caroliniana Library, University of South Carolina; Oldham Diary, Dec. 7, 1863, TSLA; "Ninth Tennessee," 1:97, Hall Papers, UNC; *CMH: Tenn.*, 114.

43. *CMH: Tenn.*, 114; *OR*, 31, pt. 2: 656, 690; pt. 3: 822-23.

44. J. W. Harris to mother, Nov. 1, 1863, Harris Letters, TSLA.

45. Harris to mother, Nov. 19, 1863, TSLA.

46. Ibid.; Watkins, *Co. Aytch*, 100; McDonough, *Chattanooga*, 63-64.

47. Stanley F. Horn, *The Army of Tennessee: A Military History* (Indianapolis, 1941), 292-95; *OR*, 52, pt. 2: 559-60; Longstreet, *From Manassas to Appomattox*, 465, 480-81. For a detailed description of the Federal success in reopening a direct supply route, and Bragg's irritation with Longstreet, see McDonough, *Chattanooga*, 79-89, 97-98, 100-101.

48. Horn, *Army of Tennessee*, 295-96; Connelly, *AG*, 272.

49. *OR*, 31, pt. 2: 685-87, 706.

50. Ibid., 664, 686-88, 692, 704, 718-19.

51. Colonel W. F. Dowd, "Lookout Mountain and Missionary Ridge," *Southern Bivouac* (Dec. 1885), 397-98; McDonough, *Chattanooga*, 130-33. Dowd led the Twenty-fourth Mississippi Regiment, and his account of the battles was ostensibly taken from his diary. Dowd was deceased by the time the excerpt was published in 1885.

52. *OR*, 31, pt. 2: 664, 693-95 (first quote, 694), 704-6 (Moore quote, 705); Dowd, "Lookout Mountain and Missionary Ridge," 398 (two Dowd quotes).

53. *Philadelphia Weekly Times*, Sept. 16, 1882 (quotes), in E. C. Walthall Scrapbook, Edward Cary Walthall Papers, Mississippi Dept. of Archives and History; *OR*, 31, pt. 2: 689, 695, 705, 731-32.

54. *OR*, 31, pt. 2: 685, 689-90, 695-96, 705, 732; Edmund W. Pettus to E. C. Walthall, Jan. 3, 1888, Walthall Scrapbook, Miss. Dept. of Archives and History.

55. *Philadelphia Weekly Times*, Sept. 16, 1882; correspondence between Daniel R. Hundley and E. C. Walthall, Sept.-Nov. 1882, and Edmund Pettus to Hundley

and Walthall, Dec. 2, 1882, all in Walthall Scrapbook, Miss. Dept. of Archives and History.

56. *OR,* 31, pt. 2: 721, 691.

57. Ibid., 721; Kinloch Falconer to BFC, Nov. 24, 1863, Cheatham Papers, TSLA.

58. McDonough, *Chattanooga,* 182-85, 205.

59. Ibid., 157-60 , 163-67.

60. Worsham, *Nineteenth Tennessee,* 100.

61. E. C. Walthall, to BFC, Mar. 17, 1876 and BFC to Walthall, Mar. 1876, both in Cheatham Papers, TSLA; *OR,* 31, pt. 2: 705-6 (both Moore quotes).

62. *OR,* 31, pt. 2: 706 (Moore quote), 690-91 (Jackson quote), 724 (Cheatham note).

63. Walthall to BFC, Mar. 17, 1876, and BFC to Walthall, Mar. 1876, Cheatham Papers, TSLA.

64. *OR,* 31, pt. 2: 727 (Brown's report), 697 (Walthall's report); Dowd, "Lookout Mountain and Missionary Ridge," 399.

65. Walthall to BFC, Mar. 17, 1876, Cheatham Papers, TSLA; *OR,* 31, pt. 2: 6A97, 6A84.

66. *OR,* 31, pt. 2: 697, 706, 727, 738.

67. Eng. G. (?) McLean to Major D. M. Hayden, Nov. 28, 1863, CSA Archives, Army Miscellany, Duke University.

68. *OR,* 31, pt. 2: 682.

69. Bragg to Jefferson Davis, Dec. 1, 1863, Dearborn Papers, Harvard.

70. "Notes of report from Dalton, of disaster at Missionary Ridge," Palmer Collection of Bragg Papers, Western Reserve; *OR,* 31, pt. 2: 664-67; Walthall to BFC, Mar. 17, 1876, Cheatham Papers, TSLA.

71. Liddell Record, Govan Papers, UNC; *OR,* 32, pt. 2: 799. Bragg's assertion that Cheatham kept a stallion obviously refers to the latter's interest in horse racing and his stint as proprietor of the Nashville Race Track, but I have been unable to find any evidence supporting the contention that Cheatham operated a saloon in Nashville. It is probable that a tavern was a part of the hotel that he ran for a time during his California sojourn, and Bragg may have assumed that drinking was a pastime which coincided with later Cheatham's operation of the Nashville Race Track.

72. Bragg to Gen. Marcus Wright, Dec. 29, 1863 (typescript copy), Wright Papers, UNC; Bragg to Sykes, Feb. 8, 1873, Claiborne Papers, UNC.

73. W. D. Gale to wife, Dec. 8, 1863, Gale-Polk Papers, UNC; *CMH: Tenn.,* 119. Gale was Polk's son-in-law.

Chapter 7

1. Joseph E. Johnston, *Narrative of Military Operations, Directed during the Late War between the States* (New York, 1874), 261; Connelly, *AG,* 34-35, 282-83; Warner, *Generals in Gray,* 161.

2. Patton Anderson, Thomas Hindman, BFC, et al. to John C. Breckinridge, Dec. 24, 1863, Patton Anderson Paper, Filson Club.

3. "Field Return of the Effective Strength, Army of Tennessee, Dec. 20, 1863," CSA Archives, Field Returns, Duke.

4. J. E. Johnston to Jefferson Davis, Jan. 15, 1864, Dalton Collection, Duke.

5. "Ninth Tennessee," 1:93, Hall Papers, UNC; I:93; Lindsley, *MAT,* 277-78.

6. "Ninth Tennessee," 1:98, Hall Papers, UNC.
7. Fielder Diary, Feb. 12, 1864, TSLA; Worsham, *Nineteenth Tennessee*, 106 (first quote); "Maney's Brigade at Missionary Ridge," *Southern Bivouac* (Mar. 1884), 298 (second quote); Lindsley, *MAT,* 162, 199, 218 (Sixth Tennessee quote).
8. Lindsley, *MAT,* 218 (quotes).
9. "Sketch of the Career of General Joseph E. Johnston, the Very God of War," *Southern Historical Society Papers* (1910), 344–45.
10. Clark Diary, 37–38, TSLA; W. J. McMurray, *History of the Twentieth Tennessee Regiment Volunteer Infantry, CSA* (Nashville, 1904), 307; Wiley, *The Life of Johnny Reb,* 53, 182–84; Watkins, *Co. Aytch,* 116–17; Edwin H. Rennolds, *A History of the Henry County Commands Which Served in the Confederate States Army* (Jacksonville, Fla., 1904; reprint ed., Kennesaw, Ga., 1961), 71–72; Melancthon Smith, "Journal of Campaign from Dalton to Atlanta," Cheatham Papers, TSLA. Melancthon Smith's journal is exceedingly valuable for tracing movements in the campaign and events associated with the artillery arm of the service. Smith was associated with Cheatham for most of the war and won promotion to colonel before the Atlanta campaign began. He served as head of Hardee's artillery. Cheatham obtained a copy of the journal in 1867, apparently after he requested information on the Atlanta campaign. The journal appears to be a combination of data kept by one of Smith's staff officers, and Smith's own wartime papers. See Smith to Abb[ott] Robertson, Aug. 13, 1867, Cheatham Papers, for information related to the journal.
11. Oldham Diary, May 1, 1864, TSLA; Watkins, *Co. Aytch,* 116–17; Worsham, *Nineteenth Tennessee,* 108–9; Rennolds, *Henry County Commands,* 72; Lindsley, *MAT,* 278.
12. Lindsley, *MAT,* 199; Smith, "Journal," Cheatham Papers, TSLA; Bromfield L. Ridley, " Camp Scenes around Dalton," *CV* (Feb. 1902), 67; LaBree, *Camp-Fires of the Confederacy,* 48–51 (quotes, 50–51).
13. LaBree, *Camp-Fires of the Confederacy,* 51 (first two quotes); Smith, "Journal," Cheatham Papers, TSLA (last quote). According to Gordon's reminiscence in the LaBree work, the Tennesseans continued battling even after conquering the Georgians. They next turned on one another, with Maney's brigade, under Col. Hume R. Feild, squaring off against Vaughan's brigade under Gordon. One source maintains that General Walker himself led his Georgia division in the snowball battle and later demanded the return of the goods stolen by the Tennesseans. Cheatham's men considered them spoils of war and kept the appropriated merchandise. See Lindsley, *MAT,* 199.
14. *OR,* 52 pt. 2: 586–95; Wheeler to Bragg, Feb. 14, 1864, Dearborn Papers, Harvard.
15. Wheeler to Bragg, Feb. 14, 1864, Dearborn Papers, Harvard; Walker to Bragg, Mar. 8, 1864, Palmer Collection, Western Reserve; BFC to General [Walker], Jan. 10, 1864, Civil War Papers, Huntington Library.
16. Connelly, *AG,* 320–21; *OR,* 52, pt. 2: 596, 608–9; Bragg to Marcus J. Wright, Feb. 6 and Mar. 6, 1864, both in Wright Papers, UNC. Though opponents of Bragg suffered, Patton Anderson turned to Bragg's mortal enemy, Polk, with news of Cleburne's idea and sought to have Polk suppress the proposal. See *OR,* 52, pt. 2: 598–99.
17. Walker to Mary [Walker], Dec. 3, 1863, W. H. T. Walker Papers, Duke.
18. Connelly, *AG,* 319–20.
19. Walker to Mary Walker, July 12 and 18, 1864; Walker to daughter, July 15, 1864, all in Walker Papers, Duke.
20. Walker to Braxton Bragg, Mar. 8, 1864, Palmer Collection, Western Reserve.

21. Louise [Chapman] to BFC, Dec. 17, 1862; Feb. 4, 1863; Mar. 22, 1863; all in Cheatham Papers, TSLA.

22. Lindsley, *MAT,* 162, 199, 298, 310; Fielder Diary, entries of Feb. 19–Mar. 1, 1864, TSLA (quote from Feb. 21, 1864 entry).

23. Worsham, *Nineteenth Tennessee,* 107.

24. *OR,* 32, pt. 2: 813–14; pt. 3, 578, 791; Fielder Diary, Mar. 1, 1864, TSLA.

25. Johnston to Davis, Jan. 15, 1864, Dalton Collection, Duke; *OR,* 32, pt. 3: 791 (Bragg's quote).

26. Gilbert E. Govan and James W. Livingood, *A Different Valor: The Story of Joseph E. Johnston, C.S.A.* (Indianapolis, 1956), 259–60, 262.

27. Richard M. McMurry, *John Bell Hood and the War for Southern Independence* (Lexington, Ky., 1982), 93; Connelly, *AG,* 313, 321; Smith, "Journal," Cheatham Papers, TSLA.

28. Fielder Diary, Mar. 10, May 21, and May 23, 1864, TSLA; Watkins, *Co. Aytch,* 112–14; I. B. Sutter to sister, Feb. 11, 1864, CSA Archives, Army Miscellany, Duke.

29. Lindsley, *MAT,* 162 (Robinson quotes), 278 (Irby quote); Col. William D. Pickett, "Re-enlistments by the Confederates," *CV* (Apr. 1902), 171.

30. Connelly, *AG,* 327–29; Govan and Livingood, *A Different Valor,* 240–41, 261–62.

31. B. F. Cheatham, "Journal of Military Maneuvers around Atlanta, 1864" (hereafter cited as Atlanta Military Journal), Cheatham Papers, TSLA; Worsham, *Nineteenth Tennessee,* 111; Watkins, *Co. Aytch,* 128–29; "Ninth Tennessee," 2: 18–21, Hall Papers, UNC (quote, 20).

32. Rennolds, *Henry County Commands,* 72–73.

33. BFC, Atlanta Military Journal, and Smith, "Journal," both in Cheatham Papers, TSLA; William R. Scaife, *The Campaign for Atlanta* (Atlanta, 1985), 8–10 (Sherman quote, 9); Perry Franklin Morgan Diary (typescript), May 9–11, 1864, Confederate Collection, TSLA; Oldham Diary, May 13, 1864, TSLA.

34. McMurry, *Hood,* 102, *CMH: Tenn.,* 128; Vaughan, *Thirteenth Tennessee,* 32 (quotes).

35. Lindsley, *MAT,* 163, 431; Morgan Diary, May 13–15, 1864, TSLA; Rennolds, *Henry County Commands,* 74–76; Oldham Diary, May 15–16, 1864, TSLA; "Ninth Tennessee," 2:20–23 (quotes, 22–23).

36. Oldham Diary, May 15–16, 1864, TSLA.

37. Ibid., May 16, 1864, TSLA; *CMH: Tenn.,* 129; Scaife, *The Campaign for Atlanta,* 26.

38. Oldham Diary, May 17, 1864, TSLA.

39. Oldham Diary, May 17, 1864, TSLA (first quote); Head, *Sixteenth Tennessee,* 128; Lindsley, *MAT,* 163; Watkins, *Co. Aytch,* 134; Charles W. Miles, Sr., "Col. Hume R. Feild," *CV* (Sept. 1921), 326 (second quote).

40. Miles, "Col. Hume R. Feild," 326.

41. Oldham Diary, May 17, 1864, TSLA.

42. Ibid., May 17–18, 1864, TSLA; Watkins, *Co. Aytch,* 135.

43. Govan and Livingood, *A Different Valor,* 271–74.

44. Oldham Diary, May 19–20, 1864, TSLA; *OR,* 38, pt. 3: 616, 983–84.

45. BFC, Altanta Military Journal, Cheatham Papers, TSLA (first two quotes); Smith, "Journal," Cheatham Papers, TSLA; *OR,* 38, pt. 3: 705–6; Morgan Diary, May 25–27, 1864, TSLA; Oldham Diary, May 26–28, 1864, TSLA (last quote from entry of May 28, 1864).

46. BFC, Atlanta Military Journal, Cheatham Papers, TSLA; *OR,* 38, pt. 3: 706–7; Fielder Diary, May 30, 1864, TSLA (first quote); Lindsley, *MAT,* 218 (second quote).

47. BFC, Atlanta Military Journal, Cheatham Papers, TSLA (first quote); Lindsley, *MAT,* 200 (second quote); Rennolds, *Henry County Commands,* 79–81; A. J. Vaughan to Capt.———, June 7, 1864, Alfred Jefferson Vaughan Papers, TSLA.

48. Smith, "Journal," Cheatham Papers, TSLA.

49. Connelly, *AG,* 358.

50. *CMH: Tenn.,* 130–31; Worsham, *Nineteenth Tennessee,* 119; Fielder Diary, June 14, 1864, TSLA; Watkins, *Co. Aytch,* 138–39.

51. BFC, Atlanta Military Journal, Cheatham Papers, TSLA.

52. Ibid.

53. Govan and Livingood, *A Different Valor,* 289–93; Scaife, *The Campaign for Atlanta,* 42–44; Samuel Robinson, "Battle of Kennesaw Mountain," in *The Annals of the Army of Tennessee and Early Western History,* ed. Edwin L. Drake (June 1878), 109.

54. *OR,* 38, pt. 1: 68–69.

55. Robinson, "Battle of Kennesaw Mountain," 109–10; BFC, Atlanta Military Journal (quote), and Smith, "Journal," Cheatham Papers, TSLA.

56. Robinson, "Battle of Kennesaw Mountain," 110–111, 113 (first quote); BFC, Atlanta Military Journal, Cheatham Papers, TSLA (Cheatham quote).

57. J. L. W. Blair, "The Fight at Dead Angle," *CV* (Nov. 1904), 533; R. H. Harmon, "Dead Angle," *CV* (May 1903), 219; Fielder Diary, June 23, 1864, TSLA; BFC, Atlanta Military Journal, and Smith, "Journal," Cheatham Papers, TSLA.

58. Robinson, "Battle of Kennesaw Mountain," 110; BFC, Atlanta Military Journal, and Smith, "Journal," Cheatham Papers, TSLA; "Ninth Tennessee," 2:29, Hall Papers, UNC; *Chattanooga Daily Rebel,* June 28, 1864; Blair, "The Fight at Dead Angle," 533.

59. *OR,* 38, pt. 1: 295–96, 632–33, 680; Sidney C. Kerksis, ed., *The Atlanta Papers* (Dayton, Ohio, 1980), 372; McMurray, *Twentieth Tennessee,* 317 (first quote); BFC, Atlanta Military Journal, Cheatham Papers, TSLA (BFC quote); Robinson, "Battle of Kennesaw Mountain," 112 (third quote); Lindsley, *MAT,* 164, 299 (last quote).

60. Watkins, *Co. Aytch,* 145; Vaughan, *Thirteenth Tennessee,* 33.

61. BFC, Atlanta Military Journal (Cheatham quote), and Smith, "Journal," Cheatham Papers, TSLA; Kerksis, *The Atlanta Papers,* 371; Diary of John W. Tuttle (captain in Third Kentucky Regt., USA), 18–19, Kennesaw Mountain National Battlefield Park (officer's quote). Both Cheatham's and Smith's journals maintain that Lieutenant Wright's two guns (from Mebane's battery) crossed fire with the eight guns to the left of the salient. The redoubt for these two fieldpieces still exists, however, and it is placed too far to the right of the salient to lend credence to Cheatham's and Smith's recollections. Still, Wright's two guns and the two left cannons from Turner's Mississippi battery no doubt assisted Vaughan's brigade and Lucius Polk's brigade in repelling the Union attack along that front.

62. *OR,* 38, pt. 1: 680; BFC, Atlanta Military Journal, Cheatham Papers, TSLA; Smith, "Journal," Cheatham Papers, TSLA.

63. *OR,* 38, pt. 1: 693, 698, 711, 724; Robinson, "Battle of Kennesaw Mountain," 112 (quote).

64. *OR,* 38, pt. 1: 711; Kerksis, *The Atlanta Papers,* 372; Watkins, *Co. Aytch,* 45; Worsham, *Nineteenth Tennessee,* 121 (first quote); "Ninth Tennessee," 2:28–30, Hall

Papers, UNC; Lindsley, *MAT,* 219; *Chattanooga Daily Rebel,* June 28 and 29, July 1, 1864 (second quote). Cheatham asserted that his men captured the Federal colors, a claim made also by the Sixth Tennessee. One member of the Ninth Tennessee Regiment boasted that a member of Company H captured a flag of an Illinois regiment, "after the seventh man had attempted to plant that flag on our works." Cavanaugh, *Obion Avalanche,* 50. Accounts in the *Chattanooga Daily Rebel* maintained that Cheatham's men captured two stand of colors, including that of the Twenty-seventh Illinois. The latter flag was allegedly seized by Sgt. W. T. Welty of the Twenty-ninth Tennessee Regiment, who leaped over the breastworks and grabbed the standard. The Union color bearer evidently surrendered as well. The paper reported that Welty carried his prize to General Hardee, and Hardee allowed the soldier to keep the flag as a reward for his bravery. *Chattanooga Daily Rebel,* June 28, 29, 1864. Capt. James I. Hall of the Ninth Tennessee wrote that the flag he saw was retrieved at great cost by the retreating Yankees, and that three men in his regiment died trying to seize the Union colors.

65. Lindsley, *MAT,* 219; Robinson, "Battle of Kennesaw Mountain," 113; "Ninth Tennessee," 2:28–29, Hall Papers, UNC (quotes 29).
66. BFC, Atlanta Military Journal, Cheatham Papers, TSLA; Lindsley, *MAT,* 219; Col. Allen L. Fahnestock Diary (microfilm copy), 37–38, Duke; "Ninth Tennessee," 2:29, Hall Papers, UNC (first quote); *OR,* 38, pt. 1: 693 (second quote).
67. J. Walker Coleman to Rev. Dr. C. T. Quintard, July 9, 1864, Quintard Papers, Duke; Robinson, "Battle of Kennesaw Mountain," 112–13; "Ninth Tennessee," 2: 28, 30 (both Hall quotes); Lindsley, *MAT,* 299 (last quote).
68. *OR,* 38, pt. 1: 69, 637 and pt. 3: 703; BFC, Atlanta Military Journal (Cheatham quote) and Smith, "Journal," both in Cheatham Papers, TSLA; Miles, "Col. Hume R. Feild," 326; *Chattanooga Daily Rebel,* July 2, 1864 (quotes referring to aid for the wounded Union soldier).
69. *OR,* 38, pt. 1: 724.
70. Lindsley, *MAT,* 219 (Sixth Tennessee quote), 299 (Eleventh Tennessee quote); Robinson, "Battle of Kennesaw Mountain," 114 (First Tennessee quote); *Chattanooga Daily Rebel,* July 2, 1864 (last quote).
71. *OR,* 38, pt. 1: 698 (Ohioan's quote), 704 (Banning's quote); Kerksis, *The Atlanta Papers,* 269 ("valor displayed" quote).
72. BFC, Atlanta Military Journal, Cheatham Papers, TSLA.
73. "Ninth Tennessee," 2:30, Hall Papers, UNC; Harmon, "Dead Angle," 219 ("corn dodgers" quote); Fahnestock Diary, 42–46, Duke; Kerksis, *The Atlanta Papers,* 376 (second quote).
74. Smith, "Journal," Cheatham Papers, TSLA; Kerksis, *The Atlanta Papers,* 377; "Ninth Tennessee," 2:30–31, Hall Papers, UNC; *Chattanooga Daily Rebel,* July 4, 1864.
75. W. L. Blair, "That Lightning Bug Fight," *CV* (Sept. 1904); W. D. Eleazer, "Fight at Dead Angle, in Georgia," *CV* (July 1906), 312 (both quotes).
76. Smith, "Journal," and BFC, Atlanta Military Journal, Cheatham Papers, TSLA; Chattanooga Daily Rebel, July 4, 1864; Fahnestock Diary, 43–46, Duke; Lindsley, *MAT,* 299; Robinson, "Battle of Kennesaw Mountain," 115–16. While Maney was definitely present during the burial truce (see Kerksis, *The Atlanta Papers,* 386), he was not in command of the brigade during the June 27 assault. That chore fell to Col. Francis M. Walker of the Nineteenth Tennessee. Col. Hume

R. Feild of the First Tennessee was the officer who most closely supervised the troops in the angle itself. Whether Maney was ill or absent from the army is impossible to ascertain.

77. Memphis Daily Appeal, July 1, 1864, cited in J. Cutler Andrews, *The South Reports the Civil War* (Princeton, 1970), 450; Lindsley, *MAT,* 436 ("never better pleased" quote), 437 (all remaining quotes).

78. Lyman S. Widney to parents, June 30, 1864 (typescript), Sgt. Major Lyman S. Widney Letters, Kennesaw Mountain NBP; Widney Diary, June 29, 1864 (typescript account compiled after the war), Kennesaw Mountain NBP; Lindsley, *MAT,* 436.

79. BFC, Atlanta Military Journal, and Smith, "Journal," Cheatham Papers, TSLA; "Ninth Tennessee," 2:32, Hall Papers, UNC.

80. For information on the battlefield, refer to William C. Davis, *Civil War Parks: The Story behind the Scenery,* (Las Vegas, 1984), 58–59, and informational brochures, Kennesaw Mountain NBP.

Chapter 8

1. James I. Hall to children, July 8, 1864, Hall Papers, UNC; Smith, "Journal," Cheatham Papers, TSLA. Melanchton Smith noted in the latter document that after June 27, " it was only necessary to expose a hand to procure a furlough."

2. Alfred Jefferson Vaughan to Elliott Danforth, May 2, 1892, Vaughan Papers, TSLA; Vaughan, *Thirteenth Tennessee,* 85 ("scanty rations" quote), 86 ("sunglass" quote); Fielder Diary, July 4, 1864, TSLA.

3. Vaughan, *Thirteenth Tennessee,* 87.

4. Oldham Diary, July 5, 1864, TSLA; Fielder Diary, July 4–5, 1864, TSLA.

5. Oldham Diary, July 16–17, 1864, TSLA; Fielder Diary, July 13, 1864, TSLA; *Chattanooga Daily Rebel,* July 19, 1864.

6. McMurry, *Hood,* 95–97, 116–22; Govan and Livingood, *A Different Valor,* 314–19.

7. *Chattanooga Daily Rebel,* July 20, 1864.

8. "Cumming Recollections," UNC, 59 (both quotes); James I. Hall to parents, May 30, [1864], Hall Papers, UNC; Watkins, *Co. Aytch,* 156–57.

9. Lindsley, *MAT,* 165 (first quote), 310 (second quote), 426; Head, *Sixteenth Tennessee,* 136–37.

10. Rennolds, *Henry County Commands,* 86–87.

11. "Ninth Tennessee," 2:34 (both quotes), 35, Hall Papers, UNC.

12. Fielder Diary, July 18, 1864, TSLA; John Henry Marsh (officer in Strahl's brigade) to the Rev. Dr. Quintard, July 26, 1864, Quintard Papers, Duke; Oldham Diary, July 18, 1864, TSLA.

13. Oldham Diary, July 18, 1864, TSLA. At least two scholars have suggested that the question of Confederate morale in the Atlanta campaign is more complex than the idea that every soldier was dismayed by Johnston's removal. This is undoubtedly true; an army of some 60,000 or so men was certain to contain individuals with highly differing opinions. It is also to be noted that a historian deals with just a fraction of the men who fought in the war, namely those who were literate enough and interested enough to record their observations, either during or after the war. Working within this admittedly narrow framework, I have not found a single source from a veteran of Cheatham's division who applauded the decision to replace Johnston with Hood; however, John-

ston's role in restoring the Tennessee regiments under Cheatham won for him a special devotion among the Tennesseans. Given this factor Cheatham's divisional members probably idolized Johnston more than did other commands. See Richard M. McMurry, "Confederate Morale in the Atlanta Campaign," *Georgia Historical Quarterly* (1970), 227–43, and William J. McNeill, "A Survey of Confederate Soldier Morale during Sherman's Campaign through Georgia and the Carolinas," *Georgia Historical Quarterly* (1971), 1–25.

14. BFC, Atlanta Military Journal, Cheatham Papers, TSLA. One of the matters complicating a study of the Atlanta campaign is the fact that hardly any reports from Hardee's corps are included in the *OR*. The probable reason for this is that Hood's army train containing army correspondence was burned at some point, according to historian Dennis Kelly of Kennesaw Mountain NBP.

15. Lindsley, *MAT,* 96–97.

16. Worsham, *Nineteenth Tennessee,* 190; Watkins, *Co. Aytch,* 158, 164.

17. Marsh to Quintard, July 26, 1864, Quintard Papers, Duke (quote); Oldham Diary, July 18, 1864, TSLA.

18. Thomas Robson Hay, "Davis, Bragg, and Johnston in the Atlanta Campaign," *Georgia Historical Quarterly* (Mar. 1924), 41; F. Y. Hedley, *Marching through Georgia: Pen-Pictures of Every-Day Life* (Chicago, 1887), 140; McMurry, *Hood,* 59, 122–23; Oldham Diary, July 18, 1864, TSLA (quote).

19. S. R. Cockrill to Cheatham, July 19, 1864, Cheatham Papers, TSLA.

20. *OR,* 38, pt. 5: 892 (quote); Fielder Diary, July 19, 1864, TSLA.

21. McMurry, *Hood,* 124–26; Connelly, *AG,* 439–40.

22. John Bell Hood, *Advance and Retreat: Personal Experiences in the United States and Confederate States Armies* (New Orleans, 1880), 165–66; Connelly, *AG,* 439–40.

23. Hardee to Gen. Samuel Cooper, April 5, 1865, Ala. Dept. of Archives and History; T. B. Roy, "General Hardee and the Military Operations around Atlanta," *Southern Historical Society Papers* (1880), 347–49 (quote, 347), 352–53.

24. *OR,* 38, pt. 5: 896–97.

25. Hardee to Cooper, April 5, 1865, Ala. Dept. of Archives and History; Fielder Diary, July 20, 1864, TSLA.

26. Hardee to Cooper, Apr. 5, 1865, Ala. Dept. of Archives and History; Rennolds, *Henry County Commands,* 88–89; Oldham Diary, July 20, 1864, TSLA.

27. "Grand Summary of Casualties in Cheatham's Division, during the First Campaign of 1864, to include July 22nd," Cheatham Papers, TSLA; Fielder Diary, July 20, 1864, TSLA (quotes).

28. T. B. Roy to Cheatham, Oct. 15, 1881, Cheatham Papers, TSLA (quote); Roy, "Hardee and Military Operations around Atlanta," 354–57; Connelly, *AG,* 445–46.

29. Fielder Diary, July 21, 1864, TSLA (quote); Oldham Diary, July 21, 1864, TSLA.

30. Oldham Diary, July 22, 1864, TSLA.

31. *OR,* 38, pt. 3: 369–70, 474–75, 545, 738; Roy, "Hardee and Military Operations around Atlanta," 360–61; "Ninth Tennessee," 2:36, Hall Papers, UNC.

32. *OR,* 38, pt. 3: 738–39; Scaife, *The Campaign for Atlanta,* 61–64; *CMH: Tenn.,* 137–38.

33. Fielder Diary, July 22, 1864, TSLA (quote); *OR,* 38, pt. 3: 731 (Lowrey's report). Sources indicating that Maney was on the Confederate left include Scaife, *Campaign for Atlanta,* 60, 62; James Lee McDonough and James Pickett Jones, *War So Terrible: Sherman and Atlanta* (New York, 1987), 224; Georgia Dept. of Natural Resources, *Georgia Civil War Markers* (Atlanta, 1982), 83.

34. "Ninth Tennessee," 2:36, Hall Papers, UNC; *OR,* 38, pt. 3: 547, 565, 573 (Union reports). Hall maintained that it was 5 p.m. before his regiment went into action. Lt. Col. Grenberry F. Wiles of the Seventy-eighth Ohio Regiment wrote in his battle report that his men "changed front" at 5 p.m. and "received the charge of Cheatham's division." See *OR,* ibid., 573.

35. "Ninth Tennessee," 2:37–38, Hall Papers, UNC.

36. Fielder Diary, July 22, 1864, TSLA.

37. *OR,* 38, pt. 3: 565 (first quote, Leggett's quote), 547 (Blair's quote), 573, 583; Oldham Diary, July 23, 1864, TSLA; Lindsley, *MAT,* 220 (Sixth Tennessean's quote).

38. *OR,* 38, pt. 3: 631 (Hood quote); Roy, "Hardee and Military Operations around Atlanta," 361. Editor R. Lockwood Tower, in *A Carolinian Goes to War,* p. 260, has noted the difference in times cited by officers as to when Cheatham's attack began.

39. Connelly, *AG,* 449, accuses Cheatham of tardiness in obeying Hood's order to attack, a charge echoed by McDonough and Jones in *War So Terrible,* 234.

40. Battle reports of Stovall's brigade (Johnson quote), and Thirty-sixth Ala. Regt., both in Cheatham Papers, TSLA; Manigault, *A Carolinian Goes to War,* 226 (quote), 291.

41. Battle report of divisional commander H. D. Clayton, reports of Baker's, Holtzclaw's, and Stovall's brigades, regimental reports for Eighteenth, Thirty-sixth, Thirty-seventh, Thirty-eighth, Fortieth, Forty-second, and Fifty-fourth Ala. Regs., all in Cheatham Papers, TSLA; Manigault, *A Carolinian Goes to War,* 227–30, 260–62, 291–94; Wilbur G. Kurtz, "The Battle for Atlanta," in *The Atlanta Cyclorama of the Battle of Atlanta* (Atlanta, 1954; reprint ed., Atlanta, 1984), 10–11; *OR,* 38, pt. 3: 546–47, 565. The battle reports cited here from the Cheatham Papers are not included in the *OR,* with the exception of Gen. Henry D. Clayton's report.

42. Connelly, *AG,* 449–50; McMurry, *Hood,* 131–32; *OR,* 38, pt. 3: 21, 29, 631.

43. Wirt Armistead Cate, ed., *Two Soldiers: The Campaign Diaries of Thomas J. Key, C.S.A., December 7, 1863–May 17, 1865, and Robert J. Campbell, U.S.A, January 1, 1864–July 21, 1864* (Chapel Hill, 1938), 103; Worsham, *Nineteenth Tennessee,* 131.

44. "Grand Summary of Casualties in Cheatham's Division," Cheatham Papers, TSLA; Marsh to Dr. Quintard, July 26, 1864, Quintard Papers, Duke; *CMH: Tenn.,* 136; Morgan Diary, TSLA. More officers were probably killed than the seventeen cited in Porter's work (*CMH: Tenn.*), since not all of the regiments in Cheatham's division are accounted for in Porter's casualty figures. Lt. Perry Franklin Morgan of the Eighth Tennessee, for instance, was mortally wounded, but is not cited in Porter's tabulations.

45. Worsham, *Nineteenth Tennessee,* 129, 209, 213 (Walker declined fellow officer's offer to lead regiment into battle); Lindsley, *MAT,* 377 (all quotes).

46. "Grand Summary of Casualties in Cheatham's Division," Cheatham Papers, TSLA; Lindsley, *MAT,* 597; Oldham Diary, July 25, 1864, TSLA.

47. Oldham Diary, July 27, 1864, TSLA.

48. *OR,* 38, pt. 3: 762–63, 767–68, 872, 927–28, 42.

49. Ibid., pt. 5: 920, 930; pt. 3: 928 (Walthall quote).

50. Connelly, *AG,* 456–57; McMurry, *Hood,* 136–37.

51. Coleman to Quintard, July 9, 1864, Quintard Papers, Duke (first quote); Oldham Diary, July 21 (second quote) and 26 (rations "for the indigent families" quote), 1864, TSLA; Smith, "Journal," Cheatham Papers, TSLA (Smith quotes).

52. Oldham Diary, entries for July 26, 29 (quote) and 31, Aug. 1, 1864, TSLA; *OR,* 38, pt. 5: 946 (Davis communication to Hood).

53. Oldham Diary, July 26, 29, and 31, Aug. 3, 1864, TSLA; *OR,* 38, pt. 5: 946.

54. *OR,* 38, pt. 5: 962–63 (Lee quote); Clark Diary, TSLA, 44.

55. *OR,* 38, pt. 1: 924; pt. 5: 420, 494–95.

56. Connelly, *AG,* 452–53, 457; Oldham Diary, July 30, Aug. 1 and 2, 1864, TSLA; Smith, "Journal," Cheatham Papers, TSLA.

57. *OR,* 38, pt. 3: 691–94, 958–61; *CMH: Tenn.,* 138; Rennolds, *Henry County Commands,* 95 (quote).

58. *OR,* 38, pt. 3: 700–01 (Hardee's report); 708 (Maney's report, quote), 764–65 (Lee's report).

59. Ibid., 709–10.

60. Ibid., 710–11.

61. Ibid., 711–12. From Maney's report it appears that the person he must have displeased was Cleburne. The two may have quarreled. If Maney's report is accurate, it is hard to fault him for his prudence. Too often in the war a series of piecemeal attacks failed to accomplish anything except produce a long casualty list.

62. Cheatham's chief of staff, James D. Porter, sheds no light on Maney's role at Jonesboro in his *Confederate Military History: Tennessee,* even though it includes a written profile on Maney. Sam Watkins wrote a nonsensical account of the battle in *Co. Aytch,* and makes no reference to Maney at Jonesboro. Few of the regimental sketches in Lindsley's *Military Annals of Tennessee* allude to Jonesboro in any detail, and none that do, shed any light on why Carter took over the division. Alfred Tyler Fielder of the Twelfth Tennessee was wounded at Atlanta, a fate he shared with James I. Hall of the Ninth Tennessee, with the consequence that their post–JULY 22 accounts, logically, deal more with hospital stays and their convalescence than with army affairs. The most informative source for Cheatham's division during the Atlanta campaign, Van Buren Oldham's diary, terminates with the entry for August 5. Oldham apparently grew so tired of Hood's leadership that he abandoned the service. His service file in the Ninth Tennessee Infantry File, NA, lists him as being a deserter who took the oath of allegiance at Nashville on October 17, 1864. From a historical standpoint, it is regrettable that Oldham, a keen observer, did not remain with the army and continue his diary. Surely he would have provided evidence of Maney's fate. Maney's obituaries in 1901 are not helpful. It is curious that someone did not at least report on the affair, either to denigrate Maney or to leap to his defense. The answer to Maney's removal may, of course, lie within a letter, diary, or memoir which I have not seen.

63. Maney's service file, First (Feild's) Tennessee Infantry File, NA. Maney was wounded during the retreat from Missionary Ridge, and when he met Gen. St. John Richardson Liddell in Mobile in late Jan. 1865, Maney complained about the pain from his injury. Hughes, *Liddell's Record,* 193. It seems highly unlikely, but Maney may have stepped down because he was not in good enough health to continue as either a brigade or divisional commander. Still, this is a development either he or Carter would probably have inserted into their reports if it affected Maney's conduct at Jonesboro. Maney is last referred to in the war records by a soldier in the First Tennessee who was captured by the Federals during the advance into Tennessee. The Confederate told his captors that Cheatham commanded the corps, John C. Brown the

division, and Maney the brigade. This information was apparently incorrect, as other sources indicate that Carter remained in charge of Maney's old regiments after Jonesboro. See *OR,* 45, pt. 1: 1094.

64. *OR,* 38, pt. 3: 696, 701–2, 712.
65. Ibid., 718–20.
66. *OR,* 38, pt. 1: 81–82; pt. 3, 712, 742–43; Lindsley, *MAT,* 221, 299–300.
67. Lindsley, *MAT,* 300; *OR,* 38, pt. 3: 633, 694–95, 992.
68. *OR,* 38, pt. 5: 777.
69. "Grand Summary of Casualties in Cheatham's Division," Cheatham Papers, TSLA; *OR,* 38, pt. 3: 638, 668–69, 676, 682; ibid., 39, pt. 2: 828, 850–52.
70. Worsham, *Nineteenth Tennessee,* 133; Rennolds, *Henry County Commands,* 99–100.
71. Fielder Diary, July 23, 1864, TSLA.

Chapter 9

1. *OR,* 39, pt. 2: 832, 842.
2. Worsham *Nineteenth Tennessee,* 134; Head, *Sixteenth Tennessee,* 145; Watkins, *Co. Aytch,* 203–4 (quote, 204).
3. *OR,* 39, pt. 2: 880–81.
4. McMurry, *Hood,* 137–38; Connelly, *AG,* 320–21.
5. New York Herald, quoted in *Charleston Daily Courier,* Aug. 15, 1864, as cited in Irving A. Buck, *Cleburne and His Command,* ed. Thomas R. Hay (Jackson, Tenn., 1959), 52–53.
6. Lindsley, *MAT,* 221. Cheatham and Cleburne apparently shared a mutual friendship and respect. Part of the discrepancy in the reputations of the two men is attributable to publicity. At least four books have been written about Cleburne and his career, including one by a staff officer, Irving A. Buck. Cheatham did not write his own memoirs received direct literary attention, as did the Irishman. Cleburne may indeed have proved to be a more competent corps commander, but his prewar experience in the British army was fairly routine, and Cheatham did see action in the Mexican War. Cleburne commanded a corps on just one occasion, at Jonesboro, when Cheatham was ill. The quality Cleburne probably excelled in, compared to Cheatham, was the discipline of his soldiers. Otherwise, writers who agree with Thomas R. Hay's description of Cheatham as a man "addicted to strong drink" feel Cleburne's personal character was higher. See Buck, *Cleburne and His Command,* 53.
7. Of the officers in the Army of Tennessee who shared Cheatham's rank, only William W. Loring possessed a commission predating Cheatham's. Loring temporarily led Polk's corps after the latter's death, but was replaced by A. P. Stewart. Loring may have been ruled out of contention for command of Hardee's corps because he had been wounded at Ezra Church. See Marcus J. Wright, *General Officers of the Confederate Army* (New York, 1911), 25.
8. James Lee McDonough and Thomas L. Connelly, *Five Tragic Hours: The Battle of Franklin* (Knoxville, 1983), 200–203 (lists BFC's corps for Tennessee campaign); Warner, *Generals in Gray,* 45 (biographical information on John C. Carter); John J. Jones, B. H. Hill, Herschel V. Johnson and G. A. Henry to [John Seddon], Feb. 12, 1863; Marcus J. Wright to Gen. Samuel Cooper, Apr. 16, 1863; Robert L. Caruthers to J. A. Seddon, Oct. 1, 1863; Robert L.

Caruthers to Jefferson Davis, Nov. 13, 1863 (quote); all correspondence in John C. Carter's service file, in Thirty-eighth Tennessee Infantry File, NA.

9. Warner, *Generals in Gray,* 109–10.
10. Ibid., 295–96; Sumner A. Cunningham, "Gen. O. F. Strahl," *CV* (Sept. 1896), 299 (quote).
11. Warner, *Generals in Gray,* 106–7.
12. Ibid., 35–36.
13. McMurry, *Hood,* 156–58; Watkins, *Co. Aytch,* 203–4 (quote, 204).
14. *OR,* 39, pt. 1: 802, 806.
15. Ibid., 718–19 (quote, 719).
16. Ibid., 717–23; Watkins, *Co. Aytch,* 213.
17. *OR,* 39, pt. 3: 785, 825; Connelly, *AG,* 472–73, 481–85.
18. *OR,* 39, pt. 1: 582–84, 588.
19. Thomas R. Hay, *Hood's Tennessee Campaign* (New York, 1929; reprint ed., Dayton, 1976), 67–70.
20. *OR,* 39, pt. 1: 797–98.
21. H. K. Nelson, "Tennessee, a Grave or a Free Home," *CV* (Nov. 1907), 508; Enoch Mitchell, ed., "Letters from a Confederate Surgeon in the Army of Tennessee to His Wife," *Tennessee Historical Quarterly* (June 1946), 174.
22. Lindsley, *MAT,* 427.
23. McMurry, *Hood,* 161–62.
24. *OR,* 45, pt. 1: 669, 730; Rennolds, *Henry County Commands,* 103 (quote).
25. *OR,* 45, pt. 1: 341, 670, 1058, 1085; Hay, *Hood's Tennessee Campaign,* 81–83.
26. Hay, *Hood's Tennessee Campaign,* 82–83; W. T. Crawford, "The Mystery of Spring Hill," *Civil War History* (June 1955), 109.
27. *OR,* 45, pt. 1: 113; Crawford, "The Mystery of Spring Hill," 109–11.
28. J. P. Young, "Hood's Failure at Spring Hill," *CV* (Jan. 1908), 36–41. Hood gave his account of the affair in his book *Advance and Retreat,* and was backed by Capt. W. O. Dodd's "Reminiscences of Hood's Tennessee Campaign," in the *Southern Historical Society Papers,* (1881), 518–24. Cheatham replied to both Hood and Dodd in an article entitled "The Lost Opportunity at Spring Hill, Tenn.— General Cheatham's Reply to Hood," which followed Dodd's account in the *SHSP* volume (pp. 524–41). Cheatham read his account before the Louisville branch of the Southern Historical Society on Dec. 1, 1881, and the text was reprinted verbatim in the *Louisville Courier-Journal* three days later. Dodd was serving as president of the historical society in Louisville at the time and may have invited Cheatham to the city to present his side of the case. The author of the first account cited in this note, John Preston Young, was a veteran of the Seventh Tennessee Cavalry who fought in the Tennessee campaign. Prior to his cavalry service, Young served at Hardee's and Cheatham's headquarters, and with the Fourth Tennessee Infantry. Being under age, he was not sworn into formal service until his enlistment with the cavalry regiment in 1864. Even then, he was only sixteen years old. After the war, he was a lawyer and city editor of the *Memphis Avalanche,* and became a justice of the peace in 1888. He was later associated with the Shelby County Court. Young turned to historical endeavors as well, writing a history of his former cavalry unit. He also spent numerous years studying the history of the Army of Tennessee for the period covering July 18, 1864, to Jan. 18, 1865, the time of Hood's command. Although a sketch of Young indicated that he planned to publish the work in book form, standard bibliographies of the Civil War indicate that

he did not do so. Both A. P. Stewart and S. D. Lee examined the manuscript, and Lee feared that Young would not find a publisher because his conclusions would offend several distinguished Tennesseans. See S. D. Lee to Ellison Capers, Nov. 12, 1902, Ellison Capers Papers, UNC. Young's information in the *Confederate Veteran* is crucial to an examination of Spring Hill, but he apparently softened his criticism of Brown to placate readers. For information on Young, refer to J. Harvey Mathes, *The Old Guard in Gray* (Memphis, 1897), pt. 1, pp. 231–32; pt. 2, pp. 140–41.

29. BFC, "The Lost Opportunity," 524–25; Young, "Hood's Failure," 31–32.
30. BFC, "The Lost Opportunity," 524–25 (Cleburne's quote, 525); Young, "Hood's Failure," 31–32; *OR*, 45, pt. 1: 268–69, 277–80, 286; John K. Shellenberger, *The Battle of Spring Hill, Tennessee* (Cleveland, 1913), 26–31 ("canine descent" quote, 29).
31. BFC, "The Lost Opportunity," 525, 539–40; OR, 45, pt. 1: 742; Young, "Hood's Failure," 31–32, 37 (quote). In one of many contradictions, Bate never relates that he met Cheatham near Rutherford's Ford. Cheatham may still have been watching Cleburne's men go forward when Bate started on his way to the front.
32. BFC, "The Lost Opportunity," 524–25, 540; Young, "Hood's Failure," 32, 37. In one of many contradictions, Bate never relates that he met Cheatham near Rutherford's Ford. Cheatham may still have been watching Cleburne's men go forward when Bate started on his way to the front.
33. BFC, "The Lost Opportunity," 525–26 (Brown quote, 525); Young, "Hood's Failure," 33–35 (Cheatham quote, 33 and 34).
34. BFC, "The Lost Opportunity," 526, 538; Young, "Hood's Failure," 33–35; "Cumming Recollections," 73, UNC (Hood's officer); S. D. Lee to Judge J. F. H. Claiborne, June 12, 1878, Claiborne Papers, UNC.
35. *OR*, 45, pt. 1: 712–13; Isham Harris, Account of the Spring Hill affair, recounted to Major Campbell Brown, 1868 (typescript), Campbell Brown and Richard Stoddert Ewell Papers, TSLA (hereafter cited as Harris Transcript); Young, "Hood's Failure," 39–40.
36. Tillman H. Stevens, "'Other Side' in Battle of Franklin," *CV* (Apr. 1903), 165.
37. Harris Transcript, Brown-Ewell Papers, TSLA; BFC, "The Lost Opportunity," 530, 532; Young, "Hood's Failure," 38.
38. "Cumming Recollections," 78, UNC (Hood's officer); *OR*, 45, pt. 1: 731.
39. Frank A. Burr, "The Battle of Franklin," *Philadelphia Press*, Mar. 11, 1883, in pamphlet form, Cheatham-Hodgson Papers, University of the South; P. B. Simmons, "The Correction Cheerfully Made," *CV* (June 1893), 163; McDonough and Connelly, *Five Tragic Hours*, 55.
40. S. D. Lee to Judge J. F. H. Claiborne, June 12, 1878. Claiborne Papers, UNC; Lee to Capers, Nov. 12, 1902, Capers Papers, UNC.
41. J. W. Ratchford, *Some Reminiscences of Personal Incidents of the Civil War* (1909; reprint ed., Austin, 1971), 62–63.
42. W. M. Pollard Diary, 8, Confederate Collection, TSLA; John Johnston, "Reminiscences," 138, TSLA (quote). In November 1903, Maury County historian Frank Smith interviewed John S. R. Gregory, a former member of Forrest's cavalry who claimed that he had been Hood's guide for the movement from Columbia to Spring Hill. Gregory asserted that he saw a number of the officers drinking during the night at the Thompson house. Gregory alleged that Cheatham was "full drunk," Cleburne and Granbury "drank quite freely," and that Walthall also "had too much liquor." See Smith, *History of*

Maury County, Tennessee (Columbia, Tenn., 1969), 238. As with other aspects of the Spring Hill affair, the accuracy of Gregory's account is hard to assess. He did have difficulty remembering just what general officers were at the house, and his age when he consented to Smith's interview (Gregory was 76) perhaps should be taken into consideration. Some Spring Hill residents later related that Absalom Thompson was a "fanatic teetotaler" and would not have permitted anyone to drink under his roof, while others have suggested that Hood may have imbibed to relieve the pain from his wounds. See David E. Roth, "The Mysteries of Spring Hill," *Blue & Gray Magazine* (Nov. 1984), 28.

43. Young, "Hood's Failure," 34–35.

44. Pollard Diary, 8, TSLA; Ratchford, *Reminiscences*, 62; Buck, *Cleburne and His Command*, 269; W. D. Gale to wife, Jan. 14, 1865, Gale-Polk Letters, UNC. A host of theories have been put forward to explain the cause of Confederate errors at Spring Hill. The most fanciful account was fashioned by author George Byram in "The Chronicle of the 656th," *Playboy* (Mar. 1968). In Byram's science-fiction yarn, a World War II unit is sent back some eighty years in time by an atomic mishap, and they shape history by helping Schofield escape and adding their firepower to the Union side at the battle of Franklin. Byram correctly identified most of the main participants on either side, with one exception. One of the characters in the story notes that the Confederate infantry operating near Spring Hill during the afternoon of Nov. 29 were from "Jackson's corps," which would no doubt have surprised the actual commander, Frank Cheatham.

45. James Harrison Wilson, *Under the Old Flag*, 2 vols. (New York, 1912), 2:44; Howell Purdue and Elizabeth Purdue, *Pat Cleburne: Confederate General* (Hillsboro, Tex., 1973), 406–7. Cheatham apparently did have an eye for the ladies. A soldier in his division noted that during an 1863 review, several women on horseback arrived to watch the display. Bragg and Polk gave their "undivided attention to the maneuvering of the troops," while "Gen. Cheatham spent his idle time conversing with the girls." Rogers Diary, 34, UNC. Trying to gauge whether Cheatham indeed visited Mrs. Peters is virtually impossible, given the uncertain time sequence of events during the late afternoon and night. The charge that Cheatham was with her comes from an interesting source, Union cavalryman Wilson. Wilson may have simply repeated neighborhood speculation; perhaps Mrs. Peters's notoriety in the Van Dorn case inspired similar rumors about potential flirtations with other Confederate officers.

46. *Louisville Courier-Journal*, Dec. 4, 1881.

47. Young, "Hood's Failure," 36–37.

48. Isham Harris to Bishop Quintard, Dec. 29, 1864, Quintard Papers, Duke.

49. *OR*, 39, pt. 3: 870 (Hood recommended BFC's promotion); 45, pt. 2: 659 (Hood withdrew recommendation for promotion), 665 (Hood asked for BFC's removal, then reversed his decision); 53: 384 (Jefferson Davis correspondence with Gen. Beauregard in regard to BFC and Hood); Harris Transcript, Brown-Ewell Papers, TSLA (Hood requested Gov. Harris's aid in winning a promotion for BFC); BFC, "The Lost Opportunity," 531–35.

50. *OR*, 39, pt. 3: 870; 45, pt. 2: 659, 665; BFC, "The Lost Opportunity," 531–35 (BFC quote, 532; Porter's information regarding a note to BFC, 534; Stewart's reception of a note, 535); Harris to Quintard, Dec. 29, 1894, Quintard Papers, Duke (Harris quotes). The *OR* contains the message from Hood to Stewart absolving Stewart from any blame at Spring Hill, and includes Hood's wish

that Stewart's corps had been "in front on that day. I feel, and have felt, that Tennessee to-day would have been in our possession." The message is dated Apr. 9, 1865; *OR,* 45, pt. 1: 713.

51. McDonough and Connelly, *Five Tragic Hours,* 57; McMurry, *Hood,* 173–74. Hood's original intention appears to have been to slip by Schofield and reach Nashville before the Union contingent did. See Quintard Diary (microfilm copy), Nov. 27 and 28, 1864, Quintard Papers, UNC.

52. Shellenberger, *The Battle of Spring Hill,* 48, maintains that a successful attack at Spring Hill "would have changed the later current of the war with results too far reaching to be estimated." Young, "Hood's Failure," 41, states that prompt Confederate action at Spring Hill would have resulted in Stanley's being crushed, the capture of the Union reserve artillery and wagons, the entrapment of Schofield "as he approached in the darkness with Ruger's division, and the remaining divisions of Cox, Wood and Kimball left at the mercy of Hood at daylight the next morning." Some modern writers have also predicted that Confederate success at Spring Hill would have had tremendous repercussions. In *Pat Cleburne: Confederate General,* 407, Howell Purdue and Elizabeth Purdue wrote: "A successful Confederate attack at Spring Hill, resulting in the destruction of Schofield's army, would have radically altered the current of the war in the west."

53. BFC, "The Lost Opportunity," 533.

54. Ibid.

55. Ibid.

56. Young, "Hood's Failure," 36.

57. Pollard Diary, 8, TSLA.

58. Burr, "Battle of Franklin," 21. Frank Burr's account for the *Philadelphia Press* has not been cited in most works pertaining to Franklin. Burr gleaned information from several sources, including Union general Jacob Cox, who later wrote a book on the battle. Burr's task was made easier by virtue of his service in the Federal army. While eighteen years separated the battle from Cheatham's and Porter's return visit, it is obvious that they retained keen impressions of the action. The intervening years figuratively dropped away as they recounted the events to Burr. In some passages, the two ex-Confederates talked more to themselves and one another than to Colonel Burr. Porter relayed news of the return visit in a letter to former army comrade Ellison Capers and also requested that Capers write an account of the battle for publication. See Porter to Capers, Feb. 12, 1883, Capers Papers, Duke.

59. Irving A. Buck, "Military View of the Battle of Franklin," *CV* (Aug. 1909), 383 (Forrest's offer to flank the enemy); Burr, "Battle of Franklin," 21 (Cheatham and Hood quotes).

60. Burr, "Battle of Franklin," 22.

61. Ibid., 22–23. For another admiring appraisal of the deployment, refer to the report of Col. Ellison Capers, in *OR,* 45, pt. 1: 737.

62. Rennolds, *Henry County Commands,* 104.

63. Burr, "Battle of Franklin," 23 (quote); Lindsley, *MAT,* 301, 427.

64. Rennolds, *Henry County Commands,* 105 (first and second quotes); Burr, "Battle of Franklin," 23–24; Lindsley, *MAT,* 222, 301 (Gordon quotes).

65. Burr, "Battle of Franklin," 22. Cheatham's men were not the only ones to make allusions to the ties between his old division and Cleburne's. Dr. J. S. Carothers, a veteran of Cleburne's division, referred to the two units as the

"Siamese twins" of the Army of Tennessee. See Carothers, "That Silver Moon Banner," *CV* (Aug. 1895), 245; also, editorial comments in "Cheatham's and Cleburne's Divisions," *CV* (Feb. 1900), 81.

66. Lindsley, *MAT,* 221-22, 302.

67. Burr, "Battle of Franklin," 24-25 (Cheatham quotes); McDonough and Connelly, *Five Tragic Hours,* 136-39, (quote, 139), 160.

68. Burr, Battle of Franklin," 24; *CMH: Tenn.,* 157-59.

69. *OR,* 45, pt. 1: 239-41; Lindsley, *MAT,* 222-23.

70. McDonough and Connelly, *Five Tragic Hours,* 132-36; Lindsley, *MAT,* 301-2.

71. *OR,* 45, pt. 1: 737; *CMH: Tenn.,* 156-59. Gen. John C. Carter's father wrote to Cheatham requesting information on the fate of his son over six weeks after the battle. Cheatham apparently had the heartbreaking duty of informing the elder Carter that his son had died on Dec. 10. See E. J. Carter to BFC, Jan. 17, 1865, Cheatham Papers, TSLA.

72. Cunningham, "Gen. O. F. Strahl," 299-300; Worsham, *Nineteenth Tennessee,* 141 (first quote), 144-46 (second quote, 144); Rennolds, *Henry County Commands,* 105-7; Lindsley, *MAT,* 377-78 (third quote, 378).

73. Burr, "Battle of Franklin," 22; Stephen D. Lee, "Johnson's Division in the Battle of Franklin," *Publications of the Mississippi Historical Society* (1930), 78-79 (Cheatham quote, 78); Lee to Capers, Nov. 12, 1902, Capers Papers, UNC.

74. Burr, "Battle of Franklin," 27; Worsham, *Nineteenth Tennessee,* 146-47 (quote, 146).

75. Burr, "Battle of Franklin," 27.

76. *OR,* 45, pt. 1: 684-86, 783, 743; Lindsley, *MAT,* 190; Quintard Diary, Dec. 1, 1864, Quintard Papers, UNC.

77. Lindsley, *MAT,* 190.

78. Ibid., 222; Rennolds, *Henry County Commands,* 108; Worsham, *Nineteenth Tennessee,* 146; Nelson, "Tennessee, a Grave or a Free Home," 509; Burr, "Battle of Franklin," 27; *CMH: Tenn.,* 190.

79. Burr, "Battle of Franklin," 27-28.

80. Hood, *Advance and Retreat,* 290; *OR,* 39, pt. 3: 636.

81. BFC, "The Lost Opportunity," 533; "Ninth Tennessee," 2:34-35, Hall Papers, UNC; Head, *Sixteenth Tennessee,* 136; "Cumming Recollections," 72, UNC; Watkins, *Co. Aytch,* 230.

82. Lindsley, *MAT,* 427 (Twenty-seventh Tennessee quotes), 310 (Twelfth Tennessee quote).

Chapter 10

1. *OR,* 45, pt. 1: 731.

2. Quintard Diary, Nov. 27, 1864, Quintard Papers, UNC.

3. *OR,* 45, pt. 1: 731, 744-46; McMurry, *Hood,* 177.

4. Brig.-Gen. J. A. Smith, Report of Cleburne's division in the Tennessee campaign, Jan. 23, 1865, Cheatham Papers, TSLA.

5. Rennolds, *Henry County Commands,* 110; Worsham, *Nineteenth Tennessee,* 151-52; Head, *Sixteenth Tennessee,* 151-52; Watkins, *Co. Aytch,* 224-25; *OR,* 45, pt. 1: 735, 738, 747.

6. H. R. Jackson to BFC, Dec. 10, 1864, Cheatham Papers, TSLA; Warner, *Generals in Gray,* 149-50.

7. Hay, *Hood's Tennessee Campaign,* 142-46, 150-52.

8. Ibid., 152; Charles B. Martin, "Jackson's Brigade in Battle of Nashville," *CV* (Jan. 1909), 12 (quotes).

9. *OR*, 45, pt. 1: 709-10, 747-48 (quote, 747).

10. *OR*, 45, pt. 1: 747-48; Hay, *Hood's Tennessee Campaign*, 156-57, 159.

11. *OR*, 45, pt. 1: 748; Hay, *Hood's Tennessee Campaign*, 157.

12. *OR*, 45, pt. 1: 748-49; J. A. Smith's Report, Cheatham Papers, TSLA.

13. William T. Alderson, ed., "The Civil War Diary of Captain James Litton Cooper, September 30, 1861 to January, 1865," *Tennessee Historical Quarterly* (June 1956), 169.

14. *OR*, 45, pt. 1: 749-50, 774-75; McMurray, *Twentieth Tennessee*, 347-48; Head, *Sixteenth Tennessee*, 153; Rennolds, *Henry County Commands*, 111; Herman Hattaway, *General Stephen D. Lee* (Jackson, Miss., 1976), 141.

15. *OR*, 45, pt. 2: 696; pt. 1: 750; Lindsley, *MAT*, 190.

16. Rennolds, *Henry County Commands*, 111-12; Worsham, *Nineteenth Tennessee*, 154-55.

17. "Cumming Recollections," 76, UNC; Martin, "Jackson's Brigade," 12-13 (BFC unable to rally troops, 73); Rennolds, *Henry County Commands*, 112; W. D. Gale to wife, Jan. 19, 1865, Confederate Collection, TSLA ("observer" quotes); Cavanaugh, *Obion Avalanche*, 50 (last quote).

18. Martin, "Jackson's Brigade," 12-13; McMurray, *Twentieth Tennessee* 348-49; Warner, *Generals in Gray*, 284.

19. *OR*, 45, pt. 1: 689; Connelly, *AG.*, 511-12; Rennolds, *Henry County Commands*, 112-113 (first quote, 112); *CMH: Tenn.*, 168-69 (second quote, 169).

20. *OR*, 45, pt. 1: 731, 750; J. A. Smith's Report, Cheatham Papers, TSLA.

21. "An Incident of Hood's Campaign," unsigned article in *Southern Bivouac* (Nov. 1884), 131-32 (BFC-Forrest quotes, intervention of Gen. Stephen D. Lee); Worsham, *Nineteenth Tennessee*, 156-57, 191 (infantrymen's vow to "shoot Forrest's cavalry"); Johnston, "Reminiscences," TSLA, 162.

22. "An Incident of Hood's Campaign," 132 (asserts that Forrest crossed first); Worsham, *Nineteenth Tennessee*, 157, 191, (asserts that BFC crossed the river first).

23. Quintard Diary, Dec. 18-19, 1864, Quintard Papers, UNC.

24. *OR*, 45, pt. 1: 726-27, 729, 757.

25. Lindsley, *MAT*, 378. Another account states that Stevenson was even more brazen, telling Hood that the cards were "d[amne]d badly shuffled." Worsham, *Nineteenth Tennessee*, 158.

26. *OR*, 45, pt. 1: 728 (first and last quotes), 727 (second and third quotes), 758-59; Lindsley, *MAT*, 190-92, 223-24, 378.

27. *OR*, 45, pt. 1: 728, 732.

28. Johnston, "Reminiscences," 171, TSLA.

29. Fielder Diary, Dec. 28, 1864, TSLA.

30. McMurry, *Hood*, 180; Watkins, *Co. Aytch*, 230.

31. Samuel A. Agnew Diary (typescript), Southern Historical Collection, UNC.

32. Luke W. Finlay, "Another Report on Hood's Campaign," *CV* (Sept. 1907), 406; *OR*, 45, pt. 2: 781, 784-85; 47, pt. 2: 1060; Fielder Diary, Jan. 4, 1865, TSLA; Rennolds, *Henry County Commands*, 114-15.

33. *OR*, 45, pt. 2: 778-79, 795-96, 800, 802.

34. "Organization of the Army of Tennessee, January 20, 1865," field return in A. P. Mason Collection, Chicago Historical Society.

35. *OR*, 45, pt. 1: 1080-81.

36. Rennolds, *Henry County Commands*, 114-15; Fielder Diary, Feb. 1-9, 1865, TSLA; Cavanaugh, *Obion Avalanche*, 15-16.

37. Lilla Mills Hawes, ed., *The Memoirs of Charles H. Olmstead* (Savannah, 1964), 177.

38. *OR,* 47, pt. 2: 1043; pt. 3: 716; Fielder Diary, Feb. 17, 1865, TSLA.

39. *OR,* 47, pt. 1: 1082-83 (Hampton quote, 1082), 1106; Worsham, *Nineteenth Tennessee,* 172 (BFC encounter with conductor).

40. *OR,* 47, pt. 1: 1083.

41. *OR,* 47, pt. 1: 1061-63; pt. 3: 773-74; *Tenn. CW,* 1:174, 193, 200; Worsham, *Nineteenth Tennessee,* 9, 175; *CMH: Tenn.,* 176-77 (quote, 177); Rennolds, *Henry County Commands,* 115-16.

42. D. G. Godwin to Miss Bettie Douglas, April 4, 1865, D. G. Godwin Letters, TSLA; Clark Diary, 51, TSLA; Worsham, *Nineteenth Tennessee,* 193 (BFC quotes, "tears ran down the faces" quote); untitled account, *CV* (July 1897), 364 (veteran's quote). See also inquiry, *CV* (Mar. 1895), 80. As two examples to support Cheatham's claim, James I. Hall of the Ninth Tennessee was wounded twice during the war, once at Perryville and again at Atlanta. Capt. Alfred T. Fielder of the Twelfth Tennessee was also seriously wounded on two occasions, at Missionary Ridge and Atlanta. Men who recuperated from one wound enough to return to active duty were again at risk, and some of them later received a mortal blow.

43. Fielder Diary, Apr. 14 and 22, 1865, TSLA; James Brown Ritchey Diary, Apr. 18, and 24, 1865, Northcut Family Papers, TSLA.

44. Clark Diary, 50, TSLA; Rennolds, *Henry County Commands,* 116.

45. Frank Porterfield to R. T. Quarles, n.d., THS Misc. Files, TSLA.

46. Hardee to Major Gen. Hoke and T. B. Roy to Gen. R. F. Hoke, both dated Sept. 8, 1865, Hardee Papers, Ala. Dept. of Archives and History; Cavanaugh, *Obion Avalanche,* 51. The amount of money given to each man is cited as a fraction over $1.17 in the *OR;* Cavanaugh wrote that he and his comrades were given $1.30 each. See *OR,* 47, pt. 3: 863.

47. *OR,* 47, pt. 1: 1066; Worsham, *Nineteenth Tennessee,* 177-78; Clark Diary, 51-52, TSLA; Fielder Diary, May 5, 1865, TSLA. While Worsham, Clark, and Fielder all agree that Cheatham wept as he bid his troops farewell, Clark and Fielder imply that he remained on horseback as he reviewed his men for the last time.

48. At some point during the war, Cheatham was introduced to the virtues of whiskey produced by fellow Tennessean Jack Daniel. Cheatham was so impressed by the quality of the product that he wrote a letter claiming that it was "beyond compare and without a doubt the finest glass of whiskey I ever tasted. Once one has sampled his first sip, it is impossible to refuse a second." The letter, which was sent to request Daniel's address, included Cheatham's assurance that the whiskey would "provide equal satisfaction to a number of gentlemen in my command." Cheatham's missive was later used as an endorsement by promoters of the sour mash whiskey, who boasted that it was the exclusive whiskey in the "Oak Room Men's Bar" at Nashville's famed Maxwell House Hotel. If Cheatham did first drink Jack Daniel's during the war, it was probably during a period when Daniel was in partnership with a whiskey maker named Dan Call. The distillery in Lynchburg, Tennessee, associated with the Jack Daniel whiskey was not registered until after the war, in 1866. See Roger E. Brashears, Jr. (Jack Daniel Distillery), to author, Oct. 16, 1985), and informational brochures available from the distillery. Cheatham's endorsement appeared on a huge cloth banner touting the Maxwell House Hotel, excursion trips on the steamboat *Burnside,* and Jack Daniel's whiskey. One of the banners is at Kennesaw Mountain NBP.

49. William T. Sherman, *Memoirs of William T. Sherman,* 2 vols. (New York, 1875), 2:387.

50. Porterfield to Quarles, THS Misc. Files, TSLA.

Chapter 11

1. *Mobile Advertiser and Register,* July 22, 1865. According to a brief notice in the paper, "Maj. Gen. B. F. Cheatham passed through Atlanta last week, on his way to his home in Tennessee. His friends will be glad to hear that he is in fine health."

2. Roller and Twyman, *Encyclopedia of Southern History,* 154, 1195; Philip M. Hamer, ed., *Tennessee: A History, 1673–1932,* 4 vols. (New York, 1933), 2:609.

3. Alex. P. Stewart to BFC, Oct. 18, 1866, Cheatham Papers, TSLA.

4. Bishop Quintard to Polk G. Johnson, n.d., Quintard Papers, Duke.

5. Quintard to Johnson, Quintard Papers, Duke; Harllee, *Kinfolks,* 3:2550; *Nashville City and Business Directory* (Nashville, 1859), 131. The story of Abbott L. Robertson, Anna's younger brother, is an interesting one. He was a student at the military institute in Nashville when the war began. The sixteen-year-old abandoned his studies and went to Union City, where he helped Cheatham by serving as a drillmaster. The Confederates apparently contemplated the establishment of a military academy similar to West Point, and young Robertson sought to be appointed as a cadet from Tennessee. Despite such heavyweight backers of his application as Isham Harris, Gustavus Henry, Cheatham, Leonidas Polk, and James D. Porter, Robertson was never appointed as a cadet. Eventually Porter requested that the lad be given a commission as one of Cheatham's staff officers, and Robertson evidently won an appointment as a second lieutenant. He was paroled in Greensboro at the end of the war, returned to Nashville, and became a lawyer. He died in 1871 or 1872, as he makes no further appearances in the city directories after those years and family information avers that he dies soon after the war. The scanty information on the status of cadets is contained in Confederate regulations: "Cadets appointed under Confederate law, shall be assigned to such duties governed by exigencies of the service, as will best promote their military experience and improvement, until a military school shall be established by the government for their instruction." See *Regulations for the Army of the Confederate States, 1864* (Richmond, 1864), 3. The copy cited is in the collection at Kennesaw Mountain NBP.

6. James Anderson to Sallie Anderson, Mar. 13, 1866, James Douglas Anderson Papers, TSLA; *Nashville Union and American,* Mar. 16, 1866.

7. Anna Cheatham to Elizabeth Cheatham, Mar. 30, Apr. 30, and Aug. 15, 1866, all in Cheatham Papers, TSLA.

8. Dorris R. Davis (present owner of Cheatham Springs Farm) to author, Apr. 15, 1985.

9. *Tullahoma News and Guardian,* Sept. 26, 1956, cited in Corrine Martinez, *Coffee County: From Arrowheads to Rockets* (Tullahoma, 1979), 76; Basil B. McMahan, *Coffee County, Then and Now — 1983* (Nashville, 1983), 228–29; Anna Cheatham to Elizabeth Cheatham, Aug. 15, 1866, Cheatham Papers, TSLA; agricultural information, Cheatham Papers, TSLA. Cheatham eventually controlled approximately 200 acres, according to records in the Coffee County Register

of Deeds Office. On a farm very near the one where Cheatham lived, J. H. Brantley purchased a black stallion which became the foundation sire for a strain of Tennessee Walking Horses. The Cheathams no longer lived in Coffee County by this time, though; see Martinez, *Coffee Coutny*, 207–10.

10. Johnston to BFC, Nov. 14, 1867; Smith to Robertson, Aug. 13, 1867; BFC, Atlanta Military Journal; Frances A. Polk to BFC, Aug. 2, 1869; W. M. Polk to BFC, Sept. 25, 1874, all in Cheatham Papers, TSLA.

11. Alice C. H. Parker to author, March 1982.

12. Hamer, *Tennessee: A History*, 2:638; *Nashville Union and American*, Aug. 2, 1868.

13. Hamer, *Tennessee: A History*, 2:638; E. Merton Coulter, *William G. Brownlow: Fighting Parson of the Southern Highlands* (Chapel Hill, 1937), 358–62; John M. Lea to BFC, Aug. 3, 1868, Cheatham Papers, TSLA (quote).

14. David Ward Sanders, "Autobiography of Maj. D. W. Sanders," *CV* (Aug. 1910), 372.

15. Roller and Twyman, *Encyclopedia of Southern History*, 1196. During this period Cheatham apparently tried to exploit his fame by selling life insurance, a not uncommon venture for former Confederate generals. The endeavor was short-lived; see *Nashville City Directory* (Nashville, 1871), 107.

16. Roger L. Hart, *Redeemers, Bourbons, and Populists: Tennessee, 1870–1896* (Knoxville, 1975), 8–14.

17. Hart, *Redeemers*, 14–15; Hamer, *Tennessee: A History*, 2:678–79; *Nashville Union and American*, Sept. 14, 1872; "Montgomery," "Brigadier General Andrew Johnson," [1872] election pamphlet, TSLA; Graf and Haskins, *Papers of Andrew Johnson*, vol. 2, *1852–1857*, 321–22, 324–26; ibid., vol. 3, *1858–1860* (Knoxville, 1972), 268–69. The 1872 election pamphlet contains several items which detail the Congressional race from Cheatham's perspective. The first, cited above, is a series of allegations against Johnson and a condemnation of his independent candidacy. Montgomery is evidently a pseudonym for the author; although there is no was to be sure of his real identity, the writer may have been the editor of the *Nashville Union and American*, a pro-Cheatham newspaper. Two other items are in the pamphlet. One is an open letter from BFC to Thomas Lowe, Sept. 6, 1872, explaining the circumstances surrounding Cheatham's nomination and defending the convention which selected him as the Democratic candidate. The letter to Lowe also includes several BFC swipes at Johnson; in one, Cheatham asserts that he had labored all of his life but never felt compelled to boast of "the dust of the shop upon my garments," a campaign phrase apparently employed by Johnson. The final item in the election pamphlet is BFC's "Circular Address to the People of the State at Large," wherein Cheatham defended his military service in the Mexican and Civil Wars, outlined his reasons for seeking the Congressional seat, extolled the virtues of presidential candidate Horace Greeley, and asked for support at the polls.

18. Hamer, *Tennessee: A History*, 2:678–79; BFC to Thomas C. Lowe, Sept. 6, 1872, in 1872 election pamphlet, TSLA; Lloyd Paul Stryker, *Andrew Johnson: A Study in Courage* (New York, 1936), 831–32.

19. BFC to Anna Cheatham, Sept. 2, 1872, Cheatham Papers, TSLA; *Nashville Union and American*, Sept. 6–7, 1872.

20. *Nashville Republican Banner*, Sept. 28 and Oct. 15, 1872.

21. *Nashville Union and American*, Sept. 7, 1872 (first three quotes); Montgomery, "Brigadier General Andrew Johnson," ("anti-southern" reference); BFC to

Lowe, Sept. 6, 1872; Gen. B. F. Cheatham, "Address to the People of the State at Large". The last three sources are all in the 1872 election pamphlet, TSLA.

22. BFC to Anna Cheatham, Sept. 2, 1872 [and Sept. 1872] Cheatham Papers, TSLA.

23. *Nashville Union and American,* Sept. 17, 1872, (first quote) and Sept. 24, 1872 (second and third quotes); BFC to Lowe, Sept. 6, 1872, election pamphlet, TSLA; Hart, *Redeemers,* 16-17; BFC to Anna Cheatham, Oct. 16, 1872, Cheatham Papers, TSLA (last quote). The *Nashville Union and American* issues of September and October provide a pro-Cheatham list of campaign stops and speeches.

24. *Nashville Union and American,* Oct. 26, 1872.

25. *Nashville Union and Amerian,* Nov. 9, 1872.

26. Hart, *Redeemers,* 17; William F. Watkins to Elizabeth Cheatham, Feb. 25, 1873, Cheatham Papers, TSLA.

27. Warner, *Generals in Gray,* 19, 36, 326; Isham Harris to Bishop Quintard, Dec. 29, 1894, Quintard Papers, Duke.

28. Hart, *Redeemers,* 25.

29. *CMH: Tenn.* 304.

30. Warner, *Generals in Gray,* 210; *Nashville American,* Feb. 10, 1906; *Nashville Banner,* Feb. 11, 1906.

31. Hart, *Redeemers,* 24-25.

32. "Biennial Report of the Superintendent of Prisons, to the Fortieth General Assembly of the State of Tennessee, January 1, 1877," in *Appendix to the Journal of the House of Representatives, of the State of Tennessee* (Nashville, 1877), 322; "Message of Governor James D. Porter to the Forty-first General Assembly of the State of Tennessee," in *Appendix to the Journal of the House of Representatives of the State of Tennessee* (Nashville, 1879), 20-21; "Report of the Officers of the Penitentiary of the State of Tennessee to the Forty-first General Assembly, January 6, 1879," ibid., 6-7; Verdel Nicley, "History of the Tennessee Penitentiary, 1865-1890" (M. A. thesis, University of Tennessee, 1933), 24-25, 27-28, 30.

33. Robert, *Nashville City Guide Book,* 36-37; Nicley, "Tennessee Penitentiary," 82-83; Superintendent's Report, *1877 House Journal Appendix,* 321.

34. Nicley, "Tennessee Penitentiary," 66-68, 82-85; Governor's Message, *1879 House Journal Appendix,* 21-22.

35. Superintendent's Report, *1877 House Journal Appendix,* 321.

36. Ibid., 321-22; "Report of the Officers of the Penitentiary," *1879 House Journal Appendix,* 3. Cheatham's younger brother John was a department warden at the camp near the Battle Creek Mines; see correspondence between the two in Cheatham Papers, TSLA.

37. "Warden's Report" and "Physician's Report," both in *1877 House Journal Appendix,* 325, 384-88; [Dr.] Albrecht F. Stimmel to BFC, June 8, 1878, Cheatham Papers, TSLA.

38. "Message of Ja[mes]s D. Porter, Governor of Tennessee, to the Fortieth General Assembly of the State of Tennessee," in *1877 House Journal Appendix,* 10-11; Governor's Message, *1879 House Journal Appendix,* 21-22.

39. Porter's recommendation, *1879 House Journal Appendix,* 22-23, which repeats an earlier 1875 plea to have the prison removed to a different site; "Warden's Report," in *Appendix to the Journals of the Senate and House of Representatives of the Forty-Second General Assembly, State of Tennessee* (Nashville, 1881), 8-9; "Report of the Officers of the Penitentiary," *1879 House Journal Appendix,* 4-5.

40. "A Synopsis of the Tennessee Penal System," information courtesy of Associate Warden Robert B. Childress to author, Jan. 19, 1983; Nicley, "Tennessee Penitentiary," 15-17, 105-7. Tennessee abandoned the convict lease system in the late 1890s, in large part because of resistance from free coal miners who resented competing with the prisoners in their occupation. The state did continue using convicts for this purpose after purchasing several mines outright, but presumably this trend diminished after the opening of the new prison in the 1890s, with its increased capacity. Construction of a new penitentiary was a topic which aroused the eventual interest of citizens and public officials in Nashville, as well as the attention of several Tennessee governors. While these parties wrestled with the problem of what to do in terms of building a new facility, a group of Coffee County citizens petitioned in the early 1880s to have the state penitentiary located near Manchester, a request that Cheatham may have instigated when he returned to the area.

41. Governor's Message, *1879 House Journal Appendix*, 21; Head, *Sixteenth Tennessee*, 323 (quotes). The correspondence and other information relating to Cheatham's superintendency in the Cheatham Papers deals with issues such as returns, salaries, pardons, and the sale of some state quarry property formerly part of the penitentiary holdings. One of the more lively moments of Cheatham's term came when a Cincinnati newspaper attacked the manner in which the state's convict labor was managed. The resulting investigation is alluded to in Porter to BFC, Feb. 12, 1878, and [Dr.] B. P. Key to BFC, Mar. 8, 1878, both in Cheatham Papers, TSLA. Additional correspondence between Cheatham and Porter may be found in Papers of the Governors of Tennessee, TSLA; see particularly BFC to Porter, Dec. 18, 1875 and John A. Cheatham to Porter, [1878], for prison-related messages.

42. Stock certificates; Blanton and Fleming to BFC, June 15, 1878, Cheatham Papers, TSLA.

43. Warner, *Generals in Gray*, 31, 93, 143, 241; Purdue, *Pat Cleburne*, 435.

44. P. J. Maxwell to BFC, July 8, 1877, Cheatham Papers, TSLA.

45. Walthall to BFC, Mar. 17, 1876; BFC to Walthall, Mar. 1876; J. E. Johnston to BFC, June 13, 1874; J. B. Hood to BFC, Jan. 13, 1878; T. B. Roy to BFC, Oct. 15, 1881; BFC to Roy, n.d., all in Cheatham Papers, TSLA; Cheatham to Gen. M. J. Wright, Jan. 5, 1879, Eldridge Papers, Huntington Library.

46. Dodd, "Reminiscences of Hood's Tennessee Campaign," *SHSP* (1881), 518-24 (quote, 521); BFC, "The Lost Opportunity," *SHSP* (1881), 524-41; *Louisville Courier-Journal*, Dec. 4, 1881.

47. Sanders, "Autobiography," 372. Sanders's account of the Tennessee campaign may be found in various 1884-1885 issues of *Southern Bivouac*.

48. Clayton, *History of Davidson County*, 458-59, 461; Harllee, *Kinfolks*, 3:2484; BFC to Porter, Apr. 30, 1878, Governor's Papers, TSLA.

49. *Nashville Banner*, Oct. 8 and 9, 1883.

50. Hart, *Redeemers*, 19; Robert Jones, *Tennessee at the Crossroads: The State Debt Controversy, 1870-1883* (Knoxville, 1977), 4-5, 9-11 (hereafter cited as Jones, *State Debt*).

51. Jones, *State Debt*, 52; John Trotwood Moore and Austin P. Foster, *Tennessee: The Volunteer State, 1769-1923*, 4 vols. (Chicago, 1923), 2:558.

52. Jones, *State Debt*, 47-50, 52, 94; Hart, *Redeemers*, 30.

53. Jones, *State Debt*, 103, 114-15; Hart, *Redeemers*, 42-46.

54. Jones, *State Debt*, 119-22, 125; Hart, *Redeemers*, 52-54; undated, unidentified

newspaper clipping in Joseph H. Fussell Scrapbooks, Joseph H. Fussell Papers, TSLA.

55. *Manchester* (Tenn.) *Times,* Oct. 8, 1931, cited in *Coffee County Historical Quarterly* (1972), 21.

56. Newspaper clipping in Fussell Scrapbooks, Fussell Papers, TSLA.

57. Jones, *State Debt,* 134; Hart, *Redeemers,* 62, 67 (quote).

58. Hart, *Redeemers,* 62–63.

59. Jones, *State Debt,* 140. Bate, Harris, and others worked out a plan whereby the debt was reduced to just under $16 million. The state took out a $10 million loan in 1913 to retire the remaining amount; see Jones, *State Debt,* 147.

60. Appointment as postmaster, in Cheatham Papers, TSLA; F. L. Mather Publishing Co., *Historical and Illustrated Memento of the Nashville Postoffice Department* (Nashville, 1896), 9, 12–13; "Children of Major General B. F. Cheatham," *CV* (Dec. 1895), 381; Colleen Morse Elliott and Louise Armstrong Moxley, eds., *The Tennessee Civil War Veterans Questionnaires,* 5 vols. (Easley, S.C., 1985), 2:502.

61. *Louisville Courier-Journal,* Sept. 4, 1886; *Memphis Avalanche,* Sept. 4, 1886 (quote); *Nashville Weekly American,* Sept. 8, 1886. Cheatham apparently did not have a photograph taken of himself in his later years, but a sketch in the Sept. 5, 1886, issue of the *Nashville Daily American* reveals that he had aged a great deal since the 1860s and early 1870s. Heart disease is listed as the cause of Cheatham's death in the Interment Book, 1855–91, Mount Olivet Cemetery Records, TSLA.

62. Quintard Diary, Aug. 28 and 31, 1886, Quintard Papers, UNC: *Louisville Courier-Journal,* Sept. 5, 1886; *Memphis Avalanche,* Sept. 4 and 5, 1886; *Nashville Daily American,* Sept. 5 and 7, 1886; *Nashville Weekly American,* Sept. 8, 1886.

63. Cheatham's death was widely reported, including in the *New York Times.* The best source for accounts of the funeral and reminiscences are the Sept. 5–7, 1886, issues of the *Nashville Daily American.* See also the *Memphis Avalanche* for the same dates and the Quintard Papers, UNC. Besides the predictable attention paid to Cheatham's battlefield exploits, the prevailing theme among those who reminisced about him was that Cheatham was open, honest, simple, and unpretentious. As one mourner stated, Cheatham was "always Frank in name and frank in nature." *Nashville Daily American,* Sept. 5, 1886.

64. *Memphis Avalanche,* Sept. 7, 1886 (both quotes).

65. *Nashville Daily American,* Sept. 5, 1886.

66. *Nashville Daily American,* Sept. 5, 1886.

Epilogue

1. Cheatham's will, dated Aug. 21, 1886, on microfilm copy of Davidson County Wills and Inventories, TSLA; *Nashville Daily American,* Sept. 5, 6, and 7, 1886, Jan. 15, 1888; Mather Publishing, *Nashville Postoffice Department,* 9, 13.

2. *Nashville Daily American,* Jan. 15, 1888; Anna's will, dated Dec. 19, 1887, Davidson County Wills and Inventories, TSLA; Interment Book, Mount Olivet Cemetery Records, 187, TSLA; "Children of Major General B. F. Cheatham," 381.

3. [Benjamin Franklin Cheatham, Jr.], Draft of speech delivered July 15, 1932, at the dedication of Stones River NMP, Cheatham-Hodgson Papers, Univ.

of the South; B. F. Cheatham, Jr., "The Tennessee Battalion: 37th U.S. Volunteer Infantry, 1899–1901," Benjamin Franklin Cheatham, Jr., Papers, TSLA.

4. *The National Cyclopedia of American Biography*, 35:476–77; *Nashville Tennessean*, Dec. 3 and 5, 1944; unidentified newspaper clipping in the Name File Index, TSLA. The last item relates information on Cheatham's selection as superintendent of Stratford Hall.

5. *National Cyclopedia of American Biography*, 35:477; *Nashville Tennessean*, Dec. 3 and 5, 1944.

6. *Nashville Tennessean and the Nashville American*, Mar. 21, 1914.

7. *National Cyclopedia of American Biography*, 31:34–35 (quote); *Nashville Tennessean*, Sept. 10, 1942.

8. Virkus, *The Compendium of American Genealogy*, 5:263–64, 6:697; Virginia Cheatham Van Ness to author, Jan. 14, 1986; Stanley, F. Horn to Ezra Warner, Mar. 28, 1956, Warner Files, Chicago Historical Society; Manuscript Guides to Cheatham Papers, UNC and TSLA.

9. *Nashville Banner*, Nov. 22, 1906. Alice's tombstone erroneously lists her birth year as 1882, instead of the actual year, 1880.

10. Rev. M. B. DeWitt, "Some Memories and Facts," *CV* (July 1900), 299.

Bibliography

Primary Materials

MANUSCRIPTS

Alabama Department of Archives and History, Montgomery
   William J. Hardee Papers
Chicago Historical Society
   John C. Breckinridge Collection
   Charles W. Carr Letters
   A. P. Mason Collection
   Ezra Warner Correspondence and Research Files
Duke University, Durham, N.C.
   Braxton Bragg Papers
   Ellison Capers Papers
   Confederate States of America Archives:
      Army Miscellany
      Field Returns
      Officers' and Soldiers' Miscellaneous Letters
   Harry L. and Mary K. Dalton Collection
   Jefferson Davis Papers
   Col. Allen L. Fahnestock Diary
   John Euclid Magee Diary
   Eugene Marshall Papers
   Leonidas Polk Papers
   Charles Todd Quintard Papers
   M. J. Solomons Scrapbook
   William Henry Talbot Walker Papers
Filson Club Historical Society, Louisville, Ky.
   Patton Anderson Paper
   Josiah Stoddard Johnston Papers
The Houghton Library, Harvard University, Cambridge
   Frederick M. Dearborn Collection of Military and Political Americana
Henry E. Huntington Library, San Marino, Calif.
   Simon Bolivar Buckner Papers
   Civil War Papers
   James William Eldridge Papers
Kennesaw Mountain National Battlefield Park, Marietta, Ga.
   John W. Tuttle Diary
   Sgt. Major Lyman S. Widney Diary and Letters

Mississippi Department of Archives and History, Jackson
  Edward Cary Walthall Papers
The National Archives and Records Administration, Washington, D.C.
  First (Feild's) Tennessee Infantry File, Confederate States of America
  First Tennessee Infantry File, Mexican War
  General and Staff Officers File, CSA
  Third Tennessee Infantry File, Mexican War
  Ninth Tennessee Infantry File, CSA
  Nineteenth Tennessee Infantry File, CSA
  Thirty-eighth Tennessee Infantry File, CSA
Southern Historical Collection, University of North Carolina at Chapel Hill
  Samuel A. Agnew Diary
  Roy Black Papers
  Ellison Capers Papers
  Benjamin Franklin Cheatham Papers
  J. F. H. Claiborne Papers
  Major Joseph B. Cumming "Recollections"
  Gale-Polk Papers
  Daniel Chevilette Govan Papers
  James Iredell Hall Papers
  W. W. Mackall Letters
  Lafayette McLaws Papers
  Charles Todd Quintard Papers
  Edmund Kirby Smith Papers
  Marcus J. Wright Papers
The Historical Society of Pennsylvania, Philadelphia
  Ferdinand Julius Dreer Collection
  Simon Gratz Collection
The South Caroliniana Library, University of South Carolina, Columbia
  Richard Irvine Manning Letters
Archives of the University of the South, Sewanee, Tenn.
  Cheatham-Hodgson Papers
  Leonidas Polk Collection
Tennessee State Library and Archives, Nashville
  James Douglas Anderson Papers
  Campbell Brown-Richard Stoddert Ewell Papers
  Benjamin Franklin Cheatham Papers
  Joseph H. Fussell Papers
  William Henry Harder Diary
  Isham Green Harris Papers
  McLaughlin Family Papers
  Mount Olivet Cemetery Records
  Northcut Family Papers
  James D. Porter Papers
  Narcissa Saunders Photo Album
  Alfred Jefferson Vaughan Papers
  Confederate Collection:
      Carroll Henderson Clark Diary
      James Caswell Edenton Diary
      Thomas J. Firth Memoirs

W. D. Gale Letters
D. G. Godwin Letters
J. W. Harris Letters
John Johnston Reminiscences
Samuel Latta Letters
Michael Mauzy Diary
Military and Financial Board Records
Perry Franklin Morgan Diary
Joseph Myrick Letters
Van Buren Oldham Diary
Gideon Johnson Pillow Collection
W. M. Pollard Diary
James N. Rosser Diary
Joe Spence Diary, 1861–1862
Oliver P. Tucker Memoir
S. T. Williams Letter
Tennessee Historical Society Collection:
   1870 Constitutional Convention Members Collection
   Alfred Tyler Fielder Diary
   Miscellaneous Files, 1688–1951
Tennessee State Museum, Nashville
   J. T. Winfrey Letter
Barker Texas History Center, University of Texas at Austin
   Braxton Bragg Letters
Western Reserve Historical Society, Cleveland
   William P. Palmer Collection

NEWSPAPERS

Chattanooga Daily Rebel
Louisville Courier-Journal
Manchester (Tenn.) *Times*
Memphis Avalanche
Memphis Commercial Appeal
Mobile Advertiser and Register
Nashville Banner
Nashville Daily American
Nashville Daily Gazette
Nashville Daily Patriot
Nashville Patriot
Nashville Republican Banner
Nashville Tennessean
Nashville Union
Nashville Union and American
Nashville Weekly American
New York Times
Philadelphia Press
Philadelphia Weekly Times

BOOKS AND SELECTED DOCUMENTS

Bennett, L. G., and Wm. M. Haigh. *History of the Thirty-Sixth Regiment Illinois Volunteers.* Aurora Ill., 1876.

Buffum, Edward Gould. *Six Months in the Gold Mines: From a Journal of Three Years' Residence in Upper and Lower California 1847-8-9.* Philadelphia, 1850; reprint ed., Ann Arbor, 1966.

Carroll, John W. *Autobiography and Reminiscences by John W. Carroll.* Henderson, Tenn., n.d.

Cavanaugh, John. *Historical Sketch of the Obion Avalanche, Company H, Ninth Tennessee Infantry.* Union City, Tenn., 1922.

Christman, Enos. *One Man's Gold: The Letters and Journal of a Forty-Niner.* Ed. Florence M. Christman. New York, 1930.

Duke, Basil. *A History of Morgan's Cavalry.* New York, 1906; reprint ed., Blooming-ton, Ind., 1960.

Gordon, John B. *Reminiscences of the Civil War.* New York, 1904.

Head, Thomas A. *Campaigns and Battles of the Sixteenth Regiment, Tennessee Volunteers.* Nashville, 1885; reprint ed., McMinnville, Tenn., 1961.

Hedley, F. Y. *Marching through Georgia: Pen-Pictures of Every-Day Life.* Chicago, 1887.

Hood, John Bell. *Advance and Retreat: Personal Experiences in the United States and Con-federate States Armies.* New Orleans, 1880.

Johnston, Joseph E. *Narrative of Military Operations, Directed during the Late War be-tween the States.* New York, 1874.

LaBree, Ben, ed. *Camp-Fires of the Confederacy.* Louisville, 1898.

Lindsley, John Berrien, ed. *The Military Annals of Tennessee: Confederate.* Nashville, 1886.

McMurray, W. J. *History of the Twentieth Tennessee Regiment Volunteer Infantry, C.S.A.* Nashville, 1904.

Malone, Thomas H. *Memoir of Thomas H. Malone.* Nashville, 1928.

Manigault, Arthur Middleton. *A Carolinian Goes to War: The Civil War Narrative of Arthur Middleton Manigault.* Ed. R. Lockwood Tower. Columbia, S.C., 1983.

Mathes, J. Harvey. *The Old Guard in Gray.* Memphis, 1897.

Morgan, Dale, ed. *Three Years in California: William Perkins' Journal of Life at Sonora, 1849-1852.* Berkeley, 1964.

Morgan, Mrs. Irby. *How It Was: Four Years among the Rebels.* Nashville, 1892.

Olmstead, Charles H. *The Memoirs of Charles H. Olmstead.* Ed. Lilla M. Hawes, Savannah, 1964.

Porter, James D. *Confederate Military History: Tennessee.* Ed. Clement A. Evans. At-lanta, 1899.

Ratchford, J. W. *Some Reminiscences of Personal Incidents of the Civil War.* 1909; reprint ed., Austin, 1971.

Regulations for the Army of the Confederate States, 1864. Richmond, 1864.

Rennolds, Edwin H. *A History of the Henry County Commands Which Served in the Confederate States Army.* Jacksonville, 1904.

[Robertson, John Blount]. *Reminiscences of a Campaign in Mexico by a Member of "The Bloody First."* Nashville, 1849.

Schellenberger, John K. *The Battle of Spring Hill, Tennessee.* Cleveland, 1913.

Sherman, William T. *Memoirs of William T. Sherman.* 2 vols. New York, 1875.

Stevenson, Alexander F. *The Battle of Stone's River.* Boston, 1884.

Stout, L. H. *Reminiscences of General Braxton Bragg.* Hattiesburg, 1942.

Taylor, Richard. *Destruction and Reconstruction: Personal Experiences of the Late War.* New York, 1879.

Tennessee, State of. *Appendix to the Journal of the House of Representatives, of the State of Tennessee.* Nashville, 1877.

———. *Appendix to the Journal of the House of Representatives of the State of Tennessee.* Nashville, 1879.

———. *Appendix to the Journals of the Senate and House of Representatives of the Forty-second General Assembly, State of Tennessee.* Nashville, 1881.

Toney, Marcus B. *The Privations of a Private.* Nashville, 1905.

Vaughan, A[lfred] J[efferson]. *Personal Record of the Thirteenth Regiment, Tennessee Infantry.* Memphis, 1897.

The War of the Rebellion: A Compilation of the Official Records of the Union and Confederate Armies. 128 vols. Washington, D.C., 1880–1901.

Watkins, Sam R. *"Co. Aytch," Maury Grays, First Tennessee Regiment; or, A Side Show of the Big Show.* Chattanooga, 1900; reprint ed., Dayton, Ohio, 1982.

Wilson, James Harrison. *Under the Old Flag.* 2 vols. New York, 1912.

Worsham, Dr. W. J. *The Old Nineteenth Tennessee Regiment C.S.A.: June, 1861–April, 1865.* Knoxville, 1902.

Wright, Marcus J. *General Officers of the Confederate Army.* New York, 1911.

ARTICLES AND PERIODICALS

Alderson, William T., ed. "The Civil War Diary of Captain James Litton Cooper, September 30, 1861 to January, 1865." *Tennessee Historical Quarterly* (June 1956).

Blair, J. L. W. "The Fight at Dead Angle." *Confederate Veteran* (November, 1904).

Blair, W. L. "That Lightning Bug Fight." *Confederate Veteran* (September 1904).

Buck, Irving A. "Military View of the Battle of Franklin." *Confederate Veteran* (August 1909).

Carnes, W. W. "Chickamauga." *Southern Historical Society Papers* (1886).

Carothers, Dr. J. S. "That Silver Moon Banner." *Confederate Veteran* (August 1895).

Cheatham, B. F. "The Battle of Perryville." *Southern Bivouac* (April 1886).

———. "The Lost Opportunity at Spring Hill, Tenn.—General Cheatham's Reply to Hood." *Southern Historical Society Papers* (1881).

"Children of Major General B. F. Cheatham." *Confederate Veteran* (December 1895).

[Cunningham, Sumner A.]. "Cheatham's and Cleburne's Divisions." *Confederate Veteran* (February 1900).

———. "Gen. O. F. Strahl." *Confederate Veteran* (September 1896).

Dupree, J. G. "Reminiscences of Service with the First Mississippi Cavalry." *Publications of the Mississippi Historical Society* (1903).

DeWitt, Rev. M. B. "Some Memories and Facts." *Confederate Veteran* (July 1900).

Dodd, Capt. W. O. "Reminiscences of Hood's Tennessee Campaign." *Southern Historical Society Papers* (1881).

Dowd, Col. W. F. "Lookout Mountain and Missionary Ridge." *Southern Bivouac* (December 1885).

Eleazer, W. D. "Fight at Dead Angle, in Georgia." *Confederate Veteran* (July 1906).

Finlay, Luke. "Another Report on Hood's Campaign." *Confederate Veteran* (September 1907).

Gilbert, C[harles] C. "Bragg's Invasion of Kentucky." *Southern Bivouac* (December 1885).

Harmon, R. H. "Dead Angle." *Confederate Veteran* (May 1903).

Lee, Stephen D. "Johnson's Division in the Battle of Franklin." *Publications of the Mississippi Historical Society* (1903).

McFarland, Judge L. B. "Maney's Brigade at the Battle of Perryville." *Confederate Veteran* (December 1922).

"Maney's Brigade at Missionary Ridge." *Southern Bivouac* (March 1884).

Martin, Charles B. "Jackson's Brigade in Battle of Nashville." *Confederate Veteran* (January 1909).

Merrill, James M. "'Nothing to Eat but Raw Bacon': Letters from a War Correspondent, 1862." *Tennessee Historical Quarterly* (June 1958).

Miles, Dr. Charles W. "Col. Hume R. Feild." *Confederate Veteran* (September 1921).

Mitchell, Enoch, ed. "Letters of a Confederate Surgeon in the Army of Tennessee to His Wife." *Tennessee Historical Quarterly* (June 1946).

Nelson, H. K. "Tennessee, a Grave or a Free Home." *Confederate Veteran* (November 1907).

Pickett, William D. "Re-enlistments by the Confederates." *Confederate Veteran* (April 1902).

Pirtle, Alfred. "Donelson's Charge at Stone River." *Southern Bivouac* (May 1887).

Porter, James D. "Col. Mosby Prizes Tribute by Gov. Porter to Gen. Grant." *Confederate Veteran* (May 1910).

Quintard, Bishop C[harles] T[odd]. "B. F. Cheatham, Major General C.S.A.: A Tribute to His Memory by Bishop C. T. Quintard." *Southern Historical Society Papers* (1888).

Ridley, Bromfield L. "Camp Scenes around Dalton." *Confederate Veteran* (February 1902).

Robinson, Samuel. "Battle of Kennesaw Mountain." In *Annals of the Army of Tennessee and Early Western History.* Ed. Edwin L. Drake. (June 1878).

Roy, T. B. "General Hardee and the Military Operations around Atlanta." *Southern Historical Society Papers.* (1880).

Sanders, David Ward. "Autobiography of Major D. W. Sanders." *Confederate Veteran* (August 1910).

———. "Hood's Tennessee Campaign." *Southern Bivouac* (1884–85).

Seay, Samuel. "A Private at Stones River." *Southern Bivouac* (August 1885).

Simmons, P. B. "The Correction Cheerfully Made." *Confederate Veteran* (June 1893).

Smith, W. H. "Melanchton Smith's Battery." *Confederate Veteran* (November 1904).

Stevens, Tillman H. "'Other Side' in Battle of Franklin." *Confederate Veteran* (April 1903).

Wells, Col. E. T. "The Campaign and Battle of Chickamauga." *The United Service: A Monthly Review of Military and Naval Affairs,* new ser. (September 1896).

Young, J. P. "Hood's Failure at Spring Hill." *Confederate Veteran.* (January 1908).

Secondary Materials

BOOKS

Anderson, James Douglas. *Making the American Thoroughbred, Especially in Tennessee, 1800–1845.* Norwood Mass., 1916.

Andrews, J. Cutler. *The South Reports the Civil War.* Princeton, 1970.

Bauer, K. Jack. *The Mexican War, 1846–1848.* New York, 1974.

Biesanz, John, and Mavis Biesanz. *The People of Panama.* New York, 1955.

Bill, Alfred Hoyt. *Rehearsal for Conflict.* New York, 1947.

Bridges, Hal. *Lee's Maverick General: Daniel Harvey Hill.* New York, 1961.

Caldwell, [May Winston]. *Historical and Beautiful Country Homes near Nashville, Tennessee.* Nashville, 1911.

Cate, Wirt Armistead, ed. *Two Soldiers: The Campaign Diaries of Thomas J. Key, C.S.A., December 7, 1863–May 17, 1865, and Robert J. Campbell, U.S.A., January 1, 1864–July 21, 1864.* Chapel Hill, 1938.

Civil War Centennial Commission. *Tennesseans in the Civil War.* 2 vols. Nashville, 1964.

Clayton, W. W. *History of Davidson County, Tennessee.* Philadelphia, 1880; reprint ed., Nashville, 1971.

Connelly, Thomas L. *Army of the Heartland: The Army of Tennessee, 1861–1862.* Baton Rouge, 1967.

———. *Autumn of Glory: The Army of Tennessee, 1862–1865.* Baton Rouge, 1971.

———. *Civil War Tennessee: Battles and Leaders.* Knoxville, 1979.

Connelly, Thomas L., and Archer Jones. *The Politics of Command: Factions and Ideas in Confederate Strategy.* Baton Rouge, 1973.

Coulter, E. Merton. *William G. Brownlow: Fighting Parson of the Southern Highlands.* Chapel Hill, 1937.

Davis, William C. *Civil War Parks: The Story behind the Scenery.* Las Vegas, 1984.

Elliott, Colleen Morse, and Louise Armstrong Moxley, eds. *The Tennessee Civil War Veterans Questionnaires.* 5 vols. Easley, S. C., 1985.

[Garden Study Club of Nashville]. *History of Homes and Gardens in Tennessee.* Nashville, 1936.

Georgia Dept. of Natural Resources. *Georgia Civil War Markers.* Atlanta, 1982.

Govan, Gilbert E., and James W. Livingood. *A Different Valor: The Story of General Joseph E. Johnston, C.S.A.* Indianapolis, 1956.

Gower, Herschel, and Jack Allen, eds. *Pen and Sword: The Life and Journals of Randal W. McGavock.* Nashville, 1959.

Graf, LeRoy P., and Ralph W. Haskins, eds. *The Papers of Andrew Johnson.* 7 vols. to date. Knoxville, 1967–86.

Hafendorfer, Kenneth A. *Perryville: Battle for Kentucky.* Utica, Ky., 1981.

Hamer, Philip M., ed. *Tennessee: A History, 1673–1932.* 4 vols. New York, 1933.

Harllee, William Curry. *Kinfolks: A Genealogical and Biographical Record.* 3 vols. New Orleans, 1934–37.

Hart, Roger L. *Redeemers, Bourbons, and Populists: Tennessee, 1870–1896.* Knoxville, 1975.

Hattaway, Herman. *General Stephen D. Lee.* Jackson, Miss., 1976.

Hay, Thomas R. *Hood's Tennessee Campaign.* New York, 1929; reprint ed., Dayton, 1976.

Henry, Robert Selph. *"First with the Most" Forrest.* Indianapolis, 1944.

———. *The Story of the Mexican War.* New York, 1950; reprint ed., New York, 1961.

Holliday, J. S. *The World Rushed In: The California Gold Rush Experience.* New York, 1981.

Horn, Stanley F. *The Army of Tennessee: A Military History.* Indianapolis, 1941.

Hughes, Nathaniel C. *Liddell's Record.* Dayton, 1985.

Johnson, Robert Underwood, and Clarence Clough Buel, eds. *Battles and Leaders of the Civil War.* 4 vols. New York, 1887–88; reprint ed., New York, 1956.

Jones, Robert B. *Tennessee at the Crossroads: The State Debt Controversy, 1870–1883.* Knoxville, 1977.

Kane, Joseph Nathan. *The American Counties.* New York, 1960.

Kelley, Sarah Foster. *Children of Nashville . . . Lineages from James Robertson.* Nashville, 1973.

Kerksis, Sidney C., ed. *The Atlanta Papers.* Dayton, 1980.

Kurtz, Wilbur G. *The Atlanta Cyclorama of the Battle of Atlanta.* Atlanta, 1954; reprint ed., Atlanta, 1984.

[Lang, Herbert O.?]. *History of Tuolumne County.* San Francisco, 1882; reprint ed., Sonora, 1960.

Lavender, David. *California: Land of New Beginnings.* New York, 1972.

Lucas, Silas Emmett. *Goodspeed's History of Tennessee.* Nashville, 1887.

McBride, Robert M., and Dan M. Robison. *Biographical Directory of the Tennessee General Assembly.* Ed. Robert M. McBride. Vol. 1, 1796–1861. Nashville, 1975.

McCown, Mary Hardin, and Inez E. Burns. *Soldiers of the War of 1812 Buried in Tennessee.* Johnson City, Tenn., 1959.

McCullough, David. *The Path between the Seas: The Creation of the Panama Canal, 1870–1914.* New York, 1977.

McDonough, James Lee. *Chattanooga: A Death Grip on the Confederacy.* Knoxville, 1984.
———. *Shiloh: In Hell before Night.* Knoxville, 1977.
———. *Stones River: Bloody Winter in Tennessee.* Knoxville, 1980.

McDonough, James Lee, and Thomas L. Connelly. *Five Tragic Hours: The Battle of Franklin.* Knoxville, 1983.

McDonough, James Lee, and James Pickett Jones. *War So Terrible: Sherman and Atlanta.* New York, 1987.

McElroy, Joseph C. *Chickamauga: Record of the Ohio Chickamauga and Chattanooga National Park Commission.* Cincinnati, 1896.

McFeely, William S. *Grant: A Biography.* New York, 1981.

McMahan, Basil B. *Coffee County, Then and Now —1983.* Nashville, 1983.

McMurry, Richard M. *John Bell Hood and the War for Southern Independence.* Lexington, Ky., 1982.

McWhiney, Grady. *Braxton Bragg and Confederate Defeat.* Vol. 1, *Field Command.* New York, 1969.

Martin, V. Covert. *Stockton Album through the Years.* Stockton, 1959.

Martinez, Corrine. *Coffee County: From Arrowheads to Rockets.* Tullahoma, Tenn., 1969.

Matloff, Maurice, gen. ed. *American Military History.* Washington, D.C., 1969.

Moore, John Trotwood, and Austin P. Foster. *Tennessee: The Volunteer State, 1769–1923.* 4 vols. Chicago, 1923.

The National Cyclopedia of American Biography. 37 vols. New York, 1892–1951; reprint ed., Ann Arbor, 1967.

Nugent, Nell Marion. *Cavaliers and Pioneers: Abstracts of Virginia Land Patents and Grants.* 3 vols. Richmond, 1977–83.

Parks, Joseph H. *General Leonidas Polk C.S.A.: The Fighting Bishop.* Baton Rouge, 1962.

Polk, William M. *Leonidas Polk: Bishop and General.* 2 vols. New York, 1983.

Pollard, Edward A. *The Early Life, Campaigns, and Public Services of Robert E. Lee, with a Record of the Campaigns and Heroic Deeds of His Companions in Arms.* New York, 1871.
———. *Southern History of the War.* 2 vols. Richmond, 1862–63; reprint ed., Freeport, N.Y., 1969.

Purdue, Howell, and Elizabeth Purdue. *Pat Cleburne: Confederate General.* Hillsboro, Tex., 1973.

Robert, Charles Edwin, ed. *Nashville City Guide Book.* Nashville, 1880.

Roller, David C., and Robert W. Twyman, eds. *The Encylopedia of Southern History.* Baton Rouge, 1979.

Scaife, William R. *The Campaign for Atlanta.* Atlanta, 1985.

Seitz, Don Carlos. *Braxton Bragg: General of the Confederacy.* Columbia, S.C., 1924.

Sellers, Charles. *James K. Polk, Continentalist, 1843–1846.* Princeton, N. J., 1966.

Smith, Frank. *History of Maury County, Tennessee.* Columbia, Tenn., 1969.

Smith, Justin H. *The War with Mexico.* 2 vols. New York, 1919; reprint ed., Gloucestor, Mass., 1963.

Smith, Col. W. D. *Battle of Stone's River, Tennessee.* Washington, D.C., 1932.

Speer, William S. *Sketches of Prominent Tennesseans.* Nashville, 1888.

Starr, Kevin. *Americans and the California Dream, 1850-1915.* New York, 1973.

Stryker, Lloyd Paul. *Andrew Johnson: A Study in Courage.* New York, 1936.

Sword, Wiley. *Shiloh: Bloody April.* New York, 1974.

Tennessee Historical Commission. *Tennessee Historical Markers.* Nashville, 1980.

Tinkham, George Henry. *A History of Stockton.* San Francisco, 1880.

Twain, Mark. *Life on the Mississippi.* New York, 1883.

Virkus, Frederick Adams, ed. *The Compendium of American Geneology: The Standard Genealogical Encyclopedia of the First Families of America.* 7 vols. Chicago, 1925-42.

Warner, Ezra. *Generals in Gray: Lives of the Confederate Commanders.* Baton Rouge, 1959.

Warner, Ezra, and W. Buck Yearns. *Biographical Register of the Confederate Congress.* Baton Rouge, 1979.

Weaver, Herbert, and others, eds. *Correspondence of James K. Polk.* 6 vols. to date. Nashville, 1969-83.

West, Ray B., Jr. *Kingdom of the Saints: The Story of Brigham Young and the Mormons.* New York, 1957.

Wiley, Bell Irvin. *The Life of Johnny Reb: The Common Soldier of the Confederacy.* Indianapolis, 1943.

Williams, T. Harry, ed. *The History of American Wars: From Colonial Times to World War I.* New York, 1981.

Wooldridge, J[ohn], ed. *History of Nashville, Tennessee.* Nashville, 1890.

THESES AND DISSERTATIONS

Cunningham, O. Edward. "Shiloh and the Western Campaign of 1862." Ph.D. disseration, Louisiana State University, 1966.

Johnson, Timothy D. "Benjamin Franklin Cheatham: The Making of a Confederate General." Master's thesis, University of Alabama, 1982.

Losson, Christopher Thomas. "Command Disorder: Benjamin Franklin Cheatham and the Army of Tennessee, 1862-1865." Master's thesis, University of Mississippi, 1978.

Nicley, Verdel. "History of the Tennessee Penitentiary, 1865-1890." Master's thesis, University of Tennessee, 1933.

ARTICLES

Byram, George. "The Chronicle of the 656th." *Playboy* (March 1968).

Cornwell, Ilene J. "Devon Farm: Harpeth Landmark." *Tennessee Historical Quarterly* (Summer 1975).

Crawford, William Travis. "The Mystery of Spring Hill." *Civil War History* (June 1955).

Fakes, Turner J., Jr. "Memphis and the Mexican War." *West Tennessee Historical Society Papers* (1948). Hay, Thomas Robson. "Davis, Bragg, and Johnston in the Atlanta Campaign." *Georgia Historical Quarterly* (March 1924).

Jacobs, Dillard. "Outfitting the Provisional Force of Tennessee: A Report on New Source Materials." *Tennessee Historical Quarterly* (Fall 1983).

Johnson, Timothy D. "Benjamin Franklin Cheatham: The Early Years." *Tennessee Historical Quarterly* (Fall 1983).

Losson, Christopher. "Major-General Benjamin Franklin Cheatham and the Battle of Stone's River." *Tennessee Historical Quarterly* (Fall 1982).

McMurry, Richard M. "Confederate Morale in the Atlanta Campaign of 1864." *Georgia Historical Quarterly* (1970).

McNeill, William S. "A Survey of Confederate Soldier Morale during Sherman's Campaign through Georgia and the Carolinas." *Georgia Historical Quarterly* (1971).

McWhiney, Grady. "Controversy in Kentucky: Braxton Bragg's Campaign of 1862." *Civil War History* (March 1960).

Popowski, Howard J. "Clash at Dug Gap." *Civil War Times Illustrated* (June 1983).

Roth, David E. "The Mysteries of Spring Hill." *Blue & Gray Magazine* (November 1984).

Index

Adairsville, Ga., 146; fighting near, 146–48
Alabama troops: Thirty-first Infantry, 124–25
Allatoona, Ga., 149
Ampudia, Pedro de, 10–12
Anderson, Patton, 65, 73, 81, 91, 126, 127, 137
Anderson, Samuel R., 28, 254
Aspinwall, Colombia, 24–25
Atlanta, battle of, 176–82

Banning, Henry B., 161
Bardstown, Ky., 63, 97
Barnes, Clay, 224
Bate, William B., 143, 178, 189, 199, 200, 254, 259, 277; and Cleburne's emancipation proposal, 137; commands division at Franklin, 218–20, 233; and at Nashville, 236–38, 239; elected governor of Tennessee, 261, 276; at Spring Hill, 204–9, 216, 268; and state debt controversy, 273–76
Beauregard, P. G. T., 44, 45, 46, 51–52, 132, 201–2
Beech Grove, Tenn., 254
Bell, John, 254
Bell, Tyree H., 78
Belmont, battle of, 33, 35–38
Bentonville, battle of, 246
Blackie, Martha (BFC's sister), 97, 117
Blair, Frank, 180, 181
Bottom, Squire Henry, 73
Bowling Green, Ky., 62, 63
Bragg, Braxton, 44, 45, 121, 132, 142, 152, 197; antagonism toward BFC, 53, 55, 56, 90–91, 95–96, 130–31, 138, 141, 172, 173, 249–50; appearance, 53; background, 52–53; and BFC's soldiers, 57, 59, 75, 96–97, 99, 113–14, 117, 119, 141;

and Chickamauga campaign, 98–102, 109–11; and Cleburne's emancipation proposal, 137–39; and Jefferson Davis, 53, 55, 78, 94–95, 112–13, 115–16, 129–30, 172; death of, 267; and Kentucky campaign, 60–65, 71, 74–76; and Missionary Ridge, 129; opinion of Polk, 53, 55, 249; photo of, 54; quarrels with subordinates, 95, 96–97, 112–13, 115–19, 129–31; and removal of J. E. Johnston, 168–69, 170, 172; reorganizes Army of Tennessee, 118–19; resignation offer after Stones River, 93–94; resigns after Missionary Ridge, 129–31; and siege of Chattanooga, 119–21, 126; and Stones River, 79, 80, 87–89, 90–92
Bragg, Elise, 55–56, 61
Breckinridge, John C., 49, 50, 80, 88, 91, 93, 127, 133
Brown, Aaron, 8
Brown, John C., 122, 128, 181, 257; challenged by BFC for governorship, 258; elected governor of Tennessee, 258, 261; at Franklin, 218–19, 221, 223–25; at Nashville, 218–21, 225; photo of, 211; as Redeemer, 261, 262; replaces BFC as divisional commander, 198–99; at Spring Hill, 204–5, 207, 210–13; and state debt controversy, 273
Brownlow, William G., 252, 257–58, 259, 272–73
Buck, Frank, 67, 73
Buckner, Simon Bolivar, 65, 73, 102, 106, 115, 254
Buell, Don Carlos, 44, 63, 64, 79
Bullock, Robert, 233
Burnside, Ambrose, 99
Buzzard's Roost, Ga., 143

Cairo, Ill., 31, 32
Calhoun, Ga., 146
Camargo, Mexico, 10, 16
Cameron, Simon, 27
Camp Brown, 28, 29, 30, 31
Camp Cheatham, 29, 294–95 n.26
Campbell, John, 51
Campbell, William B., 9
Cantey, James, 144, 162
Cape Girardeau, Mo., 31
Capers, Ellison, 192, 210, 322 n.58, 61
Carnes, William W., 66, 74, 106
Carter, Fountain Branch, 223
Carter, John C., assumes command of
    Maney's brigade, 197; background,
    197–98; mortally wounded, 225, 323
    n.71; replaces Maney as divisional
    commander at Jonesboro, 190, 317–18
    n.62, 63
Carter, Tod, 223, 228
Carter's brigade (John C. Carter), at
    Franklin, 225; at Kennesaw Mountain,
    153; at Peachtree Creek, 175–76; and
    rear guard after Nashville, 241
Cavanaugh, John, 29, 31, 61–62, 245
Cave City, Ky., 62, 63
Carroll, John W., 67
Carroll, William H., 55
Cassville, Ga., 146, 148
Centre College (Danville, Ky.), 63, 64
Chapman, Louise (BFC's sister), 41, 140
Chattahoochee River, 168, 173, 174, 198,
    199
Chattanooga, Tenn., 60, 98, 99, 100, 101,
    111, 141, 142; Bragg's siege of, 119–21
Chattanooga Creek, 99, 122
Chattanooga Daily Rebel, 93, 160, 168, 170
Cheairs, Nathaniel, home of, near Spring
    Hill, 205, 206, 209
Cheatham, Alice (BFC's daughter), 267,
    283–84; photo of, 282
Cheatham, Anderson (BFC's grand-
    father), 2
Cheatham, Anna Bell Robertson (BFC's
    wife), ancestry, 254; appointed post-
    mistress of Nashville, 280; burial site,
    284; correspondence from BFC, 260–
    61; correspondence with Elizabeth
    Cheatham, 254–55, 256; death of, 280;
    motherhood and, 257, 260, 267; photo
    of, 255; wedding of, 254; with BFC in
    Coffee County, 254–56

Cheatham, Archer, 2
Cheatham, Benjamin Franklin: adminis-
    trative talents of, 58, 251; agricultural
    activities, 3, 26, 254, 256; alcohol and,
    38, 55, 89–91, 93, 95–96, 130, 140, 249;
    altercation with Forrest, 240; ambi-
    tions of, 18; ancestry, 1, 4; appearance,
    30; baptized, 254; at Belmont, 35–38;
    boyhood, 5; business endeavors, 7–8,
    20, 26–27, 267, 327 n.15; in California,
    20–22; at Camp Brown, 28–31; at
    Camp Cheatham, 29, 294–95 n.26;
    candidate for office, 25–26, 258–61; at
    Chickamauga, 102–7, 109–12; children
    of, 257, 260, 267, 280–84; and Cle-
    burne's emancipation proposal, 237–
    40; in Coffee County, 254–56; com-
    mands Hood's corps at Atlanta, 173–
    75, 180–82; commands Stewart's corps
    after Ezra Church, 184; Congressional
    campaign (1872), 258–61; and convict
    lease system, 262, 264–66; death of,
    277; declines civil service post, 261; de-
    clines diplomatic post, 25; defends ac-
    tions at Spring Hill, 212, 215, 217, 268–
    69; education of, 5, 7; at Franklin,
    218–27, 322 n.58; fraternizes with
    enemy at Kennesaw Mountain, 162–
    63; funeral of, xiii, 277–79; historical
    reputation of, xiv–xv, 1, 279, 284–85,
    287–88; as horseman, 3, 26–27; influ-
    enced by father, 3–4, 26–27, 92; at
    Kennesaw Mountain, 153–64; in Ken-
    tucky campaign, 60–72, 73–76; and
    "Lost Cause" mentality, 287; loyalty of
    troops to, 57–59, 117, 133, 135, 142–43,
    246, 251, 288; and lynching of Jim
    Hill, 21–22; marriage of, 254–55; in
    Mexican War, 8–19; at Missionary
    Ridge, 127–31; at Monterrey, 11–12, 14;
    at Nashville, battle of, 234–39; and
    Nashville Blues, 8–9, 14; in Nashville
    mayoral race, 25–26; at Perryville,
    photos of, ii, 13, 42, 164; as postmaster
    of Nashville, 276–77; and profanity,
    29, 103; promoted to corps command,
    196–97; rejoins army at Lookout
    Mountain, 125–26; relations with:
    Braxton Bragg, 53, 55–57, 94–97, 115,
    118, 130–31, 138, 174; Patrick Cleburne,
    139–40, 222–23, 318 n.6; Ulysses S.
    Grant, 38; Isham G. Harris, 27, 95;

John Bell Hood, 212–13, 215–17; 250, 268–69; Joseph E. Johnston, 132, 172; George Maney, 48; Leonidas Polk, 53, 116–17, 152; James D. Porter, 262, 269–70, 275–76; W. H. T. Walker, 137, 139; at Resaca, 145; resignation attempt, 116–18; at Rocky Face Ridge, 143; and secession, 27; at Shiloh, 45–52; as Sky Blue, 274–76; at Spring Hill, 203–5, 207–10, 212–13, 215–17, 268–69; and state debt controversy, 272–76; at Stones River, 80–92; superintendent of Tennessee State Prison system, 262, 264–67; threatened to resign from army, 95; with Union officers at Dalton, 200; wedding, 254

Cheatham, Benjamin Franklin, Jr. (BFC's son), 257, 272, 280–81; photo of, 282

Cheatham, Edward Saunders (BFC's cousin), 2, 289–90 n.3

Cheatham, Elizabeth Robertson (BFC's mother), 4–5, 23, 41, 93, 254, 272

Cheatham, Felix (BFC's brother), 92–93, 260, 277

Cheatham, John (BFC's brother), 16, 328 n.36

Cheatham, Joseph Johnston (BFC's son), 260, 283; photo of, 282

Cheatham, Leonard Pope (BFC's father), background, 2–4; business activities, 5–7; death of, 92, 305 n.50; influence on BFC, 3–4, 26–27, 92; as postmaster of Nashville, 8; sale of Westover, 23

Cheatham, Leonora (BFC's sister), 92

Cheatham, Medora (BFC's daughter), 267, 283; photo of, 282

Cheatham, Medora Charlotte (BFC's sister), 2, 7

Cheatham, Patton Robertson (BFC's son), 260, 282, 283, 284; photo of, 282

Cheatham, Richard (BFC's great-uncle), 2

Cheatham, Richard B. (BFC's cousin), 2, 41

Cheatham, Samuella (BFC's sister), 5

Cheatham, Thomas (BFC's paternal ancestor), 2

Cheatham Bivouac, 285, 286, 287

Cheatham Hill (Kennesaw Mountain, Ga.), 156, 165

Cheatham's division: Bragg's hostility towards, 141; John C. Brown in command of, 198–99, 204–15 passim; John C. Carter in command of, 190; casualties of, 73, 89, 112, 125, 128, 150–51; 160, 183, 227–28; 247; 297–98 n.32; deserters from, 188; engagements fought at: Adairsville, 146–48; Atlanta, 178–80; Chickamauga, 102–12; Franklin, 218–21, 223–28, 230–31; Jonesboro, 189–93; Kennesaw Mountain, 153–62; Lookout Mountain, 121–25; Missionary Ridge, 126–29; Nashville, 232, 234–38; New Hope Church, 149–51; Peachtree Creek, 175–76; Perryville, 67–74; Resaca, 144–46; Rocky Face Ridge, 143; Shiloh, 45–52, 297–98 n.32; Spring Hill, 204–7, 209–10, 212; Stones River, 80–89; John K. Jackson in command of, 121–25; Mark Lowrey in command of, 236–38; George Maney in command of, 173, 178–80, 189–91; rapport with BFC, xvi, 57–59, 117, 133, 135, 142–43, 246, 251–52, 288; reorganized by Bragg, 118–19; reputation of, 161, 180, 252; reunited by Johnston, 133, 142–43; rivalry with Cleburne's division, 196–97, 221–22, 322–23 n.65; sentiment towards Braxton Bragg, 59, 75, 96–97, 99, 113, 115, 117, 119, 249–50; sentiment towards John Bell Hood, 171, 173, 187, 230–31, 241, 250; sentiment towards Joseph E. Johnston, 135, 170–72; sentiment towards Leonidas Polk, 113, 117, 119, 151–52; in snowball battle at Dalton, 136–37; surrenders in North Carolina, 248

Cheney, Hampton J., 276

Chickamauga, battle of, 102–12

Chickamauga Creek, 99, 101, 133

Clayton, Henry D., 181

Cleburne, Patrick C., xv, 76, 115, 152, 199, 200, 242, 267, 268; BFC and, 139–40, 196–97, 223, 318 n.6; at Chickamauga, 107, 109, 110; death of, 223; and emancipation proposal, 137–40; at Franklin, 218–19, 221–24; historical reputation of, xv, 196–97, 318 n.6; at Jonesboro, 189–90, 193, 317 n.61; at Kennesaw Mountain, 155; at Missionary Ridge, 126; at New Hope Church, 149–51; photo of, 222; recommended that Bragg resign, 93; at Spring Hill, 204–5, 207, 209, 216, 217; at Stones River, 80–81, 91

Cleburn's division: at Atlanta, 176–82; at

Cleburne's division (*continued*)
Chickamauga, 107, 109, 110; commanded by James A. Smith, 233; at Franklin, 218-19, 221-23, 224, 227; at Jonesboro, 189, 192; at Kennesaw Mountain, 153, 155, 157, 161; at Missionary Ridge, 126; at Nashville, 237; at New Hope Church, 149-51; at Peachtree Creek, 175; reaction after capturing black troops, 200; rivalry with BFC's division, 196-97, 221-22, 322-23 n.65; at Spring Hill, 203-5; at Stones River, 80-81
Cleveland, Grover, 276
Coffee County, Tenn., 254, 256, 258
Coltart, J. G., 81, 82
Columbia, Tenn., 203, 204, 205
Columbus, Ky., 32-33, 35, 40, 151
Colyar, Arthur S., 277
Confederate Veteran, 285
Connelly, Thomas L., xiv, 32, 151
Convict lease system, 262, 264-65
Cooper, Samuel, 55, 118, 132
Corinth, Miss., 43, 44, 45, 52, 268
Crittenden, George, 55
Crittenden, Thomas L., 63, 79, 99, 100, 101, 110, 121
Cross, Nathaniel, 7
Cumberland, Army of the (U.S.A), 141, 143, 174
Cumberland River, 4, 6, 28, 33, 41, 265
Cumming, Albert, 24

Dalton, Ga., 135, 141, 143, 170, 172; Union garrison at surrenders, 200
Davis, Jefferson (C.S.A. president), 30, 118, 252, 284, 287 and P. G. T. Beauregard, 52, 201; and Braxton Bragg, 53, 55, 94-95, 112-13, 115, 116, 129-30, 172; and BFC's promotion to major-general, 41-43; and Cleburne's proposal, 137, 138; inspection tours of, 78, 115-16, 120, 195-96, 199; and Joseph E. Johnston, 132, 168-72, 195-96; and Mississippians at Monterrey, 10, 11, 14; and Leonidas Polk, 53, 112
Davis, Jefferson C. (U.S.A. general), 155, 160
Dawson, John W., 145
Dead Angle (Kennesaw Mountain, Ga.), 158-60, 165
Deas, Zachariah, 48, 82

Demopolis, Ala., 140
DeWitt, M. B., 288
Dodd, W. O., 268
Donelson, Daniel, 65; brigade engaged at Perryville, 66-67, 70-71, 73; and at Stones River, 87, 89
Donelson, John, 109
Dowd, William F., 122-23
Duck River, 203, 240
Dug Gap, Ga., 143, 144
Dyer, Beverly L., 166

Etowah River, 149, 200
Ewing, Charles, 147
Ezra Church, battle of, 184

Feild, Hume R., 83, 89, 146-47, 148, 154, 160, 241, 242, 269, 272
Fielder, Alfred Tyler, 79, 99, 142, 150, 168, 171, 176, 178, 243, 247, 295-96 n.39, 317 n.62; and Belmont, 33, 35-37; photo of, 34; reaction to Polk's death, 151-52
Florence, Ala., 203
Flournoy, William C., 147
Foote, Henry S., 56, 93
Forrest, Nathan Bedford, xiv, 106, 202, 218, 232, 244, 257, 265, 267; altercation with BFC, 240; at Chickamauga, 102, 107, 111; and role in Ku Klux Klan, 257; quarrels with Bragg, 116; and retreat from Nashville, 240-42; at Shiloh, 48-49; and Spring Hill, 203, 204, 207
Fort Donelson, 41, 43
Fort Henry, 41, 43
Foster, Robert C., 9
Frankfort, Ky., 63, 64
Franklin, battle of, 218-28, 230-31
French, Samuel G., 269
Fussell, Joseph H., 274-75, 276

Gale, W. D., 131
Georgia troops: First Infantry, 112; Fifth Infantry, 112; Forty-first Infantry, 60, 67, 73
Gettysburg, battle of, 99
Gilbert, Charles C., 63, 64, 300 n.17
Gist, States Rights, 133, 184, 197, 198; brigade of, at Jonesboro: 190, 192; and at Franklin, 219, 225, 227; death of, 225
Glasgow, Ky., 62
Gordon, George W., 136-37, 162, 197, 198;

brigade commander at Franklin, 224–25

Govan, Daniel C., 192

Granbury, Hiram, 224

Grant, Ulysses S., 41, 234; at Belmont, 33, 35–39; at Chattanooga, 121, 127; BFC and, 38–39, 249; offered BFC government post, 261; promoted to command of all Union forces, 141; at Shiloh, 44, 50

Gwin, William M., 21

Hall, James Iredell, 51, 63–64, 133, 143, 171, 230, 295 n.27

Hamner, Hugh, 61, 73

Hampton, Henry, 246

Hardee, William J., 78, 117, 130, 140, 141, 148, 151, 153, 168, 180; assists BFC at New Hope Church, 149; at Atlanta, 176–78, 179, 181–82; background of, 45; blamed by Hood for failure at Atlanta, 195; and Cleburne's emancipation proposal, 137, 139; declines army command, 132; at Jonesboro, 189, 190, 192–93; in Kentucky campaign, 62, 64, 76; at Missionary Ridge, 129, 131; in North Carolina, 246, 248; passed over for army command, 173; at Peachtree Creek, 174–75; praises BFC, 131; recommended that Bragg resign, 93–94; recommends BFC for temporary corps command, 173; relieved from duty with Army of Tennessee, 196; at Stones River, 80, 89

Harding House (Stones River), 82, 83, 85, 89

Harney, William S., 14–15

Harper, William, 48

Harris, Isham G., 43, 56, 76, 111, 275; and BFC-Bragg animosity, 95; criticized by Andrew Johnson, 259; elected to U.S. Senate, 261; and Provisional Army of Tennessee, 28, 30; rejects Lincoln's call for troops, 27; and Spring Hill, 212, 213, 215, 268; and state debt controversy, 273–76

Harris, John W., 113–14, 116, 120, 151

Harrodsburg, Ky., 63, 64

Hart, Roger, 275

Hawes, James M., 55

Hawes, Richard, 63

Hawkins, Alvin, 273, 276

Heath, Jim, 62

Henry, Gustavus A., 41–43, 56, 93

Hickman, Ky., 32, 50

Hill, Daniel H., 98, 102, 110, 115, 116, 117

Hindman, Thomas, 101, 112, 113, 137, 139, 162–63

Hodgson, Telfair, 283

Hoke, Robert, 248

Hood, John Bell, xv, 103, 141, 145, 146, 148–49, 150, 152, 153, 184, 189, 192, 197, 199–203; and Atlanta, battle of, 176–77, 180, 181–82; background of, 173; criticized by BFC's troops, 171, 173, 186–87, 230–31, 241, 250; death of, 267; enmity towards BFC, 214–15, 250; evacuates Atlanta, 193–94; and Franklin, 217–18, 223, 227, 230–31; given command of Army of Tennessee, 169; joins Army of Tennessee, 141; and Nashville, 232–33, 234, 238; and Peachtree Creek, 174–75; photo of, 214; quarrels with Hardee, 195–96; resigns as army commander, 243; retreats from Tennessee, 240–41; and Spring Hill, 203–5, 207–10, 212–13, 215–17, 250, 268–69; target of Joseph E. Johnston's ire, 1, 256; and Wheeler's raid, 188

Hooker, Joseph, 121, 122, 123, 126, 152

Horn, Stanley F., xiv

Hornets' Nest (Shiloh), 46–47, 49, 87

Howard, Oliver Otis, 117

Hoxton, Llewellyn, 153

Hundley, Daniel R., 124, 125

Hurlbut, Stephen, 47

Illinois troops: Twenty-seventh Infantry, 159; Seventy-ninth Infantry, 107

Irby, Henry C., 142

Jackson, Henry Rootes, 233, 239

Jackson, James S., 67, 69, 70

Jackson, John K., brigade at Chickamauga, 103–4, 107, 110, 117, 119; commands BFC's division at Lookout Mountain, 124–25; criticized by subordinates, 124; at Missionary Ridge, 126–27

Jackson, Thomas J. "Stonewall," 124, 284, 287

Jackson, W. H., 208

James, R. Fred, 83, 303 n.21

Johnson, Abda, 181

Johnson, Andrew, 93, 253, 258–61, 272, 327 n.17
Johnson, Bushrod Rust, 43, 44, 46, 110
Johnson, Edward, 208, 226
Johnson, George W., 63
Johnston, Albert Sidney, xv, 40, 41, 44, 45, 49, 51
Johnston, Joseph E., xv, 76, 139, 140, 173, 174, 187, 197, 244, 269; appointed commander of Army of Tennessee, 132; in Atlanta campaign, 144–45, 148–49, 150–51, 152–53, 160, 163, 168; BFC's opinion of, 132, 135, 172; and BFC's troops, 135, 170–72; corresponds with BFC, 1, 256; at Dalton, 141–43; inspection tour of Bragg's army, 95; in North Carolina, 245–46; photo of, 134; relations with Jefferson Davis, 1, 132; relations with John Bell Hood, 1, 256; removed from command, 169–72, 195; restores BFC's division, 133, 135; surrenders to Sherman, 248
Jordan, Thomas, 46

Kennesaw Mountain, Ga., 152; battle of, 152–65
Kentucky troops: Seventh Infantry, 47, 50
King, Thomas, 109
Kingston, Ga., 146, 148
Ketcham, Thomas E., 20
Ku Klux Klan, 257

La Fayette, Ga., 101, 201
Lane, Joseph, 17–18
Latta, Samuel, 35, 36, 37
Lee, Robert E., 99, 112, 132, 284, 287
Lee, Stephen D., 182, 184, 186, 187, 189, 190, 196, 200, 202, 203
Leggett, Mortimer, 180
U.S.S. Lexington, 50, 295 n.35
Liddell, St. John Richardson, 71, 75, 113, 115, 118, 130, 317 n.63
Life on the Mississippi, 37
Lincoln, Abraham, 79
Longstreet, James, 102, 110, 111, 118, 121, 126, 129; opposes Bragg, 112–13, 115, 116
Lookout Creek, 122, 123
Lookout Mountain, 99, 101, 126, 127, 133; battle of, 122–26
Loomis, J. Q., 80, 81, 82, 83
Loring, William W., 152, 153, 318 n.7
"Lost Cause," 285, 287

Louisville, Ky., 61, 62, 63, 69; BFC travels to, 268–69
Louisville Courier-Journal, 268–69
Lowrey, Mark, 178, 189, 236–37, 238

McCook, Alexander, 63, 65, 71, 73, 79, 80, 85, 92, 121
McCook, Daniel, 155, 157
McCown, John P., 55, 76, 80–81, 90, 91
McCullough, James, 190
McDaniel, Charles, 73
McDonough, James Lee, 126
McEwen, John A., 25–26
Mackall, William W., 113
McLemore's Cove, 101, 112
McMurry, James A., 83
McMurry, L. P., 78
McMurry, Richard M., 169, 196
McPherson, James M., 141, 144, 148, 174, 175, 176, 177, 178, 180, 182
Madellin, Mexico, 15
Magee, John E., 60, 99, 115, 116
Magevney, Michael, 179
Malone, Thomas, 68, 69
Maney, George E., 77, 79, 145, 200, 277; background of, 66; commands BFC's division: at Atlanta, 173, 176–80; at Jonesboro, 189–90; at Peachtree Creek, 175; during truce at Kennesaw Mountain, 162, 313 n.76; in Kentucky campaign, 65–70; photo of, 191; postwar activities, 257, 262; at regimental reunion, 272; relinquished divisional command, 190, 192, 317 n.62, 63; at Resaca, 145–46; at Shiloh, 48–49
Maney's brigade, 168; deserters from, 188; engagements fought at: Atlanta, 177; Chickamauga, 104–5, 106–7, 111; Jonesboro, 189; Kennesaw Mountain, 153–54; New Hope Church, 149; Peachtree Creek, 175; Perryville, 67–70; Resaca, 145–46; placed under John C. Carter's command, 197; transferred to W. H. T. Walker's division, 119
Manigault, Arthur M., 80, 81, 82, 181
Marietta, Ga., 152, 166
Marsh, John Henry, 183, 228
Mason, A. P., 208
Mauzy, Michael, 76, 77
Maynard, Horace, 259, 260, 261
Memphis, Tenn., 17, 19, 31, 260, 264, 267

Meridian, Miss., 140, 143
Mill Creek Gap, Ga., 143
Missionary Ridge, 99, 101, 111, 133; battle of, 126–29
Mississippi, Army of the (C.S.A.), 53
Mississippi River, 32, 151
Mississippi troops: First Cavalry, 49; Twenty-fourth Infantry, 122–23
Mitchell, J. G., 155, 157
Monterrey, Mexico, battle of, 10–12, 14
Moore, John, 119, 125; at Lookout Mountain, 122, 123–24, 125; at Missionary Ridge, 127–28
Moore, William L., 87
Morgan, John Hunt, 78
Mount Olivet Cemetery (Nashville), xiii, 278–79, 284, 287
Munfordville, Ky., 61, 62, 63
Murfreesboro, Manchester and Winchester Turnpike, 267
Murfreesboro, Tenn., 77–78, 79, 92, 93, 96

Nashville, Tenn., 4, 7, 16, 17, 19, 23, 25, 26, 27, 28, 57, 78, 92–93, 203, 254, 258, 264–65, 272, 276–78, 280–87 passim; battle of, 232–39, 241; Elizabeth Cheatham remarks on Union occupation of, 92; surrendered to Union forces, 41
Nashville Blues, 8–9, 14
Nashville Centennial, 272
Nashville Convention, 3
Nashville Daily American, 277
Nashville Race Track, 27, 294 n.21
Nashville Union and American, 254
New Hope Church, battle of, 149–51
New Madrid, Mo., 31, 32
Noah, Tenn., 254

Ohio, Army of the (U.S.A.), 141, 148, 174
Ohio Troops: 121st Infantry, 161
Oldham, Van Buren, 101, 116–17, 119, 136, 146, 147–48, 168, 171–72, 186–87, 305 n.63, 317 n.62
Olmstead, Charles, 245
Oostanaula River, 144, 146
Opdycke, Emerson, 223–25

Palmetto, Ga., 194, 195, 199, 201
Parsons, Charles C., 67–70
Patterson, John, 73
Peachtree Creek, battle of, 174–76

Pemberton, John C., 76
Pennsylvania troops: Seventh-seventh Infantry, 107, 109
Perryville, battle of, 66–73, 97
Peters, Jessie Helen, 212, 321 n.45
Pettus, Edmund P., 122, 124, 125
Pigeon Mountain, 99, 101
Pillow, Gideon, 28, 31, 35, 40, 41, 56, 257, 267
Pine Mountain, Ga., 151, 152
Polk, James K., 2–3, 8, 14
Polk, Leonidas, xv, 31–33, 38, 44, 78, 256, 310 n.16; at Belmont, 33, 35–36, 37; Braxton Bragg and, 53, 55, 76, 94, 96–97, 112–13, 115, 139, 249–50; BFC and, 53, 116–17, 152, 249–50; at Chickamauga, 103, 110–11; and Jefferson Davis, 40, 53, 112–13, 115; corps in northern Georgia, 144, 146, 148–49; death of, 151–52; in Kentucky campaign, 63, 65, 71, 74, 76, 96–97; photo of, 114; and Gideon Pillow, 40–41; reinforces J. E. Johnston, 144; requests BFC's division, 140–41; resignation refused, 40; at Shiloh, 45, 50; at Stones River, 80–81, 88, 90, 91, 92
Pollard, William M., 218
Port Hudson, La., loss of, 99
Porter, George, 189, 190
Porter, James D., xiv, 120, 296 n.47; anti-Bragg comment, 119; as author, xvii, 269; elected governor of Tennessee, 262; and Franklin, 219, 228, 230, 322 n.58; and Nashville Centennial, 262; opposes convict leasing, 265; photo of, 263; and Polk's death, 151; praises BFC as prison superintendent, 266–67; railroad pass given to BFC, photo of, 270; as Sky Blue, 274–76; and Spring Hill controversy, 209–10, 212, 215, 268; and state debt controversy, 273–76; urges construction of new penitentiary, 265
Prentiss, Benjamin, 47, 49
Puckett, J. T., 228
Puebla, Mexico, 17
Putnam, S. M., 11, 14

Quintard, Charles Todd, 90, 183, 272, 277; baptizes BFC, 254; officiates at BFC's funeral, 278; and at BFC's wedding, 254; photo of, 229; rues losses at Franklin, 228; and Spring Hill contro-

Quintard, Charles Todd (*continued*)
versy, 213, in Tennessee campaign, 232,
241
Quitman, John A., 10-11, 14

Raccoon Mountain, 99
Rains, James E., 90, 304 n.36
Ready, Martha, 78
Religious revivals, in army, 135-36
Resaca, Ga., battle of, 144-45, 146, 150
reunion, of First Tennessee Infantry
Regiment, 272; photo of ribbon from,
271
Reynolds, Daniel H., 198
Rhodes, William, 67, 73
Rice, Horace, 163
Riggs, Samuel, 7
Ritchey, James Brown, 247
Robertson, Abbott Lawrence (BFC's
brother-in-law), 254, 326 n.5
Robertson, Abner Baldwin (BFC's father-
in-law), 254, 267, 276
Robertson, Charlotte (BFC's maternal
great-grandmother), 4
Robertson, Ciddy (BFC's maternal grand-
mother), 5
Robertson, Harriet Bell (BFC's mother-
in-law), 254
Robertson, Hattie (BFC's sister-in-law),
280, 283, 284
Robertson, James D. (BFC's maternal
great-grandfather), 4-5, 270
Robertson, Jonathan (BFC's maternal
grandfather), 4-5
Robinson, Samuel, 142-43
Rocky Face Ridge, Ga., 143, 144, 150, 183
Rogers, William J., 79, 90, 321 n.45
Rosecrans, William S., 79, 98-100, 110-11,
121
Ross, L. S., 208
Rosser, James, 35
Rucker, Jim, 61, 73

Salisbury, N.C., 246, 248
Sanders, David Ward, 269
Savage, John, 66
Schofield, John M., 141, 148, 174, 175, 201,
202-5, 207, 212, 215-16
Scogin's Georgia Battery, 106
Scott, Winfield, 15-16
Seddon, James A., 96, 118, 308 n.40
Senter, DeWitt D., 258

Shelbyville, Tenn., 92, 96, 98
Sheridan, Philip, 65, 81-83, 85
Sherman, William T., 43, 121, 126, 141, 199,
200, 245, 246; in Atlanta campaign,
141-53 passim, 160, 173-75, 181, 184, 186,
188, 193; begins march to the sea, 201;
Johnston surrenders to, 248; quoted,
251
Shiloh, battle of, 45-52
Shy, William, 236; position (Shy's Hill) at
Nashville, 236-38
Simmons, P. B., 208
Sky Blues, 274-76
Smith, Edmund Kirby, 61, 63, 74-75, 76,
93
Smith, James A., 233, 237
Smith, Melancthon, at Atlanta, 186; and
Belmont, 35; corresponds with BFC,
256, 310 n.10; at Dalton, 135, 137; at
Kennesaw Mountain, 157, 160, 162, 312
n.61; at Perryville, 74; at Shiloh, 46
Smith, Preston, 44, 75, 81, 89, 166; bri-
gade of, at Chickamauga, 104, 105,
107; death of, 107, 109; in Kentucky
campaign, 301 n.39; photo of, 108
Smith, Thomas Benton, 233, 239
Smith, Zack, 225
Snake Creek Gap, Ga., 144
snowball battle (Dalton, Ga.), 136-37, 141
Sonora, Calif., lynching at, 21-22
South, University of the, 281, 283
Southern Bivouac, 71, 300 n.17
Southern Historical Society Papers, 268
Spence, Joe, 30
Spring Hill, Tenn., action near, 203-10,
212-13, 215-17, 268-69
Stanford, Thomas, 66, 105
Stanley, David, 188, 203, 205, 210, 215, 216
Stanton, Sidney, 104, 145
state debt controversy, 272-76
Steedman, James B., 234, 236
Stephens, William H., 43, 46, 48
Stevenson, Carter L., 122, 125, 137, 143, 181
Stewart, Alexander P., 143, 145, 182, 189,
196, 202; background of, 65; brigade
of: at Perryville, 65-66, 70-71, 73; and
Stones River, 85; corps of: at Frank-
lin, 219, 226; at Nashville, 234, 236,
238; at Peachtree Creek, 174, 175; cor-
responds with BFC, 253, 268; division
of: at Chickamauga, 107; and Mill
Creek Gap, 143; opposes Cleburne's

proposal, 137; photo of, 185; quoted, 172; and Spring Hill controversy, 207, 212, 215, 268; West Point education and, 250; wounded at Ezra Church, 184

Stockton, Calif., 20, 21, 22

Stones River, battle of, 79–92

Strahl, Otho, 153, 198, 225–26

Strahl's brigade, 144, 151, 183, 228; in Chickamauga campaign, 101, 103, 104–5; engagements fought at: Franklin, 225–26, Kennesaw Mountain, 153; New Hope Church, 149; Peachtree Creek, 175; near Resaca, 144; during retreat from Nashville, 241

Taylor, Richard, 195, 201, 243

Taylor, Zachary, 10–12, 14

Tennessee, Army of (C.S.A.), xiii–xv, 1, 76, 112, 118, 125, 131, 132, 141, 142, 143, 146, 169, 173, 189, 193, 196, 210, 218, 228, 244, 247, 249

Tennessee Army of the (U.S.A.), 141, 144, 174

Tennessee River, 33, 41, 43, 45, 50, 76, 99, 100, 121, 122, 201, 242

Tennessee State Penitentiary, 262, 265–66

Tennessee troops: Infantry regiments: First, 48, 49, 67, 72, 73, 83, 85, 88, 142, 152, 155, 158, 160, 172, 195, 246, 271, 272; photos related to, 72, 158, 271; First and Twenty-seventh (consolidated), 78, 146, 153, 154, 159; Fourth, 83, 144, 228; Fifth, 144, 145, 151, 171, 194, 244, 246, 248; Sixth, 47, 67, 135, 150, 160, 180, 189, 224; Sixth and Ninth (consolidated), 142, 159; Eighth, 66, 87, 288; Ninth, 29, 47, 49, 50, 61–62, 67, 73, 75, 116, 133, 142, 145, 147, 159, 171, 186, 230, 238, 245, 246; Eleventh, 155, 160, 162, 189, 221; Twelfth, 33, 34, 35, 78, 79, 85, 109, 113, 142, 150, 179, 243, 247; Twelfth and Forty-seventh (consolidated), 78, 176; Thirteenth, 35, 36, 75, 77, 78, 79, 109, 166; Thirteenth and One Hundred Fifty-fourth (consolidated), 144; Fifteenth, 66; Sixteenth, 66, 73, 76, 77, 87, 230, 248; Nineteenth, 49, 112, 140, 183, 225, 238, 241; Twentieth, 236; Twenty-seventh, 67, 69, 73, 202, 230; Twenty-eighth, 104, 145; Thirty-first, 73; Thirty-eighth, 66, 73, 197; Fifty-first, 66; Fifty-first

and Fifty-second (consolidated), 112; One Hundred Fifty-fourth, 44, 79, 109, 179, 246

Texas troops: First Infantry, 173

Thomas, George H., 99–101, 203; in Atlanta campaign, 141, 143, 144, 153, 174, 175; at Chattanooga, 126–27; at Chickamauga, 102, 109, 110–11, 112; and defense of Nashville, 201, 232, 234, 236, 237; replaces Rosecrans, 121; at Stones River, 79, 80, 85

Thompson, Absalom, 207, 320–21 n.42

Thompson, M. Jeff, 31, 37

Trapier, James H., 55

Tullahoma, Tenn., 76, 77, 78, 96, 98, 277

Tupelo, Miss., 52, 56, 57, 59, 60, 62, 242, 243, 244

Turner, William B., 69, 71, 74, 84, 106–7, 112, 153, 157

Turner's Mississippi Battery, 69, 71, 84, 106–7, 112, 147, 153, 239, 312 n.61

Tuscumbia, Ala., 202, 213

Twain, Mark, 37

U.S.S. Tyler, 50, 295 n.35

Union City. Tenn., 28, 29, 41

Utah, territory of, 24

Van Dorn, Earl, 212, 321 n.45

Vaughan, Alfred J., background of, 166; at Chickamauga, 109; commands brigade at Stones River, 81, 84, 89; photo of, 167; succeeds Preston Smith, 109; wounded, 166–68

Vaughan's brigade, deserters from, 188; engagements fought at: Atlanta, 179, Chickamauga, 111; Jonesboro, 189, 192; Kennesaw Mountain, 152–53, 155, 159; New Hope Church, 149, 151; Peachtree Creek, 175–76; Resaca, 144–45; Snake Creek Gap, 144; Stones River, 81–82, 83, 89, 90

Vaulx, Joseph, 207

Veracruz, Mexico, siege of, 15–17

Versailles, Ky., 64

Vicksburg, Miss., 99, 125, 198

Vining's Station, Ga., 166

Walker, Francis M., 183, 313 n.76

Walker, W. H. T., 101, 102, 107, 113, 124, 133, 136; and Cleburne's emancipation

Walker, W. H. T. (*continued*)
proposal, 137–40; division broken up, 184; killed at Atlanta, 178; photo of, 138; relations with BFC, 137, 139
Wallace, Lew, 43, 44
Wallace, W. H. L., 47, 49
Walthall, Edward C., in Atlanta campaign, 184, 186; brigade of, at Lookout Mountain, 122–23, 124, 125; brigade of, at Missionary Ridge, 128, 130, 131; corresponds with BFC, 268; criticizes John K. Jackson, 124; leads rear guard during retreat from Nashville, 241–42; placed under BFC's command, 119; postwar political success, 261
Watkins, Sam R., 84, 90, 120, 152, 172, 200
Westover (plantation), 4–5, 23, 266; photo of mansion at, 6

Wharton, John A., 65, 67
Wheeler, Joseph, 65, 137, 139, 174, 175, 188
Widney, Lyman S., 163
Withers, Jones M., 60, 76, 80–81, 85, 87, 91, 94, 95, 101
Woodward, C. Vann, 261
Work, George, 21–22
Worsham, W. J., 140, 151
Worth, William J., 11, 15
Wright, Luke E., 153, 157
Wright, Marcus J., 103, 106, 111, 118, 121, 130, 138, 197, 268; brigade of, at Chickamauga, 103–4, 111; at New Hope Church, 149; at Kennesaw Mountain, 153

Young, Brigham, 24
Young, J. P., 210, 212, 319–20 n.28

Tennessee's Forgotten Warriors was designed by Dariel Mayer, composed by Lithocraft, Inc., printed by Cushing-Malloy, Inc., and bound by John H. Dekker & Sons, Inc. The book is set in Baskerville and printed on 50-Glatfelter Antique, B-16.